GOVERNMENTS
—— FROM ——
HELL

GOVERNMENTS
—— FROM ——
HELL

GOVERNMENT SPONSORED
OPPRESSION AND TERROR

CHARLES BINGMAN

GOVERNMENTS FROM HELL
GOVERNMENT SPONSORED OPPRESSION AND TERROR

iUniverse books may be ordered through booksellers or by contacting:

iUniverse
1663 Liberty Drive
Bloomington, IN 47403
www.iuniverse.com
1-800-Authors (1-800-288-4677)

Because of the dynamic nature of the Internet, any web addresses or links contained in this book may have changed since publication and may no longer be valid. The views expressed in this work are solely those of the author and do not necessarily reflect the views of the publisher, and the publisher hereby disclaims any responsibility for them.

Any people depicted in stock imagery provided by Thinkstock are models, and such images are being used for illustrative purposes only.
Certain stock imagery © Thinkstock.

ISBN: 978-1-4917-5825-0 (sc)
ISBN: 978-1-4917-5892-2 (e)

Library of Congress Control Number: 2015903564

Print information available on the last page.

iUniverse rev. date: 02/11/2015

CONTENTS

.

SECTION ONE

THE NATURE OF OPPRESSIVE
GOVERNMENTS

Over time, hundreds of public opinion polls have been conducted all over the world. These polls reflect the universal hatred of governments, the suspicion and distrust that people feel about extremist religious or racist leadership and motives, and the great fear and foreboding about the horrible threats posed by what are now dozens of vicious and rapacious terrorist groups that have become the curse of almost every country in Africa, the Middle East and much of Asia.

Hundreds of millions of people are forced to suffer governments that fail to provide security and safety, vital services, or a decent livelihood. Worse still, in a disturbing number of cases, the villains that threaten the people are the villains that control the government and the country.

The issue is not the failings that come from honest error or simple human incompetence. Even the best of leaders make mistakes. The issue is that so much of what is so horribly wrong about governments is quite deliberate and intentional. These governments range from mere thievery and corruption to unbelievable oppression and even the sponsorship by governments of terror against their own citizens.

WHY? In almost every situation confronting governments, there will be choices, good and bad. Why do so many governments deliberately ignore the good choices and deliberately choose the bad ones? What they produce is not governance designed in Heaven but governance designed in Hell.

Governments are all about power because it is their role to make decisions for the country, to deploy huge resources, and to form some kind of consensus for action. But as the British Lord Acton said "Power corrupts and absolute power corrupts absolutely." But what is there down deep in the human psyche that chooses evil and perversity when achieving positions of power? Why do ruling elites create Governments from Hell?

This book explores several dozen cases and examples of the nature of governments from Hell. Perhaps these examples help to explain how such governments operate. It is not clear that they answer the eternal question of Why.

Authoritarian governments have little interest in consultative or cooperative governance and prefer to hold dictatorial power in the hands of a small group or network of political loyalists who can be directly controlled. It can be argued that a ruling elite of some kind is historically the most common and enduring form of government, starting with kings and dictators allied with armies, aristocracies and priesthoods. Elitism and cronyism, even when essentially honest, are still narrow in vision, inherently centrist; often isolated and unrealistic in their understanding; stoutly resistant to pressures from external forces; reactionary, parochial, self-centered and self-important. Not even the current tendency for creating economic elites is new; there have been elites of aristocracies, landed gentry, or powerful industrialists and bankers.

Loyalty is to the leader and not to the people or the best interest of the country. Or the elite may be economic elite as for example in older societies where there was the "landed gentry." Many elites are based on the military, either as a direct military dictatorship or by alliance between the political and the military leadership. The advantages of the military center around the tradition of obedience to command, top-down control, and enforced discipline and loyalty to the command structure.

In modern times, the elites have been controllers of the "commanding heights" elements of the economy: banking, trade, heavy manufacturing, power generation, transportation. The elites have a natural tendency to use the power of the government to protect their superior position, though politics, the economy, and even the culture of the country. In their outward posture, they constantly display a great confidence in both the intellectual and practical "rightness" of their policies, and then the inevitable conclusion that therefore everybody else is wrong and can legitimately be opposed. Authoritarian governments will attempt to seize control of legislative bodies so that the laws can be drafted or modified in ways that protect their power. This may be done through such mechanisms as controlled elections, allocation of blocks of legislative seats for regime loyalists, bribery and corruption, pitting national groups against each other, or merely by threats and intimidation. Elites usually lack any broad or truly representative public base, and in some cases, the personal popularity of the top leader substitutes for such representative support. The whole concept of "the cult of the leader" (e. g. Kim IL Sung or Saddam Hussein) is designed to create public acceptance. But the more corrupt the elite regime, the more it is forced to turn to repression to retain power and resist needed change.

But the fact that these governments have been flawed has not meant that they were unsuccessful. The facts appear to be that State Socialism or other ideologies were widely acclaimed, but they were never really what motivated governments. The reality seems to be that there is seldom strong enough political coherence or clout exercised by "the public" to overcome the better organized and funded range of special interests. What has taken its place in every country is the formulation of **hundreds** of power bases – interest groups, local governments, unions, professional organizations, environmental advocates and many others. Here is where the leverage exists. Each of these interests is capable of organizing for two reasons: to advance their own group interests, and to leverage the political system through the exercise of "special interest politics". Political leadership thus becomes an exercise in attempting to attract the support of a critical mass of these special interests and getting them into agreeing on some central political objectives. To understand what really motivates governments, one needs to understand the uses of State Owned Enterprises (SOE) and the universal importance of special interest politics.

The great majority of governments are centrist; that is, they are driven by motivations to centralize power in the government at the cost of loss of power or capacity or freedom of action in the other elements of national society. Centrism means the extensive transfer of both control and responsibility from individual citizens to the government. It means the power and the inclination to declare any national activity to be a public responsibility which needs to be controlled by government. This assertion of responsibility then becomes the basis for demanding citizen acceptance, and the right of the government to extract money to carry out such purposes. This propensity for centrism includes the power of the central government to define what is legitimate and acceptable and what is not. In economic terms, centrism presumes the power to define the line of demarcation between public and private interests for businesses, groups and individuals.

This centrist tendency is powerful, ubiquitous and ominous. Centrism cuts across all forms of government and all political philosophies. It is the preferred style for dictators. It was the official and heavily enforced policy of all communist regimes and state socialist governments, and has been vital to socialist philosophy and as a justification for big government

There are certainly functions where national central governance makes sense. The most important include national defense, the operations of a central bank, the provision of a national supreme court, and perhaps the provision of nationwide public infrastructure such as highways, railroads, and power and communications grids. In many cases, problems obviously nationwide in character warrant uniform national regulations. In many countries, but in varying degrees, the overall development and performance of the economy is seen as a central government responsibility.

Many other functions are seen as legitimate centrist responsibilities, but there are valid options that make centrist justifications less compelling. These elements include such things as subordinate court systems, health care, unemployment compensation, regional economic development, elementary, secondary and higher education and some public infrastructure. Often too, the centrist argument is applied in terms of the division of power between the national government and state/municipal governments. Areas where the centrist argument seems weakest include housing, education, social services, law enforcement, recreation, unemployment compensation, and local economic development including the role of the private sector in a community.

It is difficult to overestimate the compelling attractions of the centrist concepts of power allocation. In both public and private organizations, it is seen as simpler, faster, and more "effective" to draw power into a small central power base, and to avoid the difficulties and negotiation and compromise with a wide range of forces at the periphery of power.

Who favors centrism? Dictators, political bosses who want to fend off opposition, elite groups of "haves" who do not want to share power with "have nots". What has also emerged in modern times is a return, in the Muslim world, of the idea of a universal Islamic state, controlled by a small minority of religious leaders whose authority must be absolute. Disaggregation will be opposed by incumbents who fear a loss of position and influence, bureaucrats who do not want to lose authority, and those who argue that disaggregating of power is messy and debilitating, and that splitting up the power base weakens the national ability to get things done.

Those who favor national redistribution of wealth argue that a strong central government is the only force that will make it possible, since the rich will never volunteer to give up their wealth and grip on economic power. Yet many economies find redistribution taking place through the functioning of the economic system whether the government is heavily involved or not, and often, government policies are dysfunctional. Where governments have intervened to attempt to redistribute wealth, the results have been positive up to a point, but often negative as well. The result seem to be that, if the government pursues the redistribution of wealth too far, its demands for money taken out of the economy can produce negative economic consequences in the reduction of funds for economic expansion, and through a middle class rejection against further taxation. Said another way, resistance to taxation usually overpowers the social motives for income redistribution. The substitution of political decision-making, the sheer contentiousness of it, and the endless opportunities for corruption and vote buying, the need to beg for favors from arrogant public officials, the unending pressures for favoritism, the "bottomless pit" of public largess – all make the public allocation of wealth ultimately less desirable than allocation through the market system, despite all of its perceived disadvantages.

A second source of argument has been that the diffusion of power is "wasteful" – that it breeds overlap, confusion, and duplication and that it stultifies action. This concept of "waste prevention" was extended to the economic arena, where the private economy was characterized as chaotic and duplicative, vulnerable to monopolistic or oligopolistic concentrations of power and oppressive for workers and citizens. It was argued that governments would be more socially responsible and would guard the public against the abuses of the private sector. A special form of arrogance grew up when centrist leaders began to believe that "only we understand what is needed."

The ultimate version of centrist governance was, of course, the command and control government of the Soviet Union and its satellites, where not only economic power and the ownership of productive resources was controlled by the central government, but also almost every element of national culture and relationships, and the lives of individual citizens. The supposed values of the centrist concept proved profoundly pathological. It became a self fulfilling justification for the elimination of opposition, not just as mistaken, but as "enemies of the state".

After WW II, various forms of State Socialism seemed triumphant. Highly centrist Socialist governments were in power in the Soviet Union, the People's Republic of China, in India, Vietnam, Cambodia, and most of Europe, including Italy, France, Sweden and Denmark.

But gradually, these centrist economies began to fail. First, there was a general decline and pervasive stagnation of the economy, even in the face of growing national needs. State controlled economies proved unable to grow and improve even enough to deal with a growing population. Ambitions for improved social services and "quality of life" had to be abandoned. The promises of socialism were not fulfilled as social services declined. The general population recognized this, and was increasingly disenchanted with their governments.

There was a withering of investment both from internal sources and from potential foreign investors. There is a world-wide shortage of capital investment money, and attracting capital is a competitive situation where "command and control" socialist countries could not or would not address. The Soviet Union, for most of its life, maintained a "closed border" policy which actively prevented foreign involvements in domestic Soviet economic affairs. This cut off huge amounts of money that might have been attracted, and contributed mightily to the stagnation of the economy.

Wages and salaries too became stagnant. There was little understanding about the relationship between productivity and management efficiency and the ability to increase wages as a consequence. Wage increases were most often granted for political reasons and often beyond what could be justified by productivity improvements. Such increases almost always proved inflationary, and produced high discontent among other workers. In fact, despite government efforts, unemployment – real or hidden – went up. Worker redundancy was as high as 40% in some industries, and workers and political leaders combined to keep it that way.

The pressures of stagnation caused governments to fail to deal with modernization and new technology potentials that might have improved productivity. Funds for modernization simply were not available, and even maintenance of current production facilities was neglected, leading to further declines in efficiency. In many socialist countries where government social services were inadequate, state owned enterprises became the providers of basic social services such as housing, education and health care for their own workers and even in part for the general population in their communities. This added to the fixed costs of the enterprises and made it especially difficult to cut costs in the face of declining economic usefulness. These high costs and rigid government price controls made state owned enterprises very expensive in comparison with their international competitors. In many cases, the state tried to cover up these problems in the short run by lying about them, or by running larger deficits, or shifting resources between parts of the economy. The decline in economic value led inevitably to a decline in public revenues and a growing inability to deliver social services. And the decline in productive work created a growing demand for such social services, especially unemployment compensation and welfare. Domestic public opinion could, in the short run, be constrained by the pursuit of false subsidy measures like cheap food, low rents, and subsidized fuels, but this made the eventual economic reckoning only worse.

This portrait of failure is equally telling in India, but less drastic. To quote Bhagwati: "The disappointment with Indian economic performance lies in her lack-luster growth for a quarter of a century. --- the framework of her economic policies (as defined by the iron fist of controls over the private sector, the spreading stain of inefficient public enterprises, and an inward-looking trade and investment strategy) has produced, not merely the dismal economic performance, but also the added sense of a senseless adherence to policies that have long been seen by others to have little rationale --- and the perception that her policies have been wittingly foolish."(1). Dr. Bhagwati thus frames one of the key elements of governmental pathology – the stubborn clinging to policies or doctrines that are generally recognized as failures. Governments tried to obscure the reality of change and refuse to adapt even in the face of overwhelming evidence of its need. This potential is especially important in developing countries that lack an advanced education system for large numbers of people, such as India where elementary and secondary education was, foolishly, not compulsory.

When governments are placed in roles that they cannot perform, they fail, and they become dysfunctional. When governments pursue perverse or self-serving motives, the distortions of reality harm the country. The government becomes the problem, not the solution. The mechanisms of government, which are supposedly designed to serve the population, are all too often simply turned around, and the public pays the elite to rob them. Even if honest, governments pursuing wrong motives can rob the public in various ways. They harm the economy by misallocating resources. They cheat the public by making them pay twice for social services: once through taxes and then through bribes. State assets are squandered. Businesses and individuals fail to pay their taxes because of influence or bribery. Public goods are mispriced when sold, and government purchase contracts are corruptly overcharged.

But all three of these ideologies are patterns for failure. Communism is dead, stringent State Socialism has generated a bad record and is in world-wide retreat, and a fundamentalist Islamic regime has with a couple of exceptions like Iran, never really happened, largely because the general public resists such regimes as best they can. A third ideology of governance has really yet to happen. That wave would be a government which is some version of a Muslim State based on and defined by a more honest interpretation of the Quran and the other holy documents of Islam.

Even if governance avoids dictatorship and authoritarian pathology it may still only rise to the level of weakness or cravenness or incompetence. It is extraordinary how fragile public programs are and how easily they fall into disrepair. And it is disturbing how easily governments lurch into corruption and pathology and how weak are the supposed defenses against them. Pathologies have stolen or squandered scarce funds, misdirected public programs, bred generations of corrupt officials and ultimately severely damaged government's capacity to function. Nobody knows how to solve these dilemmas. Nobody.

Since World War II, approximately 111 nations - more than half of the approximately 200 nations in the world -- have experienced some form of new independence. Many became independent from their former colonial rulers. Many more became independent by declaring freedom from collapsed regimes. For others, independence was internal, where dictatorships, mostly military, were overthrown. On the continent of Africa alone, a great wave of independence liberated 29 countries, and 7 more became independent in the 70's through the 90's. A second great wave of independence occurred in the 90's with the breakup of the Soviet Union and the dissolution of Soviet style centrist governments in E. Europe. Out of the Soviet Union, 15 newly independent countries emerged, and 14 E. European countries rejected their Soviet style governments in favor of some more open form of governance. This includes 6 independent nations emerging from the dissolution of the former Yugoslavia. These 29 countries have a total of about 375 million people of highly diverse cultural, ethnic, religious, and political backgrounds.

What kinds of governments emerged from these waves of independence? In all too many cases, the result was some form of heavily authoritarian regime rather than a benign and representative government. At least 45 of the newly independent governments have had dictatorships in some form during their early years of independence. An estimated 65-70 military coup took place, and in some countries, repeated military coups have alternated with brief periods of weak "democratic" rule. The universal vices of corrupt and pathological government have been pervasive, breeding stultifying incompetence, and poisoning relations between the government, the private sector, and civil society.

In many countries, the leadership that emerged during liberation has proved to be hopelessly flawed. The liberation of China produced a communist authoritarian regime that still clings to centrist power today. The initial promise of the Cuban liberation has deteriorated into a Castro dictatorship. Zimbabwe's initial leader and liberator, Robert Mugabe has become one of the most enduring tyrants in the world. N. Korea has been a brutal dictatorship for 57 years, surviving by sealing itself off from the outside world and enforcing a stunning form of national brainwashing on its citizens. Nigeria with the largest population in Africa has suffered from repeated military coups and revolts since independence in 1960, producing widespread poverty, corruption and bumbling incompetence in a country rich in resources. Indonesia, which achieved independence from the Dutch in 1949, fell under the control of Sukarno who suspended the Constitution in 1963 and had himself declared "president for life" in 1963. When he was overthrown, his successor, Suharto took over in 1968 and managed maintain authoritarian rule for another 30 years. When Iraq became a republic in 1958, its government lasted just 10 years before the Ba'ath Party took over and began to rule by dictatorial decree. Saddam Hussein seized power in 1978 and ran a terrorist regime for a further 25 years before the American invasion. Syria has been under the domination of a Ba'athist Party dictatorship for 40 years and it remains in power after long time President Hafaz al-Hassad' son Bashar al-Hassad has driven the country into a devastating civil war that promises to destroy the country. The extraordinary story of Haiti's black revolt against France in 1791-1804 has culminated in the horrible regime of the Duvaliers, father and son, who ran a terrorist regime from 1957 until elections in 1990. And Haiti's government since its first free elections in 1990 has been a further nightmare of civil conflict leaving the country in total ruin. The Sudan has been a disaster almost since its liberation in 1956, and the war between the north and the south is reported to have resulted in the deaths of 2 million people and the permanent displacement of 4 million more. The latest tragedies of government attacks against the villages of Darfur in the west are further consequences of almost 50 years of fear and hatred.

This centrist urge is common to all forms of government: democracies, dictatorships, state socialist regimes, and even in Islamic states, where many of the control mechanisms are guided or compelled by religious imperatives rather than secular principles. While the key to power is usually economic, authoritarian governments seek to extend their control to all elements of society: political, economic, social services, and even the definition of acceptable national cultural mores.

Once in power, authoritarian governments tend to become the captives of their own compelling need to hold on to power. They become very "doctrinaire"; that is, they use a doctrine or philosophy as justification for the correctness of their position and as a political justification for holding on to their power. Examples include the 65 year history of state communism in the Soviet Union, most of Eastern

Europe, Cuba, China and North Korea. Islamic states tend to rely heavily on religious doctrine as defined in the Quran and Sharia. Most political parties establish some degree of a doctrinal base as a means to attract supporters and define what the party stands for. The great wave of movement toward state socialism was elaborately defined by doctrine that emphasized the necessity for state control of national social services and large segments of the national economy, accompanied by official suspicion of the private sector. The point with authoritarian governments is that this doctrinal base is rigidly enforced, and deviations are opposed and often outlawed. Thus, authoritarian regimes almost always become highly reactionary and defensive, and feel driven to become very repressive and enforcement minded. Most centrist governments have elected presidents, parliamentary bodies with elected members, a body of defining laws, and most of the apparatus of a democratic state. But the reality is that centrist authority overpowers this democratic apparatus so that the control of the centrist elite is not challenged. Centrist regimes, paradoxically, are highly sensitive to opposition, and will go to great lengths to limit it.

IDEOLOGICAL HOPES

The last 250 years in the evolution of governance has produced an intellectually preferred pattern based primarily on the concepts of representative government, with the political leadership selected by the general citizenry through open elections, with politicians supposedly responsible to the people and functioning in a framework of separation of powers, and the primacy of the rule of law. But in truth, over the last 250 years, most governments have deliberately departed from this pattern. The real motives of the people who control governments have been to seize control and place the real power in the hands of some form of ruling elite. Some of these elites are satisfied to rule simply through raw power – no explanations, no justifications. Other centrist elites have chosen some form of ideology which appears to provide a philosophical justification and some degree of cover for what is mostly blatant political domination. The conflict is between corrupt governments and relatively honest and effective governments. The conflict involves the power seekers; the money seekers; the revenge seekers, the liberators; the zealots; the thieves -- and some who still think that governments are supposed to advance the well being of the general population.

A disturbing number of governments in the world are bad: they are corrupt, tyrannical, incompetent, or destructive. Authoritarian, self-serving leaders misallocate national resources, steal elections, terrorize citizens, and line their own pockets. Social programs are neglected, and the will of the people is ignored. Corruption becomes far more widespread and poorly resisted. Democracy and the rule of law are denied, and pathological activities are made legal. Regulations, instead of protecting the public, become instruments of tyranny and petty bureaucracy. How do these things happen? Why do governments become pathological and corrupt?

These are universal motivations, shared by people in authority the world over. All involve a spectrum of application from noble to viciously destructive. The "red line" is where the people and systems become anti-social. But by whose judgment? Most societies have answered that question by the formulation of constitutions, laws, regulations, and social mores. It is thus commonly seen as pathological where actions violate these standards and frameworks. Violation is all too easy, and the belief in "the rule of law" is not enough.

Over the course of history, there has emerged a sense of what the best of governments should be like. This consensus includes the following:

1. Better Lives for Citizens

Effective and affordable social services: health care, primary and higher education, support for the elderly, adequate housing, welfare for the poor, encouragement of the ability to help oneself, proper public facilities and infrastructure.

2. Social Justice and Equality

Prevention of corrosive conflicts between citizens: political, racial, ethnic, regional, tribal, gender, age, money, rural vs. urban, etc. All citizens of like condition should be treated equally and have inherent freedom to pursue their goals. Governments should aid rather than inhibit these needs.

3. Reduction of Centrist Elitism

Somehow, there must be a persistent and powerful effort to build protection against tyrants of all kinds. This should include serious formal sharing and balancing of the powers of governments, including a high degree of decentralized authority and independence, both to local governments and to the private sector. It is vitally important to let people understand that their ultimate best interests are served if they can commit themselves to the concept of individual self reliance. Somehow, there must be real laws against preferment, nepotism, favoritism, and limits on the power of special interests. Finally, there must be constant effort to prevention corruption in general, and as a means of lubricating power brokerage.

4. A Stronger Economy

There should be an effective means to raise the "value added" level of the economy, moving it up from primary and secondary economic levels. A key means to improve is the ability to take advantage of value adding technology such as IT and manufacturing automation. Increasingly, it is clear that a form of government is needed that facilitates value maximizing investment choices. In some cases, this means a retreat from State Socialism, a rationalization of State Owned Enterprises, and independent banking, relatively free from government manipulation.

5. A Larger Economy

The strongest possible efforts should be made to grow and expand the economy so that it is sturdy enough and profitable enough to meet the needs of the country and its people. The government should promote economic investment instead of restricting it. Favoritism for SOEs should be limited. Foreign direct investment should be encouraged. The country and the economy should be opened up to both private and international government involvements. Restrictive regulations should be very limited, including those affecting the workforce.

6. Greater Government Operational Effectiveness

The public has a right to expect relatively high levels of professional leadership; going beyond merely "a government of clerks". Maximizing the role and performance of local governments can ultimately upgrade the performance and relevance of public programs. The management of public money is crucial. Legitimate taxes should actually be collected and make it safely to public accounts. Somehow, politicians must be made to develop sensible targeted budgets. To do this it is absolutely vital to curb special interest politics.

7. Reduced/Controlled Corruption

There is a growing recognition that various forms of corruption are serious in almost every government in the world, and that the fight against public corruption must be brought to the level of constant pressure and major assaults. This is not just the responsibility of government; they are in fact often the problem. It should be the work of the whole country to develop and really use strong protective systems and rules. The key: enforcement, enforcement, enforcement! It is useless to develop a lot of laws and a lot of structure, but it is useless if it is not well used, or simply ignored. Within the government, efforts should be made to reduce the number of people who can commit the government and authorize the expenditure of public money – and then watch these people closely.

Lots of excuses have been invented to "justify" corruption, or explain it away. Here are some of the most popular.

1. "Corruption is a way of life; it has been 'built in' to the culture." Some countries/cultures are victimized by such widespread corruption that it is interpreted to be part of the culture, and therefore somehow acceptable. But in a deeper sense, it is clear that no society in history has really endorsed corruption; all consider it wrong; every religion or secular philosophy condemns it; and the laws of most countries make it specifically illegal. So the "way of life" argument is merely a feeble rationalization when tested by these broader societal views.
2. "Everybody does it; how can you stop 'everybody' "? But it is not true that everybody does it. Most people are remarkably

honest, hate corruption, oppose it where possible, hate to be its victims, and will support anti-corruption efforts.

3. "Corruption has its advantages". This kind of argument has been advanced by both political scientists and corporations. The corporations argue (especially around tax time) that bribery is a necessary business tool to avoid bureaucratic process and help to gain business. Corruption is often seen as cheaper than complying with laws and regulations and business people argue that "if we don't bribe corrupt officials, our competition will." Political scientists may have given up, decided that corruption in inevitable and therefore is justified to get the bureaucratic apparatus to perform. But the wheels do not have to be greased; most government programs can and do function well without the grease of corruption, and accepting and using corruption simply encourages more of it.
4. "Fighting corruption is too expensive and difficult". Where corruption is widespread and systematic, the means to eliminate or reduce it become so difficult and expensive that governments begin to believe that they cannot afford to eradicate it. But the cost of corruption exceeds the cost of reduction many times over; a corrupt government is never a "cost-effective" government, nor is it serving the public interest. Desperately scarce public funds are diverted into the bank accounts of cynical crooks, and vital public programs see their money stolen.
5. "In a truly representative government, democratic practices will cause corruption to disappear". Corruption can exist even in a truly democratic government. Hopefully, one of the adjuncts of a truly democratic government will be openness, transparency, lots of watchers, and managerial measures to fight corruption. But these means must be deliberately cultivated and will not happen spontaneously because a government has the democratic apparatus.
6. "In a truly market based economy, the forces of the market place will cause corruption to wither and die". Corruption is perfectly capable of flourishing in a market economy because a market economy can contain pathological forces which find corruption useful and profitable -- just as it does with straight

crime, or "cheating." When corruption becomes a means for the allocation of business/resources, it ceases to be a "market" economy, and becomes something else. Bribery provides a way to beat competitors who may have better skills or lower costs. The costs of the bribes becomes built into tax deductible business expenses, and is another form of tax on citizens, while being essentially free for the corruptors. Currently, only the U. S. makes bribery of foreign officials a crime.

7. "It is not clear exactly what 'corruption' means". This suggests that governments can't really take full measures to oppose corruption because there may be grey areas or areas of legal uncertainty as to what is wrong and what is not. But in most cases, what is corrupt/pathological in government is much the same as what is seen as corrupt/pathological in society and there is a broad range of known corrupt practices that can be attacked immediately without waiting for the perfect legal certainty. If it is not certain whether some kinds of activities are corrupt or not, then specific legal actions are available to make that determination if there is the guts to do so.

8. Better Women's Roles

Cultures must really believe in equality of all kinds – as a philosophy of governance; as the basis for laws; as an element of all government programs and activities, and as a mandate upon private companies and organizations. Most countries need a thorough reform of laws, rules, and actual practices.

9. An Honest and Effective Justice System

Independent judges and public prosecutors are an absolute necessity. Honest "serve and protect" motivated police forces must be created and sustained. The military should be kept out of civilian justice matters, or be kept in limited and defined roles. The best systems of justice would avoid of excess and apply reasonable definitions of illegality and the rules of evidence. There must be defenses against all forms of corrupt justice, illegal arrest, and improper search, seizure, assault, intimidation, or solicitation of bribes.

10. A Peaceful Citizenry

Above all, do not let the government deliberately create conflicts between elements of the population. Provide many civic means to mitigate conflict. Keep talking.

11. New Levels of Government Accomplishment

Governments must keep up with problems. To fall behind the power curve can be fatal. Governments are entitled to adequate resources, but they have no right to steal or waste them. Political stalemate must be avoided, along with special interest stultification. Create something like a philosophy of excellence – or at lease adequacy. Execute! Do more than talk. Create a culture of problem solving. Create an atmosphere of frankness and openness to the public.

In older days, this ideology has been "the divine right of kings", or the supposed God given superiority of some landed aristocracy. More recently, three forms of ideologies have come to the fore. The first is the absolute form of Communism, typified by the USSR and China, but the broader and more sophisticated version of this form of elite centralism has been that of State Socialism. And the third is seen as emerging from the more radical elements of the Muslim world. Good governance is one of the hardest, most complicated and most expensive things that human beings are called upon to do. Even very good and skilled people who try hard may not succeed. And in fact, of the 200 plus governments in the world today, about two thirds are in some form of deep trouble. In the world of governments, one should never underestimate the powerful influence of mere incompetence. Many, many governments are directed by bumblers, innocents, fools, crooks and thieves, dimwits and those that are merely totally confused. Even the honest and good hearted have often proved inept and unable to cope with their complex responsibilities. Scholarly research arrives confidently at the wrong conclusions. World class organizations such as the UN or the World Bank or ASEAN vigorously advocate courses of action which, a decade later, are seen as misguided.

Every form of government ever invented has proved highly vulnerable to pathological behavior. In the dictionary sense, pathology is defined as conditions of abnormality and/or deviations from propriety, or the assumed normal state of things. Pathological means diseased. Thus, a pathological government is one that has become sick and malfunctioning -- based on some definition of what is healthy and normal. One of the deceases of pathological governments is corruption, which is simpler to define: performance of an illegal act in violation of duty, induced by improper means. In government, it involves deriving personal and private gain from the exercise of official duty, or acts by others to induce a government official to act illegally or improperly in violation of duty.

Robert I. Rotberg, in an article in Foreign Affairs Journal (2) offers a bleak and shocking compendium of the nature of states that suffer massive failure: "Failed states are tense, conflicted, and dangerous. They generally share the following characteristics: a rise in criminal and political violence; a loss of control over their borders; rising ethnic, religious, linguistic, and cultural hostilities; civil war; the use of terror against their own citizens; weak institutions; a deteriorated or insufficient infrastructure; an inability to collect taxes without undue coercion; high levels of corruption; a collapsed health system; rising levels of infant mortality and declining life expectancy; the end of regular schooling opportunities; declining levels of GDP per capita; escalating inflation; a widespread preference for non-national currencies; and basic food shortages, leading to starvation. Failed states ultimately face rising attacks on their fundamental legitimacy."

The Rule Of Law and Why It Is Not Enough

The nature of governments is stated in constitutions, enacted laws, the enduring structure of the national justice system, a body of common laws and precedents, and a legal structure of governments in which powers and authorities are both authorized and limited. In the classic dictionary sense, the rule of law is defined as "1. A set of substantive legal principles and laws. 2. The concept of the supremacy of regular, as opposed to arbitrary power. 3. The exercise of those powers by those in authority. 4. The doctrine that any person is subject to the ordinary laws of the region, and 5. The doctrine that constitutional legal principles are the result of judicial decisions determining the rights of private individuals in the courts."

In most countries, there has been the warm and comfortable feeling that if only the rule of law is followed, all will be well. But in country after country, the rule of law is overpowered by the rule of the tyrant, because the laws themselves can be perverted, or the demands of the laws can simply be ignored. The force and effect of these legal instruments supposedly control the functioning of the government and define the obligations of government. This Rule of Law is seen as the great bulwark against government by dictatorship, or government by dangerous chaos. But even where there is such a substantial framework for the rule of law, those mechanisms can be perverted because they rest on the often invalid assumption that the laws themselves are good and proper. This has been largely true in the United States and in most other developed countries, but it is increasingly apparent that keeping the laws good and proper is an enormously complex and sophisticated process. In many countries, rules of law and the institutions mechanisms to protect them do not exist or are not strong enough. Thus, laws themselves are perverted and made to work against the very people they are supposed to protect. Anything – any pathological, corrupt, perverse, outrageous and dysfunctional thing – can and has been made legal and the law of the land. Pathological politics has proved time and time again that it can frustrate the intent of the rule of law and turn it upside down. There are countless examples in almost every country that laws are enacted that are generally seen as perverse. Laws can be enacted that prohibit free elections, forbid opposition political parties, or severely limit political activities – except by the government itself. Laws are enacted that limit the effectiveness of the nation's political structure. As the central regime control more and more power, it can pass laws that prohibit any criticism of any policy or action of the government, even by its own party members. Top level officials in government ministries and local governments are all appointed by the central elite, and these agencies benefit from further laws that allow them to control resources such as "designer" tax regulations that allow favoritism toward regime supporters, or hand out punishment for opponents. Laws can be enacted that give preferential access to public services for specific ethnic, religious or tribal groups, while denying service to others. Laws give regime officials the authority to give away or sell cheaply such valuable national assets as land, buildings, mineral rights or licenses to control monopolies for communications, transport services, banking or land development. In fact, laws enable government officials to require government approval for almost any kind of activity, with approvals awarded by political preference or the size of the bribe. Government contracts may be awarded without competition or any serious justification, and awards to relatives and political supporters are notorious.

Such legal violations are almost always manifested in highly questionable forms of economic control. Most tyrannical regimes legally own and control the banking system, first to benefit from bank earnings, but also to use the banks in a major way to advance political control. Banks will be directed to lend money to friends of the regime and to deny loans to opponents. Borrowing costs are usually highly subsidized below the rates charged to normal customers, and often, borrowers quietly "forget" to repay such loans. In those countries which have relied heavily on the use of State Owned Enterprises

(SOE), banks have been forced to lend to "loser" SOEs at next to nothing, and the government itself has been forced to use tax money to prop up and subsidize SOEs that operated at annual deficits. This has been true even when perverse laws have given what amounts to monopoly power over some crucial element of the national economy such as energy or communications, only to see such monopolies produce inferior goods or services at excessive prices.

Thus, when corrupt or pathological laws are enacted, the whole justice system becomes an instrument for the enforcement of these rotten laws. Governments can create a dilemma in which people need to be protected not from other elements of society, but from the State itself. And from this power, there is little or no recourse. Pathologies effecting control of the economy are widespread. Laws may create government monopolies, with all of their dangers. Laws that fix prices are almost always counter productive and economically distorting. The entire tax system may be perverted to favor certain interests. Worker redundancy may be mandated by law or regulation, destroying economic efficiency. Banks may be forced to lend to weak businesses, tying up limited bank lending capacity in sterile loans, and creating high default rates. Import or export licenses, quotas and tariffs may be skewed, by law, to cater to certain favored companies and punish others. Laws against foreign investment may drive off badly needed new investment capital.

Similar legal distortions may be used to disenfranchise citizens. Election laws themselves may destroy the capacity to conduct free and fair elections. Other laws may prevent creation of opposing political parties or make effective political opposition next to impossible. Laws may also be written to exploit normal diversity in society by favoring one or more ethnic, religious or tribal groups, and pitting them against others.

Many legislative bodies contribute to this problem by enacting thousands of useless laws that are murky, contradictory, pointless and often unenforceable. Prosecutors, law enforcement officials, defense attorneys and the public who want to be honest and obey the rules of law are confronted with a vague often dysfunctional body of laws that are fully understood by nobody including those who enacted them. For the corrupt official, the laws can be "selectively" enforced; those that protect the public or curb corruption are simply ignored, while new laws can be enacted that feed any form of pathology. Laws and regulations become the instruments of tyranny and are used to punish one's enemies while protecting one's own corrupt positions. Laws and regulations are slanted and made irrational by interpretation, or by some related body of regulation or administrative decisions cleverly manipulated behind the scenes and out of public scrutiny.

Further, this ponderous apparatus is usually so complicated and inefficient that it is too costly and too time consuming for average persons or small organizations to use. When the government uses the legal system as its own tool, it becomes actually dangerous because opponents can be threatened and intimidated, and because of the likelihood that the "good guys" will lose. Public prosecutors and defenders suffer from the same problems and often refrain from performing their official roles simply because they would be wasting their time.

Almost inevitably, control evolves into tyranny. The police and the military are used to suppress almost any form of civic activity. People are arbitrarily detained, arrested, and even imprisoned. Homes and businesses are entered and searched with no justification. Even very normal activities such as opening a business or joining a group can be branded as acts against the State. Intelligence services seize unlimited access to any information about private people or organizations. In some of the worst scenarios, the government sponsors and finances informal militias, paramilitary groups and other terrorist organizations to attack the regime's enemies. And sadly, some of the worst violations of the hoped for Rule of Law take place within the national justice system itself. All too often, parliaments and congresses that pass the laws are weak and captured by the regime. Court systems are seldom independent, and judges can be politically intimidated or bought off, and there is a horrible record of judges who sell verdicts to the highest bidder. Public prosecutors too can be forced to go after a regime's enemies or to forgive the transgressions of its friends.

BACKING GOOD LAWS
VS. BAD LAWS

Since anything and everything can and is locked into law, it is very important for defenders of good governance to understand what normally constitutes a good law, and how broad and interventionist the body of laws should be, because that knowledge may be the most compelling basis for public support. Is it necessary and desirable that everything in society must be law defined, driven or limited? One school of thought has been that laws should be limited to areas which civil society cannot adequately handle for itself. Important arenas such as religion or individual thought and action, or social relationships within a community are left largely free of legal intervention. Another school defends the premise that most of what happens in society will evolve properly only when defined, directed and constrained by a broad, overarching body of legal structure. The tendency has been that, as societies develop form the primitive to the complex and as the numbers and diversity of the population increase, most societies have little choice but to extrapolate the body of laws to deal with the complexities and conflicts that modern societies create. But tyrants don't care since they act to pervert the laws. But for the opponents of these tyrants it is vital to evolve some framework for defining goodness and badness. The following is an attempt to discuss such a framework.

A law may be good if it reflects and adopts the best values of the society itself, and rejects the worst values. Such laws therefore reinforce what is good and mitigates what is destructive or dysfunctional. Laws should reflect what is generally regarded as acceptable social standards of fairness and equity. These social standards may arise from social and cultural mores, religious principles, and widely held views about what is just and equitable. They may capture enduring community preferences, and even a sense of what succeeds or fails. Also, one of the greatest public concerns is the sense of outrage when laws are seen as inequitable and unfair, and when they deliberately create greater inequity in society or set out to abuse the interests of minorities. Other vague but telling phrases are used to describe bad laws, such as unethical, intolerant, undemocratic, improper, of dubious intent, socially undesirable, inappropriate, or just plain "wrong". Most people cling to the innocent assumption that their national laws are written to protect their rights and property, but government oppressors are quick to recognize that the great body of national laws can be relatively easily perverted to become the instruments of oppression. Therefore, this body of laws and related regulations becomes the battlefield between the oppressors and their victims.

Another important criterion centers around the idea that laws should reflect only those actual needs in society that require political intervention -- as opposed to the idea that laws should encompass everything. There are several reasons for this sense of wanting to limit the scope of laws. First, universal law means universal government, and there remains a deep seated resistance to such an idea. Second, it is presumed, or at least hoped, that laws will be liberating, useful, enabling and facilitative. But there is plenty of evidence that in reality, many are inhibiting, controlling and constraining, even if justified by an acceptable public purpose. Each law further creates the necessity for enforcement, which may require the reduction of individual or group freedom of choice and action. Third, the aggregate of all laws can (and usually is) so complex that it defies understanding, even by the people who must administer them. It is possible to design a government so complex that it cannot be governed, and such complexity is the enemy of democratic understanding. And experience has proved that what the people really want is often very different than what politicians think is good for them. It is useful therefore to argue that government laws should be kept as simple as possible, and within the range of what people can understand if they try. A target should be to define the "least" government that is consistent with national need and intent. As collateral to this reasoning, the more complex and confusing a body of laws become, the more possibilities are created for misuse and corruption. Therefore, laws should be written to meet the general public good and this standard should always be held up against legislation proposed merely for the advantage of some special elite or specific special interest.

Laws about the structure and authority of the government itself are of critical concern. Many a hopeful new nation has drafted a constitution and an initial package of enabling statutes, only to find out later that these documents are so vague and inconclusive that they are not only useless but dangerous. Vague, open-ended statutes or regulations are highly vulnerable to misinterpretation, unwarranted extrapolations of power, abuses of authority, and the corrupt exercise of legitimate authority. Instead of vagueness, laws should provide the public with a clear explanation of why the law is necessary, what it will authorize, who it will benefit, and how it will be implemented. Many laws are "missions impossible"; they appear to enable a response to some public problem, but prove to be impossible to carry out. Almost every country has laws that mandate "the elimination of poverty", or "university education for all", or "a clean environment", yet in fact, neither the government nor society itself may be able to achieve such goals. Also, the public has a right to expect that governments will operate with reasonable efficiency, and that public programs will in fact deliver the goods or services expected of them. While there is little direct lobbying support for "government efficiency" there is certainly a willingness to see some public money invested in a stable and competent civil service, proper maintenance and repair of public facilities, efforts to improve performance and productivity, and adaptation of the advantages of new technologies.

Most government agencies and programs are given exceedingly broad legal charters, but then the political system proves incapable or unwilling to live up to its grand promises, or to prevent the abuse of such wide-open authority. In reality, it is probably wiser to write each law so that it limits authority only to that necessary to carry out the law's defined purpose, and deliberately to limit the ability to extrapolate political and bureaucratic authority into areas that the law did not contemplate.

If there is a defining philosophy for the drafting of laws it should be that the body of national laws should reflect as closely as possible the accepted social standards and mores of the civil community, and they should be written to be empowering, facilitative, and realistically achievable rather than restrictive, constraining, prejudicial and hopelessly impractical. This does not mean that laws cannot and should not be visionary, but governments should avoid creating unattainable expectations or making promises it cannot keep.

There are similar problems with the cherished concept of "accountability". In the political science sense, this usually means accountability of the bureaucracy and of appointed officials upward to the political leadership of the executive and legislative branches of the government. But here again, what if this leadership is corrupt? Is it not pathological for corrupt leaders to demand blind loyalty as the only test of accountability? Corrupt organizations too are "accountable" but in ways that become dysfunctional since they reinforce the hand of such pathological leadership. Consider for example, the problem of an honest program official who has been ordered to do something that is inherently wrong. Is it proper for that official to be held "accountable" to bad leadership; or are there other values of the sense of accountability that apply?

In its broadest sense, accountability in government means many things, the most important being accountability to the general citizenry and this accountability should run from top to bottom. It should also mean accountability to the longer term guiding principles of good governance; to the body of general laws and regulations; to one's personal and professional ethics; responsiveness to the wellbeing of one's organization and of the organization's workers.

It is tragic the degree to which these principles are ignored and overridden. There are far too many self serving, elitist regimes whose accountability is only to themselves, and who seem easily able to pervert the laws whenever they feel like it. Yet, in every country no matter how tyrannical, there are people or groups who know better and who press, whenever and however possible, to make good laws prevail.

State Socialist Regimes

It is crucial to understand why State Socialism did not really succeed. It was a combination of powerful but erroneous concepts and an overpowering hunger for authority and control. It is amazing to look back and recognize the extent to which these twin towers of arrogance swept all else aside. In Europe, economic State Socialism was heavily mixed with concepts of societal well-being, and state provision of a full agenda of social services and public infrastructure. It was argued that the greedy selfish private sector would never support adequate social services, and that only economic control by the government would ever create the moral context and the sense of public responsibility which would produce an adequate base of social services and public infrastructure. Thus, it was argued that only the government could guarantee that the economy would be large and rich enough, and would be directed by the right priorities. This in turn justified extensive control by the government of social services delivery mechanisms and their purposes and priorities.

What is less well understood is that it dawned on a lot of rather clever and aggressive people that State Socialism provided a full blown widely supported rationale and the philosophical underpinnings for the exercise of absolute centrist power. People knew they were supposed to hate "dictators", but they thought they were supposed to respect "Socialist" leaders, or perhaps military juntas, because they clothed themselves in the garments of State Socialism.

But in the end, all over the world, State Socialism proved extensively to be a failure. Perhaps the major cause of that failure has been the fact that the whole package of State Socialist economic policies and programs almost always failed adequately to enlarge and enrich national economies. Not enough wealth was generated, and therefore the costs of welfare could not adequately be covered. The needs for public infrastructure such as roads or telephones or electric power or sewage disposal never ever got fully satisfied. State Owned Enterprises (SOE) proved to be seriously flawed in both concept and application. There came a point – at different times and places – where this reality had to be faced up to. The best possible reform pattern was when the failure was recognized at the earliest possible time and reforms were undertaken swiftly, and with a high degree of competence. The worst case was where, despite growing evidence, a regime failed to admit the need for reform, or stubbornly refused to act, or needlessly prolonged the reconstruction, or were simply not up to the task.

There are perhaps thirty seven governments in the world which have been faced with this problem. The decline of State Socialism and the redesign of a huge number of SOEs has been one of the most important tides running in the modern world over the last 30 years.

State Socialism <u>always</u> produced heavily centralized and authoritarian regimes; the whole philosophy demanded it. And this placed a heavy burden on governments, most of which loved the power but had serious difficulty dealing with the range and complexity that even simpler economies demanded. State Socialism produced two generations of leaders who could not deal with their responsibilities. Almost all Socialist regimes produced inferior results – economies that were ineffective and wasteful; economies that could not be made to grow fast enough even to keep pace with growing populations. In a number of countries, the private economy did initially justify a more interventionist government involvement. But in almost every case, the new opportunities supported by the emerging Global Economy allowed these private sectors to develop to the point where they could carry the national economy. But almost always, the ruling Socialist regime and its allies resisted that reality and continued to deny private sector capability. This resistance was, of course, explained and justified by the philosophy of State Socialism, but in country after country, this resistance proved to be mistaken and harmful. In far too many cases, Socialism got tangled up with other very serious difficulties, like the convulsions created by a military dictatorship, or heavy conflicts within society, or the destruction of aggressive terrorist enemies.

Especially during their earlier years, Socialist regimes, either deliberately or through ignorance, constipated their economies through seriously flawed policies. Many emulated the pattern of the USSR as the ultimate Socialist state, and essentially created a closed country. Many pursued a policy of import substitution where domestic enterprises, many of them state owned, were encouraged and subsidized to produce a good or service that might have been imported. Yet very early, economists almost universally demonstrated that this import substitution policy was a known failure. It usually led to local goods or services that were inferior to those that might have been imported, and they usually cost more money. As a secondary consequence of this policy, domestic producers became defenders of this bad policy because it expanded their businesses and provided a means to suck more money out of the government. Domestic labor unions also supported such policies because it created jobs that could not otherwise have been created.

One of the most important consequences of the emergence of State Socialism had been the burgeoning of the use of State Owned Enterprises (SOE), discussed in detail elsewhere. But it must be noted that, with many notable exceptions, the great bulk of these SOEs proved to be serious economic disappointments. The whole concept seemed to be wrong. SOEs proved to be highly vulnerable to political interference, much of which was bad economics. Hundreds of thousands of SOEs around the world proved to be uncompetitive and inefficient. Because they were protected and subsidized by the government, they were never compelled to face up to real competition that might have sharpened their performance. Many SOEs were in fact made national monopolies, which meant that they had no real competition at all. SOEs proved to be weakly managed, indifferent to opportunities for technological improvement, vulnerable to political foolishness, and ultimately to a rigid managerial philosophy that feared and resisted change.

This "SOE attitude" permeated whole national economies. Private entrepreneurs were frozen out of many markets because they were legally barred, or because they knew that they could never compete with the highly protected and subsidized state enterprises. Potential investors, both domestic and foreign, were scared off by government suspicion or opposition, by anti-business regulations, by closed borders and institutions, and by the dysfunctions of government banking, price controls, and blatant favoritism and preferment. State Socialist economic policy almost <u>demanded</u> a whole series of special interest choices. State regulation, justified by Socialist rhetoric, almost always exceeded the bounds of rationality and became a powerful source of both oppression and corruption. Banking systems, themselves SOEs, were mandated to adopt lending practices that were heavily biased and irrational. Friends of the regime were rewarded; enemies were frozen out. The whole tax system of many governments became the deliberate tool for a whole world of special interest dominance and preferment.

The decades of the 60's through the 80's saw both the triumph of this pattern of state socialism and the beginnings of its demise. By 1960, government, business and academic worlds all had concluded that Socialism was triumphant over the private market philosophy. By 1990, the world was no longer so sure. The great shortcoming was surely the congenital inability of Socialist economies to expand enough to keep up with reality. Not enough jobs were being created. Not enough people were being lifted out of poverty (outside of China). The system failed to control inflation, or to move the economy up the "value added" scale. Most of the policies at the heart of State Socialism had proved to be wrong and dysfunctional and often dangerous.

And then came the ultimate disenchantment. All over the world, hundreds of thousands of SOEs not only failed to produce profits for the government but were <u>operating at long term congenital deficits.</u> This broad pattern of failure produced three kinds of collateral disaster. First, the regime leadership was so committed to the Socialist scheme that they could not bring themselves to admit how wrong they had been, or how badly they had failed. This meant many years of underperforming economies that robbed people of the wealth that a reformed economy might have produced. Second, to conceal these failings, scarce funds actually had to be diverted from other crucial public needs, especially social services, to cover the cost of vast SOE deficits. Third, because of the failure to generate adequate revenues,

SOE performance got worse and worse. Customers were neglected; services were marginal; better technology never got adopted; prices remained too high; maintenance and repair was neglected; and employees never got trained. There were endless cases of people who had to wait months or even years for telephones, or water connections, or street repairs, or electrical service, or dozens of other government provided good or services. The absence of enough jobs in the formal economy of a country led to the expansion of informal economies, which, in many cases, provide half of the jobs and much of the GDP.

Further, the Socialist philosophy of centrist control, and the growing need to conceal extensive economic failure led regimes into patterns of widespread repression. No regime seemed able to bear any criticism. Huge efforts were made by almost every centrist regime to control communication in all forms, to prevent the release of information, to inhibit a free press, or to punish any person or group that criticizes the government in any way. This attitude is almost always pathological. Governments seem unable to distinguish between serious challenges and petty disgruntlement. All criticism is seen as ominous and threatening, and has produced the most astonishing and horrible repressions.

This portrait of Socialist failure has slowly become something closer to what the world now believes it understands. Since the early 90s, the battle of centrist government control of the economy vs. the private market based economy is being re-fought, but this time, market advocates are winning. This time, the debate is less theological and more realistic. Socialist economies are being dismantled or reformed out of dire necessity. They failed. They failed everywhere – Russia, China, India, Poland, Vietnam, E. Germany, Brazil, Mexico, Uganda, Syria, Turkey and perhaps thirty other nations. Thirty or more countries are engaged in trying to sell off most of their SOEs, and there are hundreds of cases of remarkable revitalizations of service provision when shifted into the hands of private organizations. People are beginning to understand the nature of these changes, and they have begun to ask "How did it get so bad?", and "Why did it take so long to recognized the need for reform?", and especially, "Why did we not know?"

Example: The Latin American Pattern

As the new nations of Latin America emerged, there was a general flow of events around certain general tendencies:

* A wide acceptance of State Socialism as a political philosophy, linked with a form of identification with other Socialist states, especially the USSR and Cuba.
* Powerful attitudes of nationalism, usually aimed in part against the United States.
* Large bureaucracies to control the economy primarily through centrist control policies such as price control, plus an endless stream of controlling regulations.
* A low quality of life for too many: crime, gangs, corruption, poverty, danger, violence against women, drug abuse, elitist inequality.
* The inability to control inflation.
* The inability to grow the economy fast enough.
* Massive and universal corruption.
* Populist subsidies to buy votes.
* A pattern of favoritism, preference given to the ruling elites, nepotism, forced bank loans, often never repaid.
* A "fat cat" power hungry military, beyond the control of the civilian government.
* Faulty economics: import substitution, export neglect, bad bank loans, damaging price controls, closed economies, negative attitudes about foreign investors, marketing boards, etc.
* Rampant special interest politics, including a cynical private sector.

In summary, Latin American leadership tended to see State Socialism as the ideal governance rationalization for heavy handed centrist control by a small and corrupt elite. The objective was almost always their own enrichment and not the well-being of the general population. As the evolution continues, much of this socialist doctrine has, of necessity, been abandoned or mitigated, but the harsh, oppressive love of centrist elitist power continues.

Special Interest Politics

One of the most important tides running in governments today is that of the universal presence and power of special interest politics. In the United States, Americans have grown up with the somewhat innocent belief that all groups that represent specific interests are "good" because they are presumed to be a form of democratic freedom of expression, and they help safeguard the public against an indifferent or wrong-headed government. But special interest politics have become far more sophisticated and, in most countries, far more ominous, and nobody particularly knows what to do about it since most political systems are ideally suited for it.

It is necessary to distinguish between special interests and "special interest politics". In essence, everybody is involved in special interests, some of them in conflict with others. Thus, a family could be concerned about the school system but oppose performance evaluation for teachers; be members of a union but vote Republican; worry about the environment but create trash and consume enormous amounts of energy, support a political party but not vote. They can be advocates of more public infrastructure and lobby for more highways and public services and still oppose any increase in the public budget. Many special interests center on powerful ideas – environmentalism or women's rights or the well-being of minorities in society. It is therefore natural and normal for people to think and act around their special interests.

Special interest politics in most countries are very aggressive and heavily pointed toward the government and what concessions can be obtained – a new program, a subsidy, a tax break, a favorable policy or the overlooking of some wrongdoing. In many cases, there is an implacable professional special interest bureaucracy that exists to lobby the government. These people have to gain something out of the political system from time to time in order to justify their work. And it must be perceived that the "something" that the government grants may be something that it was otherwise not inclined to provide. In other words, the ideal outcome for a special interest bureaucracy is to appear to have wrung concessions or resources from a reluctant government.

But the more ominous cases are those in which the influence of special interests is secret and carefully concealed, and <u>deliberately intended as the absolute antithesis of "representative democracy".</u> The history of countries is filled with this kind of "special interest" politics: the perverse collusion between corrupt officials and countless individuals and groups who are seeking to wrest wealth and power from a fumbling government. What has emerged in every country therefore is a special interest political system based on the following elements:

1. A very broad range of national interests in the hands of the government, with the political system in charge of the decision-making apparatus, and capable of allocating huge resources with some degree of discretion, ranging up to 100% in dictatorships. The more public programs there are, the more special interest groups will be created, and the more intense special interest politics will become, seeking not just money, but power.
2. The system takes place at two levels: first, there will be forms of public debate such as legislative hearings, public utterances, press releases, and endless study commissions. Then, there is a second "back room" political process of negotiation and agreement, not visible to the public, which is usually where the real threats and promises are employed. The public operations of government are deliberately designed to be essentially bland assurances, to deflect the public concerns and avoid efforts to penetrate the back room process.
3. Government's own procedures and program delivery systems which are both massive and ubiquitous are both necessary and valuable, but they can become vehicles to deliver political preference to special interests. The most important are the

public tax system, various forms of government regulations, selectively applied; items in the public budget; the award of government contracts; import and export controls, and of course, simple under-the-table corrupt payments. Both politicians and career civil servants are involved. One of the telltale signs of special interest government is when these delivery mechanisms become so extensive and so technically complex that they defy common understanding, thus giving the people in charge endless opportunities to punish or reward.

Special interest politics is enormously successful. The very broad public participation in so many forms of special interest gives them so much political credibility that political opposition seems almost unworthy. But while the "general public interest" is very broad and diffuse, special interest politics is usually very specific, and has a cutting edge that makes it easy to penetrate the political system and find backers to carry the freight. Organized special interest politics involves money, tactics and political clout specifically designed to bring pressure to bear at the key points in the political system. It is usually the ambition of special interest politics to get concessions locked into statute or regulation, since they know that it is infinitely harder to change a law or regulation than to get it in the first place. Thus, these concessions tend to be "forever", with each special interest stoutly defending and protecting them. Special interest groups tend to be implacable, insatiable and immutable – and often insufferable.

In less developed countries, special interest groups are probably more influential in their dealings with the government because there are fewer constraints. The pattern is much more cynical and aggressive than in the United States, and is more oriented toward economic advantage. In developed countries, the range and variety of special interests in greater and more sophisticated in their dealings with the government.

Why do politicians cave so easily? Special interest politics is not just campaign contribution money or short term political support. It is more importantly about the forging of longer term alliances for mutual advantage. The special interest group will continue to provide support as long as the politician continues to deliver. And once a politician is committed publicly to a position, it would be embarrassing to abandon that position, even for just cause, for fear of being perceived as weak or inconsistent, but also for fear that it will outrage special interest backers.

In the last analysis, special interest politics, as with all politics, is first and foremost about power and money. While most special interests construct an edifice of public purpose for their position, few make any pretense of seeking for a balance of judgments about the broad public interest, nor are they concerned about the success of the government itself, or the ethics of governance. Special interests can be positive and constructive, but their performance, especially in developing countries, is seriously in doubt. Too many of these special interests stop representing the interests of their supporters, and their staffs become part of the elite of the establishment, working for their own advantage.

A special interest concept has been developed around the idea of "state capture" which has been defined (3) as the actions of individuals, groups or firms both in the public and private sectors to influence the formation of laws, regulations, decrees, and other government policies to their own advantage as a result of illicit and non-transparent provision of private benefits to public officials. There are many different forms of the problem. Distinctions can be drawn between the types of institutions subject to capture – the legislature, the executive, the judiciary, or regulatory agencies, and the types of actors engaged in the capturing – private firms, political leaders, or narrow interest groups. Yet all forms of state capture are directed toward extracting rents from the state for a narrow range of individuals, firms or sectors through distorting the basic legal and regulatory framework with potentially enormous losses for society at large. They thrive where economic power is highly concentrated, countervailing social interests are weak, and the formal channels of political influence and interest intermediation are underdeveloped. The World Bank report further defines "administrative corruption" as a narrower concept involving the intentional distortion of the implementation of existing laws, rules, and regulations to provide advantages through the provision of private gains for public officials. This definition recognizes that such corruption is illicit and non-transparent, but need not be illegal per se.

At the same time, since politics is so vastly extended and interventionist, a growing proportion of the population feels threatened by governments. Yet they want help from government in protecting their specific interests and advancing causes in which they believe. People are remarkably willing to invest time, effort, and stress because they think these interests are important. People's reactions can become both assertive and defensive. They are assertive in pressing for the success of their cause or group, but defensive if they feel that their cause is being threatened or ignored. Neither of these attitudes is likely to be wholly rational; much will be emotional or uninformed. The "special interest" mentality is single minded rather than balanced.

Special interests tend to organize themselves so that they have collective influence and a more powerful voice. They will therefore tend to become more formal and bureaucratized, and much more assertive. Professional staffs are hired, recruiting stepped up, funds marshaled, a political agenda decided upon, and lobbying begun to search for allies or resist opponents. This leverage can initially be in the nature of information, education or persuasion, but as these groups press harder, they tend to phase over into "special interest politics" where they actively seek to change laws and regulations to favor their interests, or to capture funds and preferment to aid their cause.

From the political point of view, the practical consequence is that a trade takes place – a government asset traded for political support, or at least the absence of active opposition to the politician's agenda. Once these concessions are gained, they tend to be "forever" and vigorously defended. Subsequent retreat from such concessions is not only regarded as a defeat for the benefited interest group, but probably also as a "betrayal" by the political leadership. Governments therefore clash with, and collude with special interest political interests.

The former Soviet style governments sought to prevent the formation of independent interest groups, or to co-opt them. Yet, special interests emerged and became powerful because they were part of the Soviet state apparatus itself. These groups were never really regarded as speaking for the Soviet citizen – not even by their own leadership. The Soviet government in fact created and supported many specific interest groups of its own, as for example unions and trade associations, feeling that they could be used to keep people in line by serving as advocates of the official Party line at the grass roots. But in their own curious way, these captive groups still did achieve a degree of special interest power, especially as the centrist government weakened. What emerged was an embarrassing pattern of the Soviet government forced to negotiate with some of their own institutions, and the more special interests that got created, the more had to be bought off or intimidated.

The more ominous cases are those in which the influence of special interests is secret and carefully concealed, and deliberately intended as the absolute antithesis of "representative democracy". The history of countries is filled with this kind of "special interest" politics: the perverse collusion between corrupt officials and countless individuals and groups who are seeking to wrest wealth and power from a fumbling government. All governments are highly vulnerable to special interest politics. It is possible simply to accept this fact, as many governments do. It keeps the government in the enviable position of being the owner and operator of the powerful decision-making system which, at best can be reasonably proper and balanced, and at worst, totally corrupt. But special interest politics are not truly democratic nor are they reflective of the "general interest of the public". The sum of all special interests does not add up to the general public interest.

Any government that is truly based on service to its citizens must eventually face up to the need to resist and limit special interest politics. This can be done only by forcing constant adherence to the concept of balanced judgment in the general public interest. Every element of governance must constantly be put to this test, by whatever means are available, and public institutions must be designed to protect this public interest and resist the pressures of narrow special interests.

Another way to mitigate special interest leverage is to disaggregate the power and authority of governments, first and foremost by limiting their roles. Many roles and power can be passed back to the private sector as government throughout the world are now trying to do when they sell off their state owned enterprises and "privatize" government functions. In other cases, governments can return to the concepts of individual self reliance, even where this means facing up to the excruciating political pain of withdrawing public subsidies. Another major step is to hand power and authority down from the central national government to governments at the state/provincial/ regional level, and to municipalities. This can be done in many ways through devolution, decentralization, and disaggregation. As such power is shifted, special interest politics will also shift, but it can be argued that it will diminish. For example, instead of a special interest group getting a single national law out of the American government, it may have to lobby in 50 states. While this may be "messy" and sometimes "inefficient", it diffuses lobbying power to a level where government is usually more responsive to general public interests.

Another powerful line of reasoning in the design of public programs is to try and take the "money" out of special interest politics. This concept goes far beyond the narrow questions of political contributions, and must be applied to the design of hundreds of public programs. A good example is the use of open and visible competition for government contracts – as opposed to awarding contracts through political influence. Another example might be the strict and continuous application of a general philosophy and policy not to pay any government subsidy to any profit making organization, including "tax breaks" concealed in the national tax code. Another example would be to limit eligibility for public funds to the truly needy, not permitting benefits to d paid to people who can take care of themselves. The concept should be established that since public funds will always be limited and scarce they must be allocated as a scarcity and not as the distribution of plenty. Thus, national interests must be made to compete for such allocations, and a public record

41

established that the funds are going to the neediest, or those who can make the highest and best use of them. Two powerful examples: social security funds can and should be limited to the poorest and not to those who chose not to provide for their own retirement; and student loans should be limited to the most needy and not distributed to families who can provide for their own children's higher education. In fact, a valuable general concept for governments, especially in poor countries, is to shift the basis of public programs from across-the-board allocations to targeted allocations. This is a powerful message for developing countries that have great difficulty financing their social safety nets, and for former Soviet style governments now redesigning their public programs.

Legislation should be deliberately written so as to limit subsequent political interference in the drafting of public regulations, and managerial decisions implementing public programs. Many such protections are already written into public laws. Failure occurs when these limits are ignored or gamed. One powerful example has been the political attempts to control the award of public contracts, where "who you know" substitutes for "how well can you perform". The conflict between politics vs. management pervades the whole structure of public management.

Another great pool being tapped by special interests is that of public regulatory authority. Regulations supposedly must be in the general public interest, justified by some general public need. They should not be used to punish opponents or reward friends. Regulations are so complex and invisible that they have become a haven for subliminal ways for special interests to enforce their preferences. Also, regulations are too often selectively enforced to favor certain interests and ignore others.

Still another approach would be to make special interest preference illegal. This has successfully been done in such areas as patronage, nepotism, non-competitive contracting, prevention of low interest loans, and other techniques.

Another way is to make public services that favor specific groups subject to the concept of user fees. For example, the U. S. Coast Guard conducts ice breaking operations in the Great Lakes. While this may benefit "commerce" generally, it specifically benefits shippers and ship operators who do not have to pay for their own ice breaking. The Coast Guard could continue to provide the service, but could at least charge a user fee to recoup the expenses of the government.

Another way to mitigate special interest politics is to try and modify the political system itself. Examples are term limits; the enforced transparency of government activities; requirements for public review and comment of proposed public actions such as major policies or regulations. In legislation or rules, there could be enforced publication of all groups or persons who submitted or reviewed and commented on proposals and drafts, or who attended meetings in which legislation was modified. In addition, special analyses could be mandated for publication evaluating all instances where special advantages are created, and who would benefit and how – the ancient test of who benefits and who is harmed. In most governments, the government itself refuses to provide such analyses, but it is seen as crucial information by media people and public interest groups. Even though this provision would be hard to enforce, such a law would lay down a legal basis of fact that could be investigated. This might act to limit back room interventions, since a post audit could catch those who failed to disclose their interventions, or failed to report honestly in official documents – in a manner similar to post audits of tax returns. Laws could be modified to create penalties for "undue influence" in the decisions creating public authority.

Finally, there is the need to create – and enforce – laws preventing the undue influence imbedded in campaign contributions. Such laws generally exist when certain contributions are clearly defined as illegal, but laws are vague about the meaning of "undue" influence, and actual proof that some quid pro quo took place seems almost impossible. Many political bargains do not involve money, but rather the exchange of back room commitments for future support, or the mitigation of opposition.

SOEs proved to be highly vulnerable to corruption and pathological government policies and practices. The pattern of SOEs became a known failure in hundreds of specific situations in dozens of countries. But many governments did not – and often could not – face up to the economic facts of life, and clung to SOEs for pathological or doctrinal motivations. The "too important to fail" syndrome is a political motivation and not an economic reality. It caused the propping up of inherently inefficient SOEs and drained funding from other public programs. It became clear that SOEs could become tough political players themselves, capable of protecting their own obsolete institutions and serving the special interest motives that needed their survival.

In addition, great numbers of SOEs were corrupt from top to bottom. Political corruption dealt mostly with the draining of SOEs of resources to fund perverse political activities or direct corrupt payoffs to politicians. SOE bureaucracies have become corrupt on their own behalf, draining off funds into personal accounts and preserving corrupt practices instead of fighting them. These patterns of corruption seem amazingly visible. What then seems most pathological is the stubborn desires of governments to hang on to such failed institutions even when they know exactly how bad they are. This is the essence of pathological governance.

Emerging Islamic Special Interests

The Muslim world is increasingly the victim of a complex mix of serious conflicts, all of which tend to move into violence:

1. Governments vs. the people: Governments have all too often come to mean a source of conflict, rampant corruption, a neglect of social services and public infrastructure in favor of the military and foreign conflicts.
2. The ancient and implacable conflict between the Sunni and the Shia.
3. The more current deep conflict between Sunni Saudi Arabia and its allies vs. Shia Iran and its bloc of allies.

4. A vast, ever shifting set of relationships with the secular external world.
5. Splintering within each bloc into literally hundreds of terrorist groups ranging from moderates to religious zealots to greedy power hungry thugs.
6. The military vs. the civilian world.
7. Religion vs. secularism. Zealots vs. moderates.

Further, all of these factors seem to be constantly shifting and changing, but all to often for the worse. The dynamics within most Middle East countries are horrible: vicious, irrational, hateful and incompetent.

This is not a world that can be understood rationally. The prevailing environment is passionate, secretive, self-absorbed, nearly hysterical, and in the end deeply threatening and destructive. No country in the Muslim world is better off than it was 50 years ago, although some like Indonesia, Turkey and Jordan are rising up above their own pasts. Some like Afghanistan, Sudan, Syria, the Central African Republic, parts of Nigeria, and worst of all, the emergence of the hideous Islamic State in Iraq have sunk to pitiful inconceivable depths. What good do these terrorist forces offer? What have they actually produced? Death, destruction, national deterioration, poverty, ruin and a world of universal, implacable hate.

Now, countries suffer from the new "Islamic Triangle": the ruling regime vs. Sunni forces vs. Shia forces, all of them fighting each other. Occasionally there may be some other strong presence such as the large Christian community in Lebanon, or the villages and tribal strongholds in Afghanistan and Pakistan, or the Kurdish ethnic concentration in adjoining parts of Turkey, Iran, Iraq and Syria.

And again: what is the driving force that galvanizes this surge of Islamic passion in the Muslim world? Why does this passion insist on becoming vicious and hateful? What does this tide of passion promise, or seem to offer that produces hundreds of thousands of active supporters? What motivates young men (and now some women) to become suicide bombers or terrorist warriors?

Three answers are usually advanced to these questions, two of which are true but inadequate. The first answer is that the terrorist are really freedom fighters or liberators. It is argued that the ruling elite is incompetent and corrupt, and all too often, the critics are right. So, many people suffering from these corrupt regimes will buy into efforts to displace the government, hoping for something better. Usually they get the same thing or worse.

The second answer to why Islamist terrorism can be undertaken, is the broadly based call for religious jihad, originating from religious leaders. There are thousands of schools, training camps, preachers and propaganda (increasingly electronic) where a loose alliance of religious leaders call for insurgent action. This action may be a form of street protests or political maneuvering, but in fact, it is most often deliberately escalated to the level of physical attack – suicide bombers, vehicles full of explosives, armed assaults against specific elements of the targeted government or society. It is largely the zealous preaching of these Imams and Mullahs that galvanizes the suicide bombers and the Soldiers of God.

It is at this level that the Islamic world is at its ugliest and most confusing. This world is ugly because it deliberately targets the murder of the largest possible number of innocent people, on the specious and foolish premise that these murders will cause an outburst of sympathy for their cause, and the collapse of the ruling regime. The current insanity of the Islamic State in Iraq, and the horror of Hamas in Gaza are astonishing versions of this thinking. It is specious because the terrorist Imams have never really offered any superior vision of how they would govern if they should get into power. They say only that, if they come to rule, they will be honest, efficient and caring. How? By the invocation of Sharia Law and by the assertion that all people will live a pure and ideal life as defined by the precepts of the Quran. But in the limited number of cases where Islamist regimes have indeed risen to power (Iraq, Syria, Sudan, Afghanistan) the joys of pure virtue have not materialized.

There are many in the more fundamentalist element of the Muslim world who forecast the creation of a single unified Islamic world.

Muslims living all over the world would be united by their religion, and will obey a single leadership – a form of modern day Caliphate ordering and dictating the lives of all of the world's 1.3 billion Muslims.

Is such a unity possible? If so, how would it be brought about, how would it function, and what would it stand for, and what would it seek to achieve? But if such a unity is not possible, then the other questions are irrelevant. So the main question is what would make a single Muslim world (an "ummah") possible? The only potential lies in the religion, and only in some universal and extremist way. What is the likelihood of this?

The reality is that the forces in people's lives are so varied and powerful that they overpower the unreal yearnings of the Imams who are really seeking centrist power and command. To begin with, no matter where Muslims live, they are part of a society and a culture: a family, a tribe, a clan, a nation. Good or bad, these societies exert real influence over people's lives through a sense of belonging and reinforcement. These communal forces are thus needed and desirable, and they are highly varied, and thus they mitigate against the idea of a single unitary worldwide directive leadership.

It is also true that people acquire forms of professional or occupational loyalty. Doctors have developed a historic and universal set of ethics for their profession. Engineers have strong standards of responsibility for the soundness and safety for their buildings and machines. People working for an organization feel a responsibility to guard the best interests of that organization. There are millions of different organizations, and thus millions of reasons why Muslims cannot simply live under a single limited set of rules.

There is a widely held view that the Quran itself not only permits such independence but encourages it. The Quran says "God creates the capacity for you to act, and ultimately it is you who acquire a choice from among the choices God presents." Countless opinion polls conducted all over the Muslim world show that Muslims want a devout life, but one of freedom of choice, and the Quran further states that "the pattern you see on earth and in the heavens is diversity and variety."

Here again, as so often in the Muslim world, one sees a pattern of religious leadership that interprets the Quran and Sunnah in ways that support their own beliefs, which are much influenced by a yearning for power, or influence, and are not really defined by the best interests of Muslim people. Nor is it clear just what the advocates of the Caliphate hope to accomplish. They speak in general terms about returning to the perfect life that Allah desires people to have; but these interpretations can't explain how 1.3 billion Muslims can achieve such perfection. The main thrust of the theme of some Muslim religious leaders seems to be to advocate some return to the older versions of Sharia Law, and yet almost every nation in the Muslim world already lives under some degree of Sharia Law, usually augmented by necessary additional law drawn mainly from modern secular practices or from the deep historical laws and customs arising from tribes and clans from time immemorial.

DEALING WITH OPPRESSIVE GOVERNMENTS

Looking at the enormous power exercised by oppressive regimes, there is a tendency for the average person to feel powerless and hopeless, and to believe that no power can unseat them. This is especially true when the ultimate pathology has occurred and the tyrant has succeeded in perverting the governing laws themselves and making them the instruments of oppression. In the face of such evil, many people simply give up. Others manage to flee to other countries. Some hide out in hills and forests, and forge anti-government rebel bands. It may be that there is no power other than armed conflict that will ever break ultimate totalitarian control. Many tyrannies have been overthrown by revolution, massive civil unrest or military coups de etat. Tragically, the result of such horribly damaging efforts is often the emergence of a new tyranny, no better than the old.

What is most extraordinary however is not how many people give up, but how many people have the courage to battle to reclaim their lives and their countries. And times do change; totalitarians and their regimes grow old and die, and younger and hopefully better leaders emerge. Internal struggles within the ruling clique may weaken the regime and make it more vulnerable. Tyrants and their military backers may fall out. Successful counter strokes succeed. Increasingly, the globalized world has learned to apply pressure from the outside that forces changes that could not have been achieved by local forces alone. Occasionally, external invasion threats, support for dissidents, economic sanctions, or world-wide criticism force behavioral modifications for the better. In other cases, massive social or economic failures become so destructive that even tyrants are forced to change their ways.

Where totalitarianism is not "total", there are many ways in which such governments can be influenced and their power mitigated such as the following.

1. Resist centralizing too much power

A government which is highly centrist creates so much concentration of power that other elements of society cannot defend themselves and maintain their own wellbeing. Governments cannot be trusted to avoid the improper exercise of this power. Every effort must be made to see to it that the relationships between governments and the rest of a country's national institutions is structured to decentralize power and sufficient strength exists outside of the central government to modulate centrist power and create power balances. The U. S. constitution is based on this concept of shared power at two levels: first as between the central national government vs. the residual powers of the states; and second, in a sharing of power between the president, the congress and the courts. But nations need to go farther by a deliberate sharing of power between the government and private interests both individual and commercial. Further, the role of religious, cultural, social and ethnic institutions which are critical to the wellbeing of the public must be kept liberated from political control and intervention, and free to evolve as determined by their own broad public desires.

2. Deliberately Work to Create Strong Local Governments

Governments are broadly either national or local, and there is a body of knowledge and experience which supports the premise that the national government cannot and should not be the dominant level of government in the definition and delivery of local governance. This concern is best addressed by designing a "service delivery" kind of government at local levels close to and directly reachable by citizens. In order to create a strong local (i.e. state/province level or city level), the following local powers are critical:

Separate power to tax. Local authorities that are forced to rely on the national government for all or most of their money inevitably lose any real ability to control or even define the level of revenues obtained, and also lose a critical degree of control over how public funds will be spent. Funds are drained off by the national government from local resources, laundered through both the political and bureaucratic mechanisms of centrist authority, and then returned to local governments depleted and distorted by national rather than local needs and priorities. The tax system should be deliberately structured to provide a second level of revenue defined collected and spent by local governments. Local revenues should be adequate to meet their basic program operating needs. There may well be further transfers of funds from the national to local governments but each such transfer should be the subject of continuous negotiation between the two levels. It is critical in such negotiations that local governments speak from a position of some power and not total dependency.

Collateral to this argument is the need for local officials to have their own independent power base as defined by law. This means more than just having local officials elected, because such elections can still be over-ridden by centrist laws, regulations, and fund controls which can make local officials almost powerless. Therefore, in addition to financial liberation, local officials need legal and regulatory liberation. One of the best means of ratifying this local government independence is to shift the reality of where citizens go for decisions about important public services and controls from the national government to local governments, and then to provide deliberate means by which citizens and groups can influence the decisions of these local governments, and the quality of public program delivery. Finally, the managers and workers in local governments should be responsible only to their local elected leadership including not only the right to hire and fire, but the obligation to develop the government workforce up to an adequate level of performance.

3. There is no substitute for citizen self-sufficiency

A major lesson that has come out of the socialist experience in governance is that governments create a fatal mistake when they persuade the public to rely on governments for too many things as a substitute for individual self reliance. Where citizens are no longer able to provide for their own savings, or obtain their own housing, or create their own occupations or find their own jobs, or make important decisions in their lives without government approval, they have lost a critical element of democratic vigor. People expect or at least hope for a lot of things, including possibility for constant improvement in their lives and those of their children. No government yet has proved capable of meeting fully such expectations. This view runs directly counter to the philosophies of socialist governance, or even the liberal intellectual views which advocate big government. Whether a government is big or not is not critical. What is critical is whether governments function in ways that deteriorate the ability of their citizens to handle their legitimate share of their own wellbeing.

4. Sharing Power with the Private Sector

The great surge of socialist governments after World War II seemed to be the wave of the future, and perhaps its deepest and most critical element was the decision to substitute the public sector for the private sector in the control and development of the national economy. In country after country, governments took control of all, or of critical elements of economic production, finance, distribution and even marketing. This was done through the mechanism of state owned enterprises -- a middle ground between a government ministry and a true private company. State owned enterprises were supposed to be free to act like efficient private sector organizations, but still be under the policy and financial control of the government.

It is probably self obvious that the government is heavily involved in matters of the national economy. What is less obvious is the equally important point that the private sector is, and should be, heavily involved in the delivery of critical public services. But the real debate is and always has been how any society will allocate the responsibility for public services between its public and private sectors, recognizing that there is a very wide range of acceptable solutions to these allocation choices. Take for example the provision of higher education. Some countries create national university systems, with little latitude for private universities. Others rely mostly on private universities, with the government concerned with supporting the poor who can't finance higher education for their children. Most countries seem to be happy with a mix in which a combination of both public and private schools emerge in patterns that are more spontaneous than planned. The point is that the private sector has assumed a high degree of responsibility for the public service of "higher education." Similar patterns of shared responsibility can be seen in housing, health care, transportation, food production and distribution, and many others. The point is that this sharing dilutes the absolute control of governments and reduces the capacity for oppression.

5. Provide Adequate Public Revenues

A key lesson is that the question of adequate public revenues is really dominated by the question of the adequacy or size of the economy -- not by the ability of the government to tax money out of the economy. For example, the Soviet Union had almost unlimited power and legal authority to suck money out of the Soviet economy, but it still failed to provide adequate public revenues to meet even basic citizen demands. This is because the Soviet economy was neither big enough nor "value added" enough to provide adequate funds for many needs, including government needs.

This reality has dominated the fate of most of the socialist governments that found themselves unable to develop their economies enough to sustain their national commitments. The compelling role of governments is to create the conditions within the country that will permit the best possible pace of economic growth, and socialist doctrine and socialist economic apparatus is crumbling where it is perceived that it does not meet this acid test.

6. *Corruption is oppression*

Every government in the world suffers from corruption involving politicians and public officials. A lot of corruption is minor and linked with individuals, but there is a wide range of official actions that are deeply serious involving illegal and pathological programs sponsored by governments themselves against their own people or their neighbors.

These pathological excesses are so painful and destructive that they produce universal outrage in the country. This outrage may create public action. In its most moderate form, it can mean efforts within the framework of the law to create political opposition. One level up may be forms of public protests such as demonstrations or street marches. Beyond that may come the exercise of real force against the government even up to the level of the Arab Spring. Finally, terrible, oppressive governments are guilty of precipitating armed insurrections and civil wars.

Nobody on earth really seems to know how to deal with government corruption, either major or minor. Despite auditors and investigators, and inspectors and police and prosecutors and courts, the corruptors seem enduring and extraordinarily successful. Protections are too weak, and motives to be corrupt are too strong. Not least of the problems is that most of the protective mechanisms are controlled by the very people who have decided to be corrupt. For example, when the Russian Federation decided to sell of some of their state owned enterprises, it permitted the sale to be controlled by corrupt enterprise managers who put a very low value on the assets of the enterprises and then sold the new stock issues to themselves, thus effectively stealing public assets. The process was acceptable if used honestly, but totally failed to protect against those who were deliberately corrupt. No supposedly democratic government can justify this waste and illegal usurpation of taxpayer funds, and every government has a positive obligation to see to it that tax funds are spent on defined public purposes.

7. Encourage Political Competition

There are many countries where a reasonably democratic government has existed with only one political party dominant over a long period of time, and there are others where a large number of parties have not foundered the democratic environment. But a single dominant political party places the country at great risk of sinking into forms of tyranny or in a loss of impetus in moving the leadership toward more effective and representative governance. The existence of democratic mechanisms such as elections, bi-cameral legislatures, separation of powers, an independent judiciary, and a free press have not proved enough to prevent the emergence of tyrannical regimes.

Many developing countries find that there are too few talented leaders who can or will subject themselves to the trauma of politics. Such countries have great difficulty mounting two or more credible political parties at all, especially against incumbents who use the government authority to beat back political opposition. It is all too common to see opposition candidates threatened, harassed, denied access to the public and the media, or even arrested on questionable and largely uninvestigated charges. Under such conditions, it is understandable that talented and decent people are exceedingly reluctant to take on an entrenched regime. Thus, the existence of an effective political opposition must rise up from the whole of society, and can't rely simply on the courage of a few who are willing to make an extraordinary commitment. Good people must be urged to compete, but with promises of support and protection behind them. Businesses, courts, bureaucrats and police must try to function in the broader interests of the country, rising above the short-term rewards or punishments dealt out by those in power.

8. Generate Massive Bottom-Up Citizen Participation

This imperative applies even more crucially and specifically to the citizens themselves. There are some very stark options facing a national populace. In the absence of strong countervailing means to modulate the excesses of ruling elite, the public may find themselves robbed, cheated, lied to, and deprived of vital elements of their lives, as victims of their own government. And if such circumstances become unbearable, without a means to remove such a government, the only option may become the horrors of a civil insurrection of the kind that is now characteristic of the contemporary world. Considered in this light, defending and supporting valid political opposition, whatever the risks, seems far the best course.

This maintenance of political opposition means that citizens have to be committed to watching their government closely to identify its worst excesses and to form themselves into action groups to apply back-pressure on the government. This broad counter pressure is needed to defend the viability of socially protecting institutions, and to expose political corruption. It must be constant and serious, because centrist regimes, once strongly entrenched, are extraordinarily difficult to dislodge. It is right and important to say that democracy is first and foremost a state of mind, and it must become the dominant public morality. There is hope in the fact that even soldiers and police and judges and public officials are both human beings and citizens who can choose to function for the public good if pressed to do so by the common judgment of the community.

9. Avoid the Tyranny of Regulation

One of the most perplexing arenas of governance is that of public regulation, which has been a "growth industry" in almost every country. Regulation can be one of the most valuable means by which governments deploy their power, to protect the public and to advance the common good. Almost every country benefits now from proper regulation of health protection, public safety, environmental protection, and modulation of the functioning of the economy. But regulation knows few limits; there almost no ground rules to define where regulations exceed reasonable limits and become instruments of oppression and petty tyranny. Many countries have deliberately allowed the creation of hundreds of thousands of regulations because each regulation represents another form of control and potential corruption.

10. Control of the Military

Throughout history, nations have sought to maintain a strong military, and yet keep it within the control of the political leadership -- from pharaohs and kings, to presidents and legislatures. Surprisingly, governments have most often succeeded, and this tradition of civilian control is reflected in most governments today.

But the exceptions to this generalization have been many, and have, over time marked some of the worst periods in many national histories. Often, civilian and military leadership have been one and the same. In other cases, the military has overwhelmed or dominated the civilian side of government, most often with dysfunctional consequences. Sometimes, the military regards itself as a separate and equal focus of national power, or reserves to itself the role of overseers of the country, with some latent responsibility to depose what it regards as an unfit civilian government, or to meddle extensively into the functioning of the rest of government. And there is a long and mostly perverse history of military leaders using their authority over military units to overthrow the incumbent government and establish their own dictatorships.

Civilian/military relations can also be perverse in the other direction. Civilian governments have often used the military not as the national protector, but as an enforcer of their own political control, and as a means to destroy or intimidate political opposition, and a means to quash public protest.

11. Take Advantage of the Opportunities Created by Major Social or Economic Convulsions

Massive social or economic failures, while tragic, can so discredit a regime that it loses much of its power base. Such failures can also create shifts in alliances for the ruling elite, along with splintering, weakening, and even dissolution. Such failures increase the likelihood of massive civil unrest on a scale to cause an overthrow of the government.

When an arrogant regime is so embroiled in corruption that it becomes a national scandal, this alone may precipitate its own convulsion, and unite many forces in society to overturn the regime – by elections if possible, or by civil unrest.

EXAMPLE: THE DAMN DAM BUILDERS OF CHINA

After several years of planning and a lot of careful subterranean lobbying within the upper echelons of the Chinese Communist Party (CCP), China's legislature approved the construction of the huge, hugely expensive Three Gorges River Dam Project on the Yangzi River just west of Chongqing and the great regional complex of 30 million people that surrounds it. The Three Gorges Dam is now the largest in the world, in terms of its power generation of more than 20 million Gigawatts of power.

China can certainly use the energy, but there were many in China who put themselves at risk by arguing against the project. They were concerned about silting, river damage, environmental threats and cost. In addition, it was pointed out that the dam and its upriver changes would force more than 1, 250,000 people out of their homes in one of the best agricultural areas in the country.

The 1992 decision to build the dam brushed aside these scientific and engineering arguments, and ignored the human disasters it would inflict on people. It also overrode the views of perhaps one third of the members of the legislature who either opposed or abstained, at a time when it was still very dangerous to oppose the government over anything. What this whole sequence of events revealed is that the business of dam building is a highly successful example of the powers of special interest politics in China.

First, consider the admittedly important advantages of the dam as advanced by its proponents. As early as the 1930s, the need for flood control had been argued by Dr. Sun Yat-sen, considered to be the father of post-imperial China. China has spent a couple of thousand years attempting to control and harness its rivers. As a result, dam building has long been a big and powerful sector of the economy. Then, by the time of Mao Zedong in the late 50's and 60's, the second great justification for the dam emerged in the form of the demand for electricity in a rapidly growing and industrializing economy. And, as he did in so many other areas, Mao's enormous ego began to envision an enormous dam – more as a transfusion for Mao's ego than as a reflection of sober and sensible engineering.

The politics of Mao seemed to kick off the special interest players like nothing else in recent Chinese history. Organizations both in China and in other countries sensed a flood – not of water but of money. These special interests included:

a. The companies that would build the dam itself. Some of the most serious competitors included China's State Owned Enterprises (SOE), plus many companies from Japan, Europe, and the United States.

b. A second set of key players would be the organizations that would design and build the energy production facilities – the turbines and related equipment that would actually generate the electricity.

c. Then there was the next kind of organizations that would design and build and operate the energy distribution system in a wide region of China. The dam would stand just to the west of Chongqing where the central city and surrounding industrial parks, commercial complexes and residential areas contained an estimated 30 million people with a growing appetite for electrical power. Then, upstream was the rich agricultural area of the Red Basin, holding about 100 million people.

d. Other companies would seek to get on the gravy train to sell everything from secondary construction services to supplies, equipment, tools, automobiles and so much else.

e. And then there was the involvement of an extraordinary array of government bureaucratic units. The project would be managed by the huge Three Gorges Project Corporation, a

State Owned Enterprise trying to act like a business. Before the dam and related facilities were finally completed, hundreds of organizations including private corporations and SOEs would need to be selected and put under contract.

f. Dozens of government agencies at all levels were officially involved and on the hook to perform well. Most were brimming with enthusiasm over the expected opportunities to use their government powers to siphon off some of the anticipated deluge of big time money coming from the central government.

g. One of the most important responsibilities would be to organize the uprooting of 1,250,000 people in the Red Basin who were to be displaced by the new water courses, and the huge reservoir that would be created just behind the dam itself. Thirteen cities of up to 150,000 population would be inundated. Some 140 substantial towns and 1352 villages were also doomed. Rich farm land would be destroyed, and much ancient archeological history destroyed. All of this would be costly -- and badly done.

There were other commercial interests involved. Chongqing attracted cargo vessels both from upstream to the west, serving mostly agricultural interests, and from the east, all the way from the China Sea to the city. It was argued that the dam would widen the river to the west and increase the flow to the east, and that both measures would permit a considerable increase in the cargo vessel tonnage because larger vessels could be used. In a similar kind of argument, electrical power interests strongly argued for the biggest, highest possible dam because the greater length and height would allow an increase of power of output, and thus make power enterprises even happier. As earlier noted Mao, until his death in 1976 was a "monster dam" advocate, and his successors tended to continue this view largely for reasons of national pride.

And yet the despite the great risks created when one disagrees with the CCP, a growing number of analysts spoke out against the dam, or at least against the idea of a monster dam. The arguments against were numerous and serious. Most were advanced by scientists, engineers and professional managers. Consider the following:

1. <u>Dam height and width</u>. It was argued that the larger the dam the greater the structural risk. The new structure would be among the largest dams in the world, and the reservoir behind the dam would be the greatest in the world. Scientists and engineers feared that they really did not have enough precedents to say reliably what the safe size limits were.

2. <u>Earthquake potentials.</u> A collateral fear stemmed from the fact that the dam would rest on earthquake fault lines, and absolutely nobody could predict the likelihood of a quake, which would collapse the whole dam, sending an enormous wave downstream and producing absolute catastrophe. Other safety fears were seldom uttered publically; that China's notoriously corrupt contracting practices would produce faulty construction with substandard materials. It seemed certain that the project would produce corruption at least of the old traditional kind like bribes, over billing, extortion, preferment in contractor selection, and plain old theft. But such corruption could also lead to other improper practices. And this worry about corruption covered every facet of the project, including management by the central Three Gorges Dam Project Corporation. Given the almost universal ascendency of corruption in Chinese government agencies, SOEs, and private contractors, the risk of corruption was very high, and could be not only highly costly, but actively dangerous.

3. <u>The People's Liberation Army</u>. Further along these lines, the People's Liberation Army (PLA) became a major player in dam location and construction for two reasons. First, the PLA raised ominous questions about the vulnerability of the dam to foreign military attack, and second, about vulnerability to threats from "terrorists". The fact that the PLA would not, and could not be specific about the potential source of any such threats did not deter it from pushing in and throwing their weight around in the whole dam project.

4. <u>Changing the Yangzi River.</u> Other engineering studies raised all kinds of issues about the operations on the Yangzi River system, once the dam was in place. It was pointed out that the river had, throughout its history, carried heavy loads of silt from the rich farm lands of the Red Basin in the west. At worst, it was feared that the great backup of water behind the dam would begin to erode the river banks at a rate far exceeding previous experience. This would cause rapid and heavy silting into the huge reservoir that would be created immediately behind the dam. This could in turn cause two problems. First, the silt could constantly clog the intake passages to the turbines generating the power, and thus add to the cost of their maintenance. Also, the level of silt behind the dam would become a threat to the dam itself, and it was predicted that serious additional funds would constantly be needed forever just to dredge and haul away mountains of silt. Thus, these kinds of concerns added weight to the broader argument that the dam project would never be "cost effective."

5. <u>Human consequences.</u> Finally, there were very serious concerns about harm done to people. It was ultimately estimated that the displacements of people would be enormous. One and a quarter million people would be forced out of their homes, and whole cities, towns and villages would be lost. The people who studied these problems had special reasons to be fearful. China's history under the CCP in both the Maoist era and beyond was one of harsh, brutal and unjust measures to seize land and property for economic development. Many such seizures were deeply corrupt: bribes offered and accepted between developers and public officials for illegal takings, and a blatant record for under compensating the victims from whom the land and property were taken. Often, there simply was no compensation at all despite the supposed protections of the law, and much of the money available for compensations simply disappeared into the wrong pockets. Thus, the Red Basin residents had a lot of reason to fear that they would lose their very productive communities, and that they would end up in some remote desert.

6. <u>Costs.</u> Looming over the whole project was the issue of what it would cost and where the money would come from. Initially, the view of the CCP was highly optimistic. Early cost estimates were relatively low (because the bureaucracy deliberately understated them) and it was felt that large portions of the money would be "OPM" – that is, other people's money. Specifically, official investors such as the World Bank, the International Monetary Fund, the Asian Development Bank, the United Nations Development Program and various nations such as Japan, Canada, Great Britain and the United States seemed seriously interested. In addition, a whole array of the world's most powerful banks seemed poised to provide financing.

But as the less romantic and more sober evaluations of the problems inherent in the project became known, foreign sources, including the banks began to back off. "The avarice of one decade began to transmute into more considered caution. In part, the doubts arose because of a rising world-wide feeling that big dams were ill-conceived ideas; that few of them had ever realized the expectations offered for them, that all were too costly, that most caused grave environmental impacts, and that mostly totalitarian regimes favored them most notably as a way of impressing the peasantry with the ruler's energy, acumen and skill." (4).

This was surely true in China up to the hilt, where the dam was constantly cited as a fitting "Memorial to the Great Helmsman". It was also pumped up as a visible manifestation of the emerging greatness of "China's New Socialist Man."

In the end, the CCP had to conclude that it must go forward solely with Chinese resources. Part of the funding would come from the huge resources that the CCP extracts from the Chinese economy. Part would come from a new nation-wide 2% sales tax. More would come from the old (and dangerous) trick of politically forcing state banks to make preferential loans at heavy discounts to the government enterprises and private companies build and equipping the dam. These banks were State Owned Enterprises (SOE), and thus under the direct control of the Party: The Bank of China, the People's Construction Bank, the State Development Bank, and the Industrial and Commercial Bank of China. In addition, provinces and cities in China have strange and tricky laws allowing them to create "development corporations" which have the power to borrow, but little supervision, and absolutely no assurance that they will every really repay their loans. Thus, China went heavily into debt, with the serious likelihood that much of the debt would deteriorate.

Final official approval of the Three Gorges Dam Project was given by the People's Congress in 1992. After all of the technical and human arguments against the dam had been made, the pre-determined politics kicked in. But one thing is at least remarkable to note: in the tame legislative body where nobody does anything against the Party, 813 delegates out of 2613 did vote against the project, which at that time was estimated to cost $36 billion. The measure was passed with absolutely no discussion.

The profitable progress of the dam builders proceeded apace. A whole extravagant agenda of nearly 100 smaller dams in the Nu River has been undertaken, even though another group of 13 dams which required national government approval was halted by Prime Minister Wen Jiabao in 2004 because of serious environmental concerns. Another major series of approximately 20 dams were approved on the Dadu River, which enters the Yangzi west of Chongqing. A further 20 dams or more are planned on the nearby Jihnsha River and on the Lancong River which flows south into the Mekong River in Laos.

But the keystone of the dam builders agenda is the proposal to build a big new Xiaonanhai dam in Chongqing for some $5.2 billion. Many of the same arguments are raised against it that were raised about the Three Gorges Dam, and the results are the same. The political decision had already been made, records about the project have not been made available, no argument has been officially allowed. At the same time, Chinese dam builders have extended their operations around the world, usually with the substantial help and subsidy of the Chinese government.

According to the Economist "Today, authorities acknowledge that many of the predictions about the Three Gorges Dam have come true. This has led to them proposing dams upstream such as Xiaonanhai, to slow the accumulation of silt." (5).

No matter what, the damn dam builders of China and their official partners steamroller on.

HOW TO MITIGATE SPECIAL INTEREST POLITICS

One of the most compelling ideas about how to avoid special interest politics is to reduce the range of political power. But the question of what should be the range and scope of public power is at the heart of most governments today. In the United States, it has a distinct Republican vs. Democrats, or liberal vs. conservative cast. Around the world, socialism in its various forms stands for broadened and deepened involvement of government in every aspect of national life including essential control over the national economy. Not everything in society should or needs to be made political. Even if one believes in the necessity of a strong political system, it is still possible to accept that politics has its limits, and that a good argument can be made for a "de minimus" government that does all of the right things (and none of the wrong things) and stays out of affairs where it is not competent. One of the most striking forms of this debate has been taking place in countries where the socialist central control of the national economies is now in wide retreat in favor of some form of market based economic policy.

The whole Soviet experience illustrates that powerful government control forced all elements of soviet society to become special interests in their own defense against the power of the central government. When the Soviet style command and control system made the central government responsible for everything – the economy, all public facilities and services, the lives of people, the environment – then everything that went wrong was the fault of the government, and every effort to make things right had to be negotiated with the government.

But when special interests such as state enterprise managers, republic and municipal leaders, union bosses, or professional groups negotiated with the government, they found that they could seldom succeed. The problem was not the allocation of power but the fact that even unlimited power at the top did not translate into adequate capacity to solve the nation's problems. Negotiations simply revealed the near bankruptcy of the system.

Still another approach would be to make special interest preference illegal. This has successfully been done in such areas as patronage, nepotism, non-competitive contracting, prevention of low interest loans, and other techniques.

Another way is to make public services that favor specific groups subject to the concept of user fees. For example, the U. S. Coast Guard conducts ice breaking operations in the Great Lakes. While this may benefit "commerce" generally, it specifically benefits shippers and ship operators who do not have to pay for their own ice breaking. The Coast Guard could continue to provide the service, but could at least charge a user fee to recoup the expenses of the government.

Another way to mitigate special interest politics is to try and modify the political system itself. Examples are term limits; the enforced transparency of government activities; requirements for public review and comment of proposed public actions such as major policies or regulations. In legislation or rules, there could be enforced publication of all groups or persons who submitted or reviewed and commented on proposals and drafts, or who attended meetings in which legislation was modified. In addition, special analyses could be mandated for publication evaluating all instances where special advantages are created, and who would benefit and how – the ancient test of who benefits and who is harmed. In most governments, the government itself refuses to provide such analyses, but it is seen as crucial information by media people and public interest groups. Even though this provision would be hard to enforce, such a law would lay down a legal basis of fact that could be investigated. This might act to limit back room interventions, since a post audit could catch those who failed to disclose their interventions, or failed to report honestly in official documents – in a manner similar to post audits of tax returns. Laws could be modified to create penalties for "undue influence" in the decisions creating public authority.

Finally, there is the need to create – and enforce – laws preventing the undue influence imbedded in campaign contributions. Such laws generally exist when certain contributions are clearly defined as illegal, but laws are vague about the meaning of "undue" influence, and actual proof that some quid pro quo took place seems almost impossible. Many political bargains do not involve money, but rather the exchange of back room commitments for future support, or the mitigation of opposition.

The Dilemma of State Owned Enterprises (SOE)

One of the most fundamental and far reaching tides running in the post World War II era was the emergence of State Socialism and of State Owned Enterprises (SOEs) as the major fulcrum of Socialist power. These economic entities were seen as a middle ground between a standard government ministry or bureau and a true private sector organization. The key is that the SOE was designed so that it could function like an independent private entity for economic efficiency purposes, but would still be under the policy direction of the government so that each would implement some valid public purpose. State ownership was justified in part by an opposition to the private sector which was seen as excessively greedy and functioning in ways that harmed the general public interest. Thus, much of the rationale for heavy state intervention in the economy was to protect the poor from private greed and to undertake what short-sighted, unskilled and undercapitalized private actors could not." This anti private sector philosophy also rested on the premise that somehow, officials in governments would always act correctly, and that public decisions about the use of national resources would somehow always be "right". This reasoning led to the creation of hundreds of thousands of government monopolies in the form of state owned enterprises. China alone created more than 400,000 of them. The irony is more compelling in that the supposed defense against private sector monopolies would necessarily be laws and governments. But where are the protections against tyrannical government oppression and mismanagement?

Ownership by the government has been a key element in many countries, ranging from total government control to government with a 51% ownership or a substantial minority ownership sufficient to exert public policy influence. In other cases, the government has had little ownership, but remains the principal financier of the enterprise, giving it a lot of control. In many cases, the government's real control comes from its mandated participation on a board of directors, and from the oversight exerted by some supervising government ministry.

But the relationships between a government and its state owned enterprises have almost never been strictly business-like relationships. Instead, they are complex webs of political/economic tactics and strategies which define who exercises power and who benefits financially. In theory, the government creates state owned enterprises (SOEs) to provide public services, and to generate public revenue. In practice, SOEs gain a lot of political power themselves, and end up negotiating their role with the government. In fact, many countries, SOEs were given absolute monopoly over whole segments of the national economy, which then forced private sector competitors out of business. In other cases, the military was authorized to own and operate some SOEs, and they threatened and terrorized their competitors too.

These power relationships can be both good and bad, but the tide that has been running in the world for the past 30 years is that SOEs have had a reputation for poor performance, and many have survived only because they have been protected and subsidized by their governments. It has also been argued however, that much of the failure of the SOEs can be attributed to dysfunctional political and bureaucratic meddling, which has severely limited SOE ability to function like efficient businesses. According to Waterbury, "the empirical record shows that managers of public enterprises doctor their books, hoard goods, evade taxes, hide profits, and collude with other enterprises to defraud the government. So many enterprises ran forever as loss makers that the cost of propping them up contributed greatly to the fiscal troubles of their governments, and their failure meant that often decades of potential real economic development were wasted in the fruitless task of attempting to make SOEs work." (6)

As in so many other arenas, the Soviet experience is relevant. The single most pervasive phenomenon in socialist countries is the shortage of goods. In Soviet style thinking, government central planners deliberately limited access for foreign direct investment largely because of doctrinal absurdities such as economic "independence", suspicions of private capital, and fear of opening up the country in ways that let citizens learn truths that the government preferred they did not know. By denying foreign investment of capital, and by controlling even domestic potentials for generating capital investments, the government assumed the whole burden for investment capital generation. As early as the 1970's, it was apparent, if one wanted to look, that government sources were wholly inadequate despite an almost unlimited capacity to squeeze profits out of state enterprises. Adherence to the state owned enterprise system was almost total up to the point of political collapse, despite the clear recognition that many of the most important SOEs were failing to generate wealth, and instead had to be propped up with subsidies gouged out from other sources. The Soviets simply had no idea what its enterprises cost, nor any control over their total expenditures, or even knowledge of whether they were running in surplus or deficit. Schleifer and Vishny state that "industries do not keep the profits they earn from selling their products at official prices, since the taxes levied by the central authorities are close to 100%. Nor does an industry have any interest in producing a competitive output at a competitive price." (7) The only way an industry can get anything for itself is by having a shortage of the good it produces and then collecting rents in the form of bribes from quantity constrained buyers." Input costs were paid for by the State, which also covered losses. Even when prices were raised in the hope of generating greater output, the added value was largely taxed away again, and goods continued to shift out of official channels into the informal economy, thus further weakening the official institutions, and reducing the source of funds for government programs. These inevitable failure trends were clearly visible to anyone who had the independence of mind to look and to understand. But Socialist doctrine blinded those in power.

There were many perverse and corrupt ways in which governments can "game" their relationships with SOEs. Most governments exercise control of SOEs through a supervisory government ministry. For example, a Ministry of Energy will supervise all SOEs that produce oil, gas, electricity, water power, and energy distribution. This supervision usually involves review (and control of) borrowing, product lines, business location, capital investments, labor rates and prices. Governments can keep foreign competition out of the country in order to protect their domestic SOEs and private companies. Such protections include denying the right to import goods or services; imposition of heavy tariffs on imports; quotas limiting the quantity of goods that can be imported; or technical regulations that prevent certain goods from entering. Similarly, governments are usually very defensive of their SOEs. It becomes politically important that SOEs succeed -- or at least appear to succeed. This has led to the evolution of many practices which give SOEs advantages over private competitors, including the granting of a national monopoly; licensing regulations that prevent private company entry into certain markets; limits on foreign investment and/or ownership; forced allocation of market access.

The old Soviet Union, through its command and control economic planning "perfected" highly corrosive techniques for control of prices of goods and services. This might involve overall price control structures for all goods and services; selective controls on the sale of goods or services (e. g. what is paid to farmers for wheat; what prices wheat processors and distributors are allowed to charge; and what prices bakeries are allowed to charge customers). There may be mandated limits on SOE charges and profits, and forced exchange rates between SOEs. Also, the government may tamper with the costs charged for government controlled services such as power or raw materials so that some organizations are penalized while others are subsidized. The government may use regulations, or back room pressures, to control payments between SOEs and even private companies to subsidize favored SOEs. In many cases, the government has given SOEs preferential status for exchange rates.

In most developing countries, there is a central bank that is itself a SOE and it can be used by the government to control the whole national banking system, and as a means to grant further advantages and subsidies to SOEs including the following: subsidized banking loans; preference in lending over private companies; government loan guarantees; mandated "preferred customer status" vs. private banks; forgiveness of loans; or overdraft privileges. In case after case, ruling elites carried their heavy-handed kind of centrist control far beyond rationality, to the level of oppression and civic terrorism.

Chinese SOEs continue to dominate the national energy sector. They include the China Power Investment Corporation, China Export-Import Bank, China Power Grid Corp., Hydrolancang International Energy Co., Yunnan Machinery Equipment Import and Export Co., China Geo-Engineering Corp., China Gezhouba Group, China International Water and Electric Corp. Hydro China, and SINOHYDRO, now the largest dam building enterprise in the world.

It is clear that any of these games could become corrupt and they usually did. Many of the practices are inherently complex and technical, and cannot be seen or understood by the general public. Corrupt practices including the taking of bribes and/or kickbacks for preferential treatment (access to loans, access to licenses to do business, award of government contracts, insider knowledge on transactions, avoidance of audits or investigations, ignoring excessive and illegal charges, excessive prices and profits, etc.). Typically, government audit, oversight and investigation agencies are weak and understaffed -- often deliberately.

Even if SOEs were not actively corrupt, they very often proved to be highly inefficient in management terms. Most got very used to the feeling that the government was obliged to give them everything they wanted, and to bail them out of any difficulties. Most SOEs had little or no financial discipline since they were not required to live within their earnings and could get endless cheap bank loans or government subsidies that never had to be repaid. Nor was their business strategy any more rational. Production output was prized more than anything else, but there was little attention or understanding of whether produced goods could actually be sold. Output was king, and efficiency or reliability were virtually unheard of concepts. Again, what makes this inefficiency oppressive was that it was the perverse combination of pathological political motives in the face of clear understanding of the failure of these policies. Both politicians and managers knew better – but they did not care, and the public suffered for decades because of the absence of social services that the funds wasted on SOEs could have financed.

The pathology of oil in Nigeria is a pathetic example of bad economics mired in corruption. Nigeria is Africa's biggest oil producer, but the country is always short of gas and oil. The government subsidizes the price of fuel for the public, but at such a low price that local refiners cannot profit from the local market and choose instead to sell abroad. This creates an artificial shortage in the country, with long lines at retail outlets, where fuel is seldom available. Instead, fuel is diverted to the black market which is often controlled by government officials. This artificial shortage in turn creates corruption, with users having to bribe SOE or government officials to get fuel allocated to them. Even individual car owners have to bribe gas station attendants. At the same time, the people in the oil producing areas are desperately poor and benefit little from the oil wealth of the region. In the last 20 years or so, thousands of people were killed or injured in riots while stealing fuel from deliberately punctured state owned oil pipelines. Some were locals, but much of the damage was done by organized criminal gangs who steal to sell to black market channels.

While peasants were siphoning off fuel, officials in the state owned enterprise and government ministries were busy siphoning off oil profits for themselves but on a far grander scale. A previous president of the country is under investigation for allegedly stealing income and assets totaling more than $4.3 billion. Reformers in the present government find that attempts to eliminate public fuel subsidies and put fuel prices on a more market established basis are strongly opposed both by the vested corrupt interests, and by the public, which has mounted violent street protests against any increase in the subsidized price of fuel. Thus, having locked itself into a damaging economic policy, the government is almost helpless to correct its own past mistakes.

In Argentina, 50 years of the use of SOEs may have enriched government officials and SOE managers, but the country is far less sound economically than it used to be, and the gap between rich and poor has seriously widened. Starting in 2001, the government under President Menem began a serious program, as sweeping as any in Latin America, to sell off these SOEs to private interests, including water, electricity, gas, telecommunications and the state owned oil company. Since most of these enterprises were losing money and having their deficits covered by the taxpayer, their sell-off relieved the government of an enormous burden. At the same time, the effectiveness of these services improved. The new private owners finally put up the new development money that the government could never manage to produce, and service has begun to improve. For example, the waiting time for new telephone subscribers has been brought down to less than three weeks, where, in the past, many months and even years passed without response, and the total number of telephone lines in service doubled to more than 8 million in just the last three years. But these advantages were mixed blessings in a sense, because the private owners had to charge rates that made up for the loss of the subsidies regularly paid to the former SOE operators, and many service bills to consumers have risen substantially.

The relationships between a government and its state owned enterprises have almost never been strictly business-like relationships. Instead, they are complex webs of political/economic tactics and strategies which define who exercises power and who benefits financially. In theory, the government creates state owned enterprises (SOEs) to provide public services, and to generate public revenue. In practice, SOEs gain a lot of political power themselves, and end up negotiating their role with the government. These power relationships can be both good and bad, but the tide that has been running in the world for the past 30 years is that SOEs have had a reputation for poor performance, and many have survived only because they have been protected and subsidized by their governments. It has also been argued however, that much of the failure of the SOEs can be attributed to dysfunctional political and bureaucratic meddling, which has severely limited SOE ability to function like efficient businesses.

Privatization

The key to privatization success rests on the need to create new capability for effective economic competition. One main hope is that new private sector owners will be willing to make the capital investments that the government failed to make, and that privatized ventures will gradually upgrade themselves to the extent that they can sell in international markets in competition with companies in developed countries. When SOES are privatized, the government can then terminate the subsidies and national price controls that artificially propped them up. As part of this adjustment, the rates charged by the new private companies will necessarily have to be raised to eliminate consumer subsidies and bring the cost of goods and services into line with the actual costs of production. Once these changes gain hold, it is also important for the government to eliminate its further protections of domestic industry through import restrictions or export subsidies. Finally, the government will be able to reform the state controlled banking system. First, efforts must begin to dispose of the huge backlogs of bad loans that almost universally characterize the captive banks of state socialist economies. Then, governments must eliminate preferential rates that favored SOEs, and the special tax system advantages they enjoyed. All of these measures, if seriously pursued, will relieve the government of the costs of the obsolete economic apparatus, and permit the redirection of government income to urgent social services programs. Even political lobbying becomes more tolerable, since the government need no longer respond to pleas to salvage loss making enterprises.

The bigger SOEs are the harder they are to sell since it is extremely hard to find buyers with enough money. Privatization decisions are usually very complex and must be made in conditions of high political and economic change and uncertainty. When potential buyers recognize this uncertainty, they are often scared off, and will wait for better times, or invest their funds elsewhere. And few governments are trusted to avoid meddling in the affairs of the new private company. In some cases partial sell-offs may be feasible if they involve sub-elements that might be quickly separated from the main organization. The experience of many privatizations, especially in the former Soviet bloc, is that some of the bad decisions of the government must be undone in the process. Many SOES were heavily overstaffed, often as much as 40%, and there may need to be complicated arrangements for the reduction of staff redundancy and the reduction of excessive wages or employee benefits before privatization can take place. In other instances, SOEs have incurred bad debts that must be swallowed. Often, the supposed value of manufacturing plants or other activities may be grossly overstated, and a new and more realistic valuation must be determined, not relating to original cost, but based on the value of assets to generate real income.

In summary, the whole broad experience with SOEs and the unsavory exposure of the gross wastage and misallocation of scarce resources has revealed how governments which initiated and sustained these hundreds of thousands of failures in the face of reality had become the hated oppressors of their own people and institutions.

SECTION TWO

COUNTRY/GOVERNMENT ANALYSES

(See Attachment A)

Afghanistan: Failure Forever

The Soviet invasion created an enormous extremist reaction. Islamic "freedom fighters" rose to the aid of the Afghan government. When the Soviets withdrew, the surprising rise to power of the Taliban led to the American/western invasion and restoration of a more moderate government. Now, the government has a vested interest in acting against fundamentalists but they remain powerful and aggressive, and the government is dangerously bumbling and authoritarian.

Afghanistan became the first great target of international Islamist movements. By 2001, between 20-25 percent of the Taliban's combat strength came from non-Afghans who flocked to the country to take part in the jihad. The Taliban however was bankrupt as a government, and in that sense, the Taliban movement had little impact on other Islamist movements elsewhere. "The Taliban showed itself to be incompetent – it could not even feed its people, and relied almost entirely on international charity. The Taliban regime amounted to mounting repression, intolerance and self-defeating harassment even of foreign aid organizations, along with its deepening drought and famine." (8)

But the defeat of the Soviets seemed to signal the ultimate triumph of the power of armed and zealous Islam – if the Soviets could be defeated, why not the US? The victory was a Sunni one – and one that seemed to dim the luster of the Shiite triumph in Iran. But the ascendancy of the Taliban was also a first test for which the Islamists were absolutely not prepared – how to run a government. The radicals wanted the Taliban to "show the world" how an Islamic state could succeed. Yet it simply added to the record of failure of fundamentalist regimes such as those in Sudan, Iraq and for many, Iran. Afghanistan revealed once again that the real conflict in the Muslim world is S. Arabia vs. Iran – highly conservative Sunni Wahibism as practiced in Saudi Arabia vs. a Shia religious fundamentalism in Iran -- a war of extremists.

Algeria: A Succession of Government Failures

The governments of Algeria have committed serious and destructive mistakes for more than 40 years. To begin with, the government made no effort to be representative; it was really a small elite centering around the military and the middle class, with everybody else neglected and frozen out of authority. This elite group adopted many of the policies and programs of State Socialism and solicited the Soviet Union as backer and supplier of weapons. Then, with the collapse of oil prices in 1986, the whole shaky and ill conceived "planned socialist economy" utterly collapsed of it own weight, along with much of the national social structure. There were crucial failings in housing, education, health care, massive unemployment and even food shortages.

This collapse then gave rise to a surge of Islamic movements, both moderate and radical, as possible successors to the failed government. The response of the Islamic movement constituted another failure because it was not the moderate wing of this movement that rose to the fore but a more extremist and militant wing. Had the moderates succeeded, the whole future of Algeria would have been much different and better.

Starting in the mid 80's, this Islamic militancy brought it into increasing conflict with the socialist government and the military. Neither side was capable of or interested in compromise, and by 1989, the country had lapsed into full scale civil war. Even national elections conducted in 1990 were unable to resolve this conflict. The FIS – the Islamic party – had somehow forged a coalition of voting interests including urban youth who were largely unemployed and poor and highly critical of the military, plus a devout middle class, compelled by their Muslim devoutness and their disappointment with the Socialist government which they saw as anti-business, bumbling and corrupt. The FIS won many local elections of mayors and urban councilors who disbursed generous charitable funding for subsidies for the urban poor. But here again, these newly elected pubic officials failed by imposing a far too stringent set of Islamic restrictions on the public. Places like stores selling alcohol, or videos or music were forced to close. Much more stringent rules for female dress and movement were imposed and new regulations forced gender separation in many public places. A surge of government sponsored anti-secular propaganda extended the promise of yet more stringent public control measures to come.

Further, the FIS government became the sponsor of programs that called for support of Iran in its war with Iraq, including a government call for creation of a "voluntary army" to go and fight in Iraq. This program of extremist militancy was seen as a direct threat by the Algerian military, an ominous bad portent for the middle class, and a challenge for the more moderate Muslims in the country. In fact, this more extreme attitude caused serious dissent within the FIS itself. Many feared that the rise of the more radical jihadists would inevitably lead to the destruction of the FIS itself, which is in fact just what happened. This then represented another failure of the Algerian government. When the FIS came into power, it rejected moderation and mismanaged its national role to become the backers of an extremist version of Islam. This so badly divided the country that the population was totally confused, seriously worried and totally disappointed in a government that they elected. Then, when the government tried to gerrymander a lot of election districts, the public erupted into a long period of strikes, demonstrations and even riots against a government that held them in contempt. These disputes were sufficiently serious and protracted that they emboldened the military to step in, ostensibly to prevent a general uprising. It is critical to understand that, at this point, most of the population of the country was very relieved and supportive of the move.

But still, the FIS managed to win the next national election in 1992 with 47% of the vote. The consequences of this event dominated the affairs of the country for the next 20 years. The military, encouraged by its widespread public support, decided on what it thought to be a conclusive step. It seized power, removed the FIS president, and banished the FIS as a legal political party. The party structure was forcibly dismantled, thousands of militants were arrested and often interred, and many others, including known militant Imams in the mosques were placed under observation.

The Islamists fought back against this power strike, and a new civil war was precipitated that was to last for the next ten years. During the war, it was clear that the extremists had the support of al-Qaeda, in what was one of its first tests as a movement trying to extend the range of its power. In the end, the militants failed, al-Qaeda failed, and the militants were all but annihilated. A residual Islamic organization and movement continues to exist at a less militant level. The government is again failing. It is a façade, and the real power seems to have moved permanently into the hands of the military and intelligence leadership. The government blandly keeps announcing "reform initiatives" – of the bureaucracy, the budget, the judiciary, the economy, health care, education – but little is actually undertaken, and the public is well aware of it – along with the continuing eternal popularity of government corruption.

Angola: Reduced to Rubble

For the past 25 years, Angolans have been trapped between the rock of a UNITA rebel movement and the hard place of the ruling Popular Movement for the Liberation of Angola; the MPLA. In their battle for power, these two parties have reduced their country to rubble and their countrymen to poverty. For years, neither side could win, but both maintained that no reconciliation was possible. In rebel territory, anyone who did not support UNITA was killed. The MPLA preferred less direct methods. Most potential political opponents - politicians, journalists, trade unionists -- were bought off. Those who resisted were silenced with blackmail, threats and violence. Out of 150 small party organizations, perhaps 20 were genuine, and the rest were fronts for the MPLA to promote the myth of democracy. The fake parties had easy access to money; the genuine ones were broke. Fighting back, 17 of the genuine parties have formed the United Front for Change. And for the first time, Angola's churches have formed a joint body to campaign for peace and national reconciliation. Combined, the churches have a largest base of support than any other organization in the country. Miraculously, a truce was negotiated in 2002. Attention was then enthusiastically turned to other matters, and Human Rights Watch has accused the regime of having looted the treasury or squandered more than $4.2 billion over several years. Huge oil revenues have never been fully accounted for, and the government blandly blames bad accounting. Sonangol, the government's state owned oil company has never allowed access to its key financial records. The decline of public services and infrastructure are heartbreaking: no electricity, muddy streets even in cities, garbage in the streets, education seldom beyond the 4th grade, poor to nonexistent health services. The Economist says "The scraggly town of Cafunfo sits in the middle of one of the world's richest diamond fields, but most people eat nothing but funge, a barely-nutritious dough made from cassava roots. The diamond trade is largely controlled by army officers, government types and their foreign cronies."(9) And only 23 of the country's 168 municipal courts were functioning during 2003. Nobody is looking forward to the new coalition government where the leaders of the dreaded UNITA are now politicians anxious to join their old opponents in the mutual looting of the country.

Argentina: Again on the Brink

President Juan Peron was a "populist/Fascist", and master of the art of buying special interest alliances. His regime survived on populist subsidies and nationalism fed by heavy anti-American propaganda. The economy featured heavy nationalization, stiff trade barriers, subsidies for friends, and universal corruption. Inflation was almost always totally out of control; in one year, it reached 20,000%. People would carry shopping money in wheelbarrows. Big business rode the tides in order to suck money out of the purses of "no clue" bureaucrats and corrupt politicians.

Domingo Cavallo became Finance Minister in 1991, and he developed a comprehensive economic plan that reversed the mess. He eliminated import substitution policies, most trade barriers, and uncontrolled exchange rates. He undertook a program of privatization, cut redundant employment in SOEs and government agencies, and recognized the need to educate the Argentine public about complexities of "right" and "wrong" economics. The current President, Cristina Fernandez De Kirchner, has continued along these reformist lines, but her administration, like that of her husband who was president before her, is riddled with corruption. When Nestor Kirchner was elected president in 2003, the family wealth was estimated at $2.5 million dollars. In 2010, when Kirchner died, their wealth had risen to $17.7 million, with no suitable explanation offered about where the money came from. Over the years, crony capitalism has flourished; but at the same time, the cronies have turned out to be crooks. The Economy Minister had been indicted for currency manipulation; the Transportation Minister was indicted for "illicit enrichment"; and recently, the Vice President has been indicted for "bribery and influence peddling".

Meanwhile, the Argentine economy has moved into horrible disarray. Inflation is raging, foreign loans are being defaulted, the trade deficit is huge and growing, the peso has had to be devalued, and the government has bumbled and fumbled, obviously having no idea what to do to prevent disaster. The public is increasingly tortured by the prospect of serious recession, or worse, runaway inflation and economic collapse.

Bahrain: Unnecessary Brutality

Muslim Bahrain suffers from the usual problems of the region: an inadequate economy, high unemployment, lacks of adequate social services, a corrupt and inefficient government. This in turn has generated a new wave of civil protest. The government is compounding the problem by unleashing its brutal, heavy handed security police who go after any form of protest even if peaceful. The punishment of peaceful activists is now producing a surge of additional resistance to the regime.

Bosnia: Frustrating Extremist Muslim Incursions

Islamic extremists tried to preempt the freedom fight in Bosnia to create a fundamentalist state, but failed to make more than temporary penetration of the government or the military. It proved to be true that most people, even those who purported to act on religious grounds, were not religious at all in the sense that they were driven by religious beliefs. Iran intervened in Bosnia in a serious way, supplying money, weapons, training and religious "education". But after thirteen years, there is still no serious indication that a majority of Muslim Bosnians or Kosovo Albanians are disposed to embrace Islamist movements. Nationalism is a far more compelling motivator, meaning "the religion of Albanians is Albania." Saudi Arabia targeted Albania, and more than 200 mosques were funded by Saudi money and influence, but ethnic bonds proved stronger than religious coherence. A Muslim character emerged as a shared environment, cultural practices, a shared sentiment, and common experience, and not reliance on Muslim theology. Opponents of Islamist extremism included not only non-Muslims, but secular Muslims and Muslims who argued the need for a multi-ethnic and religious state. In many cases, the nations in the area see themselves as European, and seek to identify with European culture rather than stifling Middle East theologies. This tide runs despite the enduring resistance of the more radical Islamic mullahs, and the interventions of Iran. Here also were the usual patterns: the failures of governments in both economic and democratic terms; the persistence of ugly corruption, and the self-inflicted wounds of the Milosovic regime on its neighbors. The same tides were running in Kosovo. Long before Milosevic, they sought independence, but the tide was nationalistic and not religious, and the Kosovo Liberation Army was confusingly half fascist and half Marxist – and never Islamic.

Brazil: A Very Confused World Power

Brazil is another nation that suffered from an extended period of military control of the government – from 1964 to 1985. As with most military regimes, the leadership had no clue about economics but well understood corruption. Brazil at one point was so deep in debt that what it owed -- $87 billion in 1985 – was the largest government debt in the world. Inflation was so bad that the value of incomes was shrinking and Brazil could not pay its debts. Long term losers included adequate economic growth, social programs, public infrastructure, elementary and secondary education, "honesty", and trust in government.

Cardoso started out as Finance Minister in 1993, as favoring government provided welfare, but was forced to change by reality. He helped to cut the government budget, transfer some programs to states and cities, and bring inflation (1500%) under control. Brazil began the sell-off of some of its major SOEs, reduce the Civil Service, and reduce "special interest payoffs", and special interest power centers such as pernicious unions and corrupt government contractors. His punch line became "The Left is finished".

Cambodia: Government Killing Fields

Although the world has moved on, the enormity of the horrors that were perpetrated against the Cambodian people by their government and the totally incomprehensible insanity that produced such horrors are lessons that should never be forgotten. The Khmer Rouge was an exceptionally zealous and driven insurgent group harboring a very harsh view of the world, and possessing a demonic intent to remake its world if it ever came to power. When it did, by overthrowing the ruling regime in 1974, it immediately ruthlessly imposed its brutal and extremist program on the country, generally adopting some of the worst elements of the communist model developed by Mao Zedong.

The only legitimate roles accepted by the regime were the simplest forms of peasant and worker, guided by an absolute Party dictatorship. Everything and everybody else were evil and forbidden. So almost without warning, it was decided that cities and towns were not to be tolerated, and their residents were forcibly packed up and shipped to the countryside, mostly to newly formed collective farms. No one was spared. Resistance brought instant punishment. People who refused to leave were simply killed. The sick and elderly, forced to leave, died by the thousands.

All political rights, civil rights, business or family commitments, ownership of property or goods --- all were summarily abolished. Families were broken up and sent to different hard labor camps. All schools, universities, factories, hospitals -- any group or institution more sophisticated than "farmer" or "worker" -- were shut down and often destroyed. Knowledge and skill were evil and suspicious. Doctors, nurses, engineers, teachers, scientists, managers, lawyers and other professionals were virtually wiped out. Military officers were hunted down and eliminated. Music was banned; radios were evil and were destroyed; books were burned; newspapers were shut down. Every element of modern society had become immoral, hated and dangerous and all were zealously banned or destroyed.

Religion also was unacceptable. All leading Buddhist monks were killed and most temples destroyed. More than 8,000 Christian were killed, along with most Muslims. The Khmer Rouge was highly racist, and it did not tolerate ethnic Chinese, Vietnamese or Thais, and all were actively eliminated.

What happened to the urban dwellers and the skilled people driven out onto the villages and collectives? They became unpaid worker-slaves, living in miserable temporary commune huts, worked to exhaustion, and allowed to slowly starve to death. Others ended up even worse, to die in agony in prisons and forced labor camps.

<u>Civilian deaths in these four years of Khmer Rouge reign of terror, from murder, executions, disease and injury, exhaustion and starvation have been estimated to exceed more than two million victims!</u>

The Khmer Rouge had established links with Communist China; when Vietnam was accused of abusing its Chinese citizens, the arrogant Chinese invaded and "punished" the Vietnamese. This in turn sparked another kind of revenge when Vietnam attacked China's ally the Khmer Rouge, and drove them out of power in 1978. What followed was more than a decade of heavy conflict between the Cambodian puppet government and remnants of the Khmer Rouge, driven back into their role of jungle insurgents. But in these years, an additional 65,000 people were killed, and resources were wasted in destruction and disruption of the country. The national economy was all but destroyed, and the national reputation was shattered. No government in known history has ever governed worse. And yet, 25 years were to pass before a weak and gutless Cambodian Parliament finally established a special tribunal to try members of the Khmer Rouge, many of whom have since died, or are living in relatively secure retirement in Cambodia or elsewhere.

The Central African Republic: National Suicide

The mainly Muslim rebel Seleka (Alliance) force overthrew the government in March of 2013 and seized control. According to the Economist, "they looted everything, even when it was nailed down. "In one village, the courtroom's roof disappeared. Doors, hinges, even electrical wiring went." (10) Across the country, unpaid civil servants, under threat have fled. "There was no law, no security, no state." The country has been in a state of almost continuous turmoil since freedom from the French in 1960, but the current unrest is said to be among the worst ever. "Humanitarian groups say that malnutrition and disease are rife and public service almost totally disrupted. As many as 100,000 children are being recruited into armed units. Roads have deteriorated and parts of the country cannot be reached. Bands of fighters with guns and machetes strapped to their backs speed around the streets in pickup trucks bristling with rocket propelled grenades. Fighting occurs every night between the "government" and supporters of the ousted president. Mercenaries from Chad and Sudan, who have been fighting with Seleka are now demanding payment, but the treasury is empty the country is essentially bankrupt, foreign loans have dried up, and foreign investment is zero. It seems plain that this government can survive only by plunder and pillage." Western nations are almost helpless, since the violence is spontaneous, erratic and simply wanton vengeful brutality. The international peace keeping force of just six thousand troops will probably be increased, but numbers do not make the difference. That which now passes for the government is nothing but an armed mob. It will ruin the whole country for at least the next generation.

Chechnya: A Clan of Criminals

Chechnya declared its independence in 1991, but is still retained by force as part of the Russian Federation. This is a rogue state in which Islamic extremists mix with Chechen independence freedom fighters, and a bunch of corrupt criminals running drugs and other criminal activities in Russia, Europe, Central Asia, and even the U. S. It is unquestioned that the Chechens have a long history of anti-Russian and anti-Soviet activity, marked especially by rebellions in the 19th century. Chechnya is also mainly Sufi – which is esthetic, moralistic, unorthodox, and mystical. In 1944, Stalin exiled more than 400,000 Chechens to Kazakhstan, and they were not permitted to return until the 50's. After independence, a new constitution was drafted that was mostly about representative democracy and secular legal principles. Islamic law and principles were recognized, but the constitution had no reference to Islam, and instead religious liberty was emphasized.

But the Chechen conflict with Russia became one of the great targets and rallying points for the international Islamic movement, and drew Islamist fighters from across the Middle East. New Islamist religious and political leaders wrested a lot of power from the older more moderate Muslim leaders, and began the "Islamization" of the country, culminating in the declaration of an Islamic State in 1997. But it became obvious that Islamic slogans and the new laws could not provide a stable government, and government failures discredited the regime. Russia has kept control of the country, but armed conflict between the Chechen separatists and the Russian forces continues to this day.

Chile: Escaping a Dictatorial Past

When Salvadore Allende came to power in 1970, he initiated one of the most massive programs of state socialization in Latin America. He was a classic example of a dictator who clothed himself in the garb of noble State Socialist philosophy. But the result was not only harsh repression in the country, but economic chaos. This in turn led to even worse: Pinochet. Oddly, Pinochet, who seized power in 1974 opted for movement to a market based economy, supposedly because he hated "communists" and linked them with Socialism. In any event, economists from the U. S. (the "Chicago Boys") designed an economic reform program for Chile which has "done wonders" for the economy. Pinochet privatized many inefficient State Owned Enterprises (SOE), removed trade barriers, encouraged export growth, reduced wages on a more realistic level, gave the banking system more independence and latitude, and privatized the social security system.

The problem was that Pinochet did far less well with democracy than he had done with economics. He dissolved Congress and repudiated the Constitution, and he replaced hundreds of public officials who were too "socialist" with his own loyalists. He appointed military officers whom he trusted to be mayors of towns and cities. Military officers, active and retired were appointed to key civilian positions, including the presidents of universities where they enthusiastically purged the faculty of "leftists". The media were banned or controlled, and labor unions strictly controlled. A government report, issued many years later (2004) concluded that as many as 28,000 people had been mishandled and tortured by his order. Indeed, the principal characteristic of Pinochet's reign of terror is the extent that he brought it down to the level of the individual through threats, attacks, torture, imprisonment and murder. People were tortured or murdered visibly in order to terrorize whole neighborhoods.

Pinochet left office in 1988, and his chosen successor was soundly defeated in the next election in 1989. After that, two important things happened. One was the enthusiastic return of investors both domestic and foreign, and the great increase in the acceptance of Chilean products overseas. The second event was the initiation of serious investigations of the sins of the Pinochet regime. These investigations, constantly blunted, finally resulted in his forced return to Chile from G. Britain, but at that point, he was so ill that he was judged unable to stand trial. He lived in seclusion until his death in 2006. For him, crime did pay.

China and Pathological Government

As early as the mid 1970's, the Communist government of the People's Republic of China began to recognize that the state socialist economy was not capable of expanding fast enough to keep up with a growing population, and that, while the agricultural sector of the economy could be improved sufficiently to feed this growing population, agriculture was never going to be more than a subsistence sector and could not generate enough spare economic value to finance the development of other sectors of the economy.

As the Chinese economy blossomed, speculation began about the government. Very reluctantly, and after much debate and political infighting, the ruling Chinese Communist Party (CCP) was forced to recognize that a shift to a market based economy was absolutely necessary even though it abandoned many of the sacred principles and practices of the politically centralized command and control economic system. The CCP attempted to retreat as little as possible and as slowly as it could. The private sector had to be unleashed and encouraged; but politically the government sought ways to retain crucial economic control while slowly relinquishing much ownership of productive resources. Control was to be maintained through a combination of retention by state owned enterprises of the "commanding heights" portions of the economy, continued control over the state banking system, and control of the pace and shape of private sector development through regulations governing entry into business and the nature of foreign direct investment. The CCP leadership feel that they can control the nature of changes about to occur, and to sell to the population the idea that prosperity was the product of a modified version of the old state socialism. Many in China and elsewhere began to believe that the state socialist regime was doomed, and that what would emerge would be a native version of representative democracy – or something like it. Both schools of thought at this point seem to be off the mark.

What seems to be emerging is pathological governance. Their pathologies include an almost uncontrolled expansion of corruption of the political leadership from top to bottom, peddling of money and influence between the public and the private sectors, a tendency to try to hang on to failed state owned enterprises despite their economic failure, and a general neglect of public goods and services, and the accumulation of huge public debt, making the Chinese government the most heavily indebted in the world. China has persistently neglected the development of vital social services for its citizens, and it is strongly argued that China has the worst environmental problems of any government in the world, and is headed for environmental disaster. Neither the hundreds of State Owned Enterprises, nor the burgeoning private sector have yet to expand business development into socially acceptable patterns. Economic development still means breakneck urbanization, overdevelopment in manufacturing, excessive dependence on exports, expanded coal fired electrical generation capacity, heavy metals dumped into the air, and nasty chemicals dumped into the water. Water sources are extremely inadequate and yet they are recklessly dissipated. All of these problems are known. The real issue is whether the Communist

Party can change itself enough to cope with them, and then whether they have the skills to do so.

But the key to the whole structure of the Chinese economy is the unprecedented percentage of the national economy that is captured and controlled and deployed by the government, taking wealth away from almost all organizations in the country and from hundreds of millions of individuals. Even the growing middle class of the country is essentially an elite that benefits from this massive government usurpation of wealth.

Colombia: Drug Boosted Corruption

Columbia is at once the land of promise and the place of unbelievable conflict. The government has, for decades, been forced to deal with four other centers of power: the deadly world of the drug cartels; the attacks of a formidable guerilla organization; then a whole uncontrolled group of private "paramilitary" armies established by rich landowners and businessmen; and finally, a whole quarrelsome set of opponents and critics within the ruling elite itself. In a culture of corruption lasting for 100 years, there are so many who see corruption as profitable, or who think it is really not so bad, or that corruption lubricates the system, or that corruption is really simply "getting with the system". Who really wants to get out from under this oppression, and how hard will they try, and who will lead?

Cuba: Back to the Future

Cuba, once one of the poster children of the great Socialist wave, is in deep trouble. When the sainted Fidel Castro assumed power, he wholeheartedly adopted Communist State Socialism, with the enthusiastic backing and support of the Cuban public. Socialist theory required that individuals sacrifice their individual rights in favor of "all embracing socialist provision". But the government now no longer seems able to provide all necessary social services at an acceptable level. The public attitude increasingly seems to be to rcognize that the government can no longer adequately deliver, and "something" needs to change. The government continues on; it continues not only to control most of the means of production, but it dictates what consumers can buy and how much. Agricultural production is controlled, and the government has a monopoly over both the purchase and the sale of agricultural products. The strange subsidy-based economy has nevertheless satisfied a substantial proportion of the public, who remain somewhat perplexed supporters of the tattered Socialist regime.

But the government is beginning to close down free cafeterias and canteens for government ministries, which used more than $350 million in imported food each year. There are said to be 24,700 free canteens in workplaces, and is expected that most of them will be shut down as a money saving measure. Their importance lies in the fact that they are seen as a critical element of the Socialist "guarantee" of social services. Further, this move seems to reinforce the growing speculation that the government is quietly moving toward elimination or serious retrenchment of free monthly allowances for food, housing, health, education, transportation and power.

Foreign investors are spooked. After a brief period of better times when Fidel's brother Raul took over, hope again declined and most investors are looking for ways to get their money out before the disaster. The government has been forced to cut the level of approved imports by 30%, and it has cut funds for government ministries and State Owned Enterprises (SOE). The government says that it can mitigate the country's economic problems by moves to encourage the number of small businesses, but in fact, the number of licenses for small businesses has declined from 360,000 to about 200,000.

Wages are ridiculously low - $20 per month at the low end - and wages are almost 50% less valuable than they were in 1989. But of course, the government has long argued that workers are really well off because of the value of social goods and services they are provided, either free or at heavy subsidy levels. This might be nearly true – if those goods and services were in fact provided and are adequate and of reasonable quality. Public infrastructure for example is deteriorating, especially in transport and power. Cuba does have a very good reputation for its free education and a reasonably high level of health care.

Because the Cuban economy is weakening, it would appear that there is no way it can continue to provide the "cradle to grave" Socialist subsidy commitment. If many of these subsidies are abandoned, the Cuban people will face a wrenching awakening: the real world is forcing the need to create a whole new economy --- and probably a whole new government.

Democratic Republic of Congo: Tribal Destruction

In the Democratic Republic of Congo, rebels against the government have also been supported by outside governments -- mostly Rwanda and Uganda -- as an illegal instrument of "foreign policy". It has never been clear what they hoped to achieve. Tribal loyalties (Tutsi vs. Hutu) were carried outward by the same tribal divisions that existed within Rwanda. No one understands who started the war in Kisangani, nor who ended it. Meanwhile, the whole economy is in shambles, and for example, less than 10% of the country's 65 million people have access to electricity.

In the period of 1991 to 1997, Congo attempted to create the conditions for, and the apparatus of a democratic state. A new Constitution was created providing for an elected President and Prime Minister, along the lines of the French government. But the chief players managed to convert this system into an implacable source of conflict and ultimately civil war. The army, apparently seeing the clash between two reprehensible civilian contestants for power, stayed largely on the sidelines and concentrated on protecting their considerable interests and assets. By 1997, both the President, Pascal Lessouba and his main rival former president Denis Sassou-Nguesso, had built up semi-private, semi-official militia forces outside of the army.

In 1997, in the lead-up to a national election, President Lessouba was not sure he could win, so he decided to arrest some of the close associates of Sassou. But Sassou's militia managed to frustrate the army's arrest attempt, and it prevented any arrests. According to Clark (p. 96), "Lessouba subsequently sent larger and larger contingents of military forces to arrest Sassou and disarm his militia, but these efforts were met by even more numerous militia forces, who rallied to Sassou's defense --." Within days, the capital (Brazzaville) was engulfed in a full-scale civil war that soon spread to other parts of the country over the ensuing weeks. The war proved frightfully resistant to outside mediation by numerous parties. When Sassou returned to power by force in October of 1997, the Congolese experiment with democracy, begun in 1991, was over."

Sassau as President returned to the old authoritarian ways. When he staged an election in 2002, as a means of adding some degree of legitimacy to his regime, the election was generally seen as rigged and fraudulent in the old tradition. Yet the multi-party system still staggers along, three elections have been held, and a basic rule of law struggles on.

Egypt: From Wrong to Wrong

Egypt has been the long term home of Muslim movements from "Islamic socialism" to moderate Muslim development, to Arab nationalism, to Islamic extremism. Egypt had beaten back extremists, and for a while represented a middle ground with little internal trouble with extremists. The Egyptian public lost interest in utopian solutions based on obsolete doctrine. The views of the devout middle class began to emerge as the country got beyond conflict and negotiated a form of "cease fire" with the radicals. The retreat from State Socialism and the adoption of new policies of privatizing and modernizing the economy led to the emergence of a new class of entrepreneurs. In the Arab Spring of 2011, the Muslim Brotherhood (MB) played a great role, but not a terrorist one. In the subsequent elections of 2012, they won almost 50 percent of the vote, largely exactly because they had abandoned their more extremist positions and took on a moderate appearance. They won an election and formed a government. But the new regime showed itself to be so zealously "Islamic" that it frightened even the people who voted for them. Almost immediately,

President Mohamad Morsi got himself into deep trouble. (Economist, 4 May 13) More than half of his score of official advisors abandoned him, along with his vice president, his Minister of Justice, and many senior officials. His senior legal advisor, when resigning, said that Morsi "a lack of vision; failure to achieve revolutionary goals or to empower Egyptian youth, failure to accommodate or even to consult political opponents, and the overweening influence of Morsi's fellow Muslim Brothers in devising policy." Further, Morsi was accused of "pandering dangerously to the Islamic Republic of Iran, allowing an "infiltration" of Iranian money and influence."

Across the Muslim world, the millennial but long-dormant Sunni/ Shia split has deepened in recent years, largely because of competition between Iran and Saudi Arabia played out by proxy struggles from Iraq and Bahrain to Lebanon, and most viciously in Syria." According to the Economist, "Among Sunnis, the influence of Saudi-style puritanism has risen. Salifist parties fiercely reject anything alien to the "pure" faith of Islam's founding fathers, including Sufi mysticism, or Shia veneration of imams or descendents of the Prophet Muhammad. The irony is that such displays of Sunni chauvinism cause deep discomfort to the Muslim Brotherhood, the most successful Sunni champions of political Islam." Egypt is 90% Muslim and has always been solidly Sunni, and people are very confused about why their government would deal with the Shia Iranian enemy."

And what is more serious, it aroused the Army to seize power and oust an elected president. So the country is now seen as slipping back into some of the authoritarian and oppressive attitudes that created "Arab Spring" in the first place. The public is ambivalent: it does not want an army out of hand, but there is now a growing concern with lawlessness both from the street gangs of the Muslim Brotherhood and Muslim terrorist gangs in the Sinai Peninsula. It needs to be understood that the very great majority of Egyptians want more democracy. It should never be forgotten that the great majority of Egyptians are strongly against the Brotherhood, and there is little sympathy against their deposal. The Brotherhood is enthusiastically blamed for everything that is wrong in the country, and it is linked in the public mind with more extremist Islamic groups. During Arab

Spring, the Muslim Brotherhood turned out 200,000 street marchers, but <u>more than 2 million</u> of the average citizenry turned out for their own reasons. They feel betrayed by Morsi and the Brotherhood, are inclined to trust the military more than any political crowd, and will probably support the new interim government once a revised Constitution is passed and the government stabilizes. Egypt is likely to become a crucial case of a Muslim government in conflict with Muslim extremists. Excessive Islamic zeal such as the indescribable horror of the Taliban massacre of school children in Pakistan scares everybody far more than the fumbling and bumbling of some government.

Eritrea: Unending Hatred

Eritrea finally won independence in 1991. Since then, there has been a bitter, pointless dispute for ten more years over minor pieces of land along the border with Ethiopia. The government has been in long term armed conflict with Ethiopia and is now stupidly linked with the extremist Islamist terrorist groups in Somalia which are being fought by Ethiopia and other governments. Thus, the Eritrean government the country continues to be the implacable enemy of Ethiopia and of common sense.

Ethiopia: Always Another Enemy

There have been internal conflicts involving Christians versus Muslims, but the recent history has been war with Eritrea, and more recently, interventions against Islamist revolutionaries and terrorists in Somalia.

Ghana: Fumbling the Economy

Once again, Ghana is sliding into economic trouble because of the lack of intelligent leadership. The currency is sliding, having lost half of its value since 2008. In fact, oil income continues to rise – but where does the money go? Two thirds of the population lives on less than $2 per day. Populist subsidies (for the elite) and crony capitalism suck up a lot. General wages can't keep up with inflation, and unions are badly shaken. The staggering national economy is threatening much of the preferential positions unions have maneuvered for themselves. Public sector employment is out of control and salaries and benefits are so "upscale" that public sector employment costs drain off 70% of the national government budget. The President, John Mahana, has been forced to raise the prices of obsolete often erratic electric and water supply services. Inflation rates are now scary, having recently climbed over 13%. The budget deficit has quadrupled (4% to 12%) in the last few months, and the cost of food and key consumer goods have risen seriously. The government is in over its head. Unemployment is growing, especially for the young, as too few jobs are being created. Huge sums of money are "disappeared"; corruption is infamous, especially among the police, judges, politicians and petty bureaucracy. One noted success has been the peaceful and relatively honest elections in 2000 and 2008, but they seem to have produced no new leadership capable of dealing with an impending economic train wreck.

Haiti: Permanent Self-Inflicted Wounds

The finest hour for Haiti was 200 years ago when revolutionary heroes freed the country from rule by France. Few countries have suffered more from pathological governments. These two hundred years have been a permanent hell of incompetence, corruption, revolt and disruption. At independence, the country included the entire island of Hispaniola, but the eastern portion was restored to Spain in 1809. The island was reunited, but the government was so bad that the eastern half revolted and broke away to form the Dominican Republic in 1844. The government seems never to have been very stable or very effective. Constant unrest, coups, assassinations and terrorism led to occupation by the U. S. for an extended period from 1915 to 1934. Then, in 1957, Francois "Papa Doc" Duvalier seized power and instituted a brutal dictatorship. On his death in 1971, the dictatorship was inherited by his son, Claude "Baby Doc" Duvalier who ruled with equal brutality until he was finally forced into exile in 1986. This 29 year descent into hell impoverished the country, ruthlessly suppressed any semblance of democratic empowerment, neglected all forms of public service and infrastructure, ravaged the economy and built up public resentment and permanent implacable resistance to any form of government.

The first free elections in the history of the country took place in 1990 and the presidency was won by Jean-Bertrand Aristide, a highly popular activist. This created a brief period of hope that was to be dashed by a military coup in 1991 which led to further purges, with thousands of people fleeing the country, either to the Dominican Republic or in small boats to the U. S. The military government stepped down in 1994 and Aristide was returned to office with the backing of the U. S. and many other countries and international organizations, and the assistance of 20,000 American troops sent into the country by President Clinton. Aristide did succeed in getting popularly reelected in 2000, and hope stirred again. But the Aristide regime once again failed and the Parliamentary elections of 2000 were widely perceived as fraudulent and riddled with corruption. Aristide seemed to have learned nothing but bad things from his previous term as president. The country remains desperately poor and underdeveloped. 80% of its 7.5 million people are poor – the highest percentage in the Americas and one of the worst records in the world. Social indicators are hideous: high infant mortality, chronic malnutrition, the worst percentage of AIDS in the Americas, wholly inadequate social programs, a badly decayed public infrastructure, and no significant improvement in humanitarian consciousness or civic capacity building. The record of the Aristide regime since 1994 has once again created almost universal criticism in the country and a building up once again of civil disobedience. The response of the Aristide regime was brutal and repressive in the old traditional manner, adding fuel to the fire. Aristide was once again ousted by a broad coalition of forces in the country centering on its middle class with armed rebellion following fruitless civil protests.

After many years and huge sums of money, the national situation still is seemingly hopeless, and foreign intervention is seen as the only recourse. Throughout this whole sordid history, the United States, the UN, and the other supportive countries like Canada and France have come in for much criticism. But if these countries appear to have backed the wrong horse in Aristide, it must be asked whether there was ever any right horse. 50 years of self destruction cannot be solved with short term foreign aid, and 50 years of government rule has produced only tyrants and thieves and never an adequate leadership capable of achieving an effective political consensus necessary for the construction of a modern state.

India: Stubborn and Pointless

Conflicts between Muslims and Hindus led to the separation from India of Pakistan in 1947. Later, the eastern provinces of Pakistan revolted and broke off to form the country of Bangladesh with the active connivance and help of the Indian government and military forces. Two wars have been fought between Pakistan and India since then. Kashmir, which has an ethnic minority in both countries, has partitioned between them, creating a Kashmiri independence movement and constant conflict between Pakistan and India over who should control Kashmir. To some serious degree, this stupid dispute has been fostered and cherished by the military in both countries as motivation and justification of their yearning for power.

The highly popular and revered leader Jawaharal Nehru who became India's first Prime Minister was a devotee of State Socialism and an admirer of the Soviet Union, and he overcommitted the government to socialist policies that later and predictably proved to be costly failures, but he persisted in these policies beyond common sense. Nehru nationalized most of the economy, putting it into the hands of State Owned Enterprises (SOE) which almost uniformly proved to be highly inefficient and loss making. In order to control what remained as the private sector, the government vastly expanded its regulatory controls, exercised though a vast, indolent, arrogant and oppressive civil service infamously known as the "License Raj", and later, the "Regulatory Raj". There are two main national political parties, the Congress Party and the Bharatiya Janata Party, largely of Hindu origin. But the reality seems to be that both parties are pygmies compared to the size of the problems that the country faces and the public sees the political parties as "whining, complaining, back stabbing, bumbling, showing only incompetence, arrogance and downright craziness, while totally neglecting the serious issues the country faces." The tax system is a stupendous mess; the budget is in constant huge deficit and is seen as having run amok, wasting huge sums on populist subsidies; the government lives on borrowing, and almost 500 million people in India live in poverty or near destitution.

Indonesia: Governing Through Special Interest Politics

Several years ago, a bomb in a tourist nightclub in Bali was exploded – one of a series of terrorist attacks in the country. This attack was attributed to an al-Qaeda associate group, but in the last elections 2004, no Muslim party garnered any significant voter support. This is extremely important since Indonesia has the largest Muslim population of any country in the world at about 215 million people. Indonesia has largely avoided the intractable conflicts that infect Arab countries, and is enjoying a resurgence of reform, mostly in the direction of improving democracy and public wellbeing. This, along with better and more serious police and anti-terrorist activity has greatly reduced the terrorist activity.

Indonesia is a huge country, consisting of 13,700 islands and extraordinary range and variety of people from many tribes, ethnic groups, and regional identities. It has over 228 million people, making it the fourth most populous country in the world. The rulers of Indonesia banned political parties for many years, and even after 1965 when they were again allowed, it has been clear that they have exerted little influence. Instead, both Presidents Sukarno and Suharto have used a form of power brokerage which involves catering to a variety of special interest groups. In other words, special interest groups have been the only real holders of power, along with the President, in the whole country.

Indonesia is being forced to reinvent itself and face up to its elitist sins, one of which was the pattern of irresponsible power in the hands of the military, and a second was the creation of a militia that could not be controlled, and became a horrible instrument of destruction. The pathology of the Indonesian government starts with the composition of the legislative bodies. There are two legislative assemblies: the House of People's Representatives with 500 members, 400 of whom are elected and 100 appointed, including 38 seats reserved for the military. The People's Consultative Assembly has the unwieldy total of 1000 seats, but 500 of these are the members of the House of People's Representatives. All of the members of the Supreme Court members are also appointed by the President as are the heads and second level officials of the ministries of the government. Both Houses are excessively large and unwieldy and the grip of the President, through his own appointments, is sufficient to keep them out of effective decision making, which is tightly held in the hands of a small inner elite of the President's inner circle.

The most important special interest groups are, first and foremost, the armed forces. Next are worker's groups in industry, commerce, transport, and in all of the state owned enterprises. Then there are farmers and villagers, regional representatives, professionals like lawyers and doctors, youth, women, and Muslim religious scholars and academics. These special interests each have their own organizations to represent them, but the regime has further organized them into a "collective" of sorts called GOLKAR – still not a political party, but a base for negotiating power and allocating resources to each of the participating groups. There never was any serious consultation with the general public, or even with the political leaders of provinces or cities. Instead, negotiations have taken place with the leaders of the special interest groups who, in turn, seldom really represented their constituencies, much less consulted with them. Thus, the special interest leaders have been little constrained, self-serving, and often more than willing to negotiate cynically for their own personal advantage rather than the best interests of their membership or the country.

In addition, the country has been divided into regions, each of which parallels a Military District. The military commander heading each district is almost all-powerful. Finally, in most of the important state owned enterprises, top appointments are also made by the President on a patronage basis as rewards for special interest loyalty to the regime.

The entire system has been pathological; it denies any real voice in the affairs of the country to most of its 223 million people; it hugely benefits a small power elite; it gives the military excessive power in society; it rests on patronage rather than merit; and it has proved totally vulnerable to corruption, which is pushed to the hilt.

For a long time, it was thought that this system was so powerful and integrated that it was hopeless to think of overturning it because it seemed to offer something for everybody – except of course the average citizen. But a series of events became the basis for the deterioration and ultimate collapse of the GOLKAR structure. First, the arrogance of the central government and its willingness to ignore civil equity and civil rights concerns led to widespread disaffection of large numbers of regional, ethnic and tribal interests, and in a number of minor insurgencies. Second, the dictatorial powers of the president, and the widely recognized corruption of all levels of government began to erode the GOLKAR system. Third, the Indonesian economy, which features a large number of corrupt and deficit producing state owned enterprises, began to falter and weaken.

This combination of tides running in the country finally generated real insurrections in East Timor and Aceh with which most Indonesians sympathized. Heavy repression by the military was seen as an arrogant and contemptuous blow against civil government that blackened further the reputation of the military and weakened their previous national prestige. Strong new pressures for national reform began to surge in 1998-1999, culminating in the ousting of the Suharto regime and the selection of a new national parliament by more openly contested elections. Suharto's successor Abdurrahman Wahid proved so mistrusted that he too was voted out of office in favor of Megawati Sukarnoputri.

The key to these changes was constitutional amendment to require direct election of the President for a fixed five year term. [1] For the first time, parties have meaning and influence. There had been three useless parties allowed by the government; now there a dozens and they do not need government approval to function. This is making Parliament more than a rubber stamp. In addition, the courts have finally been given real independence and strong authority to review the actions of the other branches of the government. A new Judicial Appointments Commission has been established; but there is much dragging of the feet on appointments to the Commission, as well as to anti-corruption bodies.

This miracle of constitutional reform forced GOLKAR to become simply another competing political party. It proved unable to hold together the previous special interest groups, many of which shifted to other newly formed political parties, including some that represent various degrees of moderate Islamic interests. The constitutional amendments, forced through over several years, created a Senate of 128 directly elected members, four from each of Indonesia's 32 provinces, thus significantly shifting power away from the centrist elite groups. In addition, many aspects of authority over public programs were essentially decentralized to the provinces or to sub-provincial districts and cities.

In September 2004, the leader of a new reformist and secular Democratic Party (PD), Susilo Bambang Yudhoyono (widely known, thankfully, as S.B.Y.) achieved a major political upset, defeating both the incumbent party of Ms. Magawati and the "revised" GOLKAR party that had nominated a general as their candidate. At the same time, Islamic candidates, divided into five parties, garnered about 35% of the votes. While it will be difficult to say how these new political alliances will shape and change in the future, it seems clear that the old ways of special interest domination have been shattered beyond repair.

---

[1]

The ultimate special interest that remains however are the Indonesian Armed Forces. But the new constitutional amendments will further weaken military authority which has been declining over the years. The military share of the national budget has fallen from about 25% to just 4% over the last ten years. Military seats in the legislature are no longer automatic.

Meanwhile, only half of the population has access to electric power and brownouts are frequent; fewer than 20% of the poorest have access to clean water, and there is almost a total lack of proper sewage and waste disposal facilities. Roads are deteriorating fast, and there is little new investment. The oppressive nature of its previous governments has left Indonesia trying to crawl out of the 1950s.

Iran: Dividing the Muslim World

The revolutionary regime came to power by combining the frustrations of unemployed youth and the hopes of the devout middle class, along with the zealousness of the religious elite. But an important cause of the revolution was the fear of the Shahs government which was considered too secular, and too oppressive. Yet the current regime is probably worse. The fundamentalist Islamic regime really constitutes only a minority within the mainly Shia population, in a country that has Sunni and Kurdish minorities as well. The regime is widely disliked, and there has been a growing opposition against the religious minority controlling the country. Many of the motivations that drive the regime are based on authoritarian concepts of fundamentalist religious doctrine and control, and Iran is one of the very few countries in the world where it is religion rather than the grab for power that keys critical motivations.

Iran's sins include authoritarian and tyrannical shadow leadership typified by the Council of Guardians, which controls events without having to be elected or to carry direct responsibility for governance. This hidden leadership inflicts upon the country a narrow, religiously based doctrine that is rigid, uncompromising, and inappropriate for many real problems.

The government sector is excessive, unproductive, and intensely bureaucratic. Many elements of the people are discriminated against in some way (women, minorities, the "unfaithful", private businessmen, etc.). Corruption is seen as far worse than in the Shahs time, especially in terms of rewards for the regimes friends and punishments for its opponents. Many of the most important enterprises in the country have been seized by the Revolutionary Guard which has become an uncontrolled force. The economy is faltering, in part because of sanctions imposed by the UN and other countries, imposed because of their fear of Iran's program to develop nuclear weapons controlled by a regime of which the world is deeply suspicious. But even beyond these sanctions, economic policies are perverted and repressive, resources are misallocated, there are few successful attempts to diversify the economy, and private businesses are harassed or suffer from government corruption. There is no sense of accountability or consultation on the part of the hidden elites of the government including the religious leadership. And to add insult to injury, Iran now has the world's highest incidence of drug abusers, despite sophisticated government anti-addiction programs. There are the usual reasons for disenchantment: a weak economy, high unemployment, especially among young people, a good deal of urban decay. But there seems to be something else driving public decay that is somehow related to the oppressive religious environment itself.

Iraq: Sunni/Shia Hatred at its Worst

The Bush Administration overthrow of the regime of Saddam Hussein and the Baath Party unleashed the tensions inherent in the country where the majority Shia population had been suppressed for decades by the minority Sunni regime of Hussein. The minority Kurds in the north had also been harshly repressed. One of the continuing concerns in the region is that the Kurds are a coherent tribal community, yet are minorities in the three neighboring states of Iraq, Iran and Turkey, and each worries about whether the Kurds will force them toward an independent Kurdish state. The Hussein regime deliberately maintained these conflicts to justify their dictatorial control over the national economy. The Iraqi government which has taken over since the collapse of the Hussein regime has been accused of being too much under the influence of Iran, and prejudiced against the Kurds and the disenfranchised Sunni population. As a consequence, Sunnis have created terrorist organizations like the Islamic State of Iraq and the Levant (ISIL) which have constantly attacked the regime and the innocent Shia population in their market places and Mosques. The country now seems to have lurched fatally into all-out civil war. Unfortunately, the new Shia government was seen as prejudiced, largely ineffective and corrupt, and unable to keep the whole country together, although a recent election seems to have produced a more rational regime. But the possibility still exists that Iraq will become three badly battered countries for Sunnis, Shia and the Kurds.

Israel: Sixty Years of Implacable Conflict

There has been unremitting conflict between Israel and its Muslim neighbors ever since Israel was created. Muslim citizens in Israel are treated as second class citizens, with reduced legal rights. The newest threat in a series extending over the last 60 years is the specter of an Iran, with a nuclear weapon, threatening publically to destroy Israel, aided by a burgeoning and vicious Hamas regime in Gaza. An almost perfect track record for more than 65 years is one of stubbornness, implacable and inscrutable vicious conflict between Israel and the Palestinians in the Palestine Liberation Organization (PLO) and now Hamas. This has gone far beyond the issues of rightness and wrongness. It has not mattered who is in charge. It is a bitter indictment of two societies that live by hate, lead through stubborn intransigence, lack a character of humaneness, and have provided three generations of pain and damage on their people. They seem to search out the most extreme forms of stupidity and hate, and usually find them. They are implacable in driving themselves to extremes in every situation, and despite endless pompous utterances to the contrary, they have long since lost any grasp of the concepts of negotiation, compromise, rationality or consideration of the real wellbeing of their citizens.

In this mess, it is specious to expect any force – other governments, international organizations, foreign assistance – to penetrate this poisonous swamp, where everybody is wrong about everything all of the time, and they seriously work to keep it that way. They have no clue about how to change, even if they wanted to try. Foreign involvement is forced to support this lunacy. These regimes on both sides are the ultimate oppressor governments. They give people an endless burden of pain, fear, harm, hopelessness and immorality. Year after year after year, now and forever.

Kenya: Childish Misdirection

Uhuru Kenyatta, Kenya's President is under indictment by the International Criminal Court, but he won the election in his country. Now, "instead of courting governments that prize Kenya's help in the fight against Islamist extremism in the Horn of Africa, his administration has picked what one Western diplomat called "childish fights". Newly accredited European ambassadors arriving in Kenya have been told that the President has no time to receive them. Meanwhile, little mention has been made of justice for the more than 1,300 people who were murdered in the terrible post electoral ethnic violence which Kenya's two leaders are accused of masterminding in late 2007 and early 2008." The government has long been locked into a culture where corruption, preferment, patronage, and tribal rivalry have been "normal". Meanwhile, the population of the country has swollen from around 8 million in 1963 to more than 45 million now. Nobody seems to bother about running the country, and millions live in fear of their own police who are said to be "corrupt from top to bottom" and tend to violent overreaction. Hoped for improvements in social services were expected when a new layer of 47 counties were established by a new Constitution in 2010, but the cynics say that this has simply added a whole new layer of taxation, regulation and corruption.

Charles Bingman

Lebanon: An Endless Stream of Religious and Ethnic Violence.

Lebanon has long been a country very divided by its religious and ethnic minority conflicts among Sunni Muslims, Shia Muslims and Druze and Maronite Christians. The country was initially run by Amal, a loose mostly secular political/militia organization, but they survived only because the rest of the country was so divided and in conflict, including the presence of The PLO under the leadership of Yassar Arafat. Amal also cultivated Iraqi connections including the heavily Islamic group headed by Muqtada al-Sadr. The PLO in turn, cultivated links with Iran. These antagonisms led to internal civil war in 1978-79 that became an excuse for external intervention by Syria which occupied parts of the country, seeking primarily to get rid of the PLO. Because of its common border with Israel, Lebanese minorities were used to attack Israel, which in turn led to an Israeli invasion and occupation of parts of the country in 1982. For some years the PLO operated from Lebanon, and Iran funded and armed Hezbollah for that purpose. The Israeli occupation lasted until 1985, and seemed to have been largely pointless and to have led to the galvanization of Hezbollah as defender of the Faith, the protector of Muslims, the foe of the Zionists and their American Imperialist backers. The Lebanese Army was never strong enough to subdue Hezbollah, and most of the mysterious and complex relationships between ten different forces in the country continue at some level.

Meanwhile, Hezbollah itself began to change. Their hotheaded ideology had gotten them little but a part of the Beqaa Valley and a bad reputation. Many Shia in the country are becoming more prosperous and seem to want a way to stabilize the country. They are contemptuous of the corrupt governments of the past, but are fearful of excessive Hezbollah zeal, and its murky links with Iran. The idea of an Islamic Caliphate has never had much grip, especially in Lebanon with its large Christian and Druze populations. The Syrian presence has largely disappeared, after the major elections of 2005 and the assassination of the highly regarded former Prime Minister Rafic al-Hariri (killers unknown but both Syria and Hezbollah suspected). Hezbollah now seems to be a picture of confusion, anger, ambivalence, subservience to Iran and a yearning for some legitimacy. In fact, "political" Hezbollah as opposed to terrorist Hezbollah seems to be gaining ground, and once again, it should be emphasized that, as elsewhere in the Muslim world, power struggles were seldom related to religion, but were related to, well, power. Hezbollah has entered the political fray, run candidates, got people elected, and had people appointed to significant public offices. Some Shia accuse it now of apostasy.

Liberia: Dictators and Thugs

Liberia was initially established in 1820 for freed American and Caribbean slaves and it became a republic in 1847. Most of its people are native to Africa, but the former slaves tended to rule. The government was marginal but Samuel Doe, an army sergeant used the general discontent and some food rioting to attack and overthrow the government in 1980. Doe was a vicious thug and an oppressive dictator who mismanaged the economy to the point of collapse. The consequence was a civil war, eventually won by Charles Taylor, who also became an oppressive dictator. The civil war continued even after Taylor was elected as President, with an additional element in the form of a UN peace keeping mission which was trying unsuccessfully to quell the conflict. Eventually Taylor was forced to step down and go into exile in 2003. While the country is now mostly at peace, the economy remains a disaster, public services are all desperately inadequate, 250,000 people have been killed and hundreds of thousands dislocated and impoverished. The UN feels compelled to keep 15,000 troops in Liberia, with no idea when it would be possible to bring them out. Thus, Liberia has suffered from stupendously oppressive and incompetent governments for the last 35 years, with no "recovery" in sight.

An incomprehensible footnote: in 2014, none of the country's 20,000

University applicants passed this year's entrance exams, after administrators switched to a fair admissions system based on actual real marks. In the past, the whole system seems to have consisted entirely of bribes, threats or family influence and connections. This seems to be a portrait of the complete useless mess called elementary/ secondary education in the country. 3 out of 4 Liberians say that they paid a bribe to some public official within the last year. The whole country is one big universal criminal enterprise.

Libya: Extremists vs. Each Other

Muammar Gaddafi headed a so-called Socialist state, but it was really a dictatorship in which Gaddafi announced his own version of Islam. Libya had long been a sponsor and supporter and trainer of extremist terrorist Islamic groups, but this support has been largely withdrawn in recent years because of world-wide outrage. Gaddafi tried to pursue a more moderate set of policies, but it was too late. Libya is now struggling to work out a new government and define its role, but it now appears that Islamist extremists are a growing threat which the government is not capable of handling. Libya now has two competing versions of a parliament, two competing governments, two competing terrorist organizations at work, and a horrible peering into the abyss.

Malaysia: Islam in Confusion

Malaysia achieved its independence from Great Britain in 1957. Britain had imported large numbers of Indians to work in the rubber plantations, and it had encouraged the investment of Chinese merchants in trade, banking and manufacturing. As a result, Malaysia possessed a population that was half native, one third Chinese and about 15 percent Indian, and has ever since, taxed the ability of the government to maintain an equitable multi-ethnic society. It seems unfortunately true that the mass of young Malays had little or no access to the benefits of their own country, and the Chinese and the local elite controlled almost all wealth and power. This then became the heart of the campaign mounted by the militant Islamist movement offering the usual vision of an idealized Muslim society. But the main Islamist group – the Muslim Youth Movement of Malaysia –- was not the only tide of Muslim activism. The Malaysian Islamic Party was a more moderate middle-of-the road party that elected representatives to Parliament, and entered into coalitions with the government. The local version of the Muslim Brotherhood has also become more active. But there are also many fanatical sects, and even bands of armed extremists to contend with. Thus, within this one country, there were at least four major interpretations of the meaning of Islam, and of the Holy Texts.

The government decided that it must set about the definition of an acceptable form of Islam that mitigated the influence of the extremists and put the majority of Muslims in a favorable relationship with the government. One of the basic strategies employed was to expand the teaching of a conservative (Wahhabi) but modulated form of Islam in state schools. This not only served as a counter balance to the even more radical teachings in certain mosques, but it provided legitimate employment for young people at all levels in the education system. Similarly, the elite group of Islamist students were incorporated into country's governments at all levels, and began to move into positions of power and influence.

What has emerged is a pattern similar to that in Egypt: as long as Islamist organizations confined themselves to preaching and the moral values of individual religious practice, or a responsible participation in the political process, the government gave them a lot of room to function, because such religious leadership was seen as an effective counter to the more extremist views, and it was far more popular with the devout middle class of Malaysians. It was also much more accommodating to other important necessities for the country – modern technology, the expansion of the economy, the presence of foreign money and industrial operations, and a greater tolerance for non-Islamic people and ideas. Thus, Malaysia may be seen as a prototype of a new and mostly moderate Muslim state.

Malawi: Looting Public Funds

The recent shooting of a public official brought into the open a whole long series of accusations about the depredations of corrupt officials. This opened up scandal has led to dozens of arrests, including government ministers, and a freeze on foreign aid, which accounts for 40% of the national government's budget. The scam – dubbed "cash gate" - has raised deep questions about Malawi's dependence on aid, its stubborn poverty, and its inability to match neighbor's economic growth. Foreign investors and donors worry about pouring money into a leaking pot, especially since the government seems increasingly hostile to foreign investment. Malawi now ranks 171st out of 189 countries in terms of the cost of doing business, says the World Bank. The new president, Joyce Banda has made serious efforts to curb corruption, but she has a long way to go and not many allies. Meanwhile, in the mid 80s, neighboring Mozambique's income per head was less than half of Malawi's, but now it is 40% higher, and Malawi's economic record remains the worst in the region.

Mali: The Vision of Azawad

A revolt led by the Islamic fundamentalist group Ansar Eddine has allied itself with a Taureg National Movement for the Liberation of Azawad (an ancient Taureg kingdom) and they have driven the Mali army out of the eastern half of the country and declared the creation of the new nation of Azawad. The group is patterned on the al-Qaeda in Islamic Magreb, and it is said to be as close as any al-Qaeda group has ever come to forming a government. But a shaky deal has been negotiated with the government because the Taureg themselves essentially want their own secular state modeled on Egypt, while their scary Islamist allies want a full Sharia state, narrowly defined, and would be happy to steal Mali to host it. Things are further complicated when Boko Haram tends to retreat into Mali when things get too hot for them in Nigeria.

Mexico: Patronage and Corruption and Drugs

Mexico has a long term track record of running a huge patronage machine, managed by a large arrogant bureaucracy, and including massive commitments to State Owned Enterprises (SOE) – 1,100 of them at the peak. Unions, which stoutly supported the regime were

---

however notoriously crooked and venal, and the people knew it. The government was heavily committed to ISI (import substitution policies) and refused to admit its failures. The public budget, the tax system and the system of price controls were all seriously flawed and were riddled with corruption. The real "skills" of the government seem to be how to buy votes, how to get army backing, how to unite with criminals and how to get rid of political opposition. While the government officially acknowledges that state monopolies and other SOEs have become a heavy drag on the economy, it is not clear how serious reforms will ever be.

Mexico's real war with its drug cartels has had its worst impact at the local level. Local governments are congenitally underfunded, under-protected, out of their depth, and under constant threat. It is estimated that 40% of Mexico's towns and cities are under daily threat from organized crime elements, and over the last four years, 1,200 municipal officials, including 40 mayors, many council members and more than 400 police officers have been killed. Most officials say they are vulnerable to extortion and threats of death from these criminals, and that the national government in Mexico City is either helpless or unbelievably indifferent. Despite endless commissions and task forces, corruption is deeply imbedded in Mexican society. Many people do not even see it as wrong, and advance many phony arguments: "Everybody does it."; "It could be worse"; "Most of us are honest"; or "People elsewhere are worse".

Myanmar (Burma): A Blueprint For Failure

Burma has a long and dishonorable tradition of dictatorial military rule from 1965 to 2010. But the worst such regime is the one that seized power in the late '80's. It was totally caught up in Marxist socialist doctrine which justified a regime that has stifled internal dissent, concealed official statistics, sealed the country off from foreign "contamination", and deploringly damaged the national economy. This government was stupendously oppressive, almost beyond belief.

Ethnic conflict was deliberately stimulated as a device to justify tight government and military control. The entire political system was universally corrupt: rigged elections, prevention of opposition candidates, denial of media access, harassment of voter registration, rigged vote counts, threats and intimidation.

There was no reliance on skill or merit. Cronyism and preferment were widely employed, especially for military officers. Many enterprises are owned and controlled by the military, and usually, they are not taxed. Thousands of regulations deliberately form the basis for repression and corruption. Businesses routinely have to pay bribes for start-up, import/export permits, market access, land ownership, and the award of contracts or licenses. It is pointless to appeal these illegal actions to the courts because the courts and prosecutors are not independent, and are heavily controlled. The central government budget is a complete mystery, and to question any of it is seriously dangerous. The government is heavily involved with all kinds of criminal elements, with links to black marketing, smuggling, timber resources theft, and illegal land deals, especially for land owned by the government. What is smuggled? Everything -- oil and gas, drugs, timber, humans, everything! The drug trafficking is enormous; opium production and transport makes Myanmar one of the top three drug dealing countries in the world! As a result: in the corruption index, Myanmar ranks 180th out of 183 countries, making it one of the most corrupt countries in world history.

It is now however facing a new crisis that cannot be masked by Marxist doctrine – a serious health crisis. HIV, malaria, anthrax and widespread malnutrition have gotten out of hand, revealing the total neglect of the deliberately under funded health care system, which is decimating the population. But the ignorant military officers that control the country are in denial. The government claims that there are no more than 25,000 people infected by HIV, but World Bank researchers estimate the true figure to be more than 700,000 out of a total population of 48 million. The military regime has employed counter revolutionary groups and paramilitary militias that have terrorized the country. This in turn knowingly defeats the government's feeble attempts to cope with public health problems.

Where possible, hundreds of people are crossing into Thailand to seek medicines and medical services that their own government never set out to provide.

Nigeria: Divisiveness Breeds Terrorism

Section 419 of the criminal code of Nigeria makes it illegal to engage in any form of fraud. But the abject failure of the government to control **ANY** form of corruption has turned this into a bitter national joke. Everything that is corrupt, illegal, immoral or fattening is now called "a 419". For example, the phony E-mail campaigns against foreigners to swindle money is called "the 419". But if a woman finds out her boyfriend has been cheating on her, she says she "has been 419ed!" Any crooked or even unpopular action of the government is called a 419. Bribes are called 419s. Among the E-mail cheats, the cheaters frequently use local partners to hook the local suckers. In recent years, this form of 419 has been taken out of the hands of the young amateur and become part of the operations of broader and more sophisticated professional gangs.

One important element is very typical of Nigeria. The whole issue of what is corrupt is intermeshed with the normal bonds of society – the family, friends, fellow residents, members of the same tribe, and people in the same workplace. Thus, there is a conflict: what is good for the family vs. remote and often arbitrary government rules and regulations. Also, "Nigerian criminal networks manage multimillion dollar illegal schemes using ties of kinship, place of origin, ethnicity and patron-client relationships that cut across the government and private sector, and link Nigerians at home with the large Nigerian Diaspora." (11) This kind of relationship is far less common in Western circles, but well known in the Far East and other parts of Africa. Westerners have a hard time puzzling through this kind of dilemma, tending to be more accepting of the dominance of the official treatments of the concept of corruption.

The manipulation of government contracts is legendary. Government officials have, for example, simply typed up an official looking letter designating themselves as high officials authorized to select contractors for government contracts. This letter is then shown to potential contractors and/or banks. If accepted, the corrupt official can fabricate a contract competition, strike an illegal kickback deal with one of the bidders, accept a bribe, award a fictitious contract and disappear. Even if the phony letter is not believed, a crooked deal may still be possible, since finding a crooked banker is seldom difficult.

A popular version of this scam is frequently worked through a corrupt international donor or NGO. A Nigerian official can do a deal with an NGO to undertake a project for the government. The money is real; the project is not. The NGO proposes a fake project, it is approved by a corrupt Nigerian official, the money is transferred, then split between the two crooks; and later it is found that no project was even recorded, much less implemented. For the government, there are two massive failures; first, to tolerate huge numbers of corrupt officials; and second apparently to be totally unwilling or unable to catch anybody. Thus, corruption is a very safe occupation, highly profitable, and willingly adopted in nearly every facet off public life, and much of private business and personal relationships. "*Kinship--- loyalty – reciprocity.*"

Nigeria is also the ideal place to think "bottom up, top down". When the top people in a government organization are blatantly, successfully corrupt, and demand loyalty for each corrupt activity, it is impossible for the people at the middle and the bottom of the bureaucratic hierarchy to stay honest. There is an old saying: "If you are not stealing, you are either cowardly or stupid". Soon the big top down corruption links with the smaller bottom up corruption, and everybody enters a culture of common cover-up. As time goes by, the corruption becomes more sophisticated and more profitable. Often, intermediaries make a nice living linking up the bribers with potential bribees. Common excuse: government salaries are so low (and often not paid regularly) that workers fear they can't even feed their families or pay the rent. In that framework, for many, the perception of corruption changes.

In the period from independence in 1960 until today, three national presidents have been assassinated, four have been ousted from office by military officers, two have died in office, and only three have turned a military government peacefully to a civilian government. The sequence of military regimes has been tyrannical, brutal, incompetent and oppressive.

The country with the largest population in Africa at about 122 million has long suffered from the fact that 46% of the population is Christian and of the rest, 44% is Muslim. Aggressive efforts by a minority in some Muslim districts to impose a relatively restrictive form of a Sharia legal system on the entire population has led to riots and attacks and continues to feed ethnic tensions. There are constant conflicts between the Muslims and the Christians and Animists in the south – over the imposition of Sharia law and over the corrupt use of oil revenue which enriches the powerful and leaves millions of abject poor. The twelve northern states of the country, having as many as 15 million Muslims, have in fact adopted a fairly comprehensive system of Sharia Law.

These conflicts were never successfully constrained by the government, and they have now led to the emergence of the Boko Haram, a terrorist organization which loudly deplores the failures of the national government but whose real motives are to seek to break away a new Islamic country from parts of Nigeria, Niger and Chad.

The Nigerian government decided it had to spend approximately $347 million on a new soccer stadium for the All-Africa Games in 2003, despite the fact that there were already many first class stadiums including a huge one in the largest city, Lagos. But Lagos is in the south, and the new capital of Abuja is in the north. Even the President admits that the stadium was built "for political reasons." To emphasize the perverse nature of the decision, $347 million is roughly what is being spent in Nigeria for education, and it is greater than annual health care funding, both services being wholly inadequate. Meanwhile, Nigeria had to reschedule more than $23 million in foreign debt, while complaining that developed countries are not doing enough to help the poorer nations. Finally, public expectations are that the cost of the new stadium will get out of hand, and it will be further burdened with the high costs of corruption. Nigerians put up with continued fuel shortages in a country that is rich in oil. It has power blackouts and service cuts, unbridled bureaucracy, state enterprise incompetence, visible violations of the constitution and laws, a long a unsavory history of senior public officials caught taking bribes (but never convicted), and a history of large public projects being sucked dry by corruption. Why should the new stadium construction be any different?

Incidentally, the ultimate construction of the new capital at Abuja is expected to cost 25-30 billion dollars (plus corruption costs), while people in the old capital of Lagos go homeless and narrowly avoid starvation.

North Korea: The Terrorist God

Consider the case of North Korea. This extraordinary elite regime is one of the strangest in the world. It is centered on a cult of the individual leader, who is accorded almost god-like status -- deliberately to provide a justification for continuation of the regime in the face of its obvious failures. The ruling elite have not only isolated North Korea from the rest of the world; they have isolated themselves from most elements of North Korean society except the military, whose leaders are part of the elite. Extraordinarily, this pattern has succeeded. The failure to create a viable national economy or to deliver good public services has produced little national resistance. Perhaps the "cult" idea is more powerful than is commonly understood. After all, many countries bought the "divine right of kings" reasoning.

North Korea, from the very time of its creation supported policies creating and supporting terrorism both at home and in the international community. At first, the regime was so beholden to the Soviets that it was compelled to support the Soviet agenda of the Cold War against the U. S. and Western Europe. During a period of more than 40 years, from 1948 until the early 90s, North Korea actively aided and supplied Marxist movements around the world.

In Angola, the North Korean regime actually sent 3,000 troops. In addition several hundred "advisors" have operated training camps for guerilla organizations in several African countries, the Middle East, the PLO, and for the Syrian government. According to Barry Rubin, a National Security Analyst "In Lebanon during the 1970s, and in Libya and Syria from the 1980s down to the present, North Korean soldiers have also trained terrorist for many groups including the Basque Spanish ETA, the Palestinian Abu Nidal organization, the Irish Republican Army, Italian Red Brigades, the Japanese Red Army, Moro National Liberation Front in the Philippines, Turkish radicals and others. While many of these links have lapsed in the 1990s, North Korea added Hezbollah and the anti-Turkish Kurdish PKK group to its roster of clients." (12)

Thus, North Korea has supported world terrorism for more than 60 years and it continues to do so today. Extraordinarily, N. Korea has been identified as supervising the building of very extensive underground facilities for Hezbollah in Lebanon, including movement tunnels, bunkers, armories and facilities for power and communications. In addition, North Korea has reportedly sold weapons to Hezbollah, including ground to ground missiles capable of hitting Israel. These weapons are reported to be moved to Hezbollah through Iran where the North Korean agents are collaborating with the Iranian Revolutionary Guard Corps which operates Iran's terrorist sponsorship activities.

It will probably never be known what the full range of North Korean terrorist development has been, but it is clear that, for very murky reasons, the regime has been heavily committed to the advancement of terrorist initiatives all over the world, in places where the North Korean government has never had any significant interests. The explanations as to why seem particularly inadequate. For a time, it was payment for Soviet subsidies. Since the Korean War, it has been argued that the North Korean regime is "punishing" the United States by supporting terrorists who attack its friends and allies. To some extent, it has also been argued that, by selling weapons to international terrorist bad guys, North Korea earns badly need hard currency into its disastrous economy – or at least to enrich the centrist elites who control the nation's vicious dictatorship.

But there is a whole second dimension to the terrorism sponsored by the North Korean government, and that is the terrorism imposed against its own citizens. North Korea suffers from a pattern of poverty created by government policy. Despite recent experiments with economic reform, the country remains desperately poor. The World Food Program has targeted 6.5 million people out of total population of about 23 million as highly vulnerable, and seriously dependent on government handouts, including a ration of rice. Rigid controls on prices are now being reduced. Unemployment is being "solved" by moving large numbers of workers into farming even though all available land is already under cultivation. This retrograde movement ignores the fact that farming is stuck in the middle ages. There is almost no reliable power supply, no fuel for tractors, and in most cases, no tractors. Ox carts are widely used, and harvests are increasingly achieved by old fashioned hand labor. Factory workers have been hard hit. Factories are few, and are largely obsolete and rusting out. There is little money available even for maintenance of these factories, much less for industrial revitalization, and the ominous nature of the regime scares away investors even from inside of the country. Electrical power is so scarce that outside of the capital of Pyongyang most of the country is dark. Shortages of common use consumer articles are usual. These policies produced a famine of prodigious proportions in 1995-2000, and the country still suffers from that disaster. The government refuses to explain the catastrophe or publish data about it, but external estimates of the number of people who died range up to 3 million, and 5 to 10% or more of school children still suffer from the effects of malnutrition – vulnerability to diseases such as flu and pneumonia, slow learning, and physical weakness. The World Health Organization evaluates the health care system as weak to nonexistent. Hospitals are of very poor quality, most lacking staff, medicines and equipment, and some even lack running water or electricity. UNICEF says that the country is in a chronic state of emergency, but the regimes implacable opposition to outsiders makes it almost impossible to persuade donors to invest their funds in aid. UNICEF says that, for North Korea to get back to some form of adequate social services capacity would take a reconstruction effort comparable to that of Afghanistan or Iraq. Nobody believes that the current regime could devise such an effort; the economy is simply too deteriorated to produce the wealth needed to finance recovery, and the stubborn doctrinal pathological government shows little sign of tolerating change in any form.

Pakistan: Confusion Equals Catastrophe

The government has tried to have it both ways: it has supported Islamic extremists to gain credit in the Muslim world, but it postures itself as favoring "democracy" to gain U. S. support and aid. The government unwisely thought it could aid Al Qaeda and other fundamentalist Muslim terrorist groups in the struggle in Afghanistan against the USSR. Its foolish motive was somehow to do harm to India. These groups now constitute a dangerous minority within Pakistan itself since many of the extremists moved into northwest Pakistan and now require the government to use military force to suppress them. Pakistan has also used informal "militia" guerilla groups, financed by the Pakistani Army and intelligence service against Indian forces in Kashmir and against Kashmiri independence groups. This meddling came close to precipitating what might have been a nuclear war between India and Pakistan. After the attacks against the U.S on 9/11, Pakistan leadership found itself increasingly ambivalent and confused, and sympathy for insurgents is rising. It still hates India, but it seems to forget that, even after the creation of Pakistan and Bangladesh, India still has a population of about 134 million Muslims – almost as many as Egypt and Turkey combined, and the third largest population of Muslims of any country in the world. Yet Pakistan supported Islamic extremists in the take-over of Afghanistan. When Afghanistan fell, many of the extremists moved to Peshawar in NW Pakistan and have been a constant threat to the Pakistani regime itself. The country now suffers greatly from the depredations of the very Islamist terrorists it earlier sponsored. Meanwhile, the government founders and the economy deteriorates.

Palestinian Authority/Hamas: Failure One vs. Failure Two

There is now a constant clash within the Palestinian movement between the Fatah and Hamas, which is the more violent and fundamentalist. This is however not a fundamentalist issue, but it is over the future of a Palestinian state. But the fundamentalists constantly try to penetrate various elements of the movement. Both Fatah and Hamas are in constant conflict with Israel, and this is mostly about power or the lack of it. Hamas is supported and largely dominated by Iran. In 2014, Hamas chose to launch a rocket attack against Israel, which then responded with bombings, shelling, and troops on attack in the Gaza Strip. Both sides stubbornly refused to compromise, and spent months in full blown war. Major facilities in Gaza City and elsewhere in the Gaza Strip were decimated, and more than 2000 Gazans were killed and many more wounded or injured. Nobody won. Nobody understands why this insanity was necessary. Nobody knows the solution. The best hope appears to return to an earlier effort to reunite Hamas with the more moderate Fatah, and give the leadership in Gaza to some new more rational government. At that point, there might be a greater possibility of productive negotiation with Israel.

Peru: From Military Dictatorship to Fujimori

Peru suffered from a highly repressive military dictatorship from 1968 to 1980, and this regime undertook a vast nationalization program for power and profit. After the military government was replaced, Peruvians found that the civilian successor was worse: more corruption, more favoritism and patronage, oppressive control and manipulation of prices, government overspending, failure to collect taxes and inability to create enough jobs. The result was that the country essentially went broke. At the same time, there was horrible pain and destruction from the depredations of Shining Path, a highly destructive and vicious group, primarily Maoist, which killed thousands and destroyed much that was valuable, and yet nobody was ever certain what they wanted or stood for except a pointless reign of terror.

When Fujimori came to office in 1990, he was able largely to eliminate the Shining Path threat, begin the movement away from State Socialism toward a market based economy, reduce the incidence of corruption in many arenas, and retreat somewhat from the exercise of centrist power. But Fujimori proved to be another Peruvian tyrant if somewhat more moderate, and as the sponsor of the arrogant intelligence chief, Vladimiro Montesinos who made the National Intelligence Service the national headquarters for a huge range of corruption activities in the country and abroad. As a consequence, Fujimori's reputation was blasted, he lost all popular support, and the serious economic slump in the late 1990s led to his ouster in 2000, and his conviction for commitment of various crimes, while Montesinos fled the country. Governments for the last 15 years have been stable and mostly honest.

Philippines: Foreign Interference

There has been a long standing conflict between the national government and Marxist minority Moro tribes in the south. This conflict was made worse by the intervention of extremist Islamists who infiltrated an independence movement in the south, and have been supported in part by, of all things, Iranian funding. After failed negotiations, the government was compelled to launch a major military assault, which has been largely successful in decimating the guerilla movement. But somehow, it keeps resurging. Only very recently has there been the possibility of some negotiated peace agreement, but this has failed many times before during the almost 20 years of conflict.

And then there is the Philippine government. Here is an example of how it functions. (Economist, June 28, 2014). First consider the Priority Development Assistance Fund (affectionately known as the Pork Barrel), which gives every Senator in the Philippine Parliament the sum of 200 pesos ($4.6 million), and every Congressman 70 pesos, supposedly to be spent on worthy economic development projects of their choice. Next, consider the creation of fake Non Government Organizations (NGOs) to which most of this development money is transferred. Then, the NGOs invest the money in the "development" of crooked politicians as bribes, kickbacks, payoffs and other politically worthy projects. Media exposure finally resulted in some serious investigation which led to two Senators who were actually arrested and indicted. In 2013, the Supreme Court ruled that the Pork Barrel was illegal. There is some question as to whether the government can actually function without such generous funding to support its long tradition of patronage and corruption.

Russian Federation: Greed is the System

With the overthrow of its Communist/State Socialist regime, Russia had an extraordinary requirement to devise a new system to govern itself. The result was that Russia enthusiastically invented a new dictatorship. Greed is the dictator. Corruption in all facets of life is not just characteristic of the new system – it IS the new system.

An aggressive new class of greedy thieves, bribers, looters, usurpers, extortionists and "re-allocators" has seized the economy and is happily looting it. Government arrogance has revitalized the ancient Russian skills of dictatorship, oppression and terror. Once again Russia has created a world in which no resistance to the leadership is ever tolerated if it can be crushed. Once again, Russia sees itself as military muscle; civilian social services are deliberately neglected and inadequate. The president, Vladimir Putin, dreams of the recreation of the great Soviet empire, by means fair and foul.

The justice system has crashed, and in its wreckage has lost any sense of what "justice" now means in human terms. Most Russians have now been returned to the reality of great fear and loathing for the police, the courts, and protection of the law. The "rule of law" is now a threat because enforcement of unjust laws is in itself unjust and oppressive.

Beyond the corruptions of its thieves, there is the problem of how to create a balanced economy, bound by some definition of economic ethics. The collapse of the USSR threw huge numbers of Russian

State Owned Enterprises (SOE) up for grabs, and everybody in the country grabbed, and the grabbers have learned the fine arts of manipulations of political leaders, the military, the judges and the police. The country now lives largely on the earnings from its oil and gas resources, soon to be substantially augmented by new sales to China, Japan and South Korea. Thus, the fate of Russia is bound by its ability to create a more balanced economy, create a government that really wants to serve the Russian people, and get the government to rein in the national disgrace of corruption among the elite.

Rwanda: Maximum Possible Horror

Perhaps the most horrifying case of deliberate minority conflict is that of Rwanda and the infamous dilemma of the ancient tribal struggles between the Tutsis and the Hutus, extending as far back as the 15th century when the Tutsi conquered the native Hutu. Tutsi dominance persisted until the independence of the country in 1962 when the Hutu took control of the government and began the "official" oppression of their Tutsi rivals. When the Hutu president died in a plane crash in 1994, it led to massive violence and terrorism by both tribes. The Tutsi forces took over the country by force and began a campaign that can only be described as ethnic purging in which almost 500,000 Hutu (out of a total population of about 7.4 million) were brutally massacred, and an additional estimated 2 million Hutus fled the country. Further, the conflict between the two tribes spread to the neighboring states (especially Burundi) where "militias" fought each other, created havoc in refugee camps, and took sides in the disastrous civil wars in that country. Despite efforts from international organizations, and a peace accord signed with the Republic of the Congo, fighting between militia, the army and Congolese militia dragged on for years

What were the motives of the Tutsis and the Hutu? God only knows, but there is some informed speculation. The pathology of Rwanda's self torture lies in the fact that the cause of the conflict was not really, as many assume, the ancient rivalries between the two tribes. As reported in the Economist paper, "Outsiders assume that the genocide sprang spontaneously from primeval ethnic antagonism. On the contrary, it was planned over many months by its architect, Colonel Theoneste Bagosora, starting as early as 1993. Militias had to be organized, machetes bought and distributed, and Hutu peasants persuaded, through skillful propaganda, that all Tutsis were their enemies. The opportunity came on April 6th 1994, when Rwanda's Hutu president was assassinated. Bagosora and his co-conspirators seized control of one of the world's most authoritarian states, the whole apparatus of which was then turned to mass murder. The small gang of Hutus who organized the genocide was rational men in pursuit of a rational – albeit evil – objective. They wanted to stay in power, and they harnessed ethnic hatred as a means to that end." (13)

Saudi Arabia: Saudi Arabia vs. Iran

For 40 years, S. Arabia has tried to be the leader (relying heavily on oil money) of the pan-Arabic movement in the world, and it advanced the conservative, almost puritanical precepts of Wahhabi orthodoxy. Its greatest opposition has been Iran, which is even more fiercely fundamentalist. In S. Arabia itself, a fundamentalist movement supported by Iran has been contained and all but eliminated. But Iranian Shiites tried to take over the Great Mosque in Mecca in 1987, which led to rioting. After that, most Saudis seemed to rally behind the government in quashing fundamentalist meddling. Yet a third force in the Muslim world, characterized as "the Arab Spring" has emerged, and it has involved authoritarian regimes like Egypt, Iraq, Libya and Syria where the "unity" of the Muslim faith has often been used as a cover story to mask heavy centrist tyranny based on nationalist justifications. The Saudi regime has outlasted all but Iran, and in recent months, has seen a troubling resurgence of very ironic fundamentalist attacks which have labeled the Saudi government as "too liberal"!

Serbia: A Criminal Government

If one wonders why Slobodan Milosevic, the President of Slovakia, was arrested and put on trial in the International Criminal Court, the best answer lies in the fact that he "criminalized" a whole country. The normal structure of the ministries and agencies of the government were deliberately put into the hands of crooks and thugs, all appointed by the president. These ministers and their cronies almost totally ignored their primary responsibilities for delivering the social programs of the government which deteriorated to somewhere between incompetent and nonexistent. Instead, public funds were systematically looted and shifted into the pockets of the leadership. Where the state had funds to spend or assets to allocate, public need no longer determined who got what. Almost all business was done on the basis of bribery, illegal preference, diversion of funds to illegal uses, and as leverage for perpetuating the power of the ruling elite. Any pretensions of proper accounting and control of government finances were abandoned, and most ministries developed "black budgets" to conceal the funds used for pathological purposes. The legal tax system was perverted to reward the crooks and punish the honest. State assets ranging from land and buildings to business licenses and regulatory controls were awarded by the regime to its political cronies. Government owned factories or office buildings were "sold" to loyalists at a small fraction of their real worth, thus robbing the public of most of their collective value. Since the former Yugoslavia was a centrist socialist regime, the state owned enormous resources to loot. Lower level employees of state organs, taking their lessons from their top leaders, invented corrupt activities to get their own small "piece of the action."

Banks were state owned and controlled and were a powerful instruments in exercising criminal control. Subsidized loans were made to political favorites, and denied to any borrower who was in disfavor with the central clique. Often, even these highly subsidized loans were simply never paid back, and were used by the borrowers to buy up other national assets. These false loans were, of course, perfectly legal but totally pathological. Bank officials were so corrupt that the credibility of the banking system as a whole was all but destroyed. Limited amounts of money available in the country were diverted from legitimate to corrupt activities and denied to those who might have used them to improve a desperately bad economy. The corruption was so bad that whole segments of the economy simply wasted away. Businesses and individual citizens stayed out of the formal funding channels of the state owned enterprises because they were so corrupt, and falling into the clutches of government organizations could be actively dangerous. Foreign investment withered as well, since it was a dead certainty that investments would be either wasted, or stolen or diverted to further enrich the already bloated corrupt elite. Much of the Serbian economy remained in the hands of the state owned enterprises which were not only highly corrupt but totally inefficient and deteriorating. Usually, their reputation was that of delivering "less for more" -- inferior goods at excessive prices. It was fruitless to think that any of these SOEs could ever be brought up to a level of effectiveness that would allow them to compete in the international economy.

One example was the state Export-Import Bank which had funds to lend to Serbian businesses to help them buy needed equipment and materials, or to develop product lines fit to be exported. But the bank was totally corrupt and responded to directions from the regime to make loans to political cronies rather than legitimate businesses. These cronies were totally incapable of generating effective businesses, and in fact, many loans were made to people who had no business at all. Such loans, and valuable licenses to import or export were illegally sold to others at a fat profit, and in many instances, the loans themselves were never repaid because they were forgiven by the controlled bank. This pathological system of course culminated in the Bank running up an enormous number of bad loans none of which could be collected, and the Bank had to be bailed out repeatedly by the government using taxpayer funds. This had the further effect of depriving necessary social programs of adequate funding and contributed mightily to their deterioration.

SOEs and in fact many private businesses were blackmailed into making "voluntary" contributions to Milosevic's Socialist Party. At the same time, if they resisted such pressures or tried to support opposition parties and candidates, spies in the organizations would report them to government officials who took punishing retaliatory measures against them.

The fact is that the whole government under Milosevic had been criminalized. The rule of law had been perverted and the legal, ministerial, regulatory, and administrative authority of the state was turned upside down, and the very protective mechanisms that had been designed to aid and protect the public were employed instead to serve the material advantage of the small centrist elite, and against the people

Sierra Leone: Terrorist Wars

In Sierra Leone, governance has all but collapsed, and the country seems to have been reduced to the terrorist conflict of two vicious bands of terrorists one of which was created and sponsored by the government. Liberia has deliberately interfered by sponsoring rebel terrorist bands that have all but destroyed the country. The cause of this terrorist intervention was the greed of the President of Liberia Charles Taylor who was selling arms to the rebels for diamonds from mines controlled by the rebels. Taylor personally enriched himself, but there was otherwise no sane reason for the Liberian government to intervene.

The country has been torn apart by 12 years of civil war. Hundreds of thousands have died, and more than one million people have fled into exile. Warlords have fought each other to a standstill. Public infrastructure and many private houses and businesses have been reduced to rubble. There have been 12 "reconciliation conferences"; all have failed. The government operated out of three hotels that were seized when the official government buildings had been destroyed – either burned or shot full of holes. Two regions tried to declare independence from the failed central government. Almost everything of value was destroyed or stolen, from money to furniture, pots and pans, pigs and chickens.

Sierra Leone became an extreme but not untypical example of a state with all of the demands for government and none of the institutions of government. Its collapse was unusual only in its brutality: rape, cannibalism, and amputation, with children often the deliberate victims. When the UN sent in peacekeepers, Foday Sankoh (the rebel leader) tried to get them out through terror -- he captured 800 of them -- because he simply wanted to continue to plunder the country. It was also typical of the dilemma facing the UN and western countries: they badly want to stay out of meddling in the internal convulsions of hopeless countries, but they can't turn their backs on Africa since it has intervened in other (white) countries. No force can keep a peace that is implacably pursued by the natives.

To add further calamity, rebels in the interminable war in Sierra Leone initiated attacks across the border of neighboring Guinea. Guinea blamed the rebels, saying that they were supported by soldiers from Liberia. There were already more than 400,000 refugees in Guinea, most of them from Sierra Leone, and refugee camps were being used by Sierra Leone's rebels as hideouts and recruiting sources, forcing the Guinean army to counterattack. A recent UN report to the Security Council stated "there is unequivocal and overwhelming evidence that Liberia has been actively supporting the RUF at all levels, in providing training, weapons, and related material, logistical support, and a staging ground for attacks and a save haven for retreat and recuperation, and for public relations activities." (14) This is sick, pathological horrible tragedy.

Somalia: Islamist Terrorist Victim

Somalia has been in the grip of an al-Qaeda linked Islamist militia called the al Shabab for more than 20 years and it has effectively destroyed the government, killed or injured or displaced huge numbers of the population, all but terminated most public services, and left roads and other public infrastructure in a shambles. The African Union and troops from neighboring Ethiopia have been involved in reinforcing the inadequate protections of the Somali military. But recently, prospects have turned for the better. A new president is seen as honest and trusted, and he has begun to put some things back together. He heads a new Peace and Development Party which has links with more moderate Islamic elements associated with the Muslim Brotherhood. Meanwhile, al Shabab continues to function and has expanded its terrorist activities to other countries. Nobody knows why.

South Africa: Tyranny of a Minority

The struggle of the black majority in South Africa became one of the most famous examples of the tyranny of a minority in recent world history. The ultimate success of black South Africans to gain their independence is held up as a shining hope for other minorities around the world. The fact that the black government has had its serious troubles does not dim that hope.

Sri Lanka: Killing the Tiger

Sri Lanka has a majority population of Buddhist Sinhalese, and a minority Hindu population of Tamils. After independence from Great Britain, the Sinhalese government unfortunately adopted an oppressive posture against the Tamil minority who had sought a substantial degree of self rule in the regions of the country in which they were a majority. The rancor became so great that it precipitated a civil war in the early 80's, and equally unfortunately, the Tamil insurgents, called the Tamil Tigers were seriously oppressive in turn. They pursued their cause with an absolutely incomprehensive rage, using suicide bombers against government and Sinhalese civilian targets. India put 70,000 troops into the country in an unsuccessful effort to control the conflict, to no avail.

Finally, after a major Tamil Tiger victory, the government concluded that there was absolutely no possibility of a negotiated settlement and they launched an all-out military effort to win the war. During the final stages of their ultimate victory, as many as 40,000 Tamils including a large number of innocent victims, were cornered in an area in the North and systematically wiped out. For months after the war, as many as 280,000 citizens were held in camps for little or no reason. In total, more than 70,000 people were killed. This disgrace has permanently blackened the reputation of the regime, which has little to brag about at the best of times. Sri Lanka is now trying to recover both economically and spiritually from its own vicious oppressive past. In recent local elections, the Tamils have won overwhelming victories for local political offices, but the central Sinhalese government has refused to allow any substantial authority to be exercised by such provincial governments.

Sudan: Arab Oppression

In the years before 1958, Sudan had the largest Communist Party in the Arab world, and in 1958, it was able to overthrow the ruling military regime and replace it with a Socialist/Marxist regime. Thus, there were three forces at work: the Communist party; the southern clans of Christians and animists; and the Islamist movement. Then, the dictator, Gaafar Nimeiri, made a big mistake; he became angered with the Communist Party and dismantled it in 1977. This fact, plus the military's failure to win in the south, and the heavy failure of the socialist economy narrowed the base of the ruling elite, and let the Islamists into many positions of power. His regime lasted until 1985 when it was overthrown by Hassan al-Turabi. The Islamist leader, Turabi, marshaled the military, the banks, and the younger educated class into a base to seize power by a coup d'etat. This regime was heavily subsidized by the Saudis, and became the spokesmen for the devout middle class. A more purely military regime took power in 1989, setting up an Islamic dictatorship, with savage repression of the middle class and all other opposition. Purges and executions were immediately carried out in the upper ranks of the army; the same with civil officials, others of whom were forcibly "reeducated" to adopt the Islamist views. Political parties, associations, newspapers, all were banned and their leaders imprisoned. The regime was rabidly anti-west.

Sudan is now a rogue state that actively supported Bin Laden, and promotes world terrorism. It stands as the only instance in which the Sunni Islamist movement has actually gained control of a legitimate state.

It used to be easy to explain why the Sudan has been at civil war for almost 50 years. The causes were supposed to be the disparities between an Arab north and a black south, and between the Muslim religion in the north and the Christians/Animists in the south. But neither of these easy answers is really true. Of the 37 million people in Sudan, more than 70% are Muslim, and Christians and Animists are less than 10% of the population. It should be noted that the revolt was primarily against the arbitrary and brutal tactics of the government rather than a dispute about religion. In other words, there were large numbers of Muslims, Arab and blacks who did not want to be bound by a particularly conservative version of Sharia law.

The population seems to be about evenly split between blacks and Arabs. This means that many blacks are also Muslims, and there is a good deal of overlap between categories. Thus, it is possible that a Sudanese can be "a black Arab Dinka tribe Muslim." Twenty years of conflict has existed between these minorities, with a strange overlay of Marxist/Communist influence. This conflict was deliberate, motivated by strong feelings of superiority by the Arab Muslims in the North. The conflict was so bitter and hypocritical that the South fought its way to independence and has now set up the new nation of South Sudan. Meanwhile, the Arab government continues to pursue a terrorist war against the black population of Darfur in western Sudan driven by the same vicious motives.

There was yet another and very modern factor that has exacerbated the national conflict, and that is the presence of oil. In recent years, oil exploration has consistently raised the perceived extent of the Sudan oil fields to the point where it is now seen as one of the largest in the world – equal to that of Saudi Arabia. The great bulk of these oil fields lie in the South, and much of them are exactly in the area that marked the borders of the north-south conflict. A pipeline runs from these fields to the port of Port Arthur on the Red Sea, and this pipeline is particularly vulnerable to insurrectionist attack. The peace negotiations and subsequent argument between the conflicting forces the control of these lands, or the allocation of the income from oil sales is paramount and the fate of these oil fields is of vital interest to countries in the West, and to a number of international oil companies.

Khartoum has almost always acted as a totalitarian state, driven by its own, often archaic fears, and patterns of hatred against its opposition. When confronted with some crisis, it seems infallibly to have chosen the option that was most vicious and pathological. The regime hates the Christians and animists in the South because they resisted the imposition of rigid Islamic law. They hate the blacks in western Darfur because they have resisted the imposition of brutal government controls and the invasion of government sponsored Arab settlers that are allowed to seize the land and property of the native blacks. The current president, Omar Hassan Ahmed al-Bashir, is a noted anti-Semite, stemming apparently from his service with the Egyptian Army in the 1970s. The regime even hates the majority of Muslims who tend to resist the heavy enforced imposition of the Sharia. The point is that it is the government itself that has been the primary source of the tragedies of Sudan – not the people, not some vestige of colonialism, not some interference from ominous outside sources. The government represents the worst of the country's history when the regimes thought it was their divine right to be arrogant, self-serving, brutal, and dictatorial. Hatreds are implacable; fears are boundless. There is no understanding about the skills of negotiation and the political arts of compromise.

Between 1983 and 1999, some 1.2 million people died and more than 4 million have been displaced as a result of the civil war and famine, much of the tragedy was laid at the doorstep of the NIF. Thus, the NIF once again demonstrated that an Islamist-inspired regime could not create a government based on consensus, could not stop a hysterical civil war, had damaged rather that helped the economy, and became more vicious and oppressive than its ugly predecessors. Inflation ran out of control, public services disappeared or deteriorated, every force in Sudan was against them, the international community was appalled. Even the Muslim Brotherhood split away, not wanting to be tied to the debacle. The corruption of the government was amazing, even by African standards. Economic policy seemed to consist mainly of extreme predatory techniques diverting assets to party loyalists, and harassing and blackmailing traditional merchant entrepreneurs. Sudan was kept afloat mainly by its small but valuable oil industry, supported mainly by murky contracts with foreign investors. In 1999, President Bashir declared a state of emergency, and Turabi, who was then in the legislature, tried to pass legislation to curb the power of the President – and landed in house arrest where he remains today.

Sudan, post-Turabi, has shifted to a more moderate strategy. The government approved legislation to establish a democratic state and move Islamic law back from a mandate to an expressed "duty of the community". Eventually, a peace agreement was created with the Southern forces, and a new program of privatization seemed to stabilize the economy and begin to persuade foreign sources to invest in the Sudanese economy. But all of this was BEFORE DARFUR. Darfur signaled once again that the essential regime is still vicious, relying on force to rule. The failure to carry out the intent of the peace agreement culminated in the successful campaign in the south to break away from the vicious regime and form the new country of South Sudan. The two countries continue in conflict with each other, largely over the allocation of wealth from oil fields that lie on the border area between them.

Since the early 1990s, Sudan has undergone a serious shift in policy toward economic liberalization and resource allocation largely driven by greater oil income, and it has experienced considerable success. But agriculture remains the backbone of the economy providing 31% of GDP. It is a large share of export revenue and it still is the main source of livelihood for 80% of the people and of corrupt wealth for the Arab elite.

Syria: Self Destruction

The key to recent Syrian history is Hafez al-Assad, an Alawite (a subset of Shia Islam) who came to power in 1970. Alawites have a basic religious philosophy which is "polytheistic" and not the rigid monotheism of the majority of Muslims. Apart from Assad himself, it has been said that the only men who exercise power in Syria are the heads of military intelligence and the secret services, all of them Alawites.

Syria joined with Egypt to form a new joint Arab state in 1958, but this lasted only three years. During this period, the Baath Party was formed and began to grow. The Baath Party, centered around the military and led by al-Assad, was essentially both socialist and populist, and had little understanding of economics. As a result, the economy stagnated during the 70s and 80s, oil development was bungled, corruption was rampant, and most economic expansion took place in the informal economy. It was not until the '90s that al-Assad changed his thinking toward a more market based economy, but typically, change was slow, uncertain, and badly managed.

In international matters, his regime has been an unmitigated disaster. He helped to lose the war against Israel in the Six Day War of 1967; he blundered again by sending tanks to help the PLO in Jordan where they got decimated. He entered the civil war in 1976, but only made it worse. Syria lost so much of its credibility that most of the world turned against it. Egypt was able to use these blunderings to restore its leadership role in the Islamic community. And his long standing alliance with Iran has offended most of the world, and especially the Arab world.

Hassan al-Assad died in 2000, and was successfully succeeded by his son Bashar al-Assad. But the long term continuing force behind the Syrian government continues to be the *mukhabarat* – the secret police. Constant attacks and pressure from the Muslim Brotherhood (under the rhetoric of Sunni vs. Alawite) precipitated a full scale war in 1982 in which as many as 25,000 people were said to have died. Thus, Syria has been an obsolete tyranny, marked by endless, pointless leadership for more than 40 years. It is little wonder that the Syrian people have finally been forced to arm themselves against their own government, but the country has now been plunged into a totally destructive civil war which threatens to destroy the country, and the fate of Syria has become entangled with the emergence of the so-called Islamic State of radical Sunni terrorists who have seized large areas in both Iraq and Syria, and proved to be unbelievably vicious and cruel, even by regional standards.

Thailand: Religious Hatreds Unleashed

Ethnic Muslims in the south of Buddhist Thailand are using a terror campaign to scare off Buddhist and Christian residents and claim the province of Yala as an Islamic state. This is part of a decades long insurgency fed by poverty, drug-running, lack of political recognition, and discrimination. The objective seems to be not independence, but semi-autonomy. There has been a prolonged period of serious protests against the government along ethnic lines, but exacerbated by a criminal indictment against the incumbent president, Yingluck Shinawatra, brought by the National Anti-Corruption Commission. Finally, in early 2014, the army once again intervened as they had in 2006 by a military coup. The fear is that the military regime this time will be long lasting and very oppressive.

Turkey: Maximum Feasible Confusion

Turkey has been a staunchly secular state since 1924. A shock was experienced when an Islamic (but not fundamentalist) party won elections in 1996, and an Islamic Prime Minister was appointed. But he lasted less than a year, when the army pushed him out in favor of a PM who returned the country to the secular position. Yet, another moderate Islamic party has won recent elections, has proved to be moderate and competent, and is generally popular. The fear now is that government corruption and mismanagement has surged again, that President Recep Tayyip Erdogan himself or at least members of his family have been involved in some scandals, and that, under pressure, Erdogan has tended to become more authoritarian, especially against legitimate political opponents. At this point, the political environment which had been relatively stable now seems totally chaotic and uncertain.

Vietnam: A Long Way to Go

Vietnam has finally admitted the failings of its obsolete State Socialist economy and is slowly and reluctantly lurching in the direction of a "Socialist market economy", whatever that means. The national leadership is still intellectually Communist, and as in China, it will remain politically Communist forever, and it is having difficulty abandoning some of the old policies and approaches. The new Vietnam seems to want to link economic development with major upgrades of national social services, but just as the Vietnamese economy is obsolete, its social service programs are also obsolete. The old Communist regime left the country with an inadequate and deteriorating base, and the new leadership has a long way to go, including major changes in its own attitudes.

Venezuela: Chavez is Not Gone

President Hugo Chavez blindly ignored the fate of State Socialist governments elsewhere, and installed a Marxist Communist regime in the country. Under his orders, the Legislature approved the creation of communes, a Socialist entity which usurped the powers of local governments and were supposed to "regulate social and community life and guarantee public order, social harmony and **the primacy of the collective over individual interests.**" In the name of Socialism, he took over the courts, started to exert control over state and local governments, siezed control of electrical production (producing chronic shortages and outages), and instituted a whole series of anti-private enterprise policies, to the point that Venezuela now is ranked by the Global Competitiveness Index at 134th out of 148 nations. As a direct consequence, Venezuela now has the lowest rate of economic growth in the Americas. More than 40% of the workforce has been forced into the informal economy.

Venezuela is the world's 9th largest oil producer, and the third largest exporter. In the country, gas for cars sells for about 7 cents per gallon. This populist subsidy costs the government about $ 9 billion/year and it is for the benefit of the ruling elite and the middle class, since the real poor tend to use public transportation (which is also subsidized).

But Venezuela suffers from a sagging and stagnant economy, heavy inflation, a plunging currency (- 50% in 2012), an increasing number of scarcities, even such necessities as milk and eggs, and heating oil. Government subsidies were about 6.3 billion Bolivars in 1998, but by 2012 they were 48.5 billion Bolivars. The government created its own chain of food markets and deliberately filled them with subsidized products – chicken, lentils, milk, peas, beef, sugar, flour, rice, margerine. But inflation in the prices in these markets is actually higher than in private markets, and there are growing accusations of corruption – especially where food is stolen and sold at higher prices to private stores. Also subsidized is all aspects of agriculture, most fisheries, and many larger SOEs. In total, Venezuela is a heavily controlled economy, ranked 174th in global competition reports, and ranked 28th out of 29 economies in South and Central America.

While the formal economy shrank, the informal economy has been growing rapidly, and is said now to employ 2.3 million workers or about 40% of the workforce.

Here is the general perception of the characteristics of the Chavez and successor regime: There is heavy government interference in both economic and social matters, justified by Socialist theory, much of which has been proved to be failures and abandoned in other countries. Foreign exchange is government controlled, along with restrictions on both imports and exports. Venezuela has, for years, had to lowest rate of economic growth in the Americas. As part of this failed Socialist theory, the government maintains "selective" price controls which involves rewarding friends and punishing enemies. (15)

There is rampant corruption, and as control and regulation expands, corruption expands. The general policy of the government remains oriented to Socialist government control, with persistent anti-free market policies. There are serious attacks on opposing politicians and other opponents, and free speech is effectively prohibited or stringently controlled. Government control of property has meant the extensitve destruction of private property rights.

Venezuela is one of the few countries in the world that is nationaliziing private companies despite the common knowledge that even the most zealous socialist regimes are around the world are facing up to the necessity to privatize their State Owned Enterprises (SOE). The state owned electricity supplier is so inefficient that the country experiences chronic shorages and outages. Despite greatly inflated prices, there are now increasingly frequent shortages of food, clothing, consumer products and small appliances, and there have been enormous increases in all forms of crime.

Yemen: Terrorists Seizing Power

The whole country has been inflamed by extremist Muslim terrorist groups, backed by al Qaeda. Parts of the country have been taken over by these groups, and the government troops are struggling to take them back.

Throughout the region, nation building and the implacable quest for power has been far more prevalent motivations than religious zeal. What has been new is the build-up of an intellectual and educated class who prefer to be more pragmatic than their more conservative elders. Muslim religious and political organizations have remained localized along national lines, and resist any attempts toward a Pan-Asian or Pan Islam movement. In the present day, there is a continued resistance to ethnic reconciliation, and in fact such efforts are probably deteriorating, and the expansion of extreme religious conflicts is greatly feared. And there remains – forever – the irreconcilable and horribly destructive conflict within the Muslim world between the Sunni and the Shia. Thus, Islam is emerging as a cultural and social force and a religious force, but centrist governments stoutly resist the emergence of any type of political Islam as part of the basic structures of society.

Yugoslavia: Independence Produced a Dictator

Yugoslavia was never a very coherent country. It was always a collection of ethnic and religious minorities held together for a long period by force, and in more recent years by the hope that a confederation of semi-separate political entities could succeed. The country was torn apart by the aggressive use by the Serbian government of Serbian minorities in now independent parts of the old Yugoslavia. These Serbian minorities were used to agitate against the local governments in Slovenia, Bosnia/Herzegovina, Croatia and Macedonia. Wars and local insurrections were fought as each of these entities spun off their own independence, leaving Serbia to the tender mercies of the criminal government of Slobodan Milosevic whose only motives were for criminal corruption. Milosevic was finally overthrown when even the majority of Serbs had enough of him, and he was arrested and brought trial by the International Criminal Court.

If one wonders why Slobodan Milosevic was put on trial in the International Criminal Court, the best answer lies in the fact that he "criminalized" a whole country. The normal structure of the ministries and agencies of the government were deliberately put into the hands of crooks and thugs, all appointed by the president. These ministers and their cronies almost totally ignored their primary responsibilities for delivering the social programs of the government which deteriorated to somewhere between incompetent and nonexistent, in large part because public funds were systematically looted into the pockets of the leadership. Where the state had funds to spend or assets to allocate, public need no longer determined who got what. Almost all business was done on the basis of bribery, illegal preference, diversion of funds to illegal uses, and as leverage for perpetuating the power of the ruling elite. Any pretensions of proper accounting and control of government finances was abandoned, and most ministries developed "black budgets" to conceal the funds used for pathological purposes. The legal tax system was perverted to reward the crooks and punish the honest. State assets ranging from land and buildings to business licenses and regulatory controls were awarded by the regime to its political cronies. Factories or office buildings were "sold" to loyalists at a small fraction of their real worth, thus robbing the public of most of their collective value. Since the former Yugoslavia was a centrist socialist regime, the state owned enormous resources to loot. Lower level employees of state organs, taking their lessons from their top leaders, invented corrupt activities of their own to get a small "piece of the action."

Banks were state owned and controlled and were a powerful instruments in exercising criminal control. Subsidized loans were made to political favorites, and denied to any borrower who was in disfavor with the central clique. Often, even these highly subsidized loans were simply never paid back, and were used by the borrowers to buy up other national assets. These false loans were, of course, perfectly legal but totally pathological. Bank officials were so corrupt that the credibility of the banking system as a whole was all but destroyed. Limited amounts of money available in the country were diverted from legitimate to corrupt activities and denied to those who might have used them to improve a desperately bad economy. The corruption was so bad that whole segments of the economy simply wasted away. Businesses and individual citizens kept out of the formal funding channels of the state owned enterprises because they were so corrupt, and falling into the clutches of government organizations could be actively dangerous. Foreign investment withered as well, since it was a dead certainty that investments would be either wasted, or stolen or diverted to further enrich the already bloated corrupt elite. Much of the Serbian economy remained in the hands of the state owned enterprises which were not only highly corrupt but totally inefficient and deteriorating. Usually, their reputation was that of delivering inferior goods at excessive prices. It was fruitless to think that any of these SOEs could ever be brought up to a level of effectiveness that would allow them to compete in the international economy.

SOEs and in fact many private businesses were blackmailed into making "voluntary" contributions to Milosevic's Socialist Party. At the same time, if they resisted such pressures or tried to support opposition parties and candidates spies in the organizations would report them to government officials who took punishing retaliatory measures against them.

Thus, the whole government under Milosevic had been criminalized. The rule of law had been perverted and the legal, ministerial, regulatory, and administrative authority of the state was turned upside down, and the very protective mechanisms that had been designed to aid and protect the public were employed instead to serve the material advantage of the small centrist elite, and against the people.

Zambia: The More Things Change ---

In 2001, Zambia finally freed itself from the dictatorship of Frederick Chiluba, and the new president Levy Mwanawasa instigated an anti-corruption campaign, with the chief target being Mr. Chiluba. Mwanawasa immediately fired a significant number of senior officers and became his own Minister of Defense. The foreign minister resigned as a result of repeated allegations of corruption in office, and other ministers have been fired. Chiluba was first stripped of his constitutional immunity from prosecution, and then had his government retirement benefits cancelled. Finally, in February of 2003, he was arrested and charged with corruption and massive looting of the state treasury. His regime was marked by some positive achievements in paring away the obsolete socialist economy by privatizing failed state owned enterprises, but he has been accused of benefiting improperly from their sale. His regime ran a very peculiar bank account in London, ostensibly for "foreign intelligence operations"; but he and his intelligence chief have been accused of simply looting this fund, for which there is no required accounting, of as much as $30 million.

The anti-corruption task force is also attempting to investigate the ownership and use of as many as 150 properties of various kinds in Zambia and elsewhere, valued at approximately $17 million. There appear to be no clear records of how these properties were obtained, but the head of the anti-corruption task force has stated that "90% of them were obtained illegally." Many of the allegations against Mr. Chiluba have been volunteered by informers who gladly lead investigators to the suspect properties.

But now the new President, Mr. Mwanawasa is himself under fire. The International Monetary Fund (IMF) has delayed a debt relief package because large sums of unauthorized and unbudgeted money have been spent. There is a case before the Supreme Court alleging that the election of 2001 itself was rigged by Mr. Mwanawasa, who won by a very narrow margin, and with less than 30% of the total vote. Government officials in the new regime have already been accused of the excessive use of expense funds, and with appointment to a large number of top jobs in the government of people who come from the ranks of opposition parties – presumably to buy them off. Many local and provincial officials are being paid official salaries to which they are not entitled. To date, the anti-corruption campaign seems to be preoccupied with pursuit of Mr. Chiluba and his former inner elite of supporters. But corruption remains very wide spread, down to the lowest levels. Citizens have to deal with corrupt police officers, minor officials who grant licenses and approvals, and even with doctors in order to obtain treatment. It is certainly not clear whether Mwanawasa is serious about the anti-corruption effort now that he is in office, or whether he is simply paying off a new set of rascals.

Zimbabwe: The Tyrant Who Lives Forever

The regime of Robert Mugabe is surely one of the worst in modern African history. Mugabe has seldom hesitated to use force and violence to terrorize Zimbabwe's own citizens, and he has meddled in the affairs of the Congo, spending so much money that he has little left to meet even crucial domestic social needs. He has taken what was once a prosperous economy and brought it to the brink of total ruin. He is universally hated in his country, despised and condemned by most of the international community, and shunned by foreign investors and lenders.

To begin with, land reform was one of the legitimate needs of the country when Mugabe came to power in 1979. The U. S. and Great Britain offered to finance land reform to meet Mugabe's extravagant promises to resettle 162,000 families in 5 years, but on the basis that the new government would at least buy out white farmers at some fair price. Britain did in fact furnish more than 44 million pounds and 70,000 families have been resettled on almost nine million acres of land. But the government refused to undertake reasonable buyouts and instead instituted a perverse program of "land grabs", often driving off farmers by using gangs of government supported thugs. However, much of the land furnished by the government for resettlement was poor and marginal and the new farmers are still very poor. The fact that the socialist government retains legal title to the land means that it cannot be used to borrow money.

Hiding behind the rhetoric of peasant land reform, about 400,000 hectares of land has in fact been given or sold at give-away prices to about 400 of Mugabe's loyalist cronies, including cabinet ministers, army officers, government officials and greedy friends. However, since none of these people actually want to farm, they have become the new landed gentry, hiring peasants to farm for them. Mugabe has made the seizure of land from white farmers "legal" by passing a law that declared Great Britain solely at fault for the land situation, and allowing Mugabe to seize the land without compensation. The result has been a devastating decline in agricultural production so bad that Zimbabwe, which formerly exported food, now has become an importer, which drains the already bad economy, and further worsens rural poverty. In fact, donor organizations have been refusing to provide further funds until Mugabe comes up with a program to reduce rural poverty, but this he is unwilling (and unable) to do. He has avoided paying the promised funds to relocating families, and he has spent next to nothing on rural roads, schools, housing, wells, farm implements or other vital support elements. Even where farmers produce crops, the government cheats them further. The government passed a law requiring that farmers sell corn and other crops only to it. On many occasions, these farmers have not been paid, so they have had no money to buy seeds for the next growing season. Widespread food shortages are now a constant problem. Mugabe of course blames such failures on the lack of international donor funds.

The rest of the Zimbabwe economy has been similarly devastated. There is often not enough money to buy oil, and as a result, there have not only been shortages of gas for cars and trucks, but there have been frequent power blackouts and many of the factories in cities like the capital Harare and in Bulawayo have been forced to close or are reduced to three days a week of operation. Railroad traffic is down more than 50% and movement by truck is severely restricted. Real wages have been rapidly shrinking and inflation is serious. Rotberg states "Mugabe set about destroying the economic and political fabric of the country. Zimbabwe, once unquestionably secure, economically strong, socially advanced and successfully modern, has plummeted rapidly toward failure. In the last several years, Zimbabwe's per capita GDP has fallen annually by 10%, while the HIV infection rates have climbed to nearly 30%. Two thousand Zimbabweans die of AIDS each week. Life expectancy has dropped from 60 to 42 years, while annual inflation has increased from 40 to 126%. Corruption has become blatant. (Zimbabwe has sunk to 112th place in Transparency International's 2004 Corruption Perceptions Index). The central government no longer effectively provides fundamental political goods such as personal security, schooling, and medical facilities and treatment. Public order has broken down. This year (2004) many Zimbabweans may starve due to extremely serious food shortages and fuel supplies are again dwindling. Political institutions have ceased to function fully. Sizable sectional, ethnic, and linguistic fissures exist, and disaffection is everywhere. Even though the state remains intact, the government's legitimacy is now being seriously challenged." (16)

Domestic Product (GDP) shrank 7.9% in 2000, 2.8% in 2001, 11.1% in 2002, and 9.3% in 2003, and another broad decline was predicted for 2004, with worse coming. One in four adults are HIV-positive. IMF reports further noted that weak governance, corruption and the lack of respect for the rule of law have undermined confidence and led to capital flight and emigration, with negative spillover effects on neighboring countries.

Mr. Mugabe seems to have only one goal – to stay in power no matter what the cost, and to do so, he has destroyed almost every form of democratic governance, human rights, or economic capacity. He believes that he must quash the independent press, the opposition parties, and even any dissent within his own party, ZANU-PF. He does this with skill and cruelty. In the last elections, gangs were sent to rough up anyone suspected of intending to vote for the opposition MDC. Some were beaten and then dumped in a distant lion sanctuary. Tribal chiefs were ordered to herd their followers into the voting booths to back ZANU. After the election, thugs stayed behind to torture those suspected of having voted for the opposition. While few in his party still believe he is good for the country, many of the most senior and ruthless leaders, and the top generals, worry that, if he goes, they have to pay for 20 years of pocketing bribes and cracking heads. There seems to be no end in sight to his terrorist regime. Yet, the more force he uses, the angrier Zimbabweans become, and the more force he must use to keep them down.

Case Study: The Soviet Union as a Terrorist State

The problems facing the Communist Party (CP) and the new Soviet government in 1918 were enormous and intractable. The economy was not a logical response to national needs but only the weak and unbalanced residue left from the Czarist regime further deteriorated by the war and by the destructive consequences of the internal civil war. Russian society was still almost medieval. Eighty percent of the population still lived on the land where they had been serfs under the rule of an arrogant and often brutal aristocracy of rich landlords. The country lacked any really adequate systems of public social services and public infrastructure such as roads, ports, railroads and ground or river transport. Even in cities, health care was almost non-existent, and where it did exist, it was usually cash up front in amounts that few could afford. Prejudices against education were very serious and destructive. The czars and landed aristocracy agreed that the very idea of education of serfs and peasants was outrageous and probably dangerous. And of course, the idea of educating girls was seriously immoral and scandalous. As a consequence, the Soviet Union faced a long period of time with a population lacking enough education useful enough to contribute to the CP's broad agenda of plans and ambitions.

Further, the needs of the country included the need for large sums of money, either generated within the country or made available from foreign sources. As far as internal wealth is concerned, there was very little in banks, company treasuries or individual savings, but the regime had no compulsion against squeezing the 130 million peasants as much as possible in order to generate money for the financing of national economic development.

It is understandable that these problems would be excruciatingly difficult to solve even if the CP had been wise enough to undertake the best courses of action. But in fact, they seldom did. Right at the beginning, the CP made two huge critical mistakes. The first mistake was an overly enthusiastic commitment to very high speed high pressure industrialization, even when it was known that the skills to succeed in this kind of program seldom existed. The CP seemed to have understood only one thing – how to maximize production. They were very late in understanding – - or even trying to understand – - the necessity for high efficiency of production capability, or the need for safe and rapid transportation of goods, or the capacity to produce at competitive costs. Nor did they ever quite understand that how much you produce is linked to how much you can sell! Thus, the Soviet Union became famous for industrial products that cost too much, were of low quality and reliability, and which nobody wanted to buy in the first place.

Thus, the fevered program of industrialization failed to produce any great surge of improved living conditions for the workers, for whom the Revolution was supposedly designed in the first place. But an even greater tragedy was destined to descend o the peasants and the serfs. Along with the removal of the Czar went huge numbers of the landed gentry, and the government took over the ownership of all land, and reallocated most of it for use by the peasants themselves. But what followed was disaster, and it was a disaster deliberately insisted upon by Comrade Stalin, the Great Leader himself. He decided, somehow, that the peasants were guilty of instigating and sustaining all of the ills facing the new Soviet Union. He insisted that all land had to be owned and managed by the State, and he thought that the notion that land held privately by peasants was intolerable and deeply suspicious. He therefore decreed country-wide collectivization of all agricultural land. This meant that rural people were to be forced into organizations called collectives where all property was owned by "the people" but controlled and managed by supposedly skilled managers on behalf of all of the people in the community, now members of these collectives. The collective would not only own the land itself, but all homes, farm animals and farm equipment. The collective would decide what would be planted, how and when crops would be harvested, to whom they would be sold and at what prices. It is not surprising that the peasants strongly resisted this tyranny, and in some cases there were armed clashes and violent resistance.

Stalin was outraged. Given his character, he set out to punish the peasantry in the most terrible ways. The collectivization program was pushed brutally at the highest possible pace. This was of course highly disruptive of every element of rural live and the agricultural economy. The peasants were subjected to terrorist tactics, including killings, imprisonments, beatings, threats against family members, and of course the seizure of all property by the new collectives. Crops did not get planted, or were not tended or harvested. The ranks of people to produce food were decimated. An estimated 15 million people were removed through murder, consignment to labor camps, deaths in labor camps and deportations. In the peak years of 1932-1933, an estimated 10 million people died. Robert Conquest, the great chronicler of the Stalin era estimates that, during the extended period of Stalin's rule up to 1952, an estimated 20 million people died and the numbers of those "repressed" exceeded 40 million, half of them during the reign of terror from 1929 to 1933. (17)

But why did all of this turn out to be chosen government policy? Many far more reasonable options were available. More rational courses of actions could have been chosen and the pace of reform could have been less demanding. There was no inevitable compulsion for the CP to act in the vicious, harmful and irrational way that was employed. The answer to the question of why such terror was chosen lies in the character of the Party Leader Joseph Stalin.

There are those who think the answer was rather clear: Stalin was insane. He was crazy. He should have been locked up. But if one looks at the whole tide of Stalin's actions over the crucial period from 1925 to 1939, one would see the cold calculating progress of an implacable tyrant, slashing his way to ultimate power. Over the course of several years, Stalin understood better than anybody else the weaknesses and vulnerabilities of Russia's situation, and he somehow found ways to take advantage of them to triumph over his opponents. Stalin may have been the essence of evil but he was not insane.

The extraordinary disaster that he designed and implemented was a consequence of the ugly, dangerous and almost hopeless society that emerged from the war with Germany, the overthrow of the Czar and the bitter, highly divisive civil war that followed. The Communist Party was almost totally a negative force, preoccupied with its own internal vendettas and convulsions, and it gradually evolved a very strange philosophy of governance. The revolution became "The Revolution!" – almost a holy interpretation of the new mythology of what was right or wrong. Anything and everything that seemed to support the supposed objectives of The Revolution was right by definition. But the only permitted interpretation of what served The Revolution was of course by the CP leadership. And what The Revolution demanded swiftly became broader and deeper and more intense. The Party did not merely want control; they wanted total and absolute control. They did not simply want control of the "commanding heights" of the economy as proposed by Comrade Lenin, but they wanted control over even the smallest and most innocuous of enterprises. They did not just want to control bank lending policies, they wanted to own all of the banks. All land and property became government property. The CP felt compelled to control individual people, telling them who could be educated, where they could work, what they would be paid, where they could live, and what they could and could not think.

Very quickly, this attitude became pathological. It was increasingly argued and enforced that the supposed threats to The Revolution were so great that the harshest most vicious counter measures were not only permitted but required. The application of less than full terror responses by the government was seen by the Party as deeply suspicious. The very ideas of negotiation or compromise became regarded as treachery and duly punishable. The elimination of most forms of human civility, deliberately pursued in what was admittedly very difficult and uncertain times, created a dehumanized society. The Russian population, indifferent to the revolution and the party, were terrorized and cowed into acceptance of the machinations of a brutal and tyrannical state.

In that environment, the ideal leader who emerged was Joseph Stalin. Stalin was never constrained by any of the normal human motivations. He is said to have had no moral code or sense of moral obligations to anybody or any thing, and he was deeply self-centered and self-aggrandizing. It seems to have been crucial to him not only to win but to triumph, and to beat everybody down. He had two great strengths that he brought to bear. He had nerve or boldness, and he was willing to take risks that nobody else would undertake. Basically, he saw the world through a dark suspicious mind in which everything was suspect and no response was forbidden or improper if it advanced himself and his machinations. He saw the world as "after him" all the time, and once on the attack he proved to be highly vindictive and unforgiving. Enemies became enemies for life, and deserved to be destroyed.

The Great Terror thus became the principle creation of the terrible mind of this extraordinary person. One by one, Stalin captured or neutralized every element of the new Soviet society and government that might have any capacity to opposed him. The most drastic of these programs was of course the great famines resulting from Stalin's implacable enforcement of the disaster called collectivization. Initially, The Revolution was the product of military action, largely against the failures of the Czarist era. Stalin initially formed an alliance with the military, especially to enforce collectivization and other oppressions against the people. Then, as to be expected, Stalin betrayed the military, purging much of its leadership and replacing them with his own loyalists. The same thing also happened to the various elements of the justice system: the police, prosecutors, judges and especially, the prisons.

The Workers Party, which had been the bedrock of the Communist revolution suffered a similar fate and ended up, as in most Socialist countries, as a spokesman for the dictator and an enforcer of the government's authority.

The Russian economy was almost totally turned over to State Owned Enterprises (SOE), which gave Stalin absolute control over the economy, huge amounts of the national wealth, and the capacity to direct the activities of most of the national workforce. Finally, in 1933-34, Stalin purged the Party itself, and as many as one million four hundred thousand members were driven out of Party ranks.

In the later stages of Stalin's rule, he built up a cult around him. He was given the most astonishing adulation as "a genius, not only in politics but also in strategy, the sciences, style, philosophy and almost every field. His picture looked down from every billboard. His bust was carried by Soviet alpinists to the top of every Soviet peak." (18) Yet he is said to have said "It doesn't really matter who you kill, as long as you kill enough of them. The rest will get the point."

CASE STUDY: THE RUSSIAN FEDERATION NOW: WHAT MIGHT HAVE BEEN

With the overthrow of its Communist/State Socialist regime, Russia had an extraordinary requirement to devise a new system to govern itself. The optimists saw this as an opportunity; the pessimists saw it as a threat. How did it work out?

Well, Russia has enthusiastically invented a new dictatorship. Greed and corruption are the new normals stewarded by President Putin as the dictator.

Aggressive new classs of greedy thieves, bribers, looters, usurpers, extortionists and "re-allocators" has seized the economy and are happily looting it. Government arrogance has revitalized the ancient Russian skills of dictatorship, oppression and terror. Once again Russia has created a world in which no resistance to the leadership is ever tolerated if it can be crushed. Once again, Russia sees itself as military muscle; civilian social services are deliberately neglected and inadequate.

The justice system has crashed, and in its wreckage has lost any sense of what now "justice" really means in human terms. Most Russians have now been returned to the reality of great fear and loathing for the police, the courts, and protection of the law. The "rule of law" is now a threat because enforcement of unjust laws is in itself unjust and oppressive.

Two percent of the people are filthy rich. A huge percentage lives in poverty, or near poverty, or day-to-day survival. The economic middle class is both fearful and nearly hopeless. Few now feel that things can ever be better under the leadership that has emerged – not just Putin but the whole elite that has seized the country. Faced with these problems, increasing numbers of people with mobile skills or enough money are leaving the country – over 1.25 million from 2000 to 2010. Opinion polls and interviews suggest that from 25% to 40% of people consider leaving the country if possible, or at least trying to send their children elsewhere for education.

Russia is living on its energy revenues. Is that bad? From the point of view of the ruling elite, it is excellent because, one way or another, the government either controls the energy resources or controls the people who do. Thus, huge sums of money are available for anything the regime wants to do.

Much of what has been happening since the fall of the USSR is positive. Capital investment, even by crooked oligarchs has been expanded and has stimulated elements of the old, tired, obsolete Soviet economy. More elements of the economy now serve badly needed consumer needs. Wages are up, and employment has risen.

But still – in a country of 140 million people, there are 40 million pensioners, most of whom have little personal resources. The state sector employs 20 million workers, and its reputation for efficiency and cost effectiveness remains "Soviet level" bad. The private sector is almost as bad. Too much of it is in the hands of greedy oligarchs who understand looting but not good management. Meanwhile, the private sector economy beyond the energy sector remains so obsolete and inefficient that most of it can't really compete with other businesses in the world in terms of cost or quality. But when critics point out that the pace of economic activity is slackening, the regime brags about the enormous new energy markets is it tapping with its new oil and gas fields, and the new pipelines it has been building to serve prosperous new customers in China, Japan and S. Korea. Putin and his elite partners will continue to be flooded with national wealth which they can dispose of as they wish.

Why is all of this happening? Why did Russia not choose a whole range of better and wiser and more effective courses of government policy and action?

It is hard to avoid the conclusion that Russia's government after the change has presented the Russian citizen with extraordinary incompetence, invulnerable arrogance, deliberate rejection of the better options, and an abiding attention to their own greed. This is highly oppressive, and it is almost certain to persist for decades because nobody seems to have either the desire, or the will or the skill to go back and revise the disaster. Meanwhile, schools have started to charge exorbitant fees ($200 per month for families having a monthly income of from $300 to $500); public infrastructure is neglected and is deteriorating; teachers, professors, police officers and public officials are all deliberately underpaid; tax collectors must be bribed; and government contracts are up for the highest bribe. The police remain frightening and actively dangerous. Nepotism, favoritism and political preferment are the rule. Competition and merit are dying concepts. Everything is regulated, and regulatory approvals are increasingly expensive. In sum, the Russian economy is underdeveloped, the government is corrupt, and life is miserable and dangerous. Welcome to the "New Russia".

CASE STUDY: RWANDA: INCOMPREHENSIBLE EVIL

When Belgium controlled Rwanda it made a fatal mistake. In a country with a long and turbulent history of ethnic conflict between the tribes of the Tutsi and the Hutu, the Belgian colonial regime chose to pick sides, and it formed an alliance with the Tutsis. In the convulsions that followed, the Hutus managed to overthrow the Tutsi government, at which point the Belgians switched sides and allied themselves with the Hutu. Then, when the Belgians left in 1962, they had managed to leave a situation of implacable ethnic hatred, with a government in the hands of a Hutu regime which was incompetent and seriously oppressive, and as many as 30,000 people were killed in government purges and more than 300,000 fled their homes, many into exile into Uganda and Congo. In 1973, the government passed into the hands of the dictator Juvenal Habyarimana who formally defined a one party state.

Meanwhile, in neighboring Uganda, President Yoweri Museveni began to use the Rwandan exiles that had fled to his country as military allies. These exiles had arrived armed and formed the Rwandan Patriotic Front (RPF), which mounted an armed invasion of Rwanda in 1990. But the French and the government of Zaire backed the Hutu regime, and a sort of cease fire was negotiated and held until 1993 when the RPF once again invaded.

The policy that then emerged from the Hutu controlled Rwandan government was unbelievably bad. Of all of the choices it could have made, it chose the absolute worst. It decided that the only recourse to this ethnic conflict was **genocide**; to totally exterminate all Tutsis, and this decision became the basis of a long and organized program to achieve this end. The army was expanded from about 10,000 to over 35,000. The military began a protracted program of arms purchases from arms dealers and from the governments of South Africa, France and Egypt. Many of these weapons were furnished to civilian "volunteers". The French government was actively solicited as an ally and in addition to weapons, the French army helped to train the Rwandan army.

The ensuing disaster was utterly predictable. According to Feinstein "organized militias armed with fire arms and farm implements spread throughout the country, systematically killing Tutsis and any moderate Hutus who resisted the genocide. All the while, local radio exhorted further violence and greater destruction. Over the course of just three months, somewhere between 800,000 and 1,174,000 people were killed, including at least 400,000 children. Against women, rape was the weapon of choice and between 100,000 and 250,000 women were brutally raped. 75,000 children were left as orphans. The economy, which had collapsed in the late 1980s was once again devastated, and hundreds of thousands lived in serious poverty. (19)

"When the RPF finally overthrew the government in July of 1994, the full magnitude and ferocity of the slaughter became clear; mass killings in churches, entire families slaughtered by their neighbors, rotting corpses filling mass graves or left to fester in the street. It was a systematic bloodletting of incomprehensible proportions. It is important to understand: this was deliberate genocide, meticulously organized, in order to kill as many people as possible. The slaughter of thousands of Rwandans in schools and football stadiums was managed almost exclusively with automatic weapons to achieve the highest kill-rate possible." (20)

Then, horribly, the conflict spilled over into neighboring Zaire(Congo), ruled by the brutal dictator Mobutu Sese Seko. By 1996, nearly 1 million Hutu exiles had settled in eastern Zaire. But Zaire already had a substantial Tutsi population, perfectly capable of taking up the traditional hatreds of the Hutus. Thus, in late 1996, they launched a heavy attack against the new Hutu refugee camps. But the forces in these camps had come heavily armed, with weapons largely supplied by the French, and they fought back, aided by the Rwandan government and forces from Uganda. Their forces swept the eastern Congo, killing every Tutsi they encountered. Further, the Congo army, badly trained and badly led, rapidly collapsed and ran, killing, raping and looting as they fled. By mid 1997, the government of Zaire was removed, and the invaders backed Laurent Kabila as the new self appointed President, who renamed the country the Republic of Congo.

In an amazing turn of events, the Rwanda and Uganda leadership decided that Kabila was getting too independent, and that he had to be dumped. In his defense, Kabila solicited help from his neighbors and remarkably, help was provided by Zimbabwe, Namibia, Angola, Sudan, Chad and even Libya. The result was that what had become known as "The Great African War" muddled into a sort of political and battlefield stalemate, but according to Feinstein "The human suffering was grotesque; by the end of 2003, it was estimated that 3.3 million people had died as a result of violence, starvation and disease. Those left alive were barely able to scrape together a living. More than 2.3 million Congolese were compelled to move within the country, while a further 330,000 took refuge outside of its borders. Nearly 400,000 children were forced to suffer from the violence. The behavior of all of the military troops was despicable. Tens of thousands of women were raped, thousands of people had limbs amputated, young boys were kidnapped to become child soldiers, much property was destroyed and public services ceased to exist." (21)

The civil war in Rwanda horribly revealed a whole series of governments in Rwanda, Uganda, Zaire/Congo, France and elsewhere that constantly rejected potentially the best of the options available to them in favor of the worst -- some of which were evil beyond belief. There is really no explanation in human terms for the vast and implacable evil of these events. What is crucial to understand is that this evil was initiated and fed and sustained deliberately as matters of choice for three decades. Time and again, the horrible decisions made by governments were inherently evil and produced enduring evil consequences. The word evil is crucial. Choices were not simply ill informed, or misguided, or based on ignorance, or merely incompetent. The choices were evil – beyond the debate over rightness or wrongness – hugely, continuously and inexplicably evil.

CASE STUDY: CHINA AS A TERRORIST STATE

The expansion of terrorism around the world involves many groups operating independently, but it is vital to recognize that some of the worst forms of terrorism are those undertaken by governments. One of the worst terrorist governments in modern history has been that of the Chinese. For thirty years, from the rise to power of the Chinese Communist Party (CCP) in 1949 to just beyond the death of Mao Zedong in 1976, the CCP created the worst government in the world. It was a government that created wave after wave of terror and oppression, both internally and in its relationships with other countries.

Terrorism here is defined as the practices of the government that are aimed at dominating and threatening the populace through fear and intimidation. Many governments perform normally and productively and make human mistakes in the process. A government may simply be incompetent, stupid, wrong headed or misguided. But other governments are deliberate and blatant dictatorships. Others like the old USSR or Maoist China have been driven by complex philosophies which, in the end, proved horribly wrong. Other leaders may simply rule to seek power and loot. Governments have choices between many systems and ways of dealing with their citizens ranging from wise support to bland indifference to bumbling incompetence to fierce terrorism.

The Peoples Republic of China has used terrorism as an instrument of power both inside the country and in response to the external world, including terrorist threats brought against them. In general, the history of the modern-day Chinese government should be considered in two thirty year periods. The first is the Maoist era, beginning when the Communists came to power in 1949. This period was marked by one of the worst governments in the world, bringing to the Chinese population poverty, distress, obsolescence, and terrorist governance. After Mao's death in 1976, the Chinese Communist Party (CCP) was finally able to initiate its own broad range of reforms covering the thirty years from about 1980 to now, and still continuing. In this process of reform, the CCP has had to abandon the Maoist legacy, redesign the economy, reform the government itself, and manage the consequences of these reforms for the Chinese people and society. The intellectual and theological base of Communism and State Socialism has been quietly abandoned, along with most of the terrorist acts of a harsh and demanding government and military. In the new environment, the CCP still rules but tides are running to force the leadership to acknowledge other interests and pressures. The whole extensive apparatus of State control through which the domestic terror was enforced, including wage and price controls, production controls, worker job assignment, allocation of resources, structuring of government budgets, control of bank lending, and import/export controls have largely been abandoned or substantially mitigated and whole armies of enforcers and inspectors and investigators have been done away with.

But war is terror, and Maoist China was a deliberate instigator of wars with its neighbors in the name of the supremacy of Chinese Communism. Within its first year, the CCP staged the invasion and conquest of Tibet and occupied Xinjiang, with its Uighur Muslim minority population. In both cases, the Chinese government has acted implacably to suppress the local cultures and sense of independence of these two countries. There have been numerous forms of protest over the course of many years, and some of them have been brutally suppressed, with hundreds of people killed and injured. Clearly, terrorism was a major weapon of the Maoist government, used to crush any spirit of separatism or freedom. It should be remembered that this was the period in China of the "Great Leap Forward", and "The Cultural Revolution" which were among the most destructive acts of government in modern history, when terrorism was applied to the whole country. It must also be remembered that the notorious Red Guards arrested and tortured millions of people with the approval of

Mao and the CP. And because Mao forced farmers to forgo planting and made them try rudimentary industry, crops all over the country never got planted, and huge food shortages occurred, with the result that 20 to 30 million people simply starved to death.

China became the sponsor of North Korea and fought a major war, helping it invade South Korea and putting it into protracted conflict with the United States. At its peak, the People's Liberation Army (PLA) put more than 2 million soldiers into the conflict inside Korea.

Earlier, China was heavily involved in a series of assaults against other countries in S. E. Asia. In 1962, China launched two surprise border attacks against India. For more than 15 years, China strongly assisted the Vietnamese against both the French and the Americans. Mao's dark suspicions contributed fundamentally to serious border disputes with the USSR, and in the late 60's there were two border clashes between elements of the hundreds of thousands of troops that lined both sides of the border. In Indonesia, the PLA aided the Indonesian Communist Party in making an armed attempt to overthrow the government. For more than a decade, China aided the HUK communist rebels in the Philippines. In 1975, Chinese support of the Khmer Rouge helped it to seize power in Cambodia. In 1979, China attacked its old ally Vietnam in order to "teach them a lesson" about who held the power. China has continued to support the tyrannical N. Korean regime, and has also supported and armed communist rebels in Malaysia, Thailand and Burma. Thus, for most of the 30 year Maoist era, China was the most terrorist government in the world.

Only the death of Mao in 1976 saved the nation. Beginning about 1980, Mao's successors began carefully to initiate and "sell" an extraordinary reform of the government, which has been going on during the whole 30 year period from 1980 until now. What is emerging has begun with the economy and has gradually begun to deal with public needs for social services and public infrastructure. Even more slowly and cautiously is the easing of control over public opinion, social interaction, and the various forms of public communication. But it must be understood that Maoism is not totally dead. In some cases, it is the obvious policy of the government to retreat from the heady control of the Maoist systems only when forced to do so, then only as little as possible, and as slowly as possible.

In the international arena, China has, with the one exception of the province of Xinjiang, largely escaped the terrorist antagonisms of the fundamentalist Islamic world.

Returning to China's domestic condition, we need to come back again to the philosophical nature of the CCP. According to its philosophy, there is really only one absolute standard: anything that serves the interests of the Party is vital and acceptable and legitimate, whether or not it is acceptable in the country or to the rest of the world. Take for example the ethical concept of "lying". The world generally believes that lying is undesirable and unethical. In most of the world, it is thought that governments should not lie to their citizens. All governments will condemn it when citizens lie to public officials, and most such lies are punished. In China, the difference is that, while citizens may not lie to the government, the CCP and government never hesitates to lie to the people, if lying offers some advantage to the State.

This is not just a generalization. China quite openly develops the skills of necessary lying, and directs its official lying largely through a huge central government Department of Propaganda which reports directly to the CCP ruling Council. This department controls official national lying in two main arenas. First, it generates the lies that the CCP leadership deems necessary; and second, it mitigates the impact of utterances against the government by refutation, counter lies and censorship.

The Department of Propaganda is the master of the kinds of lies that employ nice soft words – vague, bland, and presumably reassuring for the public. For example, the official policy of the CCP, enunciated endlessly over three decades, is that the government seeks national harmony. Yet the real meaning of harmony is the demand, implacably enforced, that everybody agrees with the government, and conforms to the central elitist will. Harmony thus really means that no disagreement is permitted. It means that no proposals for change will be tolerated, or that no new ideas may be publically discussed. When the Department of Propaganda screens the Internet, forbidden words include "truth", "corruption", "protest", or "idea", along with "Taiwan", "Tibet", "Xinjiang", "Russian border", or "Falun Gong". More than a thousand such soft words and phrases trigger censorship investigation. What is even worse is the fact that with any form of conflict or questioning, the government stoutly maintains that the questions are always wrong, that the government is always right, and that the disturbers of "harmony" must be punished.

The Department of Propaganda has its own interpretation of the concept of "democracy". The CCP speaks constantly about its commitment to permit free elections in China, and yet observers both inside and outside of the country doubt that any really free and competitive elections have ever been held, since the Party's rise to power in 1949. Why? First, elections are allowed only at the very local level of village councils – not in districts, or counties, or provinces, or cities and certainly not at the national level. Second, all candidates who are allowed to be listed are proposed by the local party secretary, or at least approved by him. No one advocating any serious opposition to policies or actions will be permitted to make it onto the candidate list. Thus, elections as a key element of "democracy" have never been allowed to evolve.

Another element of "democracy" is the capacity for debate and discussion of the important issues facing the country and the voting jurisdiction. As with elections, the CCP maintains that such discussion is available to all citizens. But public debate is a complex, tricky and ultimately dangerous course of action, and it is getting trickier all of the time. The growth of the Internet, including the emergence of the wildly popular electronic social networks, plus the general loosening of controls over news media have significantly broadened the base of public commentary over the whole range of vital subjects. It is the intent of the government to tolerate this broadening as little as possible, as slowly as possible, and it is certain that the CCP has definite ideas about some strict limits beyond which the public dialogue will not be permitted to pass.

Example: Terrorism Produced "The Great Famine"

A monstrous famine swept areas of China in the years from 1958 to 1961, and it was not caused by drought or some other natural disaster. The horror is that at least **30,000,000 people** – and perhaps as many as 50,000,000 -- starved to death in a famine caused solely by vicious and catastrophic CCP policies. In 1958, Mao Zedong launched a new campaign called "The Great Leap Forward", as an attempt to push China into more modern industrialization under some distorted vision of the Communist Utopia. All across the country, the system of Communist communes and work brigades became the spearhead to force the peasants to form into collectives. Mao asserted that industrialization in China would soon overtake that in Britain or France, and he set a series of impossibly ambitious targets, particularly for steel production. Millions of those peasants were then forced from their fields to man "back yard furnaces" where huge amounts of steel ingots were to be produced. The forced elimination of two major planting seasons caused serious food shortages of all kinds in the cities and especially in the countryside. The old and the young died first; many survived by eating insects and "grass soup". Beyond belief, everybody "knew" – but nobody seriously opposed. Millions and millions of Chinese passively accepted the most vicious and insane directions from the top. Anybody who dared to point out the obvious disaster in the making was eliminated, and local officials sent false reports of "bumper crops" to save their jobs and lives. The ultimate result was the worst man-made disaster ever suffered in China, and one of the most horrible in modern history. And ultimately, the products of those backyard furnaces were hopeless and were simply thrown away. Was this terrorism? Yes of course. And it was terrorism planned and managed by the government.

Example: China's One Child Policy Terrorizes Mothers and Babies

In 1979, China initiated a policy that, with certain exceptions, limited every Chinese family to one child. Government utterances constantly portrayed this policy as that of a caring government helping families to design their own best futures; but in fact, the whole program was designed by an arrogant government as a way to hold down the growth of the national population at levels that could adequately be supported by the inadequate national economy. But there were many ways in which such a policy could have been pursued, and the course that the CCP chose became one of the most oppressive systems in the world – a reign of terror involving literally millions of acts of terror against Chinese parents and their children. Millions of women have suffered from forced abortions during which even living babies have been killed by the law's enforcers. Millions of families have been heavily fined, and many men have been sent to notorious "labor correction" camps. In order to enforce this policy a huge government bureaucracy was created at the national, township and village levels. At its peak, this bureaucracy had 400,000 officials at the township level and more than one million at the village level. In addition, neighborhood "snoops" were employed to rat out their neighbors. The State Planning Commission had absolute authority to set "quotas" for the numbers of children allowed at the township and village levels, and local governments were given unbridled power to enforce these quotas, often by brutal and expensive means.

In the early 80's, a Chinese peasant named Chen and some of his friends had become outraged by the local consequences of this one child policy, and had done a survey in his city of Linyi and its surroundings. He discovered that 7,000 mothers with two children each had been forcibly sterilized during the past three months, and that several hundred others had been forced to undergo abortions, even though they were eight months pregnant. The city's hospital staff admitted that, under orders, they had immersed fetuses in boiling water to make sure they did not survive. This became known as "the Linyi incident."

Chen, who was blind, and his wife went to Beijing to report his findings to an appeals commission. The police intercepted and arrested him despite the fact that his intended complaint was perfectly legal, but the Linyi incident became a famous example of the terrorist capabilities of the Chinese government. The incident became famous in part just because it became known, and in part because of the extreme official brutality it revealed. The municipal authorities had indeed published an official order directing that forced sterilizations and abortions should be carried out. According to Guy Sorman: "As this became known, terrified pregnant mothers who could do so fled the city to hide out with relatives." The Linyi police, with the full knowledge of the family planning commission, used hired thugs to track down these pregnant women and other women with two children. Parents and neighbors who failed to report them were jailed, beaten, and fined a hundred yuan a day. Entire neighboring villages then found themselves besieged, cut off from the rest of the world until they handed over the accused. Husbands who resisted their wives kidnapping were badly beaten, and often jailed. Herded into a hospital like sheep, the hapless women were summarily anesthetized and operated on, often in far from hygienic conditions. The Party cadres heaved a sigh of relief; their jobs were safe." (22)

As for Chen, he was later put under house arrest in his home. Human rights advocates trying to record how he was were beaten and chased away by the local "militia" (i. e. government thugs). The government has locked down information, and the Linyi incident has slowly disappeared. For the Chinese government, the incident was justified. For most of the rest of the world, it stands as a classic example of terrorism by the State against its own citizens.

China is very sensitive to any form of challenge to the regime and thus is very sensitive to any suggestion of terrorism, insurgency, or armed resistance. The government is very harsh against any opposition, and thus terrorists have little chance. China deliberately links the concept of terrorism, which everybody opposes, to that of dissent and separatism. Dissent might in other worlds have some legitimacy, but not in China. Separatism in China is a very serious allegation, and it refers primarily to major long standing conflicts between the Chinese government and the ethnic Muslims concentrated in the western province of Xinjiang, the population of which is mostly Muslim; against the entire region of Tibet; and against the independent Chinese populated nation of Taiwan. Thus, the CCP wants its citizens to see "separatism" not as a form of disagreement to be debated but as an ominous form of "terrorism." The same connection is maintained with the broader concept of "dissent". Thus, in the minds of the leadership, dissent equals terrorism; separatism equal terrorism.

The conflict between the central Chinese government and the Muslims in Xinjiang is decades old. It has been inflamed by government policies of diluting the Muslim population with Han Chinese imported from other regions, and by harsh and often brutal oppression of the people. This oppression takes many forms, and it is implacable. For example, a regional government has declared fasting to be illegal. Fasting is a great traditional part of the Muslim observance of the holy period of Ramadan. Police have stopped cars on the road and demanded that the occupants eat something. Refusal to do so constitutes "illegal fasting."

In general, the events of Tiananmen Square badly frightened the CCP, and caused it to tighten control of the population all over the country and not just in Xinjiang. The Peoples Armed Police (PAP) was expanded after Tiananmen Square so that it is now a national police force of about 1.5 million members, armed with heavier weapons such as tanks and artillery. New regulations supposedly created to protect the public are often really the basis of new and more powerful legal authorities which allow the government to intervene in practically anything, with the full force of "the law" behind it.

The most visible terrorist threat posed for the Chinese government is the existence of the East Turkestan Islamic Movement, a small secret group seeking to extend an Islamic "Caliphate" to Xinjiang. China attributes everything that goes wrong in Xinjiang to this insurgent group, and seems very cynical about it. This supposed threat has been substantially exaggerated, and has become the justification for the application of more oppression against Xinjiang and Muslims in general. Thus, the Chinese government brands dissidents in Xinjiang with the crime of "separatism".

In Africa, China sees its interests as under threat. More than 2 million Chinese citizens now live and work in all of the countries of Africa, and China has embassies in 49 of these countries. More than half of the population of Africa is Muslim, and countries are in some form of chaos with conflicts and crises all over the continent. Chinese people or organizations have inadvertently been caught up in these conflicts (a Chinese woman and her son were killed in the Mall attack in Nairobi Kenya for example), and a few minor incidents have occurred specifically against Chinese interests, involving al-Qaeda in the Islamic Magreb (AQIM), the Movement for the Emancipation of the Niger Delta (in Nigeria), and the Ogadan National Liberation Front in Ethiopia.

CASE STUDY: CHINA NOW: DOMESTIC TERRORISM

While China has largely escaped the terrorist conflicts elsewhere in the world, it has long maintained its terrorist and oppressive regime at home. The Chinese government has since its beginning deliberately maintained a widely oppressive and often terrorist psychology, policies and forms of government operations. It is oppressive when, in the domestic arena, governments at all levels recognize how China's people have suffered from the deliberate lack of social services and how this has been a form of government oppression. There is a growing realization of how technologically obsolete the old systems have been and how far each social service has to go in making remedial improvements to reach even basic adequacy. In China for example, only 10-20 percent of the population have access to health care insurance, and only about 15-20 percent have any form of old age protection other than the traditional reliance on their children. There would be enormous unfunded costs involved in expanding social service to the majority of citizens. In addition, professional knowledge, new equipment, major repairs and renovations to obsolete physical plant all must be brought closer to current international standards. This long term neglect means that massive efforts are now needed to create a total revenue package for social services involving continued central government fund transfers, new taxing powers, private sector responsibilities, intergovernmental cost sharing, and freedom to reallocate funds as judged against local government priorities. There is serious doubt that the central government will ever make such a massive effort, and there is the related concern that local governments are so weak and inexperienced that they are totally unable to manage such reforms, and whole new programs of capacity building must be generated.

The Chinese government is so afraid of opposition that it has created a program of government terrorism against any who speak out in any way. The government has brutally suppressed thousands of protests, putting many thousands of protesters in prisons and labor camps, all without any evidence beyond the mere fact of police arrest. All forms of communications are monitored from the most sophisticated electronic systems down to neighborhood gossip. On the Internet, about one thousand words are considered ominous and are forbidden, including such things as Falun Gong, Muslim, Tiananmen, Taiwan, Tibet, correction center, democracy, political prisoner, Russian border, corruption, protest, disruption, separation and even "truth" or "idea"!

In 2012, China executed about 3,000 people, or roughly four times more than the rest of the world together. (23) But in fact, this level was way down. In 2002, the number of executions was more than 12,000. In 1993, the number had been 24,000, and then, for several years, the average was around 15,000 each year. But it must be remembered that under Mao, millions had been executed for the vague sins of being "counter revolutionaries". In recent years, it remains the perception that the government will kill for political reasons having nothing to do with any real crime. It is a strange world where "only" 3,000 executions per year is considered a human rights triumph.

China has 60 million Protestants, and about 10 million Catholics, and more than 20 million Muslims. All of these religions have been quashed and thousands of priests, ministers, imams and other religious leaders, along with many of their followers have been imprisoned in "labor reeducation" camps. Any overt practice of any religion beyond individual activity is marked by the government and viewed with suspicion. A spiritual message from an organized religious group can be called "inciting the people to superstition".

The Family Planning System, discussed earlier, still continues to terrorize women, despite some elements of reform and promises for further future mitigation.

Corruption and the concepts of Guanxi (influence peddling) are so ubiquitous that it has been said that "anybody in China who is honest is either cowardly or stupid." The practitioners of corruption are those in the power elite. The victims are the general public. Politicians, civil servants, police, judges, prosecutors, all oppress the people with illegal demands for bribes, kickbacks, payoffs, "speed money", and other forms of harsh financial oppression. Those who refuse, or try to protest may be arrested and sent to labor camps. In the power elite the "big men" steal big, and the little men steal small. Despite strong urgings, even inside the Party, as of 2014, after 65 years of mindless oppression, the CCP has finally agreed to eliminate of these terroristic labor camps but has yet to do so.

Government control of the economy has led to a whole sophisticated system of economic oppression. What the leadership of the Communist Party think they have learned is that economic liberalization is actively dangerous for oppressive regimes. When they look at other authoritarian regimes they see: the death of the USSR; the escape from tyranny of the countries of E. Europe; the liberalization of S. Korea, the move to democracy in Indonesia and the Philippines, the conversion of Vietnam, etc. These events have frightened an always pathological elite. Even when the government has allowed greater latitude for private enterprise, it has developed and maintained a huge body of complex regulations, aimed at controlling every facet of economic life. The government controls most of the critical elements of the economy largely through government owned and controlled State Owned Enterprises (SOE), the largest of the banks, the price setting authority, and ownership of all of the land. This control is driven by the sole concept that whatever the State wants, it takes, and it is almost impossible to break through this oppressive control. But it is widely known that the higher-ups in the CCP and their families have amassed billions of dollars in corrupt property, possessions and secret bank accounts. It is disconcerting to recognize the numbers of occasions in which some government official has been found to be in collusion with smugglers, counterfeiters, or thieves. The protection of intellectual property rights is enthusiastically ignored.

According the estimates of the Chinese government itself, a large percentage of government activities, and about 40% of taxes collected have no real basis in laws, but are the product of bureaucratic discretion. Nobody knows what the law in China really means, and the leadership seems to like it that way. No genuinely competitive elections have ever been conducted in China since 1949. Where the views of the average Chinese people can be determined, one of the greatest of complaints is simply that the whole system is horribly UNFAIR!

As a deliberate fixed policy of terrorism, the People's Liberation Army has long maintained hundreds of medium range missiles in the land overlooking the island of Taiwan, and it regularly rants about how it could destroy Taiwan and murder its citizens.

Parts of the economy or of social services have been deliberately neglected for decades. Despite many technical advances, Chinese agricultural production has stagnated at the same level of productivity for the last 15-20 years. While the Chinese have expanded the number of schools, the need still far exceeds the capacity, and the quality of education is much in question. A quarter of Chinese youth seems to remain functionally illiterate, along with millions of older adults.

China has the worst environmental record of any country in the world.

Consider the judgments of expert opinions (24) both in China and from the outside, about China and the environment:

* Agricultural runoff is "the worst in the world"
* Soil erosion is "the worst in the world"
* Desertification is "the worst in the world"
* Air pollution: China is the world's largest producer of carbon dioxide
* China has 16 of the 20 world's most polluted cities
* The Yellow River is the most silt clogged in the world
* China is the world's largest user of coal, and acid rain falls in 1/3 of the country

* Almost every river in the country is heavily polluted
* 25-40% of all mercury emissions in the world come from China
* Only 20% of waste water is treated
* In the last half century, 332 Chinese dams have failed, including "the worlds worst dam disaster" – the Bauquio Dam in Henan Province which collapsed and killed an estimated 80,000 to 200,000 people.
* China suffers from "the worst river water cessation in the world"
* 300 of China's 600 largest cities (and 400 out of 700 villages studied) suffer from serious water shortages – and the shortages are chronic. 65% of underground aquifers in the major 118 cities are "severely polluted". In Beijing, 90% of the underground sources of water have been used up. This listing could go on and on.

In fact, in every one of these environmental disaster areas, the situation is getting worse and not better. This massive oppression of the populace is deliberate, since the CCP has chosen to avoid "wasting" its economic development money on costly and unprofitable environmental problems..

Protest even in mild forms, and even when true, is seldom allowed and acts of protest are highly dangerous. For example, in one case, local politicians seized farms and refused to pay the occupants. When the peasants protested, the police were called in to physically expel more than 100 peasant families. Many were beaten up, some were jailed, and 12 were killed. It was later found that the local Party officials had siphoned off most of the money that should have been paid in compensation for the seized land. In another case, peasants set up blockades around 5 heavily polluting chemical factories, built on stolen land. A clash with police lasted several hours, with people beaten and imprisoned. It became obvious that the local officials had not closed the factories because they had been bought off. These are only small incidents but they illustrate the existence of an enormous hidden problem. In 2005, a top government official admitted that China had experience 74,000 "mass incidents" in which almost

4 million people had participated, and that the number of such incidents were increasing. In 1994, only about 8700 such incidents had been recorded. The top government official asserted however that the fault was that the peasants were "terrorists".

In a country in which governments own most of the land, and in which corruption is a way of life, all too often real estate is illegally appropriated by governments and leased to investors and developers in connivance with corrupt officials, most of whom are Party officials. It should not be surprising to recognize that the average Chinese views this "system" as a severe and vicious form of oppression. The nature of some of these complaints is highly revealing; it includes the failure of employers to pay worker's wages, delayed payment of wages, underpayments, low wages, illegal enforcement of safety requirements, excessive and illegal taxes, and oppressive environmental failures such as polluted water, poisonous air, and chemically damaged soils. There are thousands of cases of illegal property seizures, property seized but not paid for, forced evictions with or without compensation and wanton destruction of private property. There have been further hundreds of thousands of complaints about demands for bribes or kickbacks or illegal payments by greedy public officials. In other words, the horrible performance of Chinese officialdom has become another major form of oppression.

Cities are becoming disasters. Limitations on the numbers of people who were allowed to become official urban residents, resulted in the creation of huge illegal neighborhoods of people working in the illegal "informal economy." In Shanghai, within sight of shiny new office buildings and apartment houses, one half of the city's 17 million inhabitants have no proper sanitation. The disparities in personal wealth are highly disconcerting. The new middle class, often a half generation out off the farm themselves, have little sympathy for the great bulk of the population which remains in poverty or near poverty.

Where does this leave the CCP and the government now? Most importantly, they have abandoned the economic principles of State Socialism because those policies did not work. This has forced the CCP to seek some new philosophy to justify their rule. They have settled for two: "successful economic development", and "nationalism", and these have been more successful, at least for the time being. The CCP can generally count on broad public acceptance and support despite its many oppressive aspects. This has meant that the political structure itself has not been forced to change and that structure is, and has always been, oppressive. This oppression is multi-faceted and deliberate. The CCP **wants** to be oppressive. Why?

Many Chinese, and not just its leaders, remember the great historic patterns of powerful leadership control exercised at the top. It is in China's DNA to yearn for the glories of the past, all the way back to the time when China was the richest and most powerful country in the world. This historic pattern was reinforced by the theology of Communism and State Socialism especially as interpreted by the tyrant Mao Zedong. This yearning for past glories is now being deliberately used to fuel growing Chinese nationalism, which in turn can be used to justify the Chinese position in dealing with foreign countries like Russia, Japan, S. Korea, India and of course the United States.

To an astonishing degree, the CCP and loyalist cadres in government ministries are morbidly afraid of any form of dissent. Time and time again, the CCP has made it clear that perhaps the most significant objective of the regime is to "**preserve national stability.**" But the true meaning of the concept of "maintaining stability" is really to "prevent opposition". This attitude is so pathological that the government can't separate serious dissent from far more modest and insignificant disagreements and disenchantments. There is no really independent justice system; every element from police to prosecutors to judges to prisons and labor camps are strictly under the direct control of the CCP. The National People's Congress and local people's congresses are deliberately weak and well controlled. None have any real oversight power. Seldom are they allowed to debate, much less approve or disapprove government budgets. No investigations are launched; no officials are ever fired or punished. Not a single bill ever proposed by members (rather than the Party) seems ever to have been passed into law.

Case Study: North Korea as a Terrorist State

What can be said about a country where people are starving and living in almost medieval squalor, and yet they love their leaders and think themselves blessed? This is North Korea – surely the strangest and most vicious and most pitiful country on earth. How did it get this way? More importantly, even while the reality of its economic and moral bankruptcy is becoming more apparent, why doe it stay that way?

North Korea has had several opportunities to move toward absolutely vital reforms, yet its leadership has rejected them all. After its freedom from Japan in 1949, Korea could have emerged as a united country, linked by a common heritage. Instead, it split itself in two. North Korea might still have achieved some success, but instead, its leaders conceded too much to the pressures of the occupying Soviet Union under the direction of Joseph Stalin, who wanted all of Korea as a Communist subordinate and ally. When the Russian troops withdrew from the country, the North Korean government could then have sought a more balanced policy of reconciliation with South Korea. Instead, they retained the antagonistic Soviet line, and two years later, in 1950, the North invaded the South. Because of the U. S. and the U. N. intervention, the war ended in a stalemate, after three years and one million deaths. Who "won" the war? Not North Korea, on its way to disaster, but South Korea, headed to remarkable economic successes.

Still, the blunting of the South Korea invasion and growing economic problems at home might have caused the North Korean leadership to undertake urgent economic and political and social reforms. Instead, they invented and perfected the worst and most vicious dictatorship in the world. Even now, with the vast superiority of South Korea (and the rest of the world) becoming more and more obvious, the North Korean national leadership refuses to learn any lessons, and fiercely maintains almost all of the terrible mistakes that have ruined the country.

The North Korea of today is the destroyed hulk of a potential nation. Its political leadership is unbelievably bad and very, very strange. Its civil service and military are paragons of incompetence, petty oppression, greed, and corruption. Its economy is a shambles and visibly getting worse each day. Nobody is dumb enough to invest in anything in the country, except of course, the natives, to their ultimate harm. There is widespread decay throughout the country. The national transportation system is pitiful. Railroads lack cars to move freight, and crops rot in the fields, and manufactured goods sit in warehouses. Railroad road beds and roads are dangerously in bad repair. Electrical power generation and distribution are totally inadequate and falling further behind demand. Meanwhile, the military spends scarce money lavishly on nuclear weapons, ballistic missiles and launch facilities in order to scare the Americans. Central heating systems work only part of the day. Water supply systems are constantly breaking down. Elevators in high rise buildings seldom seem to work, despite the powerful elites who live there. TV works about 6 hours a day, but is so horrible (political worshiping) that it seems a small loss.

This pattern of incompetence and decay has persisted for decades, and in 1994, the whole national distribution system of goods and services finally totally collapsed. How was this even possible? The basic facts at the time were that the distribution system was state owned and controlled –owned by the government, operated by the government, guided by the government along classic state socialist principles, heavily regulated, and burdened by a whole range of perverse political decisions. This state system was a perfect picture of Socialist bumbling incompetence. To begin with, most elements of production in the economy had been forced into collectives – the same pattern that had seriously hampered economies in the USSR, China, and much of Soviet dominated Eastern Europe. Collectives notoriously killed individual initiative and rewards, substituting the supposed beauties of collective action. Collectives ranged from farms and mines to manufacturing plants, transport facilities and various forms of "struggle group" decision making, all of which were unstable, high cost and low outcome.

Then, the North Korean government pursued a deeply damaging policy of rigid price controls, again drawing on the "best" of State Socialist practice. The government would, for example, pay very low prices for agricultural products so that the ultimate price for food in cities was artificially low. But such false pricing often paid farmers less than their costs, and thus, drove them out of business. This same stupidity was inflicted on almost every producer in the country. At the same time, Socialist doctrine prohibited the importation of goods from "foreign sources." The inevitable consequence of these huge blunders was the drying up of the supply of almost everything: not just food, but electrical power, machine tools, clothing, fertilizers, shoes, building materials, and much more.

The result was the total collapse of the government distribution system, starting in 1995, which had utterly unbelievable consequences in the country. People began starving to death because there was no food. Even farm animals starved. The lives of people in their villages and cities were ruined. People were eating rats and boiling grass. Much of the available food was snatched up by the Korean Army, or by black marketers selling to the North Korean elite.

This crisis persists in many ways 20 years later. It revealed not only the weaknesses and failures of the government of that time; it also revealed the inability of the government –ever – to deal with these horrible kinds of problems. And further, it has revealed, at least to those outside of North Korea, the fact that the government never even really tries. A whole different kind of government, with strange new motivations has emerged. It is not a government to help the people, or to improve the country. It is "the government of the Cult", and its purpose is self glorification, and oppression to those who do not worship.

The first leader of North Korea after liberation from Japan in 1946 was Kim Il-sung. At first, the Army largely ran the country, and for several years, it seemed that North Korea might develop well. But Kim's ego and his devotion to the concepts of State Socialism became the basis for a political party called the Workers Party that gradually rose to power in the country. It was Kim who began the formulation of the Cult – the almost endless indoctrination of the public with the mystic that Kim and his associates were always right, and always noble, and the Loving Father of the country. By the time of his death in 1994, Kim was revered as:

* The Great Leader
* The Great Guide
* The Unequaled Genius
* The Summit of Thought
* The Light of Human Genius
* The North Star of the People.

---- and three years after his death, he was designated "President for All Eternity"!

Well before his death, he and his son Kim Jong-il had begun steps for the son to succeed the father, retaining the mantle of adulation which had succeeded beyond all expectation. The Cult had become the lynchpin of the dictatorship, and Kim maintained a constant, enormous propaganda campaign to sustain this impact. But he chose to go far beyond this half-mystical grip on the North Korean public. He devised a strategy in which some element of the highly centrist government "scrutinized" every element of the life of every citizen, all of the time. Every citizen is issued an official booklet, and it is mandated that everything the citizen does must be recorded in this booklet. Dozens of different government officials, from the police to the building inspector to the dog catcher, are authorized to demand scrutiny of that booklet.

The government has developed a whole range of such "scrutiny" institutions: the police, the State Security Department, the Propaganda and Agitation Department, the Organization and Guidance

Department, the United Front Department (dealing with "spinning" all relationships with South Korea), Office 35 (intelligence) and even the Ministry of Social Security which applies the final test of "loyalty to the Leader". These organizations can scrutinize what citizens read, what TV they watch, who their friends are, what they say in public, what music they listen to, and even (or especially) what they do not do. Teachers are rigidly instructed on what to teach. Merchants are told what they can and cannot sell, and at what price. TV producers are allowed only certain kinds of programs, writers are told what to write, and musicians must perform official music, mostly in praise of the Dear Leader.

It is recognized that these organizations have been known to lie, to falsify data, to fake documents, to publish propaganda and misinformation, and to act corruptly and often illegally. Most have the power to arrest, to send people to prisons, to detain one's family or friends, to seize property, to impose fines – and to execute. Thus, the whole government is designed to terrorize. Everybody lives in fear, all of the time because the actions of these powerful organizations can be totally arbitrary and capricious. There are whole long lists of actions that are "approved" or "not approved". One can be accused of "knowledge about others", whatever that means. Even the smallest things, like listening to South Korean radio can bring punishment.

In the 1990's, North Korea created a "Cultural Revolution" in imitation of that sponsored by Mao Zedong in China. The ensuing blood bath was modest by these Chinese standards, but still, more than 20,000 cadres and their families were killed or jailed. Heavy conflicts were quickly generated between the thugs in national government agencies and provincial officials, who were accused of being the cause of all problems, and were deliberately largely eliminated, to be replaced by Kim loyalists. Other losers were deliberately the old Workers Party, factions in the military, and even Kim family members.

It also became necessary for Kim Jong-il to undertake a big-time propaganda campaign about South Korea. It was vital that the average North Korean never found out the truth about the great disparities between the miserable quality of life in the North versus the far better circumstances in the South. The laughably named United Front Department of the North Korean government spent all of its considerable effort quashing any form of rapprochement with the South. It has published a steady stream of lies about how bad life was in the South. It invented "witnesses" and "refugees" who pretended that they had just "escaped" from the terrible South. False statistics have been manufactured. Articles have been written, purporting to have been published in some South Korean source, that yearned for the South to be united – of course, under the guidance of the Great Leader as part of the northern paradise.

Meanwhile, in the paradise, people are still living on the edge. Food remains scarce, the economy is an obsolete mess, bribery has become the principle form of money exchange, corruption is mandatory for survival, people live in constant abject fear, and the whole world of North Korea is irrational, unfair, unjust and dangerous. Why? Courtesy of the terrorist government and the Dear Leader.

CASE STUDY: HAMAS: THE WORST "GOVERNMENT" IN THE WORLD

The conflict between Muslims and Israel has now lasted longer than the Cold War, and it shows no signs of abating. Over the past 65 years, the identities and characters of the Muslim organizations have changed and most have expanded their purposes far beyond the single issue of seeking the destruction of Israel. But Hamas has retained that as its main objective – in fact, virtually its only objective. Hamas has evolved out of the loose coalition of hard line Islamist groups centering around the old Palestine Liberation Organization (PLO), and going back into the 1960's. Early on, the PLO and dozens of other groups functioned out of Egypt, Jordan, Lebanon, Syria and Saudi Arabia. Hamas began life as the Islamic Compound, created in 1978 as a little brother to the Muslim Brotherhood, and loosely allied with the PLO in Lebanon. (25)

The PLO had operated for many years in Jordan, but it began to launch dangerous operations against Israel without informing the government of Jordan. The result was a nasty little war with Jordan which got the PLO expelled from the country. It then set up in Lebanon and began the same foolish tricks on the Lebanon government. This time, it precipitated an Israeli invasion of Lebanon in 1982, aimed at crushing the PLO in the country.

During the Lebanese period, Hamas began to take shape. It adopted what might be called the "Muslim Brotherhood pattern", the foundation of which is the development of a broad base of social services: aid to the poor, free food distribution, schools, health clinics or even hospitals, assistance for the aged and, especially, youth services and, where possible, job creation. Many Islamic organizations followed this same pattern, and in most cases, these services are quite genuine and much appreciated, despite the fact that people are aware that their purpose is also to gain populist support for the organization's other "product lines". It is very important to understand the nature of the Islamist strategy. It is "street" oriented and bottom up. So while the Americans and the Europeans are giving pompous speeches in the UN, or fancy generals are counting their tanks and aircraft carriers, Muslim insurgent organizations are out on the street feeding the poor – and recruiting supporters.

The next "product line" is the capacity to produce protest. If a major insurgent group wants a big noisy street protest, they might be able to turn out 100 thousand marchers, complete with signs 24 hours later. Agents for insurgent groups are routinely linked up with active supporters in universities and schools, mosques, manufacturing plants, government offices and union headquarters.

This also then explains the value of the third "product line", usually called communications, but more properly called propaganda. Far more quickly than most government agencies, insurgent groups can generate and distribute highly emotional defenses of their position. Speed is possible because the propaganda is not burdened with any obsolete concepts like "proof", or "getting the facts", or "verification". All propaganda is "spin" of the most cynical and hypocritical nature.

Islamists may or may not have two other "product lines". One is political activism. For example, the Muslim Brotherhood has participated as legitimate political parties in a number of countries, has won many elections, has people who are elected members of Congresses and Parliaments, and others who have been elected or appointed to senior government positions. And of course Hamas itself won an election to head up the government in Gaza, much to their own astonishment. The final "product line" however is outright armed conflict – from raids or attacks up to all-out civil wars, and this is where Hamas has concentrated its efforts starting in association with the PLO in the 1980s, and seriously expanded by the initiation of the al-Qassam Brigades in 1991. Hamas maintains offices and working relationships all over the Middle East, largely for the procurement of arms, intelligence, money and mutual support.

Close ties are maintained in Qatar which is a big supplier of funding, and with Iran which shares its anti-Israel hatred, and is also a big supplier of arms and money. Thus, the principle activities of the so-called Hamas government in Gaza are military and aggressive.

From its beginnings, Hamas has concentrated on war with Israel, and social services product lines for populist appeal. But it must be recognized that, despite its election, Hamas is not a real government, nor does it want to become a real government, nor does it begin to know how to run a full purpose government even if it sought to do so. To go further, the Gaza Strip, which is the only home of Hamas, was once a rudimentary real government under the PLO, but it is not a real country but really only a base for terrorist military operations. It has a modest, limited economy. Many of its 1.8 million residents must find work in Israel or Egypt, but unemployment is always extraordinarily high. In fact, some 80% or more of the funds available to support the population comes from foreign sources. There is no hope that Hamas could ever create a self-sustaining economy or country. Many residents of Gaza live in housing or camps provided, administered and financed by the United Nations. About 80% of the citizens live at or below the U. N. defined poverty level. Unemployment figures, of course, do not include the huge amount of labor that went into building the underground tunnels dug as a means of facilitating terrorist attacks against Israel. Other tunnels were dug exiting out into Egypt's Sinai Peninsula, and these tunnels, with the tacit consent of the Egyptian Army, were used to bring in food, fuel, household supplies and small industrial equipment. But of course, in their world of hatred, the Hamas leadership smuggled weapons and construction materials through these tunnels, and then sent out fighters and weapons to support certain terrorist groups harassing the Egyptian army in Sinai. As a consequence, these vital tunnels have now been shut down.

It is bitterly ironic that most of what is useful and life giving in Gaza is derived from the help and assistance of foreigners, most of them non-Muslims. And what have the residents of Gaza got from their own "government"? Hatred, blind implacable terrorist destruction, endless, hopeless war, and universal poverty or miserable, substandard lives.

Yet what Hamas says it wants is an opening up of Israeli control of its borders, so that Gaza could operate like a real independent government. But such thoughts are uttered in between Hamas diatribes about destroying Israel and killing all Jews. Such hysterical nonsense reinforces the growing world view that Hamas cannot be allowed to control anything in this world; and that Gaza can be viable only if it passes into the hands of Palestinians who are prepared to run it as a civilized entity. The current hope is that, despite its own dubious past, that leadership could be provided by Fatah, and indeed Fatah and Hamas had been approaching some agreement for combination before Hamas blew the whole thing up.

CASE STUDY: VIETNAM: SLOW RETREAT FROM OPPRESSION

Looking back on history, it is now possible to see more clearly the unbelievably complex and oppressive nature of the Communist and State Socialist regimes around the world, and the arrogance and brutality of the people who controlled these regimes. Every element of these state socialist countries was designed to control, to repress, to punish, to eliminate even the most minor objections to their centrist, elitist control.

It is hard to imagine any country that was more intense in its zeal in pursuing the Communist version of State Socialism than Vietnam. Their world was full of eager, zealous leaders – true believers, willing and capable of taking on the world in the service of their cause.

This then helps to explain why Vietnam's Communist Party (CP) seems to have been so reluctant to admit that this whole structure had failed, and they found themselves forced to abandon their sacred socialist theology and shift – as late as possible, and as little as possible, and as slowly as possible – to a form of market based economy, exactly as it had happened in the Soviet Union and in China and in India. What was also revealed was the fact that the old North Vietnam regime created a country which, despite their zealousness was not a success, and the current government now faces enormous needs for reform from an inadequate and deteriorating base. The new Vietnam seems to want to link economic development with major upgrades of national social services, a willingness that the Chinese are only now beginning to display. But just as Vietnam's economy is obsolete, its social service programs are also obsolete. If there is a bright note here it is that Vietnam is blessed with a vital, intelligent and ambitious population which could well evolve into a fabulous talent base.

There are three major elements to Vietnam's future: its economy, its governance, and its social systems, and the Communist Party clearly intends that the keystone to the future is the economy. Social services will be upgraded when it can be afforded, but the government will change not at all.

Everywhere, Vietnam is facing urgent demands for new means to rescue itself from its brutal and oppressive and inferior past. As with the Soviet Union and China, the heart of the economy is the commitment to State Owned Enterprises (SOE). One of the most fundamental and far reaching tides running in the post World War II era was the emergence of State Socialism and of State Owned Enterprises (SOEs) as the major fulcrum of Socialist power. These economic entities were seen as a middle ground between a standard government ministry or bureau and a true private sector organization. The key is that the SOE was designed so that it could function like an independent private entity for economic efficiency purposes, but would still be under the policy direction of the government so that each would implement some valid public purpose.

The failures of these institutions, embedded in the broader failings of Communist economic policies, left the country with an inferior economy – obsolete, underdeveloped, incompetent, and operating at serious deficit. It was simply forced upon the regime that this system could not provide a large enough economy to meet the needs of either the government or the nation's citizens, to generate enough jobs to meet current needs, or to hope to meet the needs of the more than one million new workers who enter the economy each year.

Within this framework, over a long period of time the detailed operations of the economic apparatus of the State was clumsy, bumbling, malfunctioning, utterly bureaucratic, oppressive and very often actively threatening. The expectation that SOEs would generate large revenues to finance the State never really materialized, and in fact, many of these SOEs operated at congenital deficits, which forced the regime to divert desperately needed funds from other vital public services. Of course, enormous resources were devoted by the regime to fight the war and unify the country. In many cases, in order to mitigate the losses of some of the most important of these SOEs, the regime created hidden subsidies as well, such as forcing down the cost for electricity or water and sewer services from suppliers (themselves SOEs), even below their actual costs. Wages were, by government policy, kept deliberately low. The centrally controlled price structure allowed SOEs to charge unrealistically high prices from customers. In some cases, SOEs were made national monopolies which not only conveniently eliminated competition but also persuaded the leaders of these enterprises that they need not exert themselves much because they were invulnerable.

The functioning of the energy sector of the Vietnamese economy is a perfect case in point. The whole sector has naturally been inherited from the Communist past, which means that it is obsolete, run down, ineffective and seriously underdeveloped. The key is the operations of Electricity Vietnam (EVN), a SOE of the old school, badly constrained by discredited Socialist laws and regulations. The law forces EVN to sell energy at heavily subsidized prices for dubious political reasons. EVN actually loses money, and it is forced to cover its shortages by borrowing heavily. The government tried to conceal how bad the system is by forcing suppliers to EVN to sell at a loss to their own operations. But EVN is so huge that these desperate measures scarcely make a dent.

What is the solution? Probably there is none. The regime has three choices. It could force the banks and other lenders to forgive EVN's huge debts, but that would probably ruin them. Or, the government itself can assume the debt, by stealing funds from other vital needs, including social services, which is political mission impossible in a populist regime faced with great numbers of people in dire poverty. The third choice would be to undertake an extraordinarily difficult restructuring of the whole energy sector from top to bottom to terminate most of the government's operational involvement and turn the sector over to the private sector. But it is not clear how much enthusiasm private interests can generate over such a monumental headache.

If there is a tide running in the country it is that the gap between the supply and national demand is growing. There is not enough money for the regime to make major capital investments. Vietnam is already in trouble. It has missed the date for the repayment of a $ 600 million loan from Credit Suisse, but it probably urgently needs something like $5 or $6 billion even to begin to try to catch up with the needs of what is now a population of more than 90 million people.

The workforce that emerged from this system is now a matter of crucial government concern. First, for political reasons, there was heavy redundancy of employment. That is, SOEs were forced to hire more employees than they could effectively use. In SOEs in other countries for example, including the Soviet Union and China, this redundancy level was estimated at up to 40 percent! As a further consequence of this extraordinarily bad policy, SOEs lost any chance of operating cost-effectively or cutting production costs. Finally, it is not often realized what this whole failed system did for the workers. It was to the political advantage to keep wages deliberately low, but it also meant that huge numbers of workers were kept in low skill, low value work, with little or no learning potential. Nor was it often important to spend money and effort in employee training or development for future advancement. Said another way, Vietnam's workforce now is all too often locked into low value obsolete skills, where they risk falling further behind the rapidly advancing tides of technological progress and change that characterizes the rest of the world. When Vietnam was a closed and internal economy, this was less important, but now that it must somehow push its way into the world economy, this lack of workforce skills has become a major problem.

Just as the CP slowly and reluctantly conceded the need to move to a market economy, they are – even more slowly and reluctantly – trying to figure out how to go about it. They have now been on their new path for almost 20 years, and it appears to be seriously disappointing how little seems to have been accomplished. The whole system needs reform. This is admittedly an extremely complex and difficult program that will truly need many years to bring off, but this simply argues for the need to sharpen their ability to bring about change rather than merely debating it.

As in many other governments in the world, the major accomplishment at the start of such reforms is words. Vietnam started with a substantial rewriting of its Constitution which, by world standards, seems to say all of the right things about everything more or less. But the one compelling element that cannot and will not be changed is the continued single party control exercised by the centrist, elitist Communist Party – no matter what the Constitution says. This means that, to some degree, the residual mind set of the CP leadership will to be to think like they thought so deeply and zealously for decades – as state socialists. When challenged by dissidents, the government mumbles: it says that dissidence "undermines national unity", or "interferes with government administration", or "causes public disorder", or worse yet "promotes reactionary ideas".

Yes, some leaders will change because of genuine acceptance of the new reality. Others will retreat out of overwhelming necessity. New younger people are pushing their way forward in the country and the government, and they are increasingly themselves asking why progress has been faster and stronger.

More than just impatience, the new wave of people remains actively afraid of their government. They see the huge residue of brutality, a phony justice system, and an enduring tradition of public and private corruption. Vietnam still illegally seizes property, conducts improper police punishment and arrest, still operates "correction centers", and almost never explains or justifies anything. While these oppressions are in decline, it is hard to explain why they still exist at all. And the new generation is especially disenchanted by a government that will not accept the new world of human intercommunication. There are no independent media. The government either directly or by regulation controls all media, limiting what can be used, suppressing that which it does not approve of, or closing down those it opposes.

The CP has done a few useful things. It has pulled back from the concept of sealed borders and resistance to imports. It has abandoned import substitution as a means of supposedly protecting SOEs and other domestic organizations. For the first time, the government is fumbling with ways to encourage and expand exports rather than inhibiting them. Rules have been relaxed for foreign investors, and foreigners can now own a higher percentage of Vietnamese enterprises. A substantial number of SOEs have been allowed to "equitize", which means that they can convert themselves into legal forms of incorporation so that they can issue private equity to show ownership and to raise capital. An "Asset Management Corporation" has quietly been set up for the embarrassing purpose of buying out the bad debts and hopeless phony bank borrowings of SOEs. A slightly higher proportion of public income is slowly making its way into social services, but much of this funding must be provided by provinces and cities.

In order to begin to understand the current state of Vietnamese social services it is once again necessary to look into the state socialist past. Looking at the key programs of health care and elementary/secondary education, what existed into the new world of unification had long been inadequate and mediocre. While Communist rhetoric trumpeted universal government support "from cradle to grave" in fact service was very selective, driven both by finance and by political preferment. Health care could be counted upon for the political ruling elite, the military, the upper reaches of the bureaucracy and the SOEs. There was (and still is) a heavy skewing in favor of better urban areas and little service for rural areas, smaller towns and urban slums. Early Communist era facilities served such areas at extremely basic levels with local health clinics, some of which were not much more than aid stations. The services provided were very valuable. They included mother/child pre and post natal help, care for minor illnesses and injuries, health information and education, some preventative medicine, and as the base for vaccination programs against outbursts of communicable diseases.

As the economy was shifted from socialist to market basing, a surge of new money created hopeful plans to upgrade and expand this rudimentary network. Hospitals could usually only be found in cities or provincial capitols, and it was planned to extend the numbers of hospitals somewhat. During the 50's through the 80's the institutional base for public service was a great system of Communist collectives, and Vietnam was soon to be reminded that almost everywhere in the world including the USSR and China, this system simply could not be made to work. Their failure to understand this reality delayed correction and the consequences were destructive for far too long.

The path of elementary/secondary education was much the same. The education system was inadequate, mediocre and selective. The children of the central elite were taken care of, but even they had difficulty getting education beyond the elementary level. The CP did try for universality at both levels, but neither their resources of their skills could handle the task. Unfortunately, the economic collapse of the early 80's also collapsed the shaky school system. By 1989, secondary education enrollment had plunged 40%, and the resources for education had seriously shrunk.

In the face of this collapse, the government instituted three new strategies which are now having some positive impact. Strategy number one was to shift the cost (but not the policy control) to provincial and local governments. This made a good deal of ministerial and pedagogical sense, but unfortunately it occurred exactly when these local governments, which were never very prosperous, were hit with their own economic collapse, and that same wave simply washed away the ineffective mechanisms of the State collectives. Ever since 1990, elementary/secondary education has passed into the hands of the civil service and it has started to become more sturdy and organized, and to get more financing.

But the second strategy for education is undoubtedly what has saved the system, and that has simply forced the parents to pay as much as possible, beyond normal taxes. The central government now finances only elementary education, and provision of secondary education exists mainly for the privileged elite. Parents pay for secondary education if their children can get that far. Costs deliberately are higher for each grade up, and there are added charges for tuition, books, construction, maintenance and repair, transportation, extracurricular activities and "extra studies". Elementary enrollment had reached a heartening level over 90 percent, but actual attendance was only about 66 percent. Lower secondary enrollment was 62 percent and upper enrollment just 29 percent.

The third strategy of the government is that, in the early 1990s, it began to allow private schools (or in the lexicon of the Communists, "semi-official" or "non-State" schools). But again, it appears that the people who can afford private education are the usual ruling elite.

In summary, an oppressive dictatorship took over Vietnam and it wanted to continue its oppressive control. It is largely economic reality that closed in on them and forced them to retreat from the most onerous characteristic of the old world. But in truth, at some point, even the Vietnamese Communist Party seems to have learned some lessons and is willing to try for reform. The current oppression lies in the fact that they are moving so slowly and reluctantly and inefficiently into the reality of the real and humanistic world.

CASE STUDY: NIGERIA:
LIFE IN THE DEPTHS

There is an old saying that "anything that can go wrong will go wrong." What has gone wrong in Nigeria? Everything.

Nigeria emerged from the wave of independence in the 1960s as the largest country in Africa in terms of population (175 million), and as a country blessed with what the whole world yearned to have – oil and gas. In addition, Nigeria has a wealth of other resources: coal, tin, cotton, cocoa, palm oil, corn, rice, plus 19 million cattle and about 200 million chickens. But the country has found itself in and out of oppressive military rule for most of its 55 years of existence. The military has often acted like conquerors, but in truth, the civilian governments presiding between military coups were seldom much better, and it is not a stretch to say that Nigeria has never produced a free and capable government in all of its existence.

The saving grace for the country should have been its natural wealth, and its active and intelligent population. And yet just the opposite has happened. Nigeria is one of the poorest countries in the world. Transparency International has rated Nigeria at 152nd place out of the total of 157 countries rated. 50 percent of the people live in poverty in a country that has seriously failed to meet the needs of its citizens for vital social services and public infrastructure.

Consider that Nigeria is one of the greatest oil producing countries in the world, yet it experiences congenital shortages of consumer gasoline. Why? Because the oil refineries that should refine this fuel are all State Owned Enterprises (SOE), which means that they are owned and controlled by the government in all of its wisdom. After nearly 40 years of oil production, the people of the oil delta are poorer, sicker, less well nourished and less well educated. Oil spill damage has been extensive. Burning of blow-off gas produces acid rain and toxic pollution, which in turn leads to skin rashes, allergies, lung problems and strange infections. The deep poverty of the delta contrasts sharply with the luxurious homes and lavish lives of the rulers, the military and their political allies. This includes the executives and managers of the Western oil companies such as Shell, Chevron, Mobil, Amoco and Texaco, who might certainly operate honest and efficient refineries of there was any political intention to do so.

Nigeria represents a major example of monumental mismanagement which the government has never attempted to cure, perhaps because they are too busy looting oil sales revenues. Then, in order to meet vital needs for gas, the government is forced to buy it at market prices from suppliers in other countries. Then, of course, for populist political reasons, this gas is sold to Nigerians at highly subsidized prices – perhaps as low as 30% of the market price. And also of course, much of the sales are handled for the government by crooks and thieves who extract their cut. The government does not seem to notice that a lot of the gas, bought at 30% of market value, is then sold by these thieves at full market value overseas.

All forms of public infrastructure are seen as basically inadequate, having never been adequate, and now suffering further decay and falling further and further behind citizen needs. Electricity is in short supply all over the country, and the expectation seems to be that the state controlled power enterprise, the Power Holding Authority of Nigeria, has no idea how to catch up, and to meet the new demands of a growing population even if were motivated to try.

Highways, roads, bridges, and the entire rail system are in bad shape. Big gaps in the water supply systems in urban areas leave large populations without reliable water supplies. These failures in turn create great pain for Nigeria's people. They reduce and impede the ability of businesses to operate, and many companies have been forced to buy power generators of their own. Farm to market transport is so bad that crops rot in the fields or warehouses for lack of transportation. Because state companies are relatively inefficient and overly costly, they often lose out to competition in foreign markets. This in turn has meant reductions in employment.

Social services seem uniformly inadequate. Health care ranges from miserable to non-existent, and care is "cash up front". Elementary/ secondary education is poor and much is obsolete, poorly managed and expensive. It suffers from lack of teacher training, poor physical plant, and congenital underfunding. Efforts to reform, especially in the north, have been brutally wiped out by sectarian terrorism and religious zeal, and unbelievable viciousness of the Boko Haram.

The whole environment in Nigeria is one of unremitting conflict between the citizens and the great arrogant and corrupt elite that controls the country. This war usually centers around the huge state owned oil and gas industry which represents so much of government funding and export earnings. But the industry has been a cash cow for 60 years or more for political manipulation and downright theft. The World Bank has estimated that something like $ 400 billion has "gone missing" over the years, and that $20 billion has somehow disappeared from the current coffers of the Oil Ministry. Yet the workers in the country suffer from low wages, high unemployment, serious underemployment, poor housing, and a general lack of public services. Life styles for most people are uniformly miserable. There are congenital and implacable shortages of vital consumer goods, industrial supplies and equipment, electric power and much else.

Crime is wildly rampant. The Economist reported that "During the first half of 2013, Nigeria had the most kidnap attempts in the world, accounting for 26% of such recorded instances in the world, or more than 500 per year. The police are so bad that nobody expects them to really catch anybody – neither citizens nor the kidnappers themselves, who are increasingly emboldened. If somehow some local police get tough, potential kidnappers or other crooks just move down the road a bit." (26)

The police are politically controlled to the great detriment of real justice. The average citizen sees the cops as brutal, savage, frightening, prejudiced, extortionist, often illegal, and universally corrupt. In the courts, money decides cases, honest judges do not survive, special interests enjoy special relationships, and everything is for sale. The public sees the upholders of justice locked into collusion with the crooks, which reflects what they see in the whole government. They see brazen subversion of elections, corrupt bureaus and government offices, more than half of the government budget squandered and misspent, wasted or stolen by government officers at all levels.

Is this sort of idiocy really corruption or mere bumbling incompetence? Probably some of both, but the outcome is oppressive. It deprives the public of vital services that the squandered funds could have paid for, and it probably forces the government to raise taxes. Realize also that Africa suffers from this kind of oppression from political and managerial misfeasance in a thousand different ways, and nobody seems to know how to mitigate it. Nobody. Even where the problems are well understood, governments lack the courage, will power and skill to face up to the massive surges of reform that this chaos demands.

What has gone wrong in Nigeria? Everything.

CASE STUDY: COLOMBIA: VERY COMPLEX CORRUPTION

The leadership of the government of Colombia has, for decades, been forced to deal with four other centers of power in the country. The most formidable continues to be the deadly world of the drug cartels. Then, over three decades, a terrorist guerilla movement wreaked havoc all over the country. The inability of the government and the Colombian military to subdue these vicious forces so terrified others – large land owners, major business firms and even local governments – that they have created yet another armed presence in the form of dozens of armed paramilitary militias to protect their own localized interests. Finally, the whole country suffers from a secret shadow world of corruption. This corruption is universal, long standing, heavily embedded, sophisticated and utterly self-serving. It has become so entangled with the "real" government that it is hard to tell when one ends and the other begins.

The worst of these forces, the drug cartels, is the genesis of a whole range of vicious, terroristic practices including deadly threats against innocent people, murders, extortion, and kidnapping, often against local government officials and even the police. In addition, the cartels have spun off other "product lines" such as smuggling, piracy, and trafficking in weapons and human beings. Over time, thousands have been killed, hundreds of thousands have had their lives destroyed or worsened, and more than one million people have been displaced and/or impoverished.

The sense of oppression stems from the infuriating question of why the government went decades without adequately facing up to the drug war that has all but ruined the country. Colombia is rich in both material and human resources. It could certainly have afforded a powerful enough military to put down both the guerrillas and the cartels. Did the government do enough fast enough? There is a lot of serious opinion that it did not. There has been formidable resistance to effective government action even from within the government itself. It is critical to understand the enormous difficulty of dealing with the war and the cartels. At times, many despaired that the government could win out. The country has been at war with itself for 50 years. There are hundreds of examples of active collusion between the cartels and officials in the Colombian military, police and government agencies at all levels. Billions of dollars have been stolen by government politicians and officials, often through the illegal deals with some cartel. In turn, the cartels have bribed officials to go on the take, or to overlook some law or regulation to favor the cartel. As these relationships evolved, they have tended to deepen and broaden and become more corrosive. Soon, elements of the government are really functioning for the advantage of the cartels and not for the Colombian people.

Huge percentages of government funds designated for urban development, health care and education seem always to get "disappeared", and some public officials become rapidly and miraculously rich. And nobody seems to be caught, and if caught, nobody is actually punished.

Recent public opinion polls are sadly revealing. When people are asked what elements of society they least trust, the results in order are: political parties; the Parliament; the police; public officials; the judiciary; and the military!

Thus, the government of Colombia stands out as one of oppression, and one so weakened by its own flaws that it is not able to deal with the problems it has faced. This failure extends to the general operations of the government which are characterized as seriously inadequate. Education is poor and surprisingly corrupt. Health care is seriously inadequate, mostly available to the elites in major cities and for the rest of the population only for cash up front. The whole law enforcement system is weak, and so riddled with corruption that entering it can actually dangerous. Government financial control is virtually nonexistent; money leaks out through countless corrupt holes. Government agencies are notorious for favoritism, nepotism, political preferment and a dazzling variety of inventive corrupt practices. Every government contract is expected to be crooked. The whole government is kept dark and impenetrable.

Fortunately, and largely because of the horrible consequences of this vicious past, more recent regimes seem to be attempting some serious reform. But it should be noted that previous reform efforts have been only marginally successful. Transparency International reported that, in the period from 2000 to 2010, the corruption ranking of Colombia got significantly worse (from a ranking of 57th to 94th). So now, as usual, the important questions remain. As reform plans and new weapons are brought to bear, will they be powerful enough to deal with such formidable enemies? Will these new weapons be used and enforced? Finally do the people of Colombia really care enough to give broad support to the government's reform action, when so many continue to benefit from the current mess? In a culture of corruption lasting for 100 years, there are many who think that much of the corruption is minor, or not so bad, or that corruption lubricates the system or that "everybody does it" or that it is simply "getting along". Or still, that corruption is still getting one's own piece of the action where the government itself is the worst corruptor of all.

Case Study: Pakistan: Government and Religion Torture Each Other

Nobody can understand "modern" Pakistan, not even the Pakistanis themselves, in part because there really is no modern Pakistan, and nobody understands the old Pakistan either. The leaders of the country have been almost feudal in their outlook, and simply don't' quite understand the consequences of their elitist arrogance, the perceived usurpation of power, the bitterness about their enormous wealth often gotten by theft and corruption. They seem to think that corruption is a way of life from which they have a right to prosper.

Few have any concept about governance as a responsibility to the public, or as a role for serving the public and for the honest provision of public services. The government has, for a long time, been locked into a deadly pattern: their neglect of the masses leads to a rising discontent and protest. The government then represses the protest, which then produces greater protest, which in turn produces greater repression. This cycle leads to revolt – everything from street marches to armed conflict.

The national leadership seems unable to think outside of this circle of oppression. Nor does it seem to understand they are able to collect only about one third of the taxes it is owed, or why both domestic or foreign investors have serious concerns about risking their capital investment money in such a risky and incompetent environment.

Part of the concern about the modernization of Pakistan lies in its weak current reality. There are 176 million people, with two thirds of the population living in the rural small town world. There are at least 75 million, both urban and rural, who are living in poverty, and another 85 million who are poor and not much farther up the prosperity scale. This population largely retains the old village and clan society which is economically and politically conservative, locked into older concepts of class and caste, family rule, family "honor" and high resistance to change. Pakistan, like India, still retains a large number of "lower caste" jobs such as sharecroppers, miners, fishermen, servants, lower trades, and animal tending. And like India, the status of women – 80 million of them – is still seen as that of an subordinate class, except of course unless their husbands or families are very rich. This culture places great value on the more traditional interpretations of Sharia Law relating to domestic matters, and on the authority of Muslim Imams rather then government officials as the proper interpreters of the laws.

The ruling elite thus continue to think and to function much along traditional lines. The government has had protracted periods in which it vigorously pushed the abandonment of state socialist policies toward a somewhat confused version of market based economic policies, but those changes are always a "work in progress" – half way completed and thus only half way understood. Petty corruption is everywhere. The legal system is a morass of bungling incompetence. Even the most trivial of cases can founder in a muddle of confusion and red tape. Cases can go on for years, demanding masses of irrelevant details. The judges are heavily but needlessly overburdened. The government certainly knows this, and it either deliberately chooses to do nothing, or it is so ignorant and incompetent that it can' figure out what to do. In either case, this oppression has harmed the country and ruined the lives of thousands.

Meanwhile, one learns how the justice system really works. There is no such thing as "truth" or "facts", or "proof". There is only money and influence. Political influence has solved far more cases than evidence. The police have their own set of rules, unrelated to the law, based on extortion and threats, and countless people are arrested for the sole purpose of extracting bribes.

In other periods, and especially during the tenure of Prime Minister Zia al Huq (1977-1988) the government pushed broadly for national "Islamification", which reversed and reduced women's rights, returned to some greater degree of nationalization of industry, and made the government more oppressive with respect to the rights of non-Muslims such as Christians, Indians, Communists, and most Westerners. Zia applied far stricter limitations on the formal "Hadd" crimes defined in the Quran: unlawful sexual intercourse outside of marriage; false accusations of such unlawful sexual intercourse; homosexuality, theft, banditry, the use of alcohol, and most importantly, apostasy.

The crimes of apostasy and blasphemy generated another form of oppression against the public, and another form of conflict between the government and the religious leadership. New anti-blasphemy laws were enacted on the premise that derogation of the government in any form was illegal in itself, but was also a form of rejection of the True Faith – i. e. apostasy. But no complete and limiting definition of either blasphemy or apostasy has been developed, and both the government and the religious establishment have used interpretations that oppress minorities, threaten opponents, significantly constrain freedom of communication, improperly change the meaning or interpretation of laws, condemn property or simply settle personal feuds.

Since apostasy and blasphemy are religious matters, these laws have greatly increased the power an influence of the religious leadership. The tide that seems to be running in the country is for the general population to move somewhat toward the right, fed by the apostasy interpretations, but also more seriously by long term public reaction to the arrogant elite, and the eternal corruption, and the long history of incompetent governments.

And yet there is a great fear about the nature of that religious leadership. In Pakistan, it has often seen that the government has been doing "deals with the Devil". The military has long allied itself with various Islamic terrorist organizations in conflicts involving Afghanistan, Kashmir, India and elsewhere. The Army thinks it can control these terrorist groups, but this has proved to be a very great failed experience. Time and time again, one terrorist group or another has betrayed the Pakistani military, humiliated its leadership and gone on to do serious damage to the country. In 2007-2009, a huge wave of more than 500 terrorist attacks, launched specifically against the government swept the whole country. More than 8900 people were killed and another 20,000 or more were wounded or injured. There was major destruction of public and private property and a breakdown of vital public services in many areas for more than two years. This crisis had been precipitated by two other terrorist events: the assassination of Prime Minister Benazir Bhutto, and the attack on the Red Mosque in Islamabad earlier that year.

The Red Mosque was an ancient and highly respected religious and education center for men but also for a population of more than 6,000 women. But by 2005, it had become a hotbed of radicalism, a purveyor of fundamentalist propaganda, and a serious opponent of the government. Its Imams preached "Jihad against America" which was an ally of the Pakistan regime. Then, when Prime Minister Pervez Musharraf initiated a "war against terror", the radicals in the Red Mosque viewed this as apostasy and a sell-out to the U. S. Several attempts were made to assassinate Musharraf which were linked to the Red Mosque in some way.

What really emerged was an exercise in political martyrdom, not unlike Hama in the Gaza Strip seven years later. The leaders of the mosque could have compromised honorably, or simply vacated the place, but they did neither. Instead, they put 200 or more heavily armed radical students in the mosque, with automatic weapons, machine guns, RPGs, explosives, and inflammatory chemicals. They knew that they could not win in a military sense, but they felt that their deaths could let them win in a political propaganda sense. Thus, the Red Mosque battle was deliberately staged to turn public opinion against the government, at the cost of at least 100 students killed and another 80 capture and imprisoned. A large number of supporters were women, drawn from the 6,000 students in the madrassah (school) attached to the mosque. At the end, many women and some children were used to surround the leaders of the revolt in the basement of the mosque to make it appear that they were being "protected".

What was the essential purpose of this martyrdom? To press for the conversion of Pakistan into a fundamentalist version of Islamic government and society.

In 2009, in the province of Swat, held by the Pakistani Taliban, the government had reluctantly entered into an agreement which would supposedly end a long-standing conflict. But after only a few months, the Taliban repudiated the agreement and returned to its attack on the government and on private citizens. The government had tried the soft approach, and gotten nothing, so in the spring of 2009, the army launched a full scale military operation against the Taliban, and in less than four months has cleared them out of the province. Buoyed by this success, and the degree of popular support it produced, the military was finally allowed to begin the far more difficult process of clearing the estimated 20,000 soldiers of the Taliban from the border province of S. Waziristan.

But in Pakistan, the military has forged a whole world of its own. According to Constable, "The military is one of the world's largest and most privileged military establishments. The military spends or controls the expenditure of 5% of the national GDP (or almost twice what is allocated for health care and education). The military, through what it calls 'welfare organizations', owns banks, drug manufacturing companies, sugar and rice mills, plastics factories, farms, fertilizer plants, an air cargo company, radio/TV stations, computer companies, insurance companies, and security services. The Bahria Foundation (Navy) even owns a real estate firm, a bakery and ---- a university!" (27)

The military has more than once seized power in the country, replacing the elected civilian government. Even when it is not in charge, it remains in control. The military has mastered the arts of scaring the political leadership with overly exaggerated and often illusory threats about India, or the fear that Kashmir will declare an independent state, or that the Chinese are increasingly aggressive. In

2010, the government of President Asif Ali Zardari agreed to divert up to 30% of its social services budget, amounting to 170 billion rupees to "security needs.

But the most extraordinary thing about the Pakistani defense establishment is the operations of its joint intelligence service which has in effect become its own government. Slowly and reluctantly in recent years, the **second government** of Pakistan is becoming more visible. This second government is officially called the Inter-services Intelligence Directorate (ISI). It is supposedly simply the joint intelligence operation for all of Pakistan's military services, and ostensibly its Director General reports to the Prime Minister. Yet its activities reach far beyond its responsibilities in the military establishment, and they extend into Pakistani politics at the national level, and to any other activity in the country that it decides to impact. It is increasingly clear that the policies and imperatives that motivate the ISI, while they may be broadly consistent with the general government leadership, may also take different courses separately arrived at and frequently at odds with those of the Prime Minister, and occasionally, of the law. These are some of the major policies that direct the actions of the ISI:

1. The ISI is, first and foremost a secret clandestine organization. It may be primarily an intelligence organization, but it goes far beyond that both domestically and in foreign affairs. Thus, it extends the cloak of total secrecy over a wide range of issues and activities where the Pakistani public really ought to know what ISI is doing. But it does not, and even the Prime Minister and the President are never fully informed.
2. ISI is strongly committed not just to Pakistani nationalism but to Islamic nationalism. It has skewed many of its actions toward support for broader Islamic imperatives. The government meanwhile must pursue a policy of equal treatment for all religious interests in the country. The government may be highly nationalistic as well, but it is Pakistani nationalism.
3. ISI has an implacable hatred of India, especially dealing with India over the fate of Jammu and Kashmir. ISI never ceases to maneuver to achieve the takeover of Kashmir as a part of

Pakistan. The government often harbors the same ambition, but it cannot afford to treat India as a bitter enemy and must exercise a degree of moderation and accommodation in this crucial relationship. It would surely like to make Kashmir a part of Pakistan, but it does not know how this can be achieved over the opposition of India, and of most of Kashmir itself which wants to be an independent state. ISI does not care about any of this.

4. ISI has, for many years, run extensive secret political and intelligence operations in Afghanistan, Kashmir, Nepal, Bangladesh, Sri Lanka, the Punjab and in India itself. Most of these operations involve relationships with Islamic groups, ranging from moderates to rabid terrorists. In Kashmir alone, ISI is said to direct, support, equip, train and/or finance 18 different insurgent groups, none of which have the interests of Kashmir at heart. The Prime Minister and Parliament may or may not know the extent of ISI operations, which spends a lot of effort denying everything.

5. ISI supports its own political party, called the Islamic Jamhoori Ittehad (IJI), and it has a tight relationship with another political party, the Jamaat–e-Islami. The IJI especially is used by the ISI to put pressure on the government, and through these political parties, ISI actively opposes many government policies and actions.

6. ISI is constantly flirting with the idea of creating some form of world-wide international global "jihad". The government opposes such an idea, fears repercussions from around the world, and tends to be much more oriented toward Pakistani nationalism and influence as their priority.

7. ISI has a complex love/hate relationship with and about the U. S. In the past, it has worked closely with the CIA, but mostly about mutual interests in Afghanistan. Now, the US black lists many of the terrorist organizations that ISI does business with. In this instance, the government too has a love/hate relationship with the U. S. ISI knew about Osama bin Laden. And so did the government, but it denies it and blames ISI for the fiasco, apparently correctly.

CASE STUDY: MONTICINOS STEALS PERU

There is a disturbing lesson to be learned about how vulnerable governments are to crime in the career of Vladimiro Monticinos of Peru.

Peru was ruled for ten years, from 1990 to 2000, by President Alberto Fujimori, and moderate political independent who faced three critical problems. The first was how to deal with a vicious Maoist terrorist group, the Shining Path, which had terrorized the whole country. Second was to take measures to bolster the Peruvian economy, and especially to bring rampant inflation under control, and then to stimulate substantial increases in capital investment by distrustful foreign and domestic sources. But the third crucial problem was invented by the Fujimori regime itself, and it was a remarkable lesson about how vulnerable governments really have become, and how ineffective government protective systems really are.

The corruption of the government centered around an extraordinary conniver and hustler named Vladimiro Monticinos, a close confidant of the President, who emerged as the de facto head of all of Peru's intelligence organizations and internal security operations. Under Monticinos, this base became a source of powerful leverage against thousands of organizations and individuals in the country. Monticinos became the master criminal against his own government, and then even outside of government. He had access, legally or illegally, to any kind of records anywhere in the country. Some of this information was of such a nature that it could be used as weapons for bribery, threats, intimidation, extortion and punishment of enemies. In addition, the intelligence connection enabled Monticinos to scrutinize almost anyone. He could and did employ illegal wiretapping, access to computers, access to personal records and private and personal affairs. He would bribe those who could be bribed; threaten and intimidate those who could be threatened; blackmail or extort those who could be extorted; and if necessary seize or murder those who could not be pushed around. What is most extraordinary about the reign of Monticinos as the "Chief Crook" of Peru was the breadth and audacity of his assaults.

What was never fully clear was how much was known by President Fujimori, but nobody ever believed he was fully innocent. It thus seemed obvious that Monticinos had the weight of the office of the President behind him, which greatly strengthened his hand. As a case in point, in a famous legal case of the time, there was a pitched battle fought over which of the owners would be given authority to run Peru's fabulous Yanacocha gold mine which, when fully developed, was destined to become the richest gold mine in the world. The battle involved a Peruvian mining company along with other companies from France, Australia and the United States. It was perceived that all parties were actively attempting to find ways to bring influence to bear. So the Newmont Mining Company of the U. S. sent a representative to speak to Monticinos who, for an alleged $4 million, spoke to Judge Jaime Beltran Queroga, who was to cast the deciding vote in the upcoming decision in Peru's Supreme Court where the case was being heard. Judge Queroga voted in favor of the American firm Newmont. Was undue influence brought to bear? After years of investigation, there was never any conclusive evidence that it had. But in many other cases that were proved, it is clear that Monticinos, with such extraordinary weapons at his command, was an extensive, enthusiastic and highly successful influence peddler.

Over the years of his remarkable career, Monticinos widely expanded his activities – into drug trafficking, arms dealing, money laundering, property seizure, contracting corruption and corporate extortion. What is most striking and ominous in this story is the fact that Monticinos was not just a private crook but he was a government crook, and it is almost impossible, even after years of investigation, to tell when his official responsibilities and authorities ended and his personal criminal activities began. He had personally recorded more than 2700 tapes of his meetings which he expected to use to blackmail or intimidate his victims. Then, in 2000, some of these tapes leaked to the press and began to be seen on Peruvian television. The public revulsion that followed was so great that it ended up bringing about the collapse of the Fujumori government. Fujimori, who happened to be in Japan at the time, submitted his resignation by FAX. Monticinos also obviously fled, but with the help of the American FBI, he was tracked down in Venezuela, extradited, and put in jail in Peru.

Consider the shocking range of the formal charges brought against him: influence peddling; abuse of power; abuse of authority; fraud; coercion; corruption; illicit enrichment; money laundering; drug trafficking; weapons trafficking; bribery; forced disappearances; torture; murder; harboring criminals; embezzlement and illegal wiretapping. Montecinos was duly convicted and is now rotting in prison where he belongs, but the government of Peru must somehow face up to some highly embarrassing and humiliating questions stemming from the Monticinos career. How could it happen – on the huge and highly visible scale that Monticinos achieved? Why didn't the rest of the government rise up and stop him? Why did all of the standard "fail safe" systems of the government fail? Can these vulnerabilities of governments be fixed? Is anybody motivated to try? If they did, could they succeed?

Section Three

Deliberate Neglect of Social Services

Perhaps the most difficult thing that people are called upon to do is to create and run an effective government. The major purposes of government – broadly, economic development, national security, social services, and public infrastructure – are in competition with one another in the formulation of national priorities, and the priorities set by government are often at great odds with the priorities felt by citizens. China is not the only country that has deliberately neglected its social services. In many countries, the order of priority seems to be most frequently economic development and expansion, the needs of the military, rewards for special interests, and corruption. Social services for the people are second last, conceding last place to environmental protection.

In most cases, economic development wins because it promises that investment now will produce prosperity in the future. In all too many cases, the military wins because they hold so much power. Social services are always stated to be one of the most important obligations of governments but usually, actual performance falls far short off political promises or moral obligations. Social services – health care, education, retirement, unemployment compensation, welfare, child and elderly care – are seldom actually at the top of national priority lists despite their critical value to individual citizens.

Social services delivery systems are complex and disturbingly fragile, and are among the worst victims of the conflicts that are suffered in so many countries. Wars, revolutions, invasions or guerrilla insurrections have destroyed public services for decades on end. Even in conditions of greater stability the functioning of a tyrannical regime can reduce social services to little or nothing. Whole segments of the population can be neglected because of racial, religious, ethnic, geographical or gender prejudices. Farmer's needs may be deliberately neglected in order to concentrate limited government funds on services for urban residents. To an extraordinary degree, corruption in government has dissipated an astonishing amount of the limited funds available. There are ominous social trends that make social services provision harder and harder: HIV/AIDS, drug abuse, terrorism and domestic violence, large population shifts, civil disobedience, youth unemployment, and aging populations.

There is also a remarkable growth of internal communities built up around things favored and things opposed, depending on commonly held beliefs of what is important including religion, ethnicity, race, geographical unity, tribalism, and clannishness. These trends have many forms of networking: political, "old boy/old girl"; extended family; tribes and clans; ethnic; religious; community; temporary-issue oriented; power protection; and unfortunately, sturdy networks for corruption. All of these are outside of official channels and often in opposition to them.

All of these trends are taking place to some degree in all economies. But there are other trends that perhaps offer some hope of social improvement. There is increasing resistance to authoritarianism, which, while not yet considered real democratization, is at least a broadening pattern of people finding ways to resist or even overthrow dictatorships. Economic improvement is producing more middle classes who are more powerful politically, more tolerant socially, more likely to understand how difficult governance can be, and less likely to swallow the false promises of loud mouthed politicians. Politics in the U. S. and most of the rest of the developed world are middle class politics. This defies the long term historical pattern of the politics of the rich/powerful.

Governance has become extraordinarily complex and difficult, and the widespread failures of government tend to cause people to overlook its successes. Government reputations as the solvers of all problems are in serious decline, paralleled by the growth of "non-government" government in the form of the emergence of hundreds of non government organizations (NGOs), volunteer movements, lobbying groups and local self help organizations that take the place of government shortfalls. Yet, as these NGOs and other organizations press to the fore, they in turn become entangled in the eternal conflict between service and power.

Along with the global economy there is a growing form of "global governance" producing global standards for social functioning in arenas such as environmentalism, human rights, citizen equality, economic equality, and responsible government, and for the provision of an adequate social safety network and skills of negotiation rather than wars.

Globalization is seen mostly as a great corporate economic tide but it has also become a fact of life for governance as well. Global institutions such as the United Nations, the World Bank, and the International Monetary Fund and the World Trade Organization have flourished and expanded and new global social organizations have been created centering on world-wide dilemmas such as environmentalism, health protection, human rights, equality, and responsiveness to emergencies, wars, and terrorism. Even those who protest outside of the World Bank against "globalism" are themselves representative of new and growing global social mechanisms.

But a social and cultural issue that has always been "global" is the treatment around the world of the position of women in social, political and economic terms. **Is the treatment of women the greatest oppression of all?** The answer is YES if attitudes are seen as deliberately "keeping women down", since such oppression impacts one half of the human race all of the time. When is this kind of oppression deliberate?

* When men seize an unequal share of scarce resources. It doesn't matter what the resources are or how adequate they are if there is a clear and deliberate policy of male preferment

pursued by men. Governments should reject any special interest that proposes to give men any form of preferment over women. Governments should eliminate any laws or regulations which convey any special interest preferment. Further, since much of special interest influence is "back room" and secretive, there needs to be constant pressure to require those men in official power serve as defenders of equality and not oppressors.

* When governments to continue to reject the clearly recognized need for reform, which denies rights to women, and the negative consequences of this failure to reform are understood and could probably have been prevented.

* When governments deliberately allow or mandate unfair disparities between what women are paid and the economic value they create, or to allow or mandate unequal compensation to women vs. what is paid to men for performance of the same work.

* When education is well understood as the great facilitator (jobs, knowledge, advancement, advantage, mobility), and education is deliberately withheld from women; or is permitted only on a scale and at levels much less than permitted for men.

* When vital information is knowingly not provided for women (family planning, mother/child care, post natal care, etc.) when it was entirely possible to provide.

* When the government takes deliberate measures to deny women the right to employment in any work that they can perform.

* Prevention of women individually or together from engaging in any economic activity, and specifically, to prevent them from forming and operating businesses of any kind.

* When the government maintains any official government policy, program, activity or process that deliberately has the effect of favoring men over women in the same circumstances.

* When the government denies to women that which is made available to men in the same circumstances.

* When, in any manner, the justice system gives women less standing before the law than men in the same circumstances.

* When the government fails to prevent the theft or misallocation of funds known to be in support of women's benefits and needs. For example, in any government budget retrenchment activity, the government should not permit funds in support of women's benefits and needs to be disproportionately reduced.
* Governments must recognize that child bearing and child rearing create a compelling special need for women, and it is oppressive not to recognize that fact and provide for it.

Women are pursuing the improvement of their status during a period when social services programs are coming under increasing pressure in a very large number of governments. Several types of new approaches are being tried. In a version of the "commanding heights" concept, central governments are beginning to abandon the old socialist "cradle to grave" commitments and are attempting to concentrate limited resources on the most important and productive elements of critical social services. This is also leading to a rethinking of the role of the private sector in countries that have previously insisted that these services were solely the responsibilities of governments. According to 2000 statement by World Bank Vice President Jean-Michel Severino, "Private sector involvement is key to any modern and effective social policy, especially in the Asian regions where growth has been built on private sector initiatives. Private sector engagement is crucial to effective social services delivery, social policy financing, social innovations, and high quality services."

At the same time, it is probably true that the national tax system in most countries may need to be redesigned to produce more revenue available for social services. The poor are, or should be, almost entirely exempt from routine taxation, especially relating to income. Tax systems that provide general subsidies to profit making organizations, including state owned enterprises should be purged of these subsidies, and the funds saved reallocated to social services programs. However, subsidies through the tax system may still have to be considered for providers of social services, at least during a period when they must expand and upgrade their performance. The private sector companies should be charged with providing at least health care and pensions for their employees and these should be taxed as acceptable business expenses.

In the Russian Federation and the Peoples Republic of China these problems were eventually dumped on local governments and they were left to their own devices. They have been learning to their disgust just how weak and deteriorated these social programs had become under national socialist leadership. Even in countries such as Hungary and the former Czechoslovakia, the system faded to the point that infant and child mortality or senior care was no better than the level found in Zimbabwe or Vietnam. In other country situations such as Japan, the long drawn out national economic recession and the huge debts being run up by the central government created a new opportunity for the prefectures and municipalities to negotiate with the central government from a position of strength, so that acceptance of greater social services program responsibility was conditioned on agreement for greater local autonomy, additional taxing powers, and more latitude to define how social services programs would be administered.

Some governments, like China still seek to retain centrist control and still feel that they can make centrist social services delivery work better than devolution to local governments. There is nothing theoretically wrong with this approach; the issue is whether the government can and will actually perform any better in the future than it has in the past. The history of the Soviet failure suggests that the Chinese approach is also doomed to failure – and probably massive systemic failure – and yet another generation of citizens will be underserved. Basic to any of these approaches is the need for making social services a higher government priority which will necessarily involve taking money from the previous budgetary "winners" of economic development and national security. But a major problem is that, if governments wait for a strengthening of the economy so that more taxes may be extracted for social services, this wait may be very long and will become an excuse for constantly delaying higher levels of social services funding. Again, the experience of Japan can be cited. In the 60's, Japanese families were said to covet the "three sacred treasures": a television set, a washing machine, and a refrigerator. In the 70's they coveted the three C's: a car, a cooler, and color TV. During these years, the government was saying "settle now for modest gains, and allow us to plow most national wealth into economic development. Ultimately, this strategy will pay off, and we'll all be rich." Such reasoning became the common excuse for shortcomings in what was generally an adequate social services system. But several years of recession have finally brought home to the government that significant structural adjustment is necessary, and one of the changes being forced upon the government is to give social services programs higher priority, finding the money wherever possible.

What seems also to have waned in the face of reality is the concept that the total package of social services provided by the government would be substantial enough to constitute a redistribution of wealth from the rich to the poor. In developed countries, the middle class resisted heavier levels of taxation and few economies have been able to generate enough wealth to redistribute. Hernando De Soto explains that "it is essential for the State to recognize that before it can redistribute the nation's wealth, the nation must produce wealth. And that, in order to produce wealth, it is necessary that the state's actions not obstruct the actions of citizens, who, after all, know better than anyone else what they want and what they have to do to get it. The State must restore to its citizens the right to take on productive tasks, a right that it has been usurping and obstructing." (28) Even those governments that made a sincere effort at redistribution found that they could not leverage the economy sufficiently to make much difference. Even the most powerful socialist governments failed at this task. It also became clear that the act of redistribution involves a heavy concentration of centrist power and authority which has often become tyrannical. A lot of the redistribution that took place using this power never reached the truly poor but ended up in the pockets of a corrupt centrist elite.

Hopefully, common sense is breaking out and governments are beginning to realize that the needs for social services are so great that all elements of society both public and private must be marshaled to address them. Innovation is needed in the creation of a total revenue package for social services involving continued central government fund transfers, new taxing powers, private sector responsibilities, intergovernmental cost sharing, and freedom to reallocate funds as judged against local government priorities. In many developing countries, local governments are so weak and inexperienced that whole new programs of capacity building must be generated. There is a growing realization of how technologically obsolete the old systems have been and how far each social service has to go in making remedial improvements to reach even basic adequacy. In China for example, only 11% of the population have access to health care insurance, and only about 14% have any form of old age protection other than the traditional reliance on their children. There are enormous unfunded costs in expanding social service to the majority of citizens. In addition, greater professional knowledge, new equipment, and major programs of repairs and renovations for obsolete physical plant all must be brought closer to current international standards. In failed or failing states everything seems to have slumped into a state of decay and governments in these countries are faced with excruciatingly difficult decisions on how to set priorities for use of severely limited funds. Finally, since the old regimes have failed to protect the public, whole new sets of regulatory protections are needed. Literally hundreds of important public regulations must be created for a social services system that is still in flux.

Governments must take more seriously the need to create a social safety net for their countries. The term "safety net" has two meanings: first, as the major, broad range of national social systems to protect the public; and second, a short term agenda of measures designed to mitigate the impact of adjustment programs. But the perception has grown that these sort term safety net measures are more important as political cover stories than for their actual impact. Safety nets as political instruments are intended to convince the public (as well as international critics) that the social costs of adjustment can be successfully managed, and that the current government is serious in doing so. There is however a nasty track record of poor performance by governments in the delivery of social services aid. This has caused lenders to turn instead to the use of Non Government Organizations

(NGOs) to deliver social services, or to put stronger limits on the ability of governments to abuse the use of donated funds. Yet it is probably true that emergency funds, if processed through normal government service delivery channels would be more cost effective. Therefore it remains important to build up regular government organizations to be more honest and effective. Said another way, short term safety net schemes do not provide the basis for long term upgrading of social services programs. The only way to improve welfare under conditions of structural adjustment is to increase the protections of the state.

In a sense, it is useless to debate whether social services should continue to be a government monopoly since it is already clear that such a pure socialist approach has never proved to be much of a success and has frequently been abandoned. But socialist states must retain the old systems until new ones evolve. The trick is not to let government controls remain too stultifying or be applied beyond their legitimate competence. There is the need in both the short run and in the longer term to retain large amounts of government funding and even developed countries recognize this. All sources of funding must be tapped, and there must be a return to the more realistic posture of personal self reliance, and the design of public programs to supplement this self reliance or to aid those who cannot achieve that goal. This is deeply unsettling for many people who have benefited from the old ways as witness the difficulties in France in dealing with labor-management relationships or in Germany in attempting to retrench excessive labor protections that have been driving companies out of Germany to less restrictive countries in Eastern Europe or elsewhere. Somehow, the concepts of "outcome effectiveness" must be given more attention and elements of programs that go beyond the concept of service to "the neediest" will have to be trimmed back. Governments get into bad habits of wasting too much precious money on program elements that are obsolete, outmoded, ineffective, irrelevant, inconsequential, corrupted and just plain stupid. The political system is the problem. It needs to become more of the solution.

"Although for much of the 1980s, revolutionary Iran and extremist movements provided the dominant note, the late 1980s and 1990s also revealed the many faces of Islamic social and political activism. Islamic movements and associations became part and parcel of mainstream institutional forces in society. Islamic activist organizations and NGOs created networks of mosques, hospitals, clinics, day-care centers, youth clubs, legal aid societies, foreign language schools, banks, drug rehabilitation programs, insurance companies and publishing houses. They fill a void and thus serve, in some countries, as an implicit indictment of the government's ability to provide adequate services, in particular for the non-elite elements of society. At the same time, they reinforce a sense of community identity as well as spiritual and moral renewal." (29)

"Many Islamic movements in recent years have eschewed violence and terrorism. Alongside the terrorist trail of unholy wars, there exists a democratic track record of Islamically oriented candidates who have been elected President of Indonesia, prime minister of Turkey, deputy prime minister of Malaysia, speakers of parliaments in Indonesia, Iran, Jordan, and Sudan, cabinet ministers and parliamentarians in Egypt, Algeria, Sudan, Kuwait, Pakistan, Jordan, Yemen, Malaysia, Indonesia, Turkey and Lebanon.

FAILURE TO COPE WITH SOCIAL CHANGES

The basic problems remain the most important -- the needs of people for food, clothing, shelter, jobs, health care, education, protection and justice. All of the heavy burdens of disease, wars, poverty and social conflict remain. There is a general sense that things are getting better as more countries manage to get a grip on their economies, and as technology improves health care, public services and general wealth production. But even so, it still leaves too large a proportion of the world's population behind this curve of rising achievement, and too few ways to share the wealth.

There are two great tides running; first, what is happening to governments in dealing with social problems; and second, what people themselves are doing, in part in response to what they see in their governments.

Perhaps the most compelling impact on social change is coming from the world economy. More wealth is being created, and despite a lot of examples to the contrary, it is being distributed more broadly. More people are benefiting directly, and a large percentage of national wealth is being absorbed by governments, mostly for the benefit of people. When the great tide of socialism took over so many governments after WW II, this was not the case. Most governments, and not just in the developing countries, have suffered intractable failures in generating enough public revenues to come anywhere close to meeting even basic public needs. The socialist promises of a "cradle to grave" social safety net seemed right at the time, and there were high expectations that added power in the government would be capable of extracting more public funds from the economy to carry out these promises. Now, the rapid decline of economic socialism and the slower withdrawing tide of social socialism seem like a loss of innocence about the capacities of governments to take on such enormous commitments. Even while there is more money available, the competition for wealth remains fierce, and governments find that they are limited in what they can extract, even when using maximum force, as in the Soviet Union. If anything, individuals, corporations, and other institutions are getting better at resisting government taxation and protecting wealth for their own use. Resistance to taxation is a growing world-wide skill.

The recognition of this failure of public revenues is becoming more widely accepted, and it is changing the nature of the social service contract. Governments must stop promising cradle to grave protection because it is clear that they will not be able to deliver, and such promises are deluding people, and ultimately cheating them. The role of governments now must increasingly be to exercise better and more realistic judgment about what the most urgent needs really are, and how to take care of those needs at an adequate level of service provision. This is especially true in the context of the world population explosion, because some countries are falling farther behind, rather than being able to raise the quality of life.

What is the alternative to the cradle-to-grave government? It is what it really always has been -- for people to learn to take care of themselves, with the government in a supportive or "safety net" role of smoothing the way, and taking care of the those not able to care for themselves. Much of what is happening in society's today centers on the struggle to redefine the relationships between governments and citizens along this watershed. Governments are being forced to choose what they can and cannot do, and this is politically tough and distasteful. What is the "objective" of this struggle? It is not just for governments to eliminate poverty. It is for societies to become middle class -- to which the poor aspire, and from which the rich emerge. The middle class is the class that, over a long span of history since the Industrial Revolution, has been willing and capable of self reliance. The middle class is essentially what powers the developed countries, and it is beginning to serve the same role in many of the less developed countries, especially in China and India.

There remains an exceptionally strong and widely shared belief that the well being of citizens must be guaranteed by governments, and perhaps this will never change. But there is also an increasing awareness that the range of governments has broadened, and there are many more formidable competitors for tax funds than just social service programs. There remains the dominance of national security demands. Many countries also give absolute priority to economic development -- even over social services -- in the belief that in the long run, the added wealth of a stronger economy will generate the public revenues that make the improved delivery of social services possible. But there are new and ominous social threats that have grown in recent years that must now be dealt with -- AIDS, drug abuse, terrorism, civil unrest and civil disobedience, ethnic and religious conflicts. Environmentalism has become a world force, capable of demanding a growing share of available money and social commitment in competition with older demands.

If greater citizen self reliance is a critical need, there are at least some positive trends to strengthen this ability. The emergence of women is an extraordinary example. More and more women are achieving the ability to take care of themselves, and as their talents are given broader scope, they are adding more and more to the world's economic and social base. The same thing is happening to all citizens in countries where too much control and been usurped by elites. While it seems inevitable that "the rich get richer" it is not self evident that the poor will get poorer. More people are finding ways to liberate themselves, enhance their own position in society, and right some of the wrongs of the past. The trend towards national independence and the growing ability of citizens to penetrate the power base are tides that are rising.

The global economy is much emphasized in economic terms, but at the same time, there is something like a global society emerging. Modern communications are a revolution in themselves. People now know more about each other, and are better able to connect with each other, and this gives them added strength and motivation. People have become more mobile at several levels. Education is central to skill building, and many of these skills are portable and not so linked to institutions such as factories or protective unions, or even government programs. People are remarkably willing to move themselves to find better jobs or less oppression, and the world is full of substantial people movements of this kind. For fifty years, there has been a mass movement of truly staggering dimensions from farms to large urban areas, and secondarily from central cities to suburbs and smaller communities. People are moving from poorer countries to richer ones, believing that opportunities will be greater for them. The universal language of democracy is becoming more believable, not at some abstract level, but because it works as a practical method for greater individual and societal achievement. The world is becoming less doctrinaire (e.g. Communist or Socialist or Democratic) and more pragmatic, even where politicians are often failing to notice the fact. It must be emphasized that these are individual decisions– not policies driven by governments – and that they are bold and courageous.

In the Russian Federation and the Peoples Republic of China these problems were eventually dumped on local governments and they were left to their own devices. They have been learning to their disgust just how weak and deteriorated these social programs had become under national socialist leadership. Even in countries such as Hungary and the former Czechoslovakia, the system faded to the point that infant and child mortality or senior care was no better than the level found in Zimbabwe or Vietnam. In other country situations such as Japan, the long drawn out national economic recession and the huge debts being run up by the central government created a new opportunity for the prefectures and municipalities to negotiate with the central government from a position of strength, so that acceptance of greater social services program responsibility was conditioned on agreement for greater local autonomy, additional taxing powers, and more latitude to define how social services programs would be administered.

Some governments, like China still seek to retain centrist control and still feel that they can make centrist social services delivery work better than devolution to local governments. There is nothing theoretically wrong with this approach; the issue is whether the government can actually do any better in the future than it has in the past. The history of the Soviet failure suggests that the Chinese approach is also doomed to failure – and probably massive systemic failure – and yet another generation of citizens will be underserved.

Basic to any of these approaches is the need for making social services a higher government priority which will necessarily involve taking money from the previous financial "winners" of economic development and national security. But a major problem is that, if governments wait for a strengthening of the economy so that more taxes may be extracted for social services, this wait may be very long and will become an excuse for delaying or further under funding. Again, the experience of Japan can be cited. In the 60's, Japanese families were said to covet the "three sacred treasures": a television set, a washing machine, and a refrigerator. In the 70's they coveted the three C's: a car, a cooler, and color TV. During these years, the government was saying "settle now for modest gains, and allow us to plow most national wealth into economic development. Ultimately, this strategy will pay off, and we'll all be rich." Such reasoning became the common excuse for shortcomings in what was generally an adequate social services system. But several years of recession have finally brought home to the government that significant structural adjustment is necessary, and one of the changes being forced upon the government is to give social services programs higher priority, finding the money wherever possible.

What seems also to have waned in the face of reality is the concept that the total package of social services provided by the government would be substantial enough to constitute a redistribution of wealth from the rich to the poor. In developed countries, the middle class resisted heavier levels of taxation and few economies have been able to generate enough wealth to redistribute. Hernando De Soto explains that t is essential for the State to recognize that before it can redistribute the nation's wealth, the nation must produce wealth. And that, in order to produce wealth, it is necessary that the state's actions not obstruct the actions of citizens, who, after all, know better than anyone else what they want and what they have to do to get it. The State must restore to its citizens the right to take on productive tasks, a right that it has been usurping and obstructing. [2] Even those governments that made a sincere effort at redistribution found that they could not leverage the economy sufficiently to make much difference. Even the most powerful socialist governments failed at this task. It also became clear that the act of redistribution involves a heavy concentration of centrist power and authority which could become tyrannical. A lot of the redistribution that took place using this power was not to the poor but to the pockets of a corrupt centrist elite.

Hopefully, common sense is breaking out and governments are beginning to realize that the needs for social services are so great that all elements of society both public and private must be marshaled to address them. Innovation is needed in the creation of a total revenue package for social services involving continued central government fund transfers, new taxing powers, private sector responsibilities, intergovernmental cost sharing, and freedom to reallocate funds as judged against local government priorities. In many developing countries, local governments are so weak and inexperienced that whole new programs of capacity building must be generated. There is a growing realization of how technologically obsolete the old systems have been and how far each social service has to go in making remedial improvements to reach even basic adequacy. In China for example, only 11% of the population have access to health care insurance, and only about 14% have any form of old age protection other than the traditional reliance on their children. Think of the almost incomprehensible task of creating a health insurance for an additional 1.2 billion people! Also, there are enormous unfunded costs in expanding social service to the majority of citizens. In addition, professional knowledge, new equipment, major repairs and renovations to obsolete physical plant all must be brought closer to current international standards. In failed or failing states everything seems to have slumped into a state of decay and governments in these countries are faced with excruciatingly difficult decisions on how to set priorities for severely limited funds. Finally, since the old regimes have failed to protect the public, whole new sets

---

2

of regulatory protections are needed. Literally hundreds of important public regulations must be created for a social services system that is still in flux.

Governments must take more seriously the need to create a social safety net for their countries. The term "safety net" has two meanings: first, as the major, broad range of national social systems to protect the public; and second, a short term agenda of measures designed to mitigate the impact of adjustment programs. But the perception has grown that these short term safety net measures are more important as political cover stories than for their actual impact. Safety nets as political instruments are intended to convince the public (as well as international critics) that the social costs of adjustment can be successfully managed, and that the current government is serious in doing so. There is however a nasty track record of such poor performance by governments in the delivery of social services aid that lenders tend to turn to non-government organizations (NGOs) for service delivery, or to put limits on the ability of governments to abuse the use of donated funds. Yet it is probably true that emergency funds, if processed through normal government service delivery channels would be more cost effective. Therefore it remains important to build up regular government organizations to be more honest and effective. Said another way, short term safety net schemes do not provide the basis for long term upgrading of social services programs. The only way to improve welfare under conditions of structural adjustment is to increase the protections of the state.

In a sense, it is useless to debate whether social services should continue to be a government monopoly since it is already clear that such a pure socialist approach has never proved to be much of a success and has frequently been abandoned. But socialist states must retain the old systems until new ones evolve. The trick is not to let government control remain too stultifying or be retained too long beyond their legitimate competence. There is the need in both the short run and in the longer term to retain large amounts of government funding and even developed countries recognize this. All sources of funding must be tapped, and there must be a return to the more realistic posture of personal self reliance, and the design of public programs to supplement this self reliance or to aid those who cannot achieve that goal. This is deeply unsettling for many people who have benefited from the old ways as witness the difficulties in France in dealing with labor-management relationships or in Germany in attempting to retrench excessive labor protections that have been driving companies out of Germany to less restrictive countries in Eastern Europe or elsewhere. Somehow, the concepts of "outcome effectiveness" must be given more attention and elements of programs that go beyond the concept of service to "the neediest" will have to be trimmed back. Governments get into bad habits of wasting too much precious money on program elements that are obsolete, outmoded, ineffective, irrelevant, inconsequential, corrupted and just plain stupid. The political system is the problem. It needs to become the solution.

China, much more quickly than the Soviet Union, recognized the need to move the economy from state socialist into a competitive market base, and it began the process as early as the 1980s, with remarkable results. China has been growing its economy an average of 9.7% over the last 20 years. But this pattern of total economic growth has been offset by a number of adverse consequences in the social services arenas. First, as in the Soviet Union, much of the provision of social services was mandated on the state owned enterprises. Each was supposedly responsible for such things as health care, pensions, and even education for their workers, and by default for many in the communities in which they operated. As China has moved to privatize these SOEs, the burden of social services was supposed to be taken up by local governments. At the same time, in order to reduce the budgets of the national government, the Chinese central government, again like the Soviets, dumped social services programs on municipalities, townships, and provinces largely without any money. As a consequence, local governments inherited huge new responsibilities without the funds to carry them out. The central government happily concluded that it had the best of both worlds: it had continued control of social services policy while dumping most of the costs onto local governments. The relief provided in the national budget was justified by the assumption that local governments would somehow make up the difference.

But most of China's townships were poor and many cities and provinces were not much better off. As a result, the substitution of local funding for national funding has been very slow to take place. At the same time, the government was also purging the central budget of the huge losses run up by these SOEs, believing that the newly created private sector would generate new wealth that could be taxed to finance the government. But most of the private sector, recognizing the lack of legal and enforcement powers of the government, has managed to avoid providing health insurance at all. National financing of health care fell from more than 60% of total health care spending to less than 40%.

These catastrophic declines in health care funds come on top of a national health care system that was wholly inadequate to begin with. Even now, only 11% of the population has access to any form of medical coverage, and only 5% of women have maternity health coverage. Paralleling the Soviet pattern, health care had been marginal in cities and almost non-existent in rural and village areas. The old pattern of subsidized clinics around the country has collapsed to the extent that perhaps 90% of the rural population has little or no access to health care, and even the cities are fortunate to be able to meet 60% of their demands. There continue to be big gaps between the provision of social services in the new economic development regions of the country and the rural hinterlands. Even where health care is available it is so relatively expensive that most poor people simply can't afford it, and even where government benefits are available they tend to be so small that they are not close to covering the needs. A recent government survey found that 60% of the rural population says that they can't afford to use the hospitals that are available. As a consequence, the true "cost" of the collapsed health care system is measured by the inability of people to get it. Diseases that had been all but eliminated such as small pox and tuberculosis are now apparently on the increase. And this collapsed system is facing an ominous new challenge in the form of the spread of HIV/AIDS, with an estimated 1 million victims now, and the prospect that this number will increase ten fold in the next 5-10 years.

CASE STUDY: THE FLAWED SOVIET HEALTH CARE SYSTEM

Under the rubric of "cradle to grave" government protection, the Soviets often cited their national health care system as one of the best in the world, and a triumph of communist governance. These assertions were intended to mask the real state of the system from outsiders. Meanwhile Soviet citizens knew better and government bragging must have been especially bitter to contemplate. But it was not until the collapse of the USSR that the true state of affairs became more fully known. The Soviet government had demanded the right to provide the health care system and had defended the necessity of top down centrist control. But having demanded this right to control all social services the government failed massively to deliver on its obligations. The entire system was in severe disarray. Lack of adequate medical services was almost universal, except for certain more visible areas like Moscow or Leningrad, and for certain groups of clientele like the Party members, the military and the bureaucracy. In other words, being unable to provide an adequate whole system, the system was drawn back to serve mostly the ruling elite. The experience of the Society health care system is worth reviewing because it illuminates the condition of most of the former Soviet bloc, and is typical of what is happening in many less developed countries.

The basic cause of the system's failure was serious congenital under funding, supplemented by cynical indifference from the top and a set of skewed priorities in the allocation of national resources. Vast sums were spent on the military establishment, and whole elements of the economy such as electronics were allotted to the military itself to make sure that their needs were met. There were probably more intelligence agents in the country than medical professionals. Funds were always available for "prestige" Soviet programs such as the space program. This misallocation of resources was conscious and deliberate, and medical costs were shifted back onto the public because the government abandoned its commitments. There were enormous personal costs and burdens created in the form of lack of access to medical treatment, untreated illnesses, inadequate treatment, lack of health care facilities in large parts of the country, poor or inadequate medical advice, and whole areas of health care such as pre-natal care that were kept at marginal levels. Most of the hospitals outside of key cities were so bad that they lacked even basic facilities and equipment – in some cases, even running water. Some "hospitals" were really no more than nursing and first aid stations. Advanced technology available in other countries was seemingly beyond reach. In rural areas and in such places as Central Asia or Siberia, service was the worst – reflecting a deliberate neglect of "non-Russian" citizens in favor of concentrating limited resources to provision of service to the Russian parts of the Soviet Union.

Even where funds were available for investment in the health care system, these funds were often poorly invested. There was an over concentration on physical plant but severe under investment is skills development. There was excessive specialization but a failure to provide enough general care physicians and "gate keeper" doctors to integrate service.

Health services suffered from major systemic incompetence. Service was usually poor and often available only after long waiting periods, and doctors were warned to avoid authorizing expensive procedures and were instructed to concentrate care on those who were favored by the regime. Vital equipment and facilities were often not available at all, or only at a few scattered hospitals. Most medical professionals suffered from poor professional training in the first place, and few opportunities for education and training to keep current with modern medical advances. The system suffered from the usual Soviet disease of unending bureaucratic red tape and delay. It is not surprising that medical care providers suffered from low morale, a feeling of indifference, and even attitudes of rudeness and contempt. The professional staffs were under trained, under paid, and overworked. The system became impervious to public protests and complaints, and seemed incapable or unwilling to correct recognized problems. Doctors and health care administrators were placed in the untenable position of covering up the patterns of failure and were forced to justify the failed system to the public. Medical associations were often used as mouthpieces for government policy rather than a means of pressing for reform. Citizen groups that protested were ignored, or threatened, abused or co-opted.

There was a puzzling lack of attention to some potentially achievable improvements, particularly the whole concept of preventative medicine. The regime seemed fully able to communicate its self serving propaganda, but was strangely silent in failing to inform and educate the public about the high personal and social costs of smoking, drinking, obesity and poor physical condition, poor nutrition, the need for pre-natal and post-natal care and protection of the elderly. For the medical profession to discuss these topics might have been interpreted as criticism of the government. There were also heavy costs of medical system failures shifted to state enterprises in the form of lost worker hours, absenteeism, lack of workplace safety and protections, and little attention to social dysfunctions in the workplace such as drunkenness. Many SOEs were required to bear the cost of health services for their employees and families, and even for other members of the community. Often, a hospital or clinic maintained by a local factory and intended for employees was required to extend services to the general community. The Soviets claimed that this was part of the "socialist design" but in truth it simply reflected the failings of government health care provision.

The government also failed to control or regulate elements of production facilities that caused illness such as environmental pollution, industrial hazards and injuries, water pollution, lack of control of agricultural chemicals, air quality, and even radiation exposure. Finally, in what seems like an almost inevitable consequence, the health care system descended into corruption. Black market medicine often replaced the official sources as doctors shifted their efforts to private unofficial patients or demanded "bonus fees" from patients before service was provided. Nurses and technicians worked outside of hospitals for private income, medical personnel sold illegal drugs, and pharmaceuticals were withheld from government hospitals and sold on the black market instead.

The Soviet health care system showed that bad politics leads to bad management. And these failures were generic; that is, the same conditions emerged in other social services programs such as elementary and secondary education, care of children and the elderly, social welfare services, and the provision of state pensions. Families had to absorb these costs and responsibilities and could expect little help from their government. The whole soviet philosophy of a controlled top down "one big system" seems now thoroughly repudiated, and it is apparent that improvement in social services generally must shift to long term incremental reform and improvement, starting with more attention to patient needs and less attention to state socialist theory.

This is a summary of the Soviet health care system, but these failures were generic - that is, the same conditions emerged in other social services programs in other socialist and less developed countries. And these sins were common in the 28 other nations that were part of the old Soviet system. There are also about 25 or 30 less developed countries that suffer from the same kinds of generic problems. If all of these social services inadequacies are considered, what emerges is a pattern of neglect that is a critical form of oppression. The long periods of neglect will have to be followed now by long, difficult years to repair these inferior systems even if done right and at a high level of competence. Do governments know how to repair the damage? Yes. The problem is not lack of understanding either of the problems or the corrections. The lack is in political will and money. The concept of competition in health care provision must be extensively introduced, both in terms of public vs. private provision, and in competition between elements of both systems to promote system effectiveness. Most former socialist countries are reluctant to abandon the basic concept of government responsibility, and are looking toward some form of managed care, with a high degree of government oversight and economic intervention. Part of this role is to redefine failed forms of cost containment: continued price fixing; rejection of fee-for-service adoption of health maintenance services; and limits on wages and professional incomes. In other words, it is clear that the whole institutional architecture of the health care system must be restructured. Under new concepts of system competition, the first and most successful elements to be privatized have been doctors into private practice, the emergence of small local clinics, the emergence of cheaper outpatient facilities and store front operations for things like pre-natal care, break-outs of dentistry and technical support services. Most countries are striving for creation of a viable health insurance system, involving government, private employers, or personal insurance plans. New packages of public regulation are needed to provide government certification of drugs, hospitals, professional qualifications, and professional practices.

CASE STUDY: CHINA: THE SAME PATTERN OF FAILURE?

China, much more quickly than the Soviet Union, recognized the need to move the economy from state socialist into a competitive market base, and it began the process as early as the 1980s, with remarkable results. China has been growing its economy an average of 9.7% over the last 20 years. But this pattern of total economic growth has been offset by a number of adverse consequences in the social services arenas. First, as in the Soviet Union, much of the provision of social services was mandated on the state owned enterprises (SOE). Each was supposedly responsible for such things as health care, pensions, and even education for their workers, and by default for many in the communities in which they operated. As China has moved to privatize these SOEs, the burden of social services was supposed to be taken up by local governments. At the same time, in order to reduce the budgets of the national government, the Chinese central government, again like the Soviets, dumped social services programs on municipalities, townships, and provinces largely without providing any additional funding. As a consequence, local governments inherited huge new responsibilities without the funds to carry them out. The central government happily concluded that it had the best of both worlds: it had continued control of social services policy while dumping most of the costs onto local governments. The relief provided in the national budget was justified by the assumption that local governments would somehow make up the difference.

But most of China's townships were poor and many cities and provinces were not much better off. As a result, the substitution of local funding for national funding has been very slow to take place. At the same time, the government was also purging the central budget of the huge losses run up by these SOEs, believing that the newly created private sector would generate new wealth that could be taxed to finance the government. But most of the private sector, recognizing the lack of legal and enforcement powers of the government, has managed to avoid providing health insurance at all. National financing of health care fell from more than 60% of total health care spending to less than 40%.

These catastrophic declines in health care funds come on top of a national health care system that was wholly inadequate to begin with. Even now, only 11% of the population has access to any form of medical coverage, and only 5% of women have maternity health coverage. Paralleling the Soviet pattern, health care had been marginal in cities and almost non-existent in rural and village areas. The old pattern of subsidized clinics around the country has collapsed to the extent that perhaps 90% of the rural population has little or no access to health care, and even the cities are fortunate to be able to meet 60% of their demands. There continue to be big gaps between the provision of social services in the new economic development regions of the country and the rural hinterlands. Even where health care is available it is so relatively expensive that most poor people simply can't afford it, and even where government benefits are available they tend to be so small that they are not close to covering the needs. A recent government survey found that 60% of the rural population says that they can't afford to use the hospitals that are available. As a consequence, the true "cost" of the collapsed health care system is measured by the inability of people to get care. Diseases that had been all but eliminated such as small pox and tuberculosis are now apparently on the increase. And this collapsed system is facing an ominous new challenge in the form of the spread of HIV/AIDS, with an estimated 1 million victims now, and the prospect that this number will increase ten fold in the next 5-10 years.

The government was shaken out of its preoccupation with economic development by the panic created by the outbreak of the severe acute respiratory syndrome (SARS) in 2003. This panic brought home not only how totally inadequate the health care system is, but a greater realization of what enormous efforts will be needed to modernize and expand it to some acceptable level, and how extraordinarily difficult it will be to find the funds to undertake such modernization. There is an urgent need for one or more systems of health care insurance. Even moderately well off people lack an adequate reserve of savings to meet a medical crisis, and there is some evidence that the very high rate of savings by Chinese is in part of reflection of the need to build up family financial reserves against an uncertain medical future. To quote the Economist "Local governments are often unwilling or unable to make the necessary contributions, especially in poorer regions. And individuals are often unwilling to pay for a service that they feel they may not immediately need. For the past two decades, local governments have gouged farmers for contributions to an almost non-existent health care system, with the money being used mostly to pay staffs (many surplus to requirements or simply non-existent), with the money being used to line official's pockets, rather than to pay for services." (30) Local governments are desperate for money, and most of them collect contributions for future social services but spend the money instead on current operating costs. Consequently, there is a huge unfunded liability, and this lying and cheating make people highly suspicious of any social services scheme controlled by the government.

The government is pinning a lot of hopes on the greater involvement of private sector investors, and many townships or cities are trying to sell off their hospitals to private investors. But such investors fear the extent of continued government involvement (most hospitals are still owned and overseen by governments), nor are they sure whether a reasonable profit can be earned except in the richest areas of the new Chinese economy. Therefore, shifting costs to the private sector will remain a slow and tricky process. Privatization has meant many improvements in services, and greater investment in equipment and training, but again, these hospitals are in wealthy parts of the country, and they are unlikely to lower costs very much elsewhere. The government policy thus seems to be to rely on an uncertain set of expectations for the private sector, meanwhile concentrating declining public funds on a smaller number of facilities. But it is clear that, for a very long time, governments at some level will have to provide health care for the masses of the rural and urban poor, and there is no private sector option in meeting that need.

CASE STUDY: SOCIAL SERVICES PROGRAMS IN INDIA

Protective social security in India covers a patchwork of unemployment benefits, medical care, maternity benefits, family benefits, family planning, injury benefits, old age pensions, and survivor benefits. It is heavily regressive, since it is restricted to employees in the formal economy--at most, 12% of the workforce. Even when paid, state benefits are inadequate and congenitally under funded. For the vast majority of the public, these programs are essentially non-existent. Social programs are a mix from the public state owned enterprises and the larger private companies. Smaller companies escape responsibility because they are low profit and hard to regulate, even though the government has many laws on the books.

Thus, the brunt of social services needs is borne by the individual with little help from major organizations. Personal relationships within the extended family are probably the real social safety net. India's record in areas such as education and health is extremely poor even in comparison with other poorer countries. Private health care is largely curative and urban oriented. The Indian government has played a heavy role in subsidizing this private sector, especially in health, but private health expenditure is 60-70% of the total. In the rural areas, only 3% of medical practitioners have the appropriate qualifications, and 62% have no medically related qualification at all.

In 1992, the government attempted social services cuts as part of a structural adjustment program and foolishly made cuts in preventative health care (e. g. malaria control, rural water and sanitation). What remained fully funded were family planning, medical education, and medical salaries. There is almost no recourse to any form of medical insurance.

India has government controlled food distribution in the form of the Public Food Distribution System and the Food Corporation of India which purchases and distributes foods, sets price supports, provides credit, and tries to streamline the system. But it is caught up in a network of other state institutions, including at the regional government level. The government defends this system as a "social service", but in fact it is an income transfer mechanism, heavily subsidized and burdened with heavy political irrationality. It appears that Indian socialism like the Soviet model produced not only massive inefficiency, but massive corruption, most intensively at the political level.

One horrible example is the almost unbelievable failure of the state owned electricity suppliers. In Uttar Pradesh, a State of more than 200 million people and heavily rural/village in character, more than two thirds of the population has no reliable source of electricity. In fact, in all of India, some 700 million people, most of them outside of cities, either have no electricity or have inadequate and unreliable sources. The Indian government says that "90% of villages have electrical power", but in fact, this often means only that a few homes are wired and a handful of businesses are connected.

The somber fact is that the Indian government is totally incapable of solving this enormous problem, now and probably for decades. This lack of power has untold adverse consequences on people's lives and the pace of critical economic development. To make the point again: this failure is a failure of governments which knew better, saw the need, failed to rise to the demand, proved to be lazy and incompetent, proved to be corrupt, proved to be stupid, and spent its time regulating and controlling and inhibiting progress. This is true oppression.

The private sector is trying to take cope itself by the development of private power generation supplies. NGOs and foreign donors are helping by promoting electric generators for villages, where schools, hospitals, businesses and some homes are provided generators and recharging stations for cell phones. These private efforts put the government to shame – but in the end, they cannot solve the shortages experienced by 700 million people.

URBAN LIFE: WEALTH VS. SLUMS

All over the world, massive shifts of population are occurring from rural and village life to urban life. This movement has been largely stabilized in the most developed countries, but in the less developed countries, a serious decline of primary level jobs (i.e. agriculture, mining, forestry, and fishing) is taking place because of the low economic value derived from these occupations, and this decline is forcing millions to move to cities in the hope of finding a better livelihood. This movement is spontaneous and irreversible. This creates two kinds of problems: first, the overburden and potential collapse of urban economies and infrastructure; and second, the collapse of rural society, despite efforts of many countries to subsidize and prop up rural economies and enhance rural development.

The great older urban centers like London, Paris, Rome, Moscow, New York, Chicago, Los Angeles, and Tokyo are being overtaken, at least in size, by cities in less developed countries. Mexico City has become the world's most populous city, surpassing New York. Cairo is as large as Los Angeles; Shanghai, Beijing, Seoul and Kolkata are all larger than Moscow. Sao Paulo exceeds Tokyo, and Mumbai is larger than Chicago. Jakarta is about the size of London, and Lagos is larger now than San Francisco.

Of 96 world cities of more than 2 million population, 51 are in developing countries. Of these, 18 are in China and India, with a total population of more than 90 million people -- roughly equal to the top 20 cities in the U. S. and Europe. But the U. S. and Europe are perhaps 75% urbanized, while China has just now reached 50% urban residence, and India is still 75% rural.

U. S. and European cities are far better off both economically and socially. They have largely stabilized their populations, have long histories and traditions of relatively effective public management, enjoy a stable and largely adequate tax base, and have accumulated a body of public infrastructure and well developed social safety nets along with a cultural tradition of civic pride and cooperation.

Compared to them, cities in less developed countries are a total mess. Most are in countries where the massive shifts from rural to urban are still taking place like uncontrolled floods. In almost all, urban infrastructure, both public and private, lags far behind demand, and many are still losing ground. Transport is chaotic and usually dangerous. Heath care ranges from poor to non-existent -- except of course for the elites. Education seldom rises above the elementary level. Poor sanitation, pollution and crime are everyday facts of life. And still the people come. Why do they do so? Rural life is hard but so is city life. But rural areas lack any real opportunity for the future, and cities at least offer hope.

China is a striking example of these changes. Despite its considerable economic growth in the last 15 years, China remains about 50% relatively poor rural, and most of these people have been untouched by economic growth. But urban dwellers are often not much better off despite government preferment, since even recent major economic advances have not been enough to raise the level of living for most urban dwellers. The Chinese government has attempted to limit the growth of major cities, but with very little success. Their policy of designating "official" or "authorized" persons who are entitled to public services was intended to keep "unauthorized" persons from coming to cities by denying them access to all social services. But the great disparities between the job opportunities and the quality of life between urban and rural residents simply overpowered these government controls and huge numbers of people came to cities and created a semi-permanent floating population living illegally despite the rules and the active opposition of the police.

Most Chinese cities were wholly unprepared to deal with the magnitude of the rapid increase in urban populations, and most public infrastructure and social services were far behind the power curve. Subsidized services included subsidized food supplies, low fee elementary and secondary education, low cost housing, and cheap public utility services. In many places, the official population having access to these services was only about 65% of the total urban population, and it was largely guaranteed only for the government bureaucracy, the military and the employees of State Owned Enterprises (SOE). Many people have now ridden the expanded and enriched economy to elevate themselves into a new middle class. But the very large informal economy remains, and despite the government, it is still the a very necessary and vital part of the economy.

Meanwhile, most countries have been marginally successful in absorbing the surge of new residents. Cities such as Mumbai or Kolkata, Jakarta, Lagos, Manila, Mexico City, Cairo, Shanghai and Beijing, and now Moscow are fighting a losing battle against the expansion of dreadful urban slums. In the Muslim world, there are many highly urbanized countries: Egypt, Lebanon, Syria, Iraq, Jordan, Tunisia and the "city states" of Qatar and Kuwait. Many of these states such as Iraq, Afghanistan, Syria, Sudan, Nigeria, Mali, Algeria and others have been extensively debilitated over long periods of time by wars, insurrections, and heavy armed conflict. Their economies are very weak and outmoded, sustained in some cases by oil money and in others by outside contributions from donors and from private remittances. But this amounts to survival money and it is not enough to galvanize the national economy. And the whole area has been marked by rule by unpopular dictators, often military, who are arrogant, tyrannical, self serving and widely hated and feared.

Many of these countries have a lot of income, based on energy rich economies, and almost all cities in the Middle East and North Africa (MENA) region are marked by wealthy high rise areas, surrounded by older residential and commercial areas, which in turn are surrounded by slums which are the home of the new transient worker populations. There is a heavy concentration in "primary" cities" such as Cairo, Algiers, Baghdad, or Amman which now holds more than half of the total population of Jordan. This concentration adds leverage to the power elite, but it overburdens the primary cities, wastes the potential of next level cities, leads to general inflation and bidding up of land prices. The economies of most of these cities are shaky, and shortages or economic setbacks fall heavily on the transient workforces. For large numbers of urban workers, poverty is just a few days away, and potential disaster can be just around the corner.

Indian cities are uniformly filthy. Urban governments all seem totally unable to deal with the rapidly increasing rivers of trash and garbage disgorged by the public. Most water flows are dangerously polluted. Land fills are totally inadequate and dangerous, and governments are seen as ignorant, apathetic, incompetent, corrupt and cowardly. Urban populations range from a relatively sophisticated upper middle class down to a poor and uneducated population who skimp out a living in the informal economy, living in squalor next to polluted sewers and mountains of unprocessed trash. In the national capital of Delhi, the lack of landfill has risen to the state of an emergency, but the effort to find new land fills is frustrated by bureaucratic delays, law suits, changes of mind, shortages of money, or simple lack of political will. Perhaps the only saving grace is that these mountains of rubbish provide a sort of living for thousands of rag pickers and recyclers in cities like Delhi, in part because the economy cannot generate any better jobs for them. For the richer residents of cities, they have the clout to siphon off scarce funds for their own support that might have gone to help the poor. As in China, the official policy for many years was to try and limit the growth of cities. This policy was foolish from the start and failed completely. Finally and reluctantly, new thinking is to turn this policy around and try to figure out how to help cities to cope with their growth. Unfortunately, "helping" turns out to be far more difficult and complex than "limiting".

Housing provision has not nearly kept pace with demand. 90% of housing investment is private, by individuals or private companies. There are now new housing financial institutions that allow people to get mortgages for home ownership, but the private housing industry is reluctant to build low cost housing, and the government has now will to step in. Also, leftover Socialist laws still make it difficult to own property in the first place, or to transfer ownership except through horrendous bureaucratic machinations. In fact, around the world, few developing countries anywhere have been able to add much housing through public programs. The poorer the country, the less likely it is that the government can play any significant role except to take care of the very poor. Public management of housing has a bad reputation, largely because of bad politics and highly successful theft of public funds. Corruption is, as usual, the one activity that succeeds.

The magnitude of informal economies illustrates the fact that every country faces a huge economic challenge -- the need to expand their national economies at a rate fast enough to provide for their own population growth, or to reduce substantially the slums and the dangers of the informal economy. This is a minimum need since it does not include the enormous demands for improvement in the quality of life among their main populations, spurred by greater recognition of the far better conditions in fully developed countries. It is not a foregone conclusion that this huge demand can be satisfied. In Jakarta, the capitol of Indonesia for example, the city population has increased almost 20 fold since 1920, and has now reached 17 million people and over 20 million if near suburbs are included. Another kind of reality is the increasing participation of women in urban migration patterns, and in many countries in addition to Jakarta. Many women use their housekeeping and home making skills to start their own work relationships, or even to own their own businesses in such arenas as domestic services, child care, food preparation, laundry and dry cleaning and elderly care. Also, young women are favored in many commercial and light manufacturing facilities where they are seen as more efficient, more dexterous, less contentious – and willing to work for less money.

Africa has been and still is predominantly a rural population, but the fact is that the future of the continent is now in its cities. Cities tend to become overwhelmingly the center of everything; of the economy, of the government, of the ebb and flow of money, and as the dictator of national life. Today, perhaps half of Africa's population professes Islam, but as the colonial powers left, the newly independent countries set up secular governments, often with a heavy adoption of State Socialist policy. But Islamic interpretations of the world are largely antithetical to governments, and to secularism in general. Also, many countries have experienced horribly corrosive wars, revolutions, insurrections, coups d'etat and rampant terrorism. Finally, many have an older powerful undercurrent of clans and tribalism that retains relevance and tends to resist intrusive centrist government. These tribal interests are source of stubborn resistance to government authority, and the source of serious conflicts between tribes.

African cities found themselves without the kind of economic elements that would allow them to support the flood of people who were coming to the cities. In the past, national exports were usually natural resources such as gold, copper, iron or agricultural products such as cotton, coffee, wood products, or fish and fruits. In order for cities to survive, there had to be intensive development of manufacturing or commerce, and so during the period since the 1960s, most governments have turned to a policy of encouraging manufacturing, both through private companies and through State Owned Enterprises (SOE). As usual, funds for such development was initially gouged out of the hides of farmers, and false policies of import substitution were widely adopted to protect (the inefficiency of) local producers. Governments mistakenly believed that they could stem the tide of rural populations coming to the cities, and they tried a variety of means of doing so: the requirement for a written permit from the police; limits on terms of work; deliberately low wages, denial of public services; denial of places to live; even the denial of water supplies. But almost universally, the growth of urban populations simply overpowered these measures.

While education systems have become somewhat better, over a long period, graduates have had serious difficulty finding jobs that take advantage of their knowledge and talent, and one of the great problems of these underpowered economies is the widespread underemployment of the workforce. Many governments took large numbers of young people into government agencies or in SOEs, and the degree of employment redundancy can be as high as 40% of an organization's total workforce. In addition, the competition for jobs has led to widespread nepotism, preferment, tribal loyalties, and simple corruption.

Urban labor continues to be gender divided, even when they are better than the practices in the countryside. Urban job opportunities are severely limited for women for several reasons: they tend to get less education; they are diverted for child bearing and rearing; they must counter a cultural prejudice that men are "the breadwinners" and thus are entitled to first preference for jobs.

Rural Life: Victims Of Governments: Taxes, Subsidies and Votes

The most notable land reform program in history was probably the Soviet conversion of all farming into collectives; a form of organization in which the government owned the land itself and most of the equipment, and the management of the collective was provided by politically appointed collective managers. The land was worked on a communal basis, and the profits, if any, were shared out at the discretion of the management. This collective farm system was widely adopted by governments around the world, and was both a political and an economic disaster. Some countries such as Poland and Bulgaria are now benefiting from the fact that they never took this course. China and Vietnam failed their people by employing massive programs of collectivism and communes, even when they should have known better. Modern Venezuela has moved along this path despite the overwhelming evidence of its failure. Decades were wasted until these governments finally faced up to their mistakes, and they are now weaseling out from under their own political collective ownership at the local government level.

In the late 19th and first half of the 20th centuries, several great tides of expansion and development of agriculture had emerged. The first was the urgent desire was to strengthen the agricultural sector of each national economy through expansion, research, mechanization, and improved farm techniques. Enormous advances were made in farming itself: in planting and harvesting techniques, irrigation, land reclamation, mechanization, soil conservation, research, education, pesticides, insecticides, and fertilizers. Government assistance was highly popular and prevalent through crop loans, crop insurance, home ownership assistance and so on.

The second tide occurring around the world was urban migration, driven in part by the poverty of the countryside, and in part by the creation of new jobs and a far broader range of opportunities in cities. But in countries like the United States and Japan, these two tides reinforced each other. Industrialization demanded a greater urban workforce, and better farming released workers to the cities without reducing food production. Equally powerful was another tide -- the conversion of the small family farming into larger consolidated holdings, with a similar consolidation taking place among the processors resulting in what is now called agribusiness. Despite huge public subsidies, the growing and harvesting of crops remains a marginal economic sector in most national economies, and there is the growing realization that the beneficiaries of government subsidies have increasingly been the large agribusiness corporations. But governments are more likely to see rural areas as the source of populist votes.

The Triumph of Agribusiness

Farming is universal and is still found in almost all countries. Until the latter part of the 20th century, the bulk of the population still lived on farms or in rural areas, and this remains true now in less developed countries. But in China for example, for the first time in its history, more that 50% of the population how lives in urban areas.

While government policy is focused on "the poor farmer", the reality is that the whole agriculture sector has been moving toward agribusiness because of the economics of the industry. This kind of intensive and specialized farming requires larger capital investment – millions of dollars – and such demands drive out small farming everywhere.

Despite the fact that there are fewer farms and fewer farmers, overall food production has soared. Much of the increase is attributable to research and technology: newer seeds, better farming techniques, concentration on highest productivity lands, better fertilizers, and better herbicides and insecticides. One of the tragedies of food production is that, in developing countries there are still food shortages largely attributed to failed government policies. Governments have failed to assist their farmers in understanding and adopting modern farming techniques. Thus, local agriculture is inefficient and in many cases, food must be imported. But some of these countries are so poor that even the cost of food can scarcely be afforded. It is outrageous to recognize that often corruption and mismanagement dissipates the money that might have gone for food, and oppresses large numbers of people. It is not just that enough food can't be produced, but that the related functions of food processing, transportation and distribution are also neglected, leaving valuable food rotting in the fields, storage facilities, or on the street. Also, as the farm base has changed and shrunk, it has produced a kind of collateral revolution in small towns, and small supporting businesses that were designed to serve large rural populations.

CASE STUDY: AGRICULTURE IN AFRICA

It is absolutely amazing to realize the degree to which governments around the world have oppressed and neglected their rural populations. Almost every country has had heavy majorities of their citizens living on farms and in small villages, and there are still many where the rural population runs from 70-80%. While cities are growing, many of their residents are one generation or less removed from the farm. In a sense, "they" are "us." Yet country after country has a history of harsh treatment of their rural populations, and in no place is this truer than on the continent of Africa. Many African governments have deliberately sucked as much money as possible from the rural population in order to finance the expansion of cities or the industrial base of the country. There are dozens of cases where, when it is possible for a country to improve social services such as education or health care, the money is spent on the cities, and the rural world is deliberately neglected. In many less developed countries (LDC) the conflict between rural and urban interests is still sharp and divisive; and it is still true that the farmer is usually the loser. For example, in the 70's and 80's, the People's Republic of China began its drive toward economic development by using their command and control authorities to squeeze the farmers – who represented most of the population. How did they squeeze? By over-taxation and under-investment, and the deliberate unwillingness to provide even crucial social services. Funds were extracted from rural areas to finance new industrial development. Rural areas lack roads and transportation, electricity, communications, and healthy water sources. Almost nowhere do skimpy pension systems extend to the rural areas. Bank loans are hard to get, and taxes are inordinately and deliberately high. Governments never hesitate to seize land for economic development, and farmers or villagers are lucky if they see any compensation. The quality of government management is usually distressingly bad; leadership is incompetent, corruption is universal, the police are greedy, the bureaucrats are petty tyrants enforcing what seems like thousands of rules and regulations. Above all, governments use this power of regulation to enforce a system of price controls, largely through marketing boards, which underpay farmers for their produce in order to subsidize urban residents and enrich the regime's friends.

One of the consequences of this outrage is that farming is so unrewarding that agricultural production has actually declined in many countries. For example, George B. N. Ayittey reported that, in Africa, "Food production per capita has declined steadily over the decades after Independence in the 1960s, continuing well into the 90s. For example, with 1989-1991 as the base year, the World Bank food production per capita Index for Africa was 105 in 1980, but 92 for 1997. Countries such as Kenya, Malawi, Nigeria, Sierra Leone and Zimbabwe that were self sufficient now face sharp escalation in their food import bills." (32)

As a result, there is a real threat of the rise of hunger on the continent. Again to quote Ayittey, "In September 2001, the International Food Policy Research Institute released a report that stated 'The study concludes that, without massive investment in irrigation, roads to take the harvest to market, and crop research, Africa might have 49 million malnourished children by 2020 – a rise of 50 percent. African governments would need to invest $133 billion over the next 20 years to avert the predicted sharp rise in malnutrition.'" This kind of highly sophisticated program has never been undertaken by any African government, and it is highly doubtful that they have the will and the skill to do so now.

Meanwhile, the food gap has been increasingly been filled by expensive food imports, which rose between 1988 and 1997 by a startling 65 percent ($8.9 billion to $14.7 billion). By 2000, the cost had risen to almost $19 billion. African nations remain too dependent on primary commodities, mainly cotton, coffee, cocoa, and copper for which there is little domestic demand. Exports of these basics count for 90-95% of all exports. The exceptions are some countries in N. Africa, plus Nigeria and Chad which are oil producers. But there is growing competition in these commodities, mostly in other LDCs. Coffee production has expanded in Indonesia, Columbia and Vietnam in addition to the traditional coffee growers such as Brazil and Columbia. In cocoa, the competition comes from Indonesia and Malaysia. It is now likely that, in Nigeria, Brazilian pineapples will cost less that native grown fruit because of inefficient production and distribution. The deteriorating export trade reduces government revenues, costs jobs, and reduces attractiveness for foreign investors. Banking, finance, insurance, transport -- all are oriented toward export business. The failures of economic development and provision of adequate social services directly reflect an appalling lack of national leadership in country after country. Studies conducted by the World Bank indicate that only about 15% of Africans live in states having any serious potential for economic growth. At least 45% of Africans live in poverty now, and the depth of such poverty is almost unfathomable. If sub Saharan Africa could somehow miraculously achieve and sustain a growth rate of 6-7%, it would still only cut the gap between them and moderately developed countries by 50% over the next 15 years. Instead, that gap continues to grow, and sub Saharan African countries are all near the bottom of almost every measure of social welfare.

The World Bank first advocated and then later abandoned two failed policies: import substitution and expansion of primary products. The failure of these economic approaches is evident in the fact that most of the African countries have not successfully achieved much diversification or reliable growth. Most are still stuck in an import substitution mode, and populist motives for developing high employment but low value types of industry. Import substitution was reinforced by policies for regional self reliance through various regional economic organizations. But preferential trading blocs have not worked, here or elsewhere. After 20 years of existence, these communities remain a very small share of total trade, usually less than 10%. In fact, preferential trade blocs have collapsed or stalled everywhere in the developing world. They tend to be protectionist, suspicious of foreign investment, still too small in terms of market size for most commodities, and likely to be used to justify government control of inputs and outputs. Most are heavily subsidized.

Much of the political rhetoric coming from various sources tends to put the blame for much of this economic dilemma on the World Bank and IMF for insisting on structural reforms, and on the developed world generally for not supplying adequate levels of financial aid. Yet the fact is that, while developed countries provide about $55-60 billion dollars of aid per year with about 20% of it going to sub Saharan Africa, it is estimated that lost trade revenues stemming from poor economic policies amount to about $700 billion. External aid, even if substantially increased could never have the same impact as trade development and promotion. Nor is it possible to estimate accurately the negative impact of corrosive government corruption which misallocates scarce funds, reduces government program effectiveness, ruins the national reputation, and outrages citizens. It is sad but true: crime does pay, and many people see corruption as perfectly acceptable and understandable, and preferable to a wrong headed, indifferent and badly managed government.

It is hard to escape the conclusion that sub Saharan African leadership has failed repeatedly and disastrously in their economic development responsibilities, and that this failure is a form of oppression. Domestic producers are being shown up to be less productive and competitive than foreign producers. Sub Saharan Africa cannot even feed itself, and the penetrations of foreign competitors is in large part a recognition that domestic food production can't defend itself from external competition. It is also true that, where governments seek to protect local producers against lower priced foreign goods it finds itself defending weakness and it is depriving local consumers of access to cheaper and usually better imported products. The causes of local failure are many, and most of them go right back into government failures. For example, the lack of transportation facilities such as farm to market roads makes movement of goods too slow and two expensive. It has also contributed to the lack of development of food processing plants and export shipment facilities, both of which depend heavily on rapid, cheap transportation.

Africa's share of world agricultural exports has fallen drastically from about 8% of the world total to about 2%. In addition, total domestic farm output has actually declined despite heavy government subsidies. Since 1965 (the time frame for most colonial liberation) cultivated land has fallen by 40%, and the sub Saharan area has become a net importer of food. In the critical period of the 70's and early 80's, when other countries were modernizing their agriculture sectors, Africa failed to respond. During this period global per capita farm output grew by 25%, but output in Africa fell by 14%. African nations seem unable to adopt the kinds of improvements in farming methods, and the introduction of new varieties of crops that have been successfully mastered in Latin America and parts of China, India and other Asian countries. There is the additional concern that African nations are doing little to stem the degradation of much of their best land, even though techniques for land preservation and soil conservation are known, tested, and relatively inexpensive. Thus, Africa is hurting itself, by its lack of professionalism in agriculture. And this is true even without the notorious interventions of wars, revolutions, terrorism, and genocide and property destruction characterizing the region for more than 50 years. So what have African governments been doing? Fighting wars and creating oppressive and terrorist governance.

In almost every country, public policy remains locked in obsolete concepts of what the agriculture sector of the economy is. This lock-in is largely political and highly pathological. But government supports for farming in many countries including the United States have often proved to be subsidies for big agribusiness, or exercises in expensive vote buying. For example, tax breaks justified to help the small farmer have been snapped up and far more extensively used by agribusiness to the point that highly profitable companies pay little or no taxes, and the small farmer actually gets little or nothing. Bitterly, most governments know this – and couldn't care less.

Drastic changes in farm policy are needed in most countries. Subsidies to large agribusinesses are unwarranted and should be avoided. Farming must be shifted from government subsidy to a market based and market driven economy. But in many LDCs the conflict between rural and urban interests is still sharp and divisive;

and it is still true that the farmer is usually the loser. Land reform was only one of many techniques by which authoritarian governments sought to milk money from the agricultural sector of the economy. Crop price supports were common, distorting both the domestic markets, and the prices of crops in international trade, but yielding a lot of political support in the cities. Governments relied heavily on price controls to skew the costs of production, distribution and processing. In many countries, the government itself insisted on being the main purchaser and distributor of agricultural products through government purchasing and selling agencies, so naturally these organizations became profitable sources of corruption. Import controls were used in an attempt to protect domestic production, but at high cost to consumers

Rural Development

In corrupt and incompetent governments around the world the pattern remains to neglect rural areas in favor of cities, and to overtax the peasantry to finance economic development elsewhere. These countries may now begin to invest in rural development, and there finally some growing emphasis on making sure that government programs are available in rural communities: education, health care, social services, community services, and others. There is also an effort to pay more attention to rural community revitalization. Rural/small town communities themselves are taking such steps, whether the national government participates or not. There is a deliberate effort to sweep away the vestiges of the old Socialist communes and collective farms in favor of the development of rural cooperatives for everything from equipment sharing, to volume discounts on purchases of seeds, marketing cooperatives, and community development projects. This appears to be a real success and is a pattern that can be made to apply in any country.

Rural Economic Dilemmas

In an area where almost 75% of the population lives on farms or in small villages, why can't this huge area even feed itself, much less export for profit? Why do Africans pay relatively more for the food they consume? To begin with, African agriculture functions remarkably close to marginal subsistence. African farmers are the poorest in the world, and they seem to be losing ground. Since 1965, all trends are down: 40% less land is under cultivation; the land itself is degrading and becoming less productive; governments are reducing their expenditures on the agricultural sector; foreign aid to African farmers dropped by 50%. At the same time, agricultural production in other parts of the world, including other Less Developed Countries (LDC) has been constantly improving and being more productive, and thus Africa is falling further behind its competition. In the ten year period from 1972 to 1982, global agricultural output per capita was rising by 25%, but it was falling by 14% in Africa. These growing disparities are so serious that Africa may never be able to recoup its lost ground. Nor has the political leadership shown any wisdom. One official of the New Partnership for Africa's Development (NEPAD) said "Significant poverty reduction will not be possible in Africa without rapid agricultural growth. Only improved agricultural productivity can simultaneously improve welfare among the two thirds of Africans who work primarily in agriculture, as well as the urban poor, who spend over 60% of their budget on food staples." (16) But this desirable statement was not made until 2003 rather than in 1965. Almost 40 years have passed since the independence period for most African countries, and agriculture seems worse off than it has ever been. African governments that neglect these crucial tides through indifference or failure to understand are guilty of severe national oppression.

Ghana's woes are a case in point. It isn't that the country can't grow fine food products, but that they don't seem to know what to do next. There is a great gap in the industrial facilities to process these foods. Pineapples are plentiful in Ghana and of very good quality, but there is virtually no way to process them. There is also no effective means for distributing pineapples in the country, with farmers either trying to hasten them to cities or sell them in roadside stands before they rot. But the farm-to-market roads are poor, there are far too few trucks, gasoline is too expensive -- and 40% of the crops are lost. Because so many farmers are attempting to sell their pineapples at the same time, the glut drives down local prices, and the inability to process and export means the missed opportunity to sell at far higher profits in Europe or elsewhere. The same pattern seems to be true for coconuts and other crops.

For most of the last hundred years, the most important crop in Ghana has been cocoa which involved about 50% of all cultivated land and created almost 60% of its export earnings. But cocoa production is down, and it appears that the government itself has been the principle cause of the decline. When Kwame Nkrumah became the country's first president at the time of independence from the British in 1957, he nationalized the cocoa crop and instituted a policy in which cocoa could only be sold to the government at government fixed prices. Even very sophisticated governments such as Japan or the former Soviet Union have botched up such controlled market approaches. In Ghana, even had the government been sincere it would have had difficulties, but in fact the government was corrupt in the old fashioned way. It fixed the price paid to farmers at about one half of the world market price, then sold products at world prices and pocketed the profits. Some of the money went to questionable development schemes (some of which were famous failures), and some of it simply disappeared. While Nkrumah was removed in a military coup in 1966, the new military dictatorship knew a good thing when they saw it and kept cocoa market controls. But the long stretch of the unrealistically low prices (down to 10% of world prices!) destroyed much of the incentive to grow the crop, and production fell to new lows. In fact, price controls generally were so bad that they caused foreign competitors to enter Ghana's domestic market where they could sell more cheaply than the natives. Ghana consumers can eat chickens from Brazil, rice from the Far East, canned goods from Europe, and even – ultimate insult – chocolate from Indonesia. In every instance, foreign producers are much more efficient that those in Ghana. In 2003, the current government began making some initial moves to increase farm prices, but 46 years of damage to agriculture cannot be overcome by a few bonuses.

One vital reform still has to be faced up to. The government owns most of the land, and it is really controlled by tribal authorities in each area, so that farmers cannot use the land as security for loans. Private ownership comes up against ancient tribal forms of governance. Similarly, transport remains very rudimentary, and will be expensive to upgrade. Nor does Ghana seem able to capitalize on the use of new varieties of crops and better farming methods that energized agriculture in Latin America and parts of India 50 years ago.

In case after case, destructive armed conflicts have wreaked havoc on agricultural systems. In African countries such as Egypt, Sudan, South Sudan, Uganda, Kenya, Tanzania and Zaire there have been highly destructive conflicts that destroyed existing capabilities, scared off investors, reduced economic development, destroyed social services, shattered human wellbeing and wasted huge sums of scarce funds. In Sudan for example, almost since independence in 1956, there has been a constant series of conflicts between the government in Khartoum, Christian/Animists in the southern part of the country, and between the government and the western province of Darfur which is almost totally agricultural. The results, after 50 years, is the universal deterioration of public facilities of all kinds, an economy that has been seriously damaged, tens of thousands of people killed, injured or displaced and forced to leave their farms and homes and, ultimately, a long and vicious civil war. According to the National Geographic (2007), "under the stress of civil war, the water infrastructure has crumbled. At least one third of existing waterworks, such as hand pumps, water yards and "hafirs" (small ponds used for irrigation and watering livestock) in the region are broken. Water, potable and otherwise is in desperately short supply. Only 40% of the rural population has access to any clean water. Homes may be miles from the nearest remaining water source. Water distribution systems such as water pipelines and indoor plumbing are nearly non existent in places like the Nuba Mountains, where more than 600,000 people were displaced by the fighting of the civil war." (34)

India: The Complex World of Village Life

Village life in India has evolved over centuries into an enormous and infinitely complex kaleidoscope of life on farms and in villages. This life is far broader than the issues of agriculture as a sector of the economy. Two thirds of the national population, or about 750 million people depend on this rural/village/small town world for their livelihoods, including about 240 million who are classified as rural poor. Farms are small, poor and inefficient. They average only about 2.5 acres, yet they support huge numbers of unemployed and underemployed workers earning $1.3 dollars/day.

The reaction of the government of India is typical. Their farms and villages are the great enduring bastions of the old traditions. But as farms have been getting smaller and as costs have risen, the government's response has been to fill the gap with expensive government subsidies which are politically popular but create as serious overload of the government's budget and did little to raise agricultural productivity. Subsidies include irrigation, water, power, fuel, seeds, fertilizers, insecticides. But in typical Indian fashion, these subsidies end up enriching the wealthiest large scale farmers and business people, and the truly poor tend to get frozen out. It seems clear that the political leadership does not want to deal with the rural population in social assistance terms, but prefers to see them as reservoirs of votes that can be lured or bought. There is far too little connection between Indian national economic growth, and the efforts and resources devoted to upgrade lives in rural areas.

Despite these agricultural subsidies, the government of India has also been involved in large and expensive programs to subsidize the cost of food for the consumers. But the results as so weak that Amarta Sen, the Nobel Prize winning economist asks: 'Why is it that large expenditures on food subsidy do not achieve more in reducing undernourishment? The answer centers around the fact that the food subsidy program is really aimed at keeping food prices paid to producers high, but the producers that benefit are large farmers and agribusiness enterprises. Thus, small farmers benefit little, and consumers of food actually pay more. Meanwhile, there is the cost of a big staff of government employees to manage the system." (34)

In truth, the richer states in India have no interest whatever in dealing with their agriculture sector. There is no connectivity between the increasing wealth in the industrial sector, and lagging agricultural sector. Strangely, for a country that remains predominantly rural, there has never been a conscious, consistent, substantial strategy to increase agricultural productivity, build up non-agricultural employment in rural areas, or to find ways to enhance rural quality of life. Also strangely, there are government policies that still maintain heavy restraints on the exportation of agricultural products which reduces rural incomes and hurts the health of the whole economy.

CASE STUDY: JAPANESE POLITICAL SUBSIDIES

The whole history of the agricultural sector of Japan is one of unreal policies driven by bad politics. In this sense, it is no better or worse than the experience of the United States or the European Union and thus it can stand as an illuminating lesson about the fine arts of government subsidy.

After WW II, the Japanese government developed an almost morbid fear that somehow Japan could never get enough food and thus there emerged an urgent public policy purported to guarantee the wellbeing of farm families and to maintain the food supply of the nation. The government got itself committed to a whole series of policies and programs aimed at protecting the agricultural sector. The keystone of these policies was a broad range of crop price supports and subsidies aimed at maintaining farmer incomes. But as in the United States, these programs took the farm sector farther and farther away from market realities, and created excessive demands on the national budget, and greater tax burdens on the other elements of Japanese society.

Thus, the basic policy of the government for most of the post WW II period has been one of "agricultural self sufficiency." The national governments of the time developed an amazing array of support and aid programs for its farming sector, most of which were defined in the Fundamental Basic Agricultural Law of 1961, and most of which are still in effect today. These programs included the following:

1. Crop price supports
2. Government direct control and marketing of many commodities such as rice, wheat, barley, and manufactured

milk products. That is, the government directly purchased all domestic supplies, and all imports, established a controlled price structure, marketed these products to users, and stored surpluses to maintain high domestic market prices.

3. Land reforms. In later years, this has taken the form of attempting to persuade landowners to "rationalize" their holdings into larger, more productive farms where economies of scale could operate.

4. Import quotas and/or tariffs on many food commodities to protect domestic producers from foreign competition.

5. Farmer education programs encouraging modern farming techniques.

6. A low income tax structure for farmers, and extremely low inheritance taxes on farm land.

7. Government financed or sponsored irrigation and land reclamation programs

8. Rural community development, including farm to market roads, village services, rural education, promotion of cooperative farm organizations to generate programs for joint land use, sharing of equipment, crop insurance, home loans and mortgage guarantees and joint financing arrangements.

9. Funding to promote agricultural mechanization, including subsidies to encourage introduction of tractors, modern farm planting and harvesting equipment, rice paddy harvesters, and better farm buildings.

10. Programs to promote shifts in crops -- especially away from rice farming and into beef and dairy cattle, vegetable crops, more wheat and pulses, and more fruits.

11. Assistance to farm families in finding non-farm jobs and the promotion of non-farm small industries in rural areas.

This essentially is everything anybody could ever think of to subsidize farmers. There is a very important political reality behind the richness of this agricultural subsidy policy. Loopholes exist for frozen foods, prepared foods, specialty items, or partially processed foods (e.g. cake mixes). Japanese markets are now full of asparagus from Taiwan, mushrooms from Canada, and pumpkins from Mexico. Many imports have sold at 50% or more under the prices for comparable domestic produce. Even so, there has been the perception that the profits of distributors and processors are excessively high, and if even more competition could be introduced into this segment of the market place, prices on most agricultural products would not be allowed to fall.

But it remains true that the rural world of Japan has long been the unshakable bastion of political support for the long ruling Liberal Democratic Party, and this garden is carefully tended, at whatever cost.

China: In and Out of Collectives

The plight of China's rural and village people has been the same for thousands of years – too many people, too little land, too little value, too many landlords and overlords – a world of neglect, abject poverty, ignorance, no hope, and no future. In the period of 1945 to 1980, the overlords of the Chinese Communist Party (CCP) gouged money out of peasants and used it as capital for industrializing China's burgeoning cities. It was not until Mao's death in 1976 that the CCP finally began to think about how to improve life in the countryside.

First and foremost, the leadership was forced to abandon key elements of Communist theory. By 1956, all land had been seized by the government and had been put into the hands of farm collectives similar to those in the USSR. These collectives were a form of control, but they were expected to be so productive that they would generate far more revenue for the government to use. Twenty years later, it was clear to everybody but the government that these collectives were a failure, and had produced little increase in either farm production or productivity. In addition, until the 1980's rural areas political control was placed under the control of political communes which were large collective groups of around 2,000 families. Communes were in turn organized into work brigades and production teams, and given control over all forms of public services. Here again, these mechanisms proved to be inefficient as providers of public services compared to a professional civil service staff. With the advent of new leadership after the death of Mao, townships began to take the place of the communes, and the management of rural affairs also became more professional and better.

But out of a total rural workforce of 350 million, only about 140 million were needed for agriculture, while another 90 million are working in villages and towns in non-agricultural work. Farmers and village people have fled to the cities by the millions upon millions, despite the serious efforts of governments to prevent the flow. The 140 million who remain in agriculture are typically under employed, underpaid, and living in abject poverty. In addition, another huge pool of about 135 million people in cities has been working in the informal economy and has also been abjectly poor. One of the real successes of modern China is the fact that, in the last 30 years, the abandonment of Communist economic theory and the shift to a market based economy has raised perhaps 200 million workers out of such abject poverty, even if they remain as "near poor."

The Consequences of Government Price Meddling

Another manifestation of the arrogance of centrist governments has been the belief that governments can control the prices of goods and services as they are created, bought and sold, and somehow keep everything cheap and affordable. Politicians ignored market reality in part out of genuine ignorance of the ways in which economies set prices, but often because they saw populist political advantage in controlling the customer price of certain goods (such as bread or rents) or they saw certain corrupt political opportunities. Low bread prices for consumers, for example, were seldom the result of great economic efficiencies, but rather the skewing of prices set for agricultural products. This might start with government pressure on suppliers of vital inputs for farmers (seed, fertilizers, equipment, and fuel) to supply these necessities at subsidized costs to the farmers, even at the risk of harm to their own enterprises. Similar pressures could be brought to bear on millers, bakers, and distributors of bread so that the customer could buy cheaply and praise their leaders. But the reality in so many cases is that the government's price structure was so low that they were confiscatory and the whole tortured system became an unnecessary form of oppression. As a consequence of these mistaken policies, farmers and processors increasingly were forced to sell their products on the black market as the only alternative to being forced out of business. In many cases, governments set up official marketing enterprises to control the acquisition and distribution of products, but most of them produced pathological results – a reduction in production, skewed allocation of scarce resources, payment of subsidies to weak and inefficient enterprises, and ultimate distrust of the government itself. Most of these marketing enterprises were clearly perceived as drab, bumbling, cost-inefficient, poorly performing and corrupt. The consequence was that the network of official state stores was empty of both goods and customers, and most of the public's needs were being met in back alley black markets which were officially illegal, meaning that the police had to be bribed. However, the political leadership displayed its usual tendency to mask such failures by paying marketing organization deficits, suppressing competition by other than state suppliers, and fiddling with the exchange rate to protect domestic suppliers. But such fiddling was often outrageously dysfunctional. The exchange rate was often overvalued, and this made exports too expensive and imports very attractive. This led to a natural tendency to seek out imports in preference to overpriced domestic products, even in the face of widely practiced import substitution policies.

There appears to have been a high degree of government use of these pathological practices all across Africa. The result has been a reduction of farmer incentives to produce in the face of disastrous price setting policies, plus a dampening of foreign donor interest in funding agricultural sector reforms. In worst cases, donors found that their money was being substituted for that of local governments instead of supplementing it.

One form of farmer assistance – agricultural credit projects – seemed always headed for disaster. All public sector credit banks in Sub-Saharan Africa had become financially insolvent by the mid-1990's, and could be sustained only by government subsidy or reluctant foreign donor funds. It is ironic to note that state banks lent money to politically favored borrowers and to agribusinesses, yet small farmers almost always demonstrated better repayment rates. In the agricultural sector as elsewhere, the lending institutions were characterized by lots of uncollectible bad loans, high operating overheads, and reputations for corruption and political connivance.

HOW GOVERNMENTS
CREATE POVERTY

The discussion of failed state owned enterprises in Section I is a compelling case in point; government preoccupation with their own massive failures over decades has squandered enormous resources that would have been better spent on "bottom up" poverty alleviation programs. The constituencies behind these massive institutions form a political barrier against money for the poor. Political resistance to structural adjustment has kept governments committed to declining industries and ineffective economic policies. An example is Venezuela where an obsessive dictatorship is far along in crippling the economy and creating a newly impoverished citizenry. To quote the Economist paper: "Venezuela's economy contracted by 29% in the first quarter (of 2003), compared to the same period last year. This spells hardship for millions of Venezuelans. According to Datanalysis, a market research firm, 72% of households say they have cut back on food; only half now eat three meals a day. Unemployment stands at 20%. Of those officially counted as employed more than half work in the informal economy. Many forecasters expect a decline of 12% or more for the year. Foreign exchange controls have choked off economic activity; black market dollars now cost 50% more than the official rate. Opponents of the regime see the official dollar shortage as a deliberate ploy (by a socialist government) to strangle Venezuela's beleaguered private sector. But what it has done is to continue Venezuela's deindustrialization, one of Mr. Chavez's main gifts to his country. Six out of ten of the manufacturing businesses in existence when the president was first elected in 1998 have since shut down, according to the industrialist's association. These shut downs are permanent and cannot easily be reversed. Thus, unemployment can be expected to get worse in the months to come. What is really perverse is that Venezuelan citizens seem not to understand what the government is doing, despite vigorous and vocal opposition in the country. Chavez continues to be popular even in death, and his successor continues to pursue these pathological policies in the face of all reason." (35)

North Korea shows an even worse pattern of poverty created by government policy. Despite recent experiments with economic reform, the country remains desperately poor. The World Food Program has targeted 6.5 million people out of total population of about 23 million as highly vulnerable, and seriously dependent on government handouts, including a ration of rice. Rigid controls on prices are now haltingly being reduced. Unemployment is being "solved" by moving large numbers of workers into farming even though all available land is already under cultivation. This retrograde movement ignores the fact that farming is stuck in the middle ages. There is almost no reliable power supply, often no fuel for tractors, and in many cases, no tractors. Ox carts are widely used, and harvests are increasingly achieved by old fashioned hand labor. Factory workers have been hard hit. Factories are few, and are largely obsolete and rusting out. There is little money available even for maintenance of these factories, much less for industrial revitalization, and the ominous nature of the regime scares away investors even from inside the country. Electrical power is so scarce that outside of the capital of Pyongyang most of the country is dark. Shortages of common use consumer articles are usual. These policies produced a famine of prodigious proportions in 1995-2000, and the country still suffers from that disaster. The government refuses to explain the catastrophe or publish data about it, but external estimates of the number of people who died range up to 3 million, and 5 to 10% or more of school children still suffer from the effects of malnutrition – vulnerability to diseases such as flu and pneumonia, slow learning, and physical weakness. The World Health Organization evaluates the health care system as weak to nonexistent. Hospitals are of very poor quality, most lacking staff, medicines and equipment, and some even lack running water or electricity. UNICEF says that the country is in a chronic state of emergency, but the regimes implacable opposition to outsiders makes it almost impossible to persuade donors to invest their funds in aid. UNICEF says that, for North Korea to get back to some form of adequate social services capacity would take a reconstruction effort comparable to that of Afghanistan or Iraq. Nobody believes that the current regime could devise such an effort; the economy is simply too deteriorated to produce the wealth needed to finance recovery, and the stubborn doctrinal pathological government shows little sign of tolerating change in any form.

These illustrations are intended to make the point that governments themselves are often the creators of the very poverty they say they want to alleviate. A rethinking of such perverse policies could rescue wasted money and permit it to be redirected to poverty alleviation. An examination of a typical government tax system reveals many ways in which profit making companies or special interest groups avoid paying taxes. If such loopholes were closed, and tax subsidies and waivers eliminated, more revenues would be generated and more funding available for poverty. Similarly, an examination of a typical government annual budget is likely to show large highly questionable commitments for the military, industry, and special interests. If poverty alleviation were made the absolute top priority of the government, it would justify challenging many of these less valuable expenditures. The use of funds to bring the informal economy into the economic main stream would add relatively modest costs that would be offset by bringing more taxes to the income stream. Re-pricing or restructuring of government goods and services programs so that expensive subsidies are eliminated would further enhance funds for poverty.

Poverty Reduction: Mission Definitely Not Impossible

There are two ways to look at the human condition, one that is optimistic and the second that is pessimistic. The optimistic view becomes visible when long term tides in the human condition are examined. In this view, poverty in absolute numbers went up steadily until about the 1980s when it began to decline. The essential cause of this decline was the reduction of poverty in China and India, which have one third of the world's 6 billion people but 60% of the world's extreme poor. Between them, they have created the most spectacular reduction of poverty in world history. According to a British scholar "On a world scale of risk the intensity and severity of poverty has fallen more sharply in the past 50 years than in the preceding one thousand years." (37) In the early 1970s, more than half the people of Asia lived in extreme poverty. That figure is now less than one third. Average life expectancy is up to 65, and 70 per cent of the people are literate. In even broader perspective, the total world population has doubled from 3 to 6 billion from 1965 to the present and it is expected to double again in the next 40 years, and yet the quality of life for billions has actually improved.

In 1900, we lived for an average of 30 years: today we live for 67 years. In 1970, 35% of all people in developing countries were starving or undernourished; this figure has declined every year since then and was down to 18% in 1996 and is about 14% today. In fact, the rate of population growth has slowed from 2.17% worldwide in 1961 to less than 1.26% in 2000, and is estimated to go below 1% in the next 15 years. There seems to be an inverse correlation between wealth and population growth. The United Nations has a classification of a "medium development" standard of living in terms of income, assets, education and health care. In 1975, 1.6 billion people met that standard; today, that number is up to 3.5 billion. Huge numbers of people are living better than their parents – and most of them are in developing countries.

To quote one observer "Global hunger is in mild retreat. An estimated eight hundred million people in the world today are malnourished, a heartbreaking figure; but this huge number is driven by population growth. The *percentage* of the globe's people who are malnourished is dropping steadily; more than a billion were malnourished just one generation ago, and now the total is smaller even though the total world population is much larger. While an estimated 9 million people worldwide (2002) died from hunger or hunger related illness, just 20 years ago, that number was 15 million. Food production has risen faster than population growth everywhere – except sub-Saharan Africa. Food prices have fallen dramatically; down 68% from 1957 to now. Total food production is way up; we grow 23% more food/ capita now than in 1961. Child mortality is strongly down, in part due to a decline in child malnourishment. Child deaths before the age of five has declined from 28 percent fifty years ago to just 10% today."(38) Worldwide, the <u>rate</u> of population growth has slowed: from 2.17% worldwide in 1961 to less than 1.26% in 2000 and it is estimated to go below 1% in the next 15 years. There seems to be an inverse correlation between wealth and population growth, and the decline in such growth is easing the pressure on national economies.

In another report, the World Bank "World Development Report: 2000/2001", the total number of people living in poverty has remained about the same from 1987 t0 1999, but very large declines have taken place in East Asia. There were 486 million in poverty in 1990, but this number was down to 279 million in 1999. A large percentage of this decline took place in China, which has achieved one of the most extraordinary reductions of poverty in human history. China's poor declined from 376 million to 222 million by 1999. In Asia excluding China, the decline was from 114 million to 57 million. Looking at world regional figures, every region of the world except Sub-Saharan Africa and Central Asia showed marked declines in the percentage of people living in poverty, and the world total shrank from 23.7% to 19.5% The South Asia region which includes India shared this decline, going from 45% in 1990 to 36.6% in 1999.

No one suggests that these advances have solved the problems of poverty in the world, but they repudiate the sense that poverty alleviation is hopeless. Nor do long term improvements help very much in the lives of the estimated 1.8 billion Asians and the millions in Africa and Latin America who are very poor.

Thus we return to the second scenario about the human condition which is a look at current reality of people in pain and governments unable or unwilling to deal effectively with the demands for social services. It is not tolerable to suggest that we can all just sit back and let the rising tides of world economic development solve the poverty problems. Instead, these broad statistics act to show that the alleviation of poverty is not impossible and that governments can and should act vigorously and across a broad front to reinforce the forces bringing about improvement. It has been said that "the poor will always be with us", and while this is undoubtedly true, it need not be taken as an excuse not to attempt to alleviate poverty. The fact is that, while all politicians speak in solemn tones about the need to deal with the problems of the poor, an astonishing number have few successful programs to do so and no serious motivations to try. Those who believe the problem to be one of greater and greater assistance from the government are no longer in the majority and most are being forced to rethink the causes for their lack of success. Even the largest and poorest countries like China and India need not consider the problem as insurmountable because many successful examples of poverty reduction are already available from which lessons can be learned. One thing that is being learned is that the pathologies of governance in the form of wars, terrorism, ethnic and religious conflict corruption and theft of public resources all descend harshly on the poor and are keeping them in poverty and pain. It is impossible to understand why governments that could do a very great deal to alleviate poverty seem unwilling or unable to mount the best possible anti-poverty programs. It now seems clear that "charity" or public subsidy is not the answer. Most countries are far too poor to ever offer adequate levels of social well being solely through government programs. Therefore the basic approach in these countries should be to recognize that people must be as self-sufficient as possible, that government policies must be deliberately designed to support this self sufficiency and that people should not be deluded into thinking that the government can provide adequate levels of assistance to all.

But the key to poverty alleviation remains economic development, and the greatest economic debate of the last 50 years since the end of WW II has been that of state socialism vs. the market tested economy, including doctrinal debates over which system produces the greatest social equity. But there are indications that are very encouraging, whatever the political system. According to a recent report "The long term global trend toward greater inequality prevailed for at least 200 years; it peaked around 1975. Since then, it has stabilized and possibly even reversed. The chief reason for the change has been the accelerated growth of two large and initially poor countries: China and India. Second, a strong correlation links increased participation in international trade and investment on the one hand and faster growth on the other. The developing world can be divided into a "globalizing" group of countries that have seen rapid increases in trade and foreign investment over the last two decades – well above the rates for rich countries – and a "non-globalizing" group that trades even less of its income than it did 20 years ago. The aggregate annual per capita growth rate or the globalizing group accelerated steadily from one percent in the 1960s to five percent in the 1990s. During that latter decade, in contrast, rich countries grew at two percent, and non-globalizers at only one percent. Economists largely agree that openness to foreign trade and investment (along with complementary reforms) explains the faster growth of the globalizers." (39)

"--- contrary to popular perception, globalization has not resulted in higher inequality within economies. Inequality has indeed gone up in some countries (such as China) and down in others (such as the Philippines). But those changes are not systematically linked to globalization measures, but stem more from domestic education, taxes and social policies. In general, higher growth rates in globalizing developing countries have translated into higher incomes for the poor. Even with greater inequality, for example, in China has seen the most spectacular reduction of poverty in world history – which was achieved by opening its economy to foreign trade and investment."

Programs to Alleviate Poverty

It is useless to debate whether social services should continue to be a government monopoly – it is clear that such a "pure" socialist approach has never proved to be much of a success and every country is moving toward a sharing between the state, the individual and the private sector. No socialist country has "cured" poverty and few have ever managed to raise their social services systems up to the level of effectiveness of free market based economies. But as reforms are considered, many services will continue to be supplied by governments, especially where personal or private sector responsibility is not a valid option, such as elementary education. There is the need in both the short run and in the longer term to retain large amounts of government funding. Even the most developed countries recognize this. Here, the trick is to add as much funding as possible, for whatever source is available, and not to get hung up on doctrinal debates. There are many hard decisions being faced. In some cases, the abandonment of the cradle to grave policy means the abandonment of many social program elements that can't be justified or afforded.

Psychologically it is difficult to return to a strategy of personal self reliance as the conceptual base for program design after decades of reliance on the government, but even the most intense socialist efforts failed to provide a social safety net that was fully adequate. Few countries even came close to the goals of universal well being guaranteed by the government. Consequently, there must be a shift in government thinking away from universal coverage to concepts of targeting on the neediest – that is, the concentration of scarce public funds on the places in society where the needs are greatest or that represent the greatest and most realistic opportunities to have real impact on the poor. This means that the concept of public programs as entitlements is being challenged, because politically many entitlement programs have become bottomless pits of expectations that will always exceed any practical capacity to be filled. This means that many forms of aid to the public are being trimmed back. Governments should provide a "no frills" safety net of social services with categorical programs based on need and not on politically popular general distributions of benefits.

This is deeply unsettling for many people and organizations that have benefited from generous programs, as witness the difficulties of France in reconsidering its 35 hour work week policy or of Germany in attempting to retrench excessive labor protections that have been driving companies out of Germany to less restrictive governments in Eastern Europe or elsewhere. Somehow, the concept of "outcome effectiveness" must be given more attention, and elements of programs that go beyond the concept of service to the neediest will have to be trimmed back. Governments get into bad habits of wasting too much precious money on the obsolete, the outmoded, the ineffective, the irrelevant, the inconsequential, the corrupted, and the just plain stupid. The political system is the problem; it needs to become the solution.

But what is the alternative? In many cases, it is for individual people to take care of themselves. The whole discussion of the informal economy is relevant to this self reliance argument. The informal economy is both a refutation of the government's ability to provide a social safety net and a valuable lesson about the ability of people to be self reliant. Further, it is legitimate for governments to expect other elements of society to bear some of the burden. This is especially true of private profit making organizations which can make the provision of social services such as heath insurance, training, unemployment protection and retirement pensions a part of a "social services" package for their employees.

Most developing countries for example are deeply locked into a health care delivery system that relies on the absolute guarantee of the centrist governments, and most of these commitments have been broken. When the State insists on providing health care for all, it usually sets out to create a state monopoly based on a stringent need for efficiency. Options and variations are seen as messy and expensive. Few such options were available and even people with some money to spend on their own health care are not always free to do so. There are negative incentives throughout such systems. Citizens tended to over-use them because they were "free". There was too little strategic targeting of services even where the need was compelling, such as pre and post natal care. As usual, there is never enough money, and since most or all of the funding came from general revenues it was usually felt that the political visibility of appearing to hold down costs counted for more than providing adequate systems funding. Professionals were poorly paid, had few opportunities for skills development, and thus generally produced low productivity. New technology was "too expensive" and its lack usually meant loss of quality of treatment. Maintenance was often neglected.

In many cases, the money that was available was wasted in poor investment decisions. Large high volume (and high visibility) hospitals were emphasized at the cost of local hospitals, outpatient clinics, and public health services. There was a tendency to create many narrow specialists, and to undervalue the generalist diagnostician.

Each specialist would seek as many patient references as possible, but the "gate keeper" doctors were constantly torn between this pressure and the pressure from management to deny treatment, and reduce expensive procedures in order to cut system costs. Purchase of more expensive diagnostic or treatment equipment simply never could get approved. The condition of most of these archaic health care systems is very sobering and most are decades away from achieving adequate health provision. Thus, each country is struggling to work out the design of some whole new national health plan and to inject some coherence and urgency into the revitalization of their systems.

Most are looking at some form of managed care which retains a high degree of government oversight and economic intervention. They find it exceedingly difficult to contemplate allowing greater entry into health care by the private sector or the element of competition between public and private provision. Yet it seems inevitable that the health care system can reach satisfactory levels only if both sectors are involved, and work together to promote system efficiency. Most governments still feel the need for price fixing and control but this is unwise. Fee-for-service is likely to take a back seat to forms of Health Maintenance Organization (HMO) approaches with the government as the ultimate overseer. It can be expected that gradually doctors will be freer to enter into private practice, small local clinics and outpatient clinics will multiply, and specialization will be used to drive quality. There is no reason why all forms of technical services cannot immediately become competitive.

Money is hard to obtain for financing government programs, especially in developing countries, but if the alleviation of poverty were seriously to be designated as a nation's number one priority, the necessary funds could in fact be found. After all, money has been found for useless armies, state owned enterprises that run deficits, executive jets for government officials, and an infinite variety of graft and corruption. Why do governments not make the alleviation of poverty their top priority? All of them say that they do, but the facts in many countries do no show such results. In some instances national leadership gives up, decides that poverty can't be substantially reduced, and concentrates on other things. In many countries the leadership is busy ruining the country and creating poverty. In others, leaders have simply proved bumbling and incompetent. Corruption and pathological laws and policies spend scarce funds on useless and irrelevant activities. There is no magic formula for alleviating poverty but there is a wide variety of sound approaches which, if carefully selected and persistently followed could achieve a far greater degree of alleviation than has been the case to date.

One lesson learned from the regeneration of Russia and eastern European countries is that property ownership is a compelling advantage. Not only does it give people a sense of ownership and higher motivations for improvement, but property becomes a resource for borrowing money for home and business development which is a powerful basis for self sufficiency. Governments can simply give farm property and the land and buildings of former state owned property to poor individuals for their own use. Government financed small business loans can be made cheap, easy to administer, and often profit making. The experience in repayment of such small loans is extremely good; often far better investments than lending (or giving) large sums to loss making state owned enterprises. Revolving funds have been set up so that repayments of such loans can be retained and invested in new small loans. The result is that there is little or no drain on the annual budgets of the government. Further, such small loans can help solve two other problems; first, there is a real opportunity to bring women actively into the main stream of economic activity. Women have been very successful in starting small businesses, first in areas in which they have normal homemaker skills (e. g. child care, house cleaning, laundries and seamstress services), and then as experience is gained, in a wider range, especially in consumer related ventures. Second, a small business loan program can be accompanied by more supportive recognition of the values of the informal economy, and small entrepreneurs who are running illegal businesses can be invited into the main stream and lent money to legitimize and expand their informal enterprises.

As in so many cases, the concept of decentralization of centrist public power has relevance here too. The national government is not the most advantageous place for the operation of a small business loan program and the range of such efforts can be multiplied much more quickly and effectively if based in cities and urban counties. Community loans can occur in hundreds of places, and the repayment of loans can be reinvested to maintain such programs. National governments should use whatever funds are available to start such community efforts rather than to provide direct lending to individuals.

There are also some major institutional changes that could yield funds for reprogramming. Where governments are facing up to the privatization of their SOEs, the proceeds from the sale of these enterprises could be captured and put in special protected trust funds for poverty reduction. In some cases, special development banks have been established for specific development purposes, and such a bank for poverty alleviation is very feasible and would not represent a continuing drain of the annual government budget. Many development banks have proved capable of obtaining private funding to supplement funding provided by governments. Governments are heavy spenders on large public works, and while it is hard to fault this kind of effort, such contracts are lobbied by the special interests in the construction industry, and are very sensitive to bribery, corruption and mismanagement. Perhaps some of this money would be better spent on government goods and services for the poor. Finally, there is the long standing recognition that efforts to improve the quality, knowledge and experience of the government civil service can be made to produce significant improvements in the value and effectiveness of all public programs. It is often bitterly apparent that this possibility is often deliberately neglected by a cynical political leadership claiming to want to "hold down the cost of government" by paying low salaries and benefits. This attitude is extended to opposition and neglect of staff training and development, and an unwillingness to adopt management reforms and improvements even when sound proposals are brought forth by the professionals.

In communities where the government is not able to live up to its education commitments, the private elements of the community have been willing to step into the gap. In most cases, community financing has primarily been to provide ways to meet excess demand. But community financing may also be voluntary, to create alternative forms of education. In Islamic communities there is an ancient tradition for the provision of education through the mosques but there is also a dominating bias for Islamic schools to teach religious principles and to be reluctant to deal with secular subjects that would help people obtain better jobs.

Support from the community may be in money or "in kind", including the allocation of land to generate revenue for schools. Even teachers may accept part of their pay in housing, food, or transportation. Assistance could be provided by special cooperatives or by the efforts of community organizations such as unions or social clubs. In many countries, parent-teacher organizations are really designed as fund raising organizations and will mount programs either for capital facilities or for operating funds. Many schools charge parents school fees in order to raise revenue, as well as making the parents pay for things like uniforms, books and supplies. Many communities will create special school taxes.

One of the messes inherited by successor governments in the former Soviet Union and Eastern Europe is that of housing. Where the State became the provider of housing the consequences once again were pathological. There was a chronic scarcity of places to live, and a very high proportion of constructed units were shoddy and poorly made. Soviet cities for example created vast stretches of sterile unattractive neighborhoods, lacking adequate consumer services, and suffering from a whole series of ominous government controls inhibiting the formation of social services related activities. The great advantage of state provided housing was that it was usually very cheap and often free. These advantages were offset by the fact that maintenance became very expensive and had to be borne by the tenants. Heating systems and elevators frequently broke down, plumbing was hideous, electrical wiring failed often, floors warped, windows could not be opened. The pattern of housing emphasized concentrations of cheap high rise apartments, and this in turn dictated the inconvenient allocation of schools, stores, child care facilities, and the availability of other factors such as transportation. Poor quality high rises were obviously favored for "cost effectiveness" reasons, but for the same reasons, little money was spent on amenities in or around the buildings.

Housing control was almost always accompanied by social control. The allocation of housing became a dominant concern in the assignment of people to jobs, and acted as a great deterrent to job mobility, especially between cities. If a worker found a better or higher paying job elsewhere, a job shift was possible only if the housing allocation problem could be solved. Ominously also, each multiple family unit had assigned to it one or more spies or informers to help the authorities monitor the residents. This system made little or no provision for personal desires or preferences, and all people were captives of a third rate system. Governments everywhere make poor landlords. Bureaucratic managers were remote and non-responsive. A lack of money – often deliberate - meant that maintenance and repair was hard to come by, and a lack of motivation and will meant that there was little effort to face up to social problems such as drug dealing, vandalism, or domestic violence. Individual residents of course had little motivation for caring for the property, and did so at their own expense only for necessary repairs to plumbing and electrical problems. And of course, the whole process of housing allocation and maintenance became an almost universal swamp of petty corruption, ranging from the official who allocated housing in the first place down to the janitor who had to be bribed to fix the plumbing.

Social service programs should be decentralized as much as possible to state/province and municipal levels. There is a broad professional agreement that putting the responsibility in the governments closest to the people is producing better government service. This also means that local governments must be given more direct and substantial power to tax to support these social responsibilities. There is no reason that continued funding from the central government cannot continue for some purposes, but supplemented and balanced by local tax sources. The main reason that this idea of decentralization is resisted appears to be the perverse desire of centrist politicians and bureaucrats to hold on to the power.

Decentralization also means the movement of some forms of social services from governments to the private sector. In those governments where state owned enterprises were prevalent, the sell-off of SOEs required that the social services that they had provided had to become the responsibility of local governments, except those services that the private companies should continue such as health care, unemployment compensation and retirement benefits for their own employees. But the major concerns here are two fold. First is whether the government (or the people) can make the private sector accept and live up to social services commitments since most might prefer to dodge the whole issue. The second is the ability of local units of government to face up to their new responsibilities for general and wide spread social services provision.

Section Four

Pathological Economics

The most important role of governments in the world today is to deal with the state of their national economies. Of the 201 countries in the world, perhaps fifty of them are facing some form of serious economic dilemma and most of the rest face major challenges to keep their economies up with the demands placed on them. After the fall of the U. S. S. R. the 15 nations that emerged and the countries of the former Soviet bloc in Eastern Europe are all struggling to abandon their soviet style governments and economies and accommodate to a "market tested economy" that few of them seemed initially to understand. Most of the nations of Sub Saharan Africa have economies that are so weak that they are scarcely able to support even basic public services, especially where tyrannical and incompetent governments are mired in wars, rebellions and the incursions of terrorist war lords. In the Far East, China, India, Vietnam and other state socialist governments are also being forced to abandon much of their socialist economies and retreat slowly and reluctantly into some form of market economy. Armed conflicts in a score of countries are destroying what little economic advancement has been achieved. Thus, economic development is seriously constrained by terrorism and State oppression.

Unfortunately, these realities come at a time when the more developed countries of the world are evolving into a complex new "globalization" world which widens the gap between developed and less developed economies. A large part of this greater complexity relates to the ability to absorb new technologies, and to shift the economy of a country away from low value economic activities to those that produce a higher rate of wealth generation.

It is not easy for government leaders, especially in former state socialist countries to understand these emerging powerful economic trends. According to one commenter, "There is an overwhelming propensity for the leadership, when confronted by poor results, to do the same things only harder. It is very difficult to challenge the premises behind present strategy, and the tendency is simply to repeat the thinking that is now in disrepute. The evaluations and judgments that inform action are automatic, highly abstract and inferential. It is frightening how quickly individuals will jump to such judgments as if they were concrete and self obvious conclusions. And the political interpreter of events is almost always captured by the obvious, as reflected by reactionary clientele." (40)

Perhaps the greatest movement in governments in the present world is the decline of the great tide of state socialism which has been the predominant form of government in the world. No other form of government has even come close. Socialist government came in many manifestations. A total of about 28 countries with a total population of approximately 375 million people with highly diverse cultural, ethnic, religious and economic circumstances were ruled under some form of "Soviet style" government. And when the USSR itself broke up, 15 new countries emerged, all of which are attempting to shed their Socialist past. Many other countries which were neither communist nor officially socialist were in fact heavily socialist in character, with the Soviet model as their frame of reference. Think for example of such diverse countries as India, Argentina, many in sub-Saharan Africa, and even New Zealand.

While the numbers and purity of socialist governments is declining, that does not mean that socialism is dead as a political force. What is happening is that former socialist regimes are seeking new combinations of more open and market tested economies with retained social programs continuing heavy government support and protection. Such "semi-socialist" states or "social socialist" states vary across a broad range of experimentation and are very much works in progress. Many are being limited not by doctrine but because of the growing realization that added taxation to support the former "cradle to grave" social program commitments simply could not be brought off, in part because economies were not strong enough, but increasingly because of a rising tide of citizen tax resistance.

One of the collateral elements of the post-war rise of socialism and the commitments to state owned enterprises was the condemnation of capitalism and national private corporate enterprise. Philosophically, the two were linked. That is, the real and imagined failures of the private sector were used to justify the need for the expansion of the public sector in the form of state owned enterprises which were given control of production assets that might have been private. This commitment to public ownership and control was then used to argue against the need for government support of the private sector, and indeed to justify high levels of private sector taxation and economic regulation. Finally, the growth of the state owned enterprises justified high levels of citizen taxation, since socialist governments needed to finance industrial development in addition to the traditional commitments for public infrastructure and services.

The primary justification for the expansion of State Socialism was the concept of governments willing and able to provide all or most of the principal needs of citizens -- the idea of "cradle to grave" social safety net. This concept meant not only the absorption by the state of much of the production elements of the economy, but a similar assumption by the state of most health, education, and welfare delivery systems previously provided by individuals for themselves, or through private sector mechanisms. There was never any doubt about the urgency of citizen need. There had been failures in the capitalist system in terms of providing for the poor, for excess unemployment, and for lack of provision of adequate public facilities. But most socialist governments predicated that the capitalist system was irreparable, and that sufficient levels of public revenue could never be achieved unless the government itself seized the sources of wealth and extracted a larger share of them for public purposes to finance the admittedly huge costs of its cradle to grave program commitments. This meant that, during the expansion of socialism, higher levels of taxation were justified and tax systems were extensively changed to contain elements of redistribution of wealth -- but not directly from the rich to the poor, but from private sources to public treasuries and ministries as the intermediaries in their redistribution into public programs and state owned enterprises.

The nature of the perceived threats from the private sector has not changed:

* The fear that it will grow so powerful that it can dominate countries and societies; and lately, through the "global economy", the whole world.

* The fear that their power cannot be curbed by any force -- even governments. The whole argument of the global economy adds to this fear; it is felt that governments can't come to grips with powerful corporations beyond their own jurisdictions, or that governments, in attempting to become global themselves, will also become too powerful. Thus, all of the fears of big government and big business are multiplied by the "world scale" argument.

* The concern that big corporations may be competitive among themselves, but will be anti-competitive in relation to individuals. These kinds of concerns are made much more serious by all of the trumpeting of the "global economy" and the current wave of corporate consolidations.

* The fear that super corporations will be able to frustrate environmental protections, and that they will dissipate earth's natural resources.

* The presumption that corporations will not help the poor, and will be able to limit their tax payments to government through their economic power, leaving governments with all of the high risk, high cost societal obligations while avoiding their fair share of both obligations and costs.

* The concern that the private sector will increasingly become bi-level or even tri-level; a level of huge extremely rich and powerful global corporations; a next layer of smaller, struggling private enterprises trying to avoid being crushed by the powerful; and a third highly marginalized level of the "informal economy".

But at the same time, there are remarkable changes taking place in how wealth is generated. Land is no longer the main source of wealth, and the main source of power and influence, as it has been for a landed gentry. Control of land is no longer the way to have a grip on people. Then, for a hundred years, manufacturing became the paramount generator of wealth, but for the last 20-30 years, in the most developed countries, there has been a shift from a manufacturing economy to a service economy. Fixed industrial facilities are no longer the place where most people work, and thus they are no longer so much at the mercy of the factory owners. Nor do people derive as much benefit from organized labor unions. Today's economies are far more diverse, much more flexible, very mobile, very demanding for workers with more education, and very responsive to individual motivations in the workplace.

The sad case of Cuba is a continuing reminder of when socialist economics fail. The average salary in Cuba is less than $20 per month. The economy remains under direct government control, despite some loosening around the edges. As an example of the consequences of Cuba's distorted economy, the Economist reported that "cars can only be bought through state-owned enterprises, all cost a fortune. A 2013 Peugeot 508, marketed in Europe as an affordable saloon car costing around $30,000 has a price tag of more than a quarter of a million dollars at a rundown showroom in Havana. A Chinese Geely car, with more than 50,000 on the clock is on sale for around $30,000." These costs are laughable and suggest that the whole thing is just a weak attempt to pretend that Cubans can buy new cars. All businesses must be approved by the government. No occupation of line of work can exist unless listed by the government. So thousands of entrepreneurs and individuals have become very inventive about how to subvert their own government, and smuggling is a growth industry." (41) President Obama's restoration of diplomatic relations with Cuba may dislodge some of the old failed structures and open up more potential for the Cuban people to rid themselves of their obsolete governing apparatus.

In Milosevic's Serbia in the 80's, banks were state owned and controlled and were a powerful instruments in exercising criminal control. Subsidized loans were made to political favorites, and denied to any borrower who was in disfavor with the central clique. Often, even these highly subsidized loans were simply never paid back, and were used by the borrowers to buy up other national assets. These false loans were, of course, perfectly legal but totally pathological. Bank officials were so corrupt that the credibility of the banking system as a whole was all but destroyed. Limited amounts of money available in the country were diverted from legitimate to corrupt activities and denied to those who might have used them to improve a desperately bad economy. The corruption was so bad that whole segments of the economy simply wasted away. Businesses and individual citizens kept out of the formal funding channels of the state owned enterprises because they were so corrupt, and falling into the clutches of government organizations could be actively dangerous. Foreign investment withered as well, since it was a dead certainty that investments would be either wasted, or stolen or diverted to further enrich the already bloated corrupt elite. Much of the Serbian economy remained in the hands of the state owned enterprises which were not only highly corrupt but totally inefficient and deteriorating. Usually, their reputation was that of delivering inferior goods at excessive prices. It was fruitless to think that any of these SOEs could ever be brought up to a level of effectiveness that would allow them to compete in the international economy.

Economic Oppression

The United States government officially designates governments which it determines are state sponsors of terrorism, and it authorizes the imposition of penalties of various types against these countries. These sanctions are:

1. A ban on arms related exports and sales.
2. Congressional approval is required for the U. S. export of any dual-use items that could significantly enhance the terrorist-list country's military capability or its ability to support terrorism, either domestic or international.
3. Prohibitions on economic assistance to these countries.

4. Official U. S. opposition to loans by the World Bank or other international financial institutions.
5. Allowing families of the victims of terrorism to file civil law suits in the U. S.
6. Denying companies and individuals of tax credits for income earned in terrorist-listed countries.
7. Denial of duty-free treatment of goods exported into the U. S.
8. Giving the Treasury Department authority to grant, or deny licenses for U. S. citizens to engage in a financial transaction with a terrorist-list government.
9. Prohibition against the award of any DOD contract in excess of $100,000 to any company controlled by terrorist-listed states.

International organizations such as the World Bank, the International Monetary Fund, the United Nations, the European Union and the Association of Southeast Asian Nations have initiated dozens of counter measures to try and deal with these monumental problems. In each of the 58 countries dealt with in this book, all have deliberately chosen to engage in acts of oppression and terrorism against their own citizens and in the broader world. In these countries, there are many forms of opposition to centrist tyranny, but the difficulties in ousting or even successfully opposing these tyrants are staggering. One of the most hopeful courses of action, as advocated by these international organizations is to work along the lines of changing the nature of the economy and the degree to which a central elite can control the whole economy. The need for such structural adjustment is almost always critical. Whether it can be accomplished in any specific country is a matter of politics and of economic policy.

The World Bank has attempted to define what it considers to be the basic essential elements of any national program for structural adjustment, including the following:

1. Control of inflation, strong central bank, a tight money supply.
2. Concentration of the developing country's strategy for economic development on export development (not import substitution).

3. Limit borrowing only for economic development purposes, not financing of day-to-day government operations. A key mandate is that international debts must be honored and gradually paid off, but loans can be refinanced or even forgiven if "adequate" structural adjustment progress is being made.

4. Bring all prices into line with market reality – wages, consumer goods, industrial transfers, financing of state enterprises.

5. Reduce trade barriers to a minimum.

6. Eliminate redundancy in the labor force, particularly in government agencies and in state owned enterprises.

7. Privatization: the sell-off of many/most state enterprise, unless economically justified.

8. Environmental sustainability.

9. Major improvements in education and training.

Economically underdeveloped countries have tended to pursue policies that subsidize the local economy with heavy reliance on many of the centrist policies of Socialist economics, government creation and/or support of local companies, and the establishment of State Owned Enterprises to fill economic gaps in the national economic structure.

When developing countries fall into economic trouble, it has almost always also involved short term international debt, and government loss of fiscal control. But increasingly, external lending institutions have had to admit that many of the governments to which they have been lending have deliberately become intolerably oppressive and corrupt. And these faults have had the effect of undermining the economic structure that lenders think they are helping. In some cases, the structure of a nation's economy has become so weak and out of balance that it cannot produce adequate economic results. For example, there may be too much concentration in low value agriculture or primary natural resources development, and too little strength in manufacturing. Or there may be too much investment in heavy industry and too little development in the service sector, or the economy is so gutted by crooked politicians and business people that it urgently needs massive reform and redesign.

For example, Argentina, with plenty of natural resources and a strong and vigorous people has nevertheless been led into a state of near economic collapse and has been teetering on the brink for years. 22 million people – 58% of the population - live in poverty and 18% of the workforce is really living on government handouts. Real wages declined 40% in 2004 alone, and unemployment – congenital and structural – hovers around 18%. The government has never done much to assist in the development of the private sector, and as general economic conditions repeatedly founder, private investors are scared off. The country has reneged on payments of the national debt and loans from international banks, and an effort to devalue the currency failed miserably. As a result, there has been a severe decline in foreign investment and Argentine citizens themselves are increasingly sending their money out of the country. The government is often part of the problem and seldom part of any solution. It is brassily committed to corruption in all known forms. The many state owned enterprises follow this lead and are seen as corrupt beyond control. Labor unions have to be bought off, but still stubbornly resist most proposed changes. The bureaucracy is excessive, inefficient, and preoccupied with their piece of the corruption action, largely through a morass of punitive and incomprehensible regulations. These symptoms reflect that the economy is stuck in the past and has failed to achieve any degree of economic efficiency, and the people of Argentina are forced to suffer the consequences of oppressive government incompetence.

Pakistan with over 150 million people has the sixth largest population of any country, but it has been preoccupied with internal wars, military coups, conflicts with India and Kashmir, and often disastrous consequences of its interference in the Afghan wars. Successive governments have finally embarked on programs of structural adjustment which involve trimming the bloated civil service, cutting populist subsidies on energy prices, cleaning up the balance sheets of nationalized banks, more serious efforts to collect tax revenues and accelerating an economic privatization process.

Mexico committed itself after WW II to a long period of state socialism and the concentration of economic power in state owned enterprises. In the 50's and 60's, the governments of the day built on initial successes after the war when the recovering countries bought from Mexico. But when this business dried up, the government turned to a program of import substitution, imposing high tariffs to protect local industries from foreign competition. The economy flourished during the 20 years between 1950 and 1970, but in truth, much of the expansion was financed by foreign sources attracted by Mexico's more than 100 million people and abundant natural resources. Much of the money from loans and profits were used by the government to gain direct control of most of the economy through the expansion of state owned enterprises from 84 in 1970 to 845 in just seven years. But nationalized industry became introverted – concentrating on an often monopolistic capture of the domestic markets, and showing little interest or skill in exporting. As a consequence, the long term economic tide was a lack of foreign earnings, a growing trade deficit, and a reduced capacity to pay back enormous foreign loans from both public and private lenders.

The expansion of the oil industry and the benefit of the oil sellers market created by OPEC in the mid 70s was a boon for the country and stimulated the economy generally. But the government made a pathological mistake. Against a lot of advice to the contrary, the regime assumed that the good times would continue indefinitely, and the Mexican government continued to borrow heavily, often at excessively high rates of interest. Further, corruption in the oil industry dominated by state owned enterprises was unbelievable even for Mexico. Oil company executives appointed to their positions by the government, awarded contracts to companies owned by themselves and their relatives and friends. Bribery was the rule in obtaining sales of oil. PEMEX and other SOEs became heavily involved in undercover financing of political campaigns, bribery of public officials, and other blatantly illegal irregularities. The government further added to its colossal political mistakes by nationalizing the banks with their huge burden of defaulted loans, thus adding a further $80 billion in debts to foreign lenders for the government and the taxpayers to deal with. By 1988 the economy was in crisis, the currency had collapsed, and the value of the currency had shrunk by 97%.

As a consequence, PEMEX, once the pride of the Mexican socialist government is perennially in deep trouble. Still owned by the government, it is now being squeezed by two government pressures; on the one hand, much of its budget is furnished by the government and it is the victim of short-sighted fiscal cutbacks. At the same time, taxation of PEMEX by both national and local governments has become excessive since it is still regarded as a cash cow for all to milk. As a result, the enterprise is being forced to face reality and it is doing it badly. It can no longer rest on the comfortable presumption that it is "too important to fail" and that the government will bail it out of difficulties. More careful public scrutiny means that it can't use corrupt practices so blatantly to secure its political position. It can no longer rely on some of the state subsidies it could count on such as cheap electricity and bank loans. In recent years, it has fallen badly behind in its ability to finance oil exploration, systems maintenance and repair, and improved technology. As a consequence, it is less and less able to compete well in the highly competitive international energy market. Yet efforts of the government in recent years to privatize it have been strongly resisted. The government has been forced to bail out contracts where the contractors were incompetent – having won their contracts by deliberate underbidding and bribery. The electricity generation industry shares these same pathologies, and is facing perhaps the most immediate crisis.

The following represent the most important motivations -- good and bad -- for undertaking major transformations of a national economy:

1. The country may be too reliant on low value added sectors such as agriculture or fishing. Further, wasteful subsidies have been lavished on rural/small town populations as populist ways to woo votes. Without lessening these important arenas, countries should seek further diversification, especially in economic sectors with higher payoff and an abandonment of political squanderings.

2. It may be necessary to force the pace of economic development because the current pace is obviously too slow to keep up with the growth in the population, much less enabling improvements in the national standards of living. This

motivation is often paramount when countries decide to borrow heavily from private banks or international lending organizations. But government, in the hands of greedy thugs terrorizes potential investors. Before an economy can be upgraded, oppression and corruption must, somehow, be controlled.

3. It is usually a wise economic policy to diversify the nature of the economy. Often, this has meant denying the agriculture sector needed resources in order to fuel diversification elsewhere in the economy such as manufacturing, consumer services, and most recently, information technology. But here again, too many governments blatantly and deliberately ignore these potentials out of greed or incompetence.

4. Sometimes it is possible to use economic restructuring to lessen the grip of existing class structures such as rich landholders, foreign corporations, or some form of economic elite. One of the most effective means for this change is for the government deliberately to aid in the development of small/middle sized companies. In Russia and other former Soviet style governments, this has been very important since it involves breaking up the old state owned enterprises, and either privatizing them, or letting their work be absorbed by new private competitors. One way to force restructuring is for the government deliberately to foster competition where it has not existed -- even competition with its own state owned enterprises. But who forces the government to become competent and responsible? Breaking up SOEs is a formidable task, and has a high potential of going wrong, even in relatively honest governments.

5. Many countries are being forced to rethink their own version of the "military-industrial complex" which gave the military establishment great leverage over elements of the economy and generally exempted it from full accountability and effective civilian scrutiny. As many as 40 states have been the victims of military coups and of endless intimidation of civilian governments of military leadership. In some countries, the "military" has little to do with national protection and a lot to do with getting rich and meddling in politics.

6. It is often legitimately necessary for governments to step in and assume – or share – the costs of very large investments which the private sector cannot or will not undertake. Examples may include dams, rail lines, and power generating stations, power distribution networks, or telephone systems. But corrupt governments incredibly expand this arena, in the name of State Socialism because it provides huge sources of power, leveraging of resources and corrupt money diversion opportunities.

7. Some countries have assumed control of the banking system, either to enlarge its resources, or more cynically, to control who gets access to lending. Governments often seek to achieve reallocation of economic development out of marginal or unproductive sectors such as declining manufacturing enterprises into much more value added lines such as electronics and information technology. But there is a long and unsavory history of the perversion of national banking systems. Why control banks? Because that is where the money is!

8. Finally, in countries with large systemic unemployment or underemployment, governments may seek to create enterprises that are worker intensive to sop up some of that unemployment. However, most of these efforts appear to yield marginal economic returns and they are a dangerous short term gamble producing a nasty track record of excessive worker redundancy, low labor productivity, large inflationary wage settlements, and politically powerful unions.

In summary, the socialists in many countries stressed income redistribution, job creation, industry at any cost, containment of the private sector, and especially the dominance of the economy by the public sector, largely through state owned enterprises. The conservative elements in a country tend to emphasize fiscal restraint, higher productivity, more value added and profitable endeavors, and the need to stimulate the private elements of the economy. In many countries, these two philosophies exist side by side, often with a good deal of acceptance of the State as the orchestrator of all aspects of the development process. Over time, the conservatives have gained the ascendancy and have begun the process of turning around the ground rules for economic development. But often, the real "winner" under either scenario is the crook, the corrupter, the oppressor, the terrorist, or merely the politically incumbent incompetents.

Pakistan with over 150 million people has the sixth largest population of any country, but it has been preoccupied with internal wars, military coups, conflicts with India and Kashmir, and often disastrous consequences of its interference in the Afghan wars. Successive governments have finally embarked on programs of structural adjustment which involve trimming the bloated civil service, cutting populist subsidies on energy prices, cleaning up the balance sheets of nationalized banks, more serious efforts to collect tax revenues and accelerating an economic privatization process.

One example was the state Export-Import Bank which had funds to lend to Serbian businesses to help them buy needed equipment and materials, or to develop product lines fit to be exported. But the bank was totally corrupt and responded to directions from the regime to make loans to political cronies rather than legitimate businesses. These cronies were totally incapable of generating effective businesses, and in fact, many loans were made to people who had no business at all. Such loans, and valuable licenses to import or export were illegally sold to others at a fat profit, and in many instances, the loans themselves were never repaid because they were forgiven by the bank. This pathological system of course culminated in the Bank running up an enormous number of bad loans none of which could be collected, and the Bank had to be bailed out repeatedly by the government using taxpayer funds. This had the further effect of depriving necessary social programs of adequate funding and contributed mightily to their deterioration.

In famously corrupt Nigeria, "a debt verification investigation in 1989 found that over $4.5 billion equivalent funds in supposed debt was found to be spurious and fraudulent, and much of the money paid out on this fake debt ended up in the overseas bank accounts of corrupt officials." (42)

In the Democratic Republic of Congo, the most important resource for the country is its mining industry, where most of the mines are owned by the government and they have, for many years, been sold or leased at far less than their real value.

In India, banking is still very much a government system, but it's State Owned Banks, which are responsible for three fourths of all bank loans are also where bad debts are overwhelmingly concentrated. Even the State Bank of India holds a portfolio where 25% are non-performing. Thus, the system is so shaky that, in a serious downturn, it may be in danger of collapse. Further, India also has a history of government financing of large infrastructure projects largely funded by loans from state banks, and many of these are in financial trouble, although still afloat. The whole system reeks of high politics and low management.

Import Substitution: Bad Politics Equals Bad Economics

In a study of state enterprises and their import substitution policies over more than forty years in Egypt, India, Mexico and Turkey, John Waterbury put it this way: "The need to protect and subsidize public enterprises led to multiyear planning, heavy regulation of all economic activity, administered prices, control or modulation of normal market forces, subsidization, cross subsidization, partial or even total control of banking/lending, heavy government oversight of enterprise performance and the politics of state control." He goes on further to condemn SOEs in general: "The track record of one of disappointment in the performance of the SOEs – chronic losses, inability to avoid import reliance, the high cost of sheltering both industries and labor, and a growing realization of the failure to capitalize in real export development potentials" (43)

There are two similar but more moderate versions of the failed import substitution policy – a "domestic content" policy and a "mandated exporting" policy. The domestic content policy loosened up control of an economy to the extent that it permitted foreign direct investment, but the goods and services produced could not exceed some arbitrary percentage of the total, usually 50%. The purpose of such a policy is to force foreign investors to partner with domestic enterprises and use locally produced raw materials, fabricated parts or subassemblies, and domestic labor. This policy is almost purely political and is widely used; it is even popular in the U. S. Opposition to foreign investment generally comes from labor unions, populist politicians, and locally subsidized or protected industries. Mandated exporting policies are also based on the political urge to assist domestic industry, and the usual approach is to use government mechanisms such as tax waivers for export earnings, fast depreciation of assets used in exporting, preferences in the granting of export licenses, waiver or reduction of export fees, and even government help in exploring overseas markets.

The point is that all of these centrist government policies proved to have value only in the short run and only in cases where a country private sector was very weak, but all proved to be pathological in the longer term. Import substitution had the effect of depriving national consumers of superior foreign products in favor of what all too often proved to be inferior local products. Domestic content regulations were almost always quickly abandoned simply because they seriously inhibited the willingness of foreign investors to invest in a country where the government officially forced them to combine with obsolete or inefficient local enterprises. It also appears true that when such a domestic content involvement is mandated, the venture begins perversely to act more like a "protected industry" and less like a dynamic private enterprise. Most will lobby to retain and enhance their subsidies, and there is a high risk that, unless the government is very skilled, they will subsidize enterprises that are never capable of making it on their own and will survive only as long as the government props them up. Export encouragement has often failed because the government's policy makers proved to have an almost pathetic lack of grasp of the markets their subsidized enterprises were trying to enter, and the real oppressive nature of import substitution mandated by the government is that most governments hung on to such policies long after the whole world knew that they were failures, and thus the government was guilty of depriving its citizens of cheaper and higher quality goods for years and a time.

What has emerged is several dozen nations seeking new ways to retain a socialist political power base with some degree of movement of the economy into market based patterns. In China, this is called "a market economy with Chinese characteristics." This "semi-socialist state" is viewed with skepticism by purists at both ends of the political and economic spectrum. The pure socialist intellectuals see this as betrayal and apostasy. The pure free marketers see it as infeasible, inadequate in scope, and ultimately unworkable. The advocates of democratic governance see it at best as a transitional course in which centrist socialism will inevitably give way to the will of the people. But it can be argued that even supposedly representative democracies heavily mistrusted market economics are rather muddled combinations of private market systems and heavy government involvement in the provision of social services. The hope and expectation in these several dozen governments is that, by experimentation or muddling through, they will find a middle ground that proves to be stable and successful, and in this sense, all governments in the near future may well be "semi-socialist" states.

In India, after a protracted effort at full blown state socialism, and excessive use of state owned enterprises, the Indian government now seems to on a track which permits two parallel economies -- one public and one private -- to be pursued more or less at will. But the overall allocation of roles between the two sectors remains in the hands of the government, which shifts its views from regime to regime so that the evolution of these roles is a loose pragmatic one. The astonishing success of some elements of the Indian economy such as IT has been pushing the government to give ground more widely. Social programs remain almost entirely the responsibility of government, with richer people able to buy some services such as education and health care from private sources. Government social programs remain hopelessly inadequate, and private provision of social services is growing, but at relatively high costs.

But wait: India is still capable of horrible economics. The recent Indian power blackout was surely the biggest electricity failure in history, affecting a staggering 640 million people. Thus, the power outage has exposed the greatest vulnerability of the Asian economic miracle; it is fundamentally underpowered. In the past 10 years, according to BP, India's coal consumption has more than doubled, its oil consumption has increased by 52%, and its oil consumption has jumped by 131%. For China the figures are, respectively, 155 percent, 101 percent, and 376 percent. The McKinsey Global Institute expects India's economy to grow at an average rate of between 7 and 8% up to 2030. The bad news is that Asia's creaking institutions are not able to cope with the staggering social consequences. Urban population will increase from 340 million in 2008 to around 590 million by 2030. India will then have 68 cities over a milllion, and three with more than 10 million. India therefore needs to invest at least $1.2 trillion over the next 20 years to upgrade urban infrastructure. "India's electricity system is so dilapidated that 27 percent of power it carries is lost as a result of leakage and theft. And 300 million people – 25% of the total population – do not even have access to the system.

In a country such as Turkey, the approach is a form of the commanding heights approach in that the government maintains a large public sector in which much of the larger elements of the economy are regarded as the "commanding heights" that really control the economy. The private sector is conceded primacy in small and intermediate sized businesses, the services sector, non-manufacturing industry, and the rest of the non-basic enterprises. Like India, social services are necessarily a responsibility of the government and poorly done.

The essence of these approaches is much the same as it is in all other countries; how far must a government go in relinquishing centrist power -- both to corporations and to individuals -- in order to create a more effective and growing economy, versus how much real power can be retained in the government to control or modulate economic affairs. But there is an important form of reality in this "socialism vs. market economy" debate. Because of the fact that highly socialist and centrist regimes of the past have failed, the key question centers around how far the socialist retreat may have to go to reach economic viability, and is it so far that a real socialist regime ceases to have meaning? Is there some watershed in economic evolution beyond which the socialist framework no longer survives? If retreat from heavy socialist control is widely acknowledged to stimulate the economy, is not the knowing failure to take advantage of these opportunities a form of government oppression?

There is a growing feeling that the current policies being applied to European economic revitalization are dysfunctional. (44) The key policies are austerity and structural adjustment. But economists now admit that the recessionary impact of austerity has been more serious than initially thought. The new thinking is to go more slowly on austerity but harder on structural reforms. Nobody seriously suggests fiscal stimulation; instead there is more attention to removing regulatory and other impediments to economic activity, measures to boost productivity and cost effectiveness, reducing the negative impacts of "obstreperous unions", and creating more efficient public administration. There is a growing recognition of the incestuous relationships of some business special interests. Everywhere, there is outrage against dysfunctiional politics. There seems to be more interest in enhancing single market mechanisms, such as a full banking union, and permitting shopping on Sundays.

Once again for example, Ghana is sliding into economic trouble because of the lack of intelligent economic leadership. The currency, the ceti, has lost half of its value since 2008. Oil income continues to rise and therefore the general economy has survived (2011 = 14%; 2012 = 8%; 2013 = 7%). But where does the money go? Two thirds of the population lives on less than $ 2 per day which is the World Bank definition of "near poverty" as opposed to absolute poverty. Populist subsidies and crony capitalism suck up a lot of national income, and public sector wages consume up to 70% of the national budget. General wages can't keep up with inflation. Much of the urban population lives in make-shift hovels with no real address. Huge numbers of youths graduate school and can't find any kind of job. Corruption is infamous, especially among the police, judges, sitting politicians, and petty bureaucracy. As per usual in many countries around the world, Ghanian labor unions sell their votes and oppose any cuts in wages or benefits. Patronage is the core of election campaigning. All of this despite peaceful elections in 2000 and 2008, which seem to have changed little.

Egypt began a process for reform of its state controlled economy in 1991, and is trying to back away from its heavy control, and the resistance of its special interests against change. A major problem has always been the long term bureaucratic tendency to create regulations, down to an increasing level of detail. The bureaucracy has become a vast unchanging, unpredictable, corrupt, venal and irrational force in the country. In addition, bad politics has produced expensive and unproductive subsidies for health insurance, utilities, customs imports and exports, bank lending and much else. State Owned Enterprises are required to hire hundreds of thousands of redundant workers so that the political leadership can pretend that there is low unemployment.

Case Study: The Sea of Aral

One of the classic examples of how a stupid and stubborn government wreaked economic havoc and serious oppression in people's lives is the infamous case of the destruction of the Sea of Aral, which is bordered on the north by Kazakhstan and on the south by Uzbekistan. Until the 1990s, both were part of the old Soviet Union, and most of the real power was exercised in Moscow. In the late 1950's this leadership made a series of disastrous decisions. First, economic planners pushed hard on the concepts of "import substitution" where the government aided local production of goods and services within the USSR. (Over time, this policy proved to be seriously flawed in country after country, and had to be abandoned). As the Soviets proceeded with their import substitution programs, they quickly found out that most were infeasible without heavy government subsidy. So the Soviets made their second major mistake by deciding to commit to these subsidies. As a result, they ended up with local producers producing inferior goods and services, at costs for consumers greater than they would have paid for imports. The Soviet government provided free or cheap state owned lands, cheap subsidized loans, often forgiven, subsidized inputs such as electrical power, and a workforce forced to work for near slave labor rates. Usually, SOE taxes were forgiven at all levels of government. The cost of subsidizing loss-making state enterprises created the third major error: money had to be diverted from other government programs, which turned out not to be the military or the bureaucracy, but social services, health care, education and public infrastructure, public pensions and mitigation of environmental threats, and these shortages harmed millions upon millions of people.

One of the import substitution programs which the Soviet government initiated had to do with the growing of cotton. It was decided that large areas of both Kazakhstan and Uzbekistan were land capable of producing good cotton, and these new cotton fields could be sustained by using water from the Sea of Aral and the Syr Darya and the Amr Darya rivers that fed the sea. And so the fourth big mistake was that the Soviets began an immense project to create cotton farms, often by diverting lands from existing crops such as grain, fruits or vegetables. The excessive magnitude of these projects was the fifth major policy mistake.

The great Soviet Central Plan was seriously overzealous. The great minds in Moscow never researched reality and no idea of what they were doing. The Plan mandated cotton production far beyond the reasonable capacity of the land. This in turn created the demand for (cheap) labor, brought into the region to live in substandard conditions, to work the farms. Even worse, all of this land had to be irrigated and hundreds of miles of irrigation canals were built to distribute water out of the Sea of Aral and its river systems. The huge costs of these irrigation systems drained funds from other public needs, and the general quality of life in the region deteriorated, a serious mistake number six.

Worse still, the diversion of water for irrigation reduced the flow of the two rivers and thus the flow into the Sea of Aral, so the level of the sea began to sink. As it shrank, it exposed large deposits of salt, sands and other chemicals on the fringes of the lake, and local winds picked up these chemicals. Much of the region began to experience serious toxic wind storms. Major mistake number seven became apparent when the irrigation water began to raise the water table in the land where the cotton was growing. This poisoning of the land began to reduce the production of the cotton itself – a consequence directly the result of the master planners had sought.

Major mistake number eight followed inevitably. In order to get production back up again, the government mandated the greater and greater use of (expensive) fertilizers and pesticides. But this in turn created mistake number nine –the runoff from these chemicals began to poison the water sources vital to the people in the region, and thus began the creation of many forms of serious illness: respiratory infections, digestive system failures, hepatitis, nervous system complaints, food poisoning, kidney problems, and many secondary consequences. At one point, the Kazakhstan/Uzbekistan region began to experience the highest incidence of infant mortality in the USSR, and in fact, in all of Europe.

The Sea of Aral fiasco infamously became the center of a range of further failures of the Soviet government. For example, the medical profession and the political leadership both were well aware of the medical/health problems in the region. Critical assistance could have been marshaled elsewhere and sent to the region, but almost nothing of the kind was ever done. In fact, doctors and officials were under orders to lie to the public and conceal how great the threats to health had really become.

Similarly, production of cotton was in fact, embarrassingly low given the immense efforts that had been invested to increase it. But officials lied about production in two miserable ways. First, they lied to make the figures look good to protect the mistakes of the bosses. Second, some reported less than had actually been produced so that they could "disappear" the unreported cotton on the black market for personal profit. This corruption is not a direct consequence of this cotton program. It is simply the universal corruption in the great Russian tradition.

Perhaps the greatest and most disturbing major mistake in the whole Sea of Aral saga is the blind, stupid insistence of the Soviet leadership to resist any reform. Over many years, the leadership, the grand Soviet Central Plan office, the Ministry of Agriculture and everybody else knew beyond doubt the nature of the disaster they had created, and they were either unable or unwilling to do anything about it. This was deliberate oppression of the people of the region, who were required to suffer so that the regime in Moscow could conceal their stubborn incompetence.

What may have finally saved the Sea of Aral and its rivers (in greatly reduced condition) has the collapse of the Soviet Union. In that deluge, Kazakhstan and Uzbekistan became independent nations, and both are attempting to mitigate the long term damage that the Soviets created. While the Sea of Aral surface area shrank by 90%, a dam has been constructed, sealing off the north of the sea, and the lake behind the dam is slowly filling up. The region still produces cotton, but no longer at the insane pace of the old Soviet program.

The Informal Economy

The informal economy is defined by De Soto as "the refuge of individuals who find that the costs of abiding by existing laws in the pursuit of legitimate economic objectives exceed the benefits. It is essential that the state remember that before it can distribute the nation's wealth, the must *produce* wealth." (45)

Every country in the world contains an informal sector of its economy. A distinction is usually made between the informal economy and the so called "underground" economy which is broader and includes illegal activities such as drugs, prostitution, illegal betting and smuggling. The size and variety of the informal economy is directly related to the capacity of the formal economy and its ability to generate enough economic strength to support its people. When the formal economy is too weak, people often have no option but to enter the informal economy as a means of survival. One of the pathologies of many governments is that they fail to recognize this reality, and view the informal economy as a form of crime, often called a "black market" existing only to avoid taxes and escape regulations. Thus, incompetent governments oppress the people by attacking that element of local economies that save the most people from poverty, and in truth, in many countries the informal economy is saving the country from economic collapse. The government can and does use laws and police enforcement to suppress the informal economy even when it knows that it provides employment and income that the state has failed to provide, and that kind of callous pigheadedness is simply another form of government oppression.

Anybody capable of performing a service or providing a good can enter the informal economy and become a provider. The most likely types of work in the informal economy are casual laborers, construction workers, and personal services providers such as servants, janitors, trash collectors, porters, messengers, errand runners, delivery people, child care providers, street vendors, and even panhandlers. In addition, if some capital is available, other people may be able to become small retailers or customer service providers. One of the most frequent such service is transportation in urban areas where networks of jitney cars and minivans supplement scarce and inadequate public transportation. Small scale manufacturing is widespread, including the fine arts of making cheap copies of Gucci handbags and Omega watches. Many crafts are represented, including carpenters, plumbers, masons, electricians, tailors, and auto mechanics, and many of these entrepreneurs are capable of working in both the formal and informal economies at the same time, depending on what work is available and where the money is.

The informal economy has many obvious downsides, most of which are tied to oppressive government policies. First, even while these activities may be legal in the formal sense, they are illegal when they escape the tax collection system or avoid most government regulation. In many cases, there are added costs of business for bribing the police, or to buying off inspectors. Property ownership is also dangerous because it thwarts the government tax collector, and this makes the protection of physical facilities more difficult. Informal operators may be the victims of thieves and protection rackets since it is difficult to appeal for police protection. There is seldom any real job security, with too many workers seeking too few jobs. Few work benefits such as health care or unemployment compensation are possible. But surprisingly, wages in the informal sector often compare favorably with those in the formal economy, where the excess of workers also keeps wages down. The informal economy, especially in poor countries, is often the only starting point for young people who do not have the education or skills to enter more formal businesses.

The World Bank has estimated that, in many less developed countries, the informal economy employs between one third and one half of the national labor force. Various studies estimate that, in 2000, the informal economies in developing countries were about 40% of their official gross domestic product. In Zimbabwe, the figure is around 70%, and it clearly reflects the terrible damage inflicted on what was once a prosperous country by the pathological policies of the dictator, Robert Mugabe. Other countries such as Turkey, Brazil, Egypt, and the new Russia, the figure ranges from 40 to 60%. Even in developed countries, the number averages about 18%, and there seems to be a direct correlation between the size of the informal economy and a country's total tax burden and the intrusiveness of its economic regulation. Thus, among rich countries Spain, Belgium, Italy and Greece have large informal economies and the United States, Canada, Switzerland and Great Britain have far lower levels.

As these realities are finally recognized, it appears that the attitudes of governments are undergoing some change, becoming less oppressive and more supportive. It all starts with the essential issue – can the formal economy generate enough national wealth to maintain a reasonable standard of living for its citizens? If the answer is yes, and if the government in fact delivers on its commitments, the value of the informal economy is lessened, and it makes sense for the government to attempt to recapture lost revenues to help finance its social agenda. But if the answer is no, then it would be wiser for the government not only to tolerate the informal economy but to encourage it. For example, there is now a great deal of evidence and many examples where women have been able to use the informal economy to create successful business enterprises, where such opportunities simply could not be achieved in the formal, more controlled and more elitist formal economy. Governments that refuse to recognize this reality limit the economic wellbeing of their women and thus they are deliberately oppressive. In Muslim countries, this economic oppression is reinforced by religious limitation on the roles of women in society, and also by long-standing cultural inhibitions. The informal economy also helps young people who never got more than a rudimentary education or skills training, and who have trouble finding a work opportunity in the more structured formal employment scene

Dozens of bright ideas have evolved about how a government with a less oppressive attitude could aid an abet those in the informal economy instead of figuring out how to further oppress them. Programs to provide low interest loans for women and young people are cheap, easy, highly popular and highly successful. Almost always, the timely repayment rate for holders of such small loans have proved better than the record of large, arrogant, loss making State Owned Enterprises.

Every government has its share of bad economic policies, economic cul de sacs, failed investments, or just plain economic mismanagement. The socialist tendency for economic centralism is replete with lessons learned (or not yet learned) about how economies go wrong. The general decline and pervasive stagnation of Socialist economies was particularly harmful because it took place in the face of growing national needs.

In these kinds of oppressive regimes, wages and salaries too became stagnant. There was little understanding about the relationship between productivity and management efficiency and the ability to increase wages as a consequence. Wage increases were most often granted for political reasons. The motives of the regime were mainly to buy loyalty, or at least to mitigate labor unrest as workers suffered from the consequences of an inadequate economy. Phony increases almost always proved inflationary, and produced high discontent among other workers. Worker redundancy was as high as 40% in some industries occurred because workers and political leaders combined to keep it that way.

The pressures of stagnation caused governments to fail to deal with modernization and new technology potentials that might have improved productivity. Funds for modernization simply were not available, and even maintenance of current production facilities was neglected, leading to further declines in efficiency. In many cases, the state tried to cover up these problems in the short run by lying about them, or by running larger deficits, or shifting resources between parts of the economy. In many less developed countries, such economic pathologies have been covered by overseas borrowing from both public and private sources. The decline in economic value led inevitably to a decline in public revenues and a growing inability to deliver social services. And the decline in productive work created a growing demand for such social services, especially unemployment compensation and welfare. Domestic public opinion could, in the short run, be constrained by the pursuit of false subsidy measures like cheap food, low rents, and subsidized fuels, but this made the eventual economic reckoning only worse. Deliberate lying and self delusion proved to be enormously oppressive.

This portrait of failure also plagued India. The economic structure was defined and strictly enforced by the extremely popular President Pandet Nehru who was intellectually enchanted by the early Soviet model, plus some elegant but mistaken Fabian socialist theory from Great Britain. Economic policies were enforced by the iron fist of regulatory controls over the private sector, the spreading stain of inefficient public enterprises, and an inward-looking trade and investment strategy. This produced not merely dismal economic performance, but also "the added sense of a mindless adherence to policies that have long been seen by others to have produced little real success, plus the perception that national policies have been wittingly foolish." (46) Dr. Bhagwati thus frames one of the key elements of governmental pathology – the stubborn clinging to policies or doctrines that are generally recognized as failures. Governments are, or should be, the leaders in testing reality and instigating change where needed. Instead, they too often tend to obscure the reality of change, and refuse to adapt even in the face of overwhelming evidence of its need, and become obstacles to those forces in their societies that are urgently trying to emerge. This is truly pathological.

Many governments have subsidized both their state owned enterprises and some purely private companies, usually justified by a philosophy of import substitution. But the problem then becomes that even temporary aid tends to become permanent. Government motives to protect their native producers and political allies were thus essentially political, but India also fell into the trap of thinking that subsidizing big SOEs was a short cut to achieving rapid economic growth. Foolish concentration on trying to salvage huge loss-making SOEs seems to have so preoccupied the attention and resources of governments that they neglected realistic opportunities they might have seized to foster and assist small businesses.

India's 25 years of lack luster socialist economics was a cul de sac from which India must now spend further years in withdrawing. The total collapse of the Soviet style of command and control economics has left Russia and perhaps 30 other nations with the enormous task of reinventing their economic institutions. Tyrannies such as that of Saddam Hussein in Iraq, the Hassads in Syria, or Robert Mugabe in Zimbabwe, forcefully pursuing false motives, produced economies in protracted decline over 15-20 years – ground that may never be made up. Wars, rebellions, warlords, tribal feuds, terrorism, all interrupt any serious prospect of vigorous economic development.

An analysis of national programs of economic development cannot be left to the economists. To an extraordinary extent, each country is driven by philosophical and conceptual patterns many of which are essentially irrational. They arise from ego, ambition and arrogance, and usually culminate in harmful excess.

Most of the governments committed to State Socialism have finally, slowly and reluctantly been forced largely to abandon almost all of these failed concepts and policies. Even the most dictated socialist zealot governments – the USSR, China, India, Egypt, Vietnam, Argentina, N. Korea, Mexico, Italy, Tanzania and many, many others have been forced to face up to the conceptual and practical failure of these policies – in other words, practicality has finally won out over philosophy. All powerful Central Plan organizations are gone, or are reduced to "advisory" bodies. The absolute imposition of residence controls and people movement controls are mostly gone, and now it is the people themselves and not the government who decide where they will live and work. Even China, which, for decades used harsh measures to keep people from moving to cities, has relented. It now not only admits that this policy was wrong because it never worked. With the removal of movement controls, a whole new dynamic surge has occurred because people can now search out the best and most profitable places to invest their talents.

Perverse Labor Management Relationships

Unions have been a fairly recent evolution, and came into being largely as a direct result of the tyranny of perverse employers, taking advantage of their economic power. In many countries, unionism has had a long and valuable place in the "rebalancing" of that power. But unions have not been the only means by which this rebalancing has been addressed. Increasingly, governments took on the role of the protector of workers and as the constraint on the abusive employer. Increasingly, workers, acting as part of civil society, have joined other organizations that have enhanced their wellbeing. What is saddening and disturbing however is how the political system has seized upon the power of the unions and turned it to their advantage. Unions have responded both as big winners and big losers.

First is the enormous growth and increasing complexity of all forms of economic activity. This has required the development of very large numbers of employees possessing higher orders of skills and knowledge, and greater ability to fit into the new forms of complex organizations. The ancient skills of farmer, fisherman or miner are still important, but they have been reduced in significance by the growth of manufacturing, transport, distribution or retailing. Companies in every economic sector have strategies to move beyond rudimentary operations into those that are more complex but create higher "value added" outputs. Thus, it is to the advantage of the whole society of each country to actively strengthen the level and sophistication of its technology, enabled by a higher level of education of its young citizens.

Unions have been caught up in this evolution as well and in general, union leadership has not responded effectively. Many of the sectors of the economy where unions have had their strength are the very areas such as manufacturing, mining, transport and distribution which, in developed economies, are declining in employment. At the same time, unions have not succeeded in attracting large numbers of workers in the burgeoning services sectors. In developed countries, services now represent the majority of jobs, and are creating up to 70% of all new jobs including education, government, communications, banking and insurance. In less developed countries where the bulk of jobs are relatively unskilled, unions have done better, but unfortunately, these unions are often suspected of serving the interests of the leadership rather than the upgrading of pay and working conditions for their members.

Governments tend to intervene in labor markets in three ways: broad economic policies aimed at enhancing economic development and thus creating jobs; regulatory interventions aimed at protecting worker interests, often in preference to employer interests; and in specific regulatory interventions aimed at the actual work environment. To a large extent, it is felt that each of these approaches has failed or produced undesirable negative consequences. The whole great tide of state socialism swept the countries of the world has essentially set the framework for each nation's workforce as part of state controlled economies.

But the state socialist economic tide has turned, largely because state intervention proved unable to create the dream of a superior economic world. In fact, failed government economic policies have deprived economies of much economic dynamism that would have created the very jobs that the states were seeking. Governments proved unable to understand or recognize the importance of innovation as an instrument of job creation, and they tended instead to anguish over the short term restructuring problems facing workers. When new technology such as automated production lines or electronic information processing has reduced the need for workers, both unions and governments have a history of resisting its introduction. Most governments remarkably seemed not to understand the concepts of productivity enhancement and the improvement of operational effectiveness and efficiency, and the fact that such improvements increase profitability and raise wages. They saw the unions as a counter force against corporatism and as a way to leverage corporate compliance with government rules. This in turn led to a system of favoritism for certain unions (but not all unions) which included government backing for higher wages, subsidies to union organizations and to economic rewards for union leaders personally. Governments permitted closed shop laws, skewed labor relations laws, largely unsupervised union pension funds, and lavish health and safety provisions. In many countries, these relationships became rigid and oppressive, and this oppression was detrimental to the economy.

As one author put it "The basic formula has been for the state to create a single dominant and even monopolistic confederation of trade and labor unions with leaders carefully chosen by the state. Labor forgoes strikes and confrontation in exchange for a constant stream of material benefits and virtually inviolable job security. Labor leaders enforce the deal among the rank and file, and as they become corrupted over time as distributors of the spoils, they lose the ability to lead unions into questioning or challenging the government. Public sector employment (in SOEs) becomes the instrument by which the state could most expeditiously deliver the benefits. But it is the public employee that is the most difficult to resist politically." (47)

Many governments also sponsored policies of labor redundancy, where both state owned enterprises and private corporations were required or "urged" to hire employees that could not be justified by the nature and volume of work. The basic political motive was to create jobs for political reasons. Since these jobs were false, they have been in the long run a destructive policy, even for the people who held them. Once these redundant positions have been created, they have been strongly defended both by the unions and the political leadership, often against the judgment of the professional managers. This skews human resources toward low quality redundant jobs and away from higher value genuine jobs.

What is most disturbing is the fact that far too many governments have bad track records about corrupt relations with unions, and a blindness of attitude about seizing opportunities to expand job markets, add value to goods and services, and upgrade the skills of the national workforce.

It is popular now for various interests to get all lathered up about "globalization" – both for and against. But this is scarcely a new issue, and corporate decisions to internationalize their operations are not causes but rather consequences of the great tides of economic change that have been running since the Industrial Revolution. The tide of internationalization has been driven for more than 150 years not by corporate conspiracies but by new opportunities created by new technologies, by vastly better communications and transportation, and the emergence of world-wide means for deploying and controlling money. Whole new or substantially expanded economic sectors have been created such as information technology, pharmaceuticals, insurance, aircraft/airports, and hundreds of consumer oriented products and services such as television, entertainment, health care, and education.

Unions are civic institutions and have never been the same as, or representative of the whole workforce, nor have they ever actually represented the majority of the workforce employed in any economy. The basic concept of unionism remains sound – an intermediary organization to protect the interests of workers relative to the greater economic leverage of employers. But unions all too often seem unwilling to ride the tides of new technologies even when experts urge that these technologies will greatly add to total job opportunities. Unions too have tended to be protective of their existing membership and have resisted stepping forward to help women and minorities. The expansion of the service sectors in most countries has produced whole new classes of professionals and white collar workers for whom unions have little relevance. Unions are almost inevitably opposed to corporate practices of foreign plant location, downsizing, outsourcing and privatization of SOEs in dozens of countries. In many cases, the crucial link for organized unions in no longer with their employers or even with their worker members, but with their governments.

But workers themselves are making some decisions that challenge to grip of the elites. Increasingly, one needs to consider the difference between "unions" and "the workforce". The great majority of workers in most countries are not members of unions. The only exceptions may be in those countries with a long history of state Socialism including most European nations. When governments deal with issues of the well being of the workforce, this is not the same as advancing the well being of unions. State Socialist countries have tended to control their unions, or even formulate and manage unions as an element of the government. As State Socialism has faded, so has the grip on unions. Some of the most significant tides running in the world-wide workforce are being decided not by corporations or governments by the workers themselves, often over the opposition of officialdom. Hundreds of millions of farmers have left the farms and rural poverty to move to cities. History shows many very large migrations of people from poor countries to those of greater work opportunity, and the post WW II era has become one of those historic periods, with millions and millions of workers relocating themselves and their families. Further millions have invested enormous personal efforts to learn the new skills demanded by the new economies. Women and minorities have broken old barriers in sector after economic sector and have added huge numbers to the overall workforce. Often, workers are more sensitive to economic reality than companies or governments, and people have shown a remarkable ability to change jobs, change their homes, and acquire new skills. There are major lessons to be learned from the nature of entrepreneurship in informal economies, especially in less developed countries with weak private sectors and governments. One of the lessons is that, while governments tend to become politically preoccupied with attempting to prop up declining industries, the real economic dynamism is coming from the bottom up through both the informal economy and the entrepreneurial spirit of millions of small businesses across the entire spectrum of economic endeavor. While unions have tended to see technology as a threat, the small entrepreneur sees opportunity. While governments subsidize large loss-making state owned enterprises with taxpayer money, small companies are prospering, taking business away from their cumbersome SOE rivals.

Example: Egyptian Labor Organizations

In Egypt, the main sectors of the economy are divided up into labor federations, and then, sitting at the top, is the General Federation of Trade Unions (GFTU) which is the product of the great wave of socialist state building of President Abel Nasser in the 50's and 60's. The GFTU was established as the monopoly representative of workers in Egypt, and even after Nasser, it has exercised serious power in the country, and is now frequently the opponent of central government policies. As a consequence, the regime has sought to stack the leadership of the various separate federations, especially at the local level, with loyalists as the instruments of top down government control. In any event, no labor organization in Egypt seems genuinely to represent the interests of the workforce.

In the private sector, workers are allowed to form committees to seek to join a labor federation in their industry, but in fact, anyone who tries is usually quickly fired. As usual, most public sector enterprises (plus government agencies) are substantially overstaffed. When a SOE is privatized, it results in big losses from the elimination of obviously redundant workers, and the GFTU has been unable to do much about it. There is a law preventing mass layoffs after privatization, but this has been frustrated by big staff layoffs in the SOEs prior to privatization through "early retirement" techniques. FGTU has of course fought such tactics fang and claw, but the pressures on the government to reform the economy now far outweigh the traditional clout of the union. Independent unions have been created to dispute the GFTU monopoly, but have not often succeeded, especially in the face of the general panic over privatization

Nasser created GFTU and a whole series of perquisites for workers: high wages, annual bonuses, annual Cost of Living increases, subsidized health care, anti-firing rules, good pensions, subsidized loans, factory provided housing, and job training and retraining. The government is in turmoil, and will have to spend many years in dealing with the country's enormous economic problems. One of its toughest problems will now be to deal with the politics of trying to pare back the costs of worker largesse without precipitating a major labor war.

Example: Venezuela and Its Unions at Odds

In Venezuela, Hugo Chavez built an extraordinarily popular regime largely on the basis of populist politics and generous subsidies and wage increases, and much catering to the unions. His successor, Nicholas Maduro is seeking to retain this support by further labor laws favoring unions. Maduro is attempting to forge a new political philosophy called "21st Century Socialism" which is a tacit admission that the old 20th Century Socialism was a failed experience in so many countries including Venezuela itself. That failure was mostly economic, since socialism seldom produced enough economic growth and enrichment to keep up with a rising population, much less with dreams for a better future. But the failure was social and political as well. In Venezuela, the social shortcomings are masked because those who oppose government policy or point out obvious failings are severely inhibited. The political consequences of State Socialist failures have yet to be felt, and President Nicolas Maduro believes that a retread of old Socialist program can be made to succeed.

The Maduro program has three main anchors. One is nationalism, and this is tied to strong rhetoric about "crushing capitalism", linked to a deliberate and cynical campaign against the ultimate capitalist boogie man, the United States. The second anchor is the retention of the highly successful Chavez populist programs of subsidizing the poor, the unemployed, the working poor and the teachers and unions. The costs of subsidizing food, housing, electricity, and especially gas prices has become difficult for the government to sustain, and the resulting tax levies have started to produce a political backlash, but in truth, these programs did a lot of good for a lot of people, and are justifiably popular. The third main anchor upon which the Maduro regime hopes to rely is the enthusiastic support of the unions, and to a certain extent, the working non-union poor.

Under the Maduro administration, it remains exceedingly difficult for an employer to dismiss an employee, and most of the time the approval of some government official would be required. The work week has been shortened, wages have been arbitrarily increased, most union actions are officially supported, and union leadership is granted wide access to the inner circle of the regime. And yet, it is not really clear whether the real world disadvantages of these policies outweigh the somewhat unreal perceptions of political advantage. Business people in the country are the implacable foes of those policies that freeze employment and flatly forbid firings. The short term consequences of such policies have been a growth of employee indifference to the idea of competitive hard work, a really serious increase in absenteeism, and an expectation of an almost guaranteed sequence of pay increases. In the longer term, companies face the prospect of overstaffing, and many have therefore frozen hiring, or expedited the movement to labor saving devices. In many cases, staff retention laws have been flanked by the simple process of bribing unwanted employees voluntarily to resign.

And remarkably, even the unions are increasingly unhappy. No level of preferment is ever enough. Public unions object to the fact that workers in government jobs and as employees of State Owned Enterprises (SOE) are generally exempted from these favorable laws and regulations. And it remains true that the government will never stand for any opposition even from labor unions, and many union leaders have ended up in jail when they crossed the regime in some way. All unions must register with the government, which could deny them the right to operate if they chose to do so, and the unions know it. The government continues to control decisions about wages, and these decisions are made almost always in response to political motives having little relationship to economic reality, or to the views of the companies whose wages are increased unilaterally.

Meanwhile, the general relationships between the unions and the government have continued to deteriorate. Hundreds of collective bargaining agreements have been allowed (or forced) to expire, including most of the public sector workforce of 2.6 million. Labor disputes have become more frequent and more serious in a period in which the national economy is in big trouble, inflation is just about uncontrollable, the supply system even for vital things has been breaking down, and the low productivity of Venezuela's companies has finally caught up with them and has all but destroyed their ability to compete in international markets. The Venezuelan government has succeeded in making everybody in the country equally unhappy—and scared.

The same kinds of dilemmas plague almost every country, and in most, it is likely that the tide is brushing unions aside or substantially reducing their impact and value to society. What are the principal causes of union decline?

1. Technology has resulted in the decline of numbers of workers, and a decline in the skilled trades that form the backbone of many unions. Unions have failed to expand the range of jobs which they seek to unionize. Whole new categories of jobs (most of them professional, semi-professional and services related), are untouched by the union movement. For whole broad sectors of the workforce, unions are simply irrelevant and unwanted.

2. In many countries, privatization has resulted in the diminishment of unions.

3. Other forces have stepped up to fill part of the role unions have regarded as theirs. Corporations have, in many cases, grown more sophisticated in meeting worker needs and desires, thus preempting the unions. In many cases, workers are getting their workplace protections from the government, which also reduces the perceived need for unions. Deregulation and the enhancement of the competitive environment in many countries have also resulted in the decline of the old protected unions. Many companies have adopted a policy of "exporting" manufacturing and service work when unions are seen as a drag on either productivity or profitability.

4. Unions themselves as organizations have come under increasing criticism. There is a growing perception in many countries that benefits received by unions are excessive and must be trimmed back. At the same time, unions are

congenitally anti-consumer in their policies, and this has produced a lot of citizen disenchantment. Finally, many unions have suffered from disastrous leadership -- either incompetent, or corrupt, or both – and their incestuous relationships with cynical and self-serving political leadership is deeply resented.

China and Economic Reforms

Two main fears have haunted the thinking of Chinese Party leaders: first, that, if some greater degree of freedom was allowed, the pressure for more and more would be irresistible and would overwhelm the government and destroy the command and control system that has been at the heart of state socialist theory and justification; and second, that a stampede to economic freedom would also undermine the ability of the government to provide the "cradle to grave" social services that the government uses to control society. In short, the Party worried that society and the economy would learn to manage without them, and people would start asking "Who needs the Party?" The Party finally and reluctantly recognized that the old system would have to give way to a new and more market based economy, but they felt that the economy could be opened up in controlled ways without the loss of ultimate centrist control. Four main mechanisms were to be relied upon to retain that essential control: government's continued control of most of the land; the retention of a substantial number of critical State Owned Enterprises; effective control of the national banking system; and the redesign and retooling of the centrist state bureaucracy, including the creation of the capacity to regulate the new market economy. So far, these mechanisms seem to working, and the Party retains both control and a reasonable degree of public support.

In order to put together more development capital for investment in its "new wave" market economy, the Chinese government has finally been forced to face up to the inefficiencies of its state owned enterprises. At first, in the 1980's, the Chinese government sought to upgrade the performance of SOEs by pressing for better management, usually through the form of performance management contracts between the government and each enterprise. This effort failed in large part because the motives for difficult upgrading did not exist, and in part because of the limits placed on SOEs by the government itself (e. g. no funds for new technology). In another effort, the central government fobbed off many enterprises onto provincial and municipal governments and told them to cope.

But then, fiscal and economic reality closed in and forced what the Chinese government had most dreaded --the closure of many SOEs that have not been able to respond to improvement efforts, and can no longer afford to carry millions of redundant workers on the payroll. The Chinese government is notoriously unwilling to publish any reliable figures about its economy, but sources seem to indicate that an extraordinary 24 million jobs have been lost in failed SOEs in the last 10 years. Most were in economic areas such as agricultural collectives, mines and primary manufacturing, including many of the very large manufacturing SOEs. But despite these draconian reductions, still more cutbacks and closures appear necessary. In banking for example, some 45,000 offices have been closed, and 250,000 people laid off. The shear magnitude of the reductions simply highlights the degree to which these enterprises were overstaffed in the first place. Many of the workers who have been rendered unemployed receive a stipend for three years while they seek other employment; these workers are not counted as unemployed until the stipend is completed, but unemployed they are. Millions will succeed in finding new jobs in the burgeoning private sector, but others will be forced into the informal economy, thus increasing competition, and lowering incomes for all. Others in rural areas can retreat back onto family farms, but this is the same marginal economic environment from which they fled to the cities in the first place. In all, the official government figures suggest an unemployment rate of 3-4% or about 8.4 million workers but the truth may be that it is closer to 11-12% and 20-25 million. Chinese economic development policy faces an additional dilemma: the kind of high tech economic organizations that they need to meet the standards of the international economy, are also the types of organizations that have least to offer in the way of creation of large numbers of jobs to help soak up all of that unemployment.

A second major way in which the Chinese government has sought to retain control of the economy is to continue the policy of state ownership and control of almost all land. This gives the government control of who is allowed to use the land, and thus it has control over the location and pace of development of housing, factories, businesses of all kinds, shopping centers, and various forms of transportation. As this form of government control has been decentralized to provinces and municipalities, it quickly got out of hand, and became an evergreen source of corruption. All potential land users found that "who you know" and "how much will you pay" had become the criteria on which land use permits were determined. The continued use of land also rested on willingness to continue some form of "kick-back" forever. In addition, public officials became dictatorial and perverse in throwing people off land holdings to make way for economic development, and there is now a rising tide of public indignation against such oppression, especially since the government often failed to provide adequate compensation or relocation of displaced persons to other locations. Banks of course were part and parcel of these abuses. Government corruption often extended to forcing banks to lend to favored developers including local governments and SOEs, usually with totally inadequate security, and without regard to actual risk or asset quality. When it came time for the borrowers to repay their loans, they often declined to do so, and relied on their political allies to protect them. As a result of these practices, **China's banks have outstanding loans in excess of 145% of GDP – the highest ratio in the world**.

In addition, provincial and municipal governments played the same pathological game, often forcing banks to "lend" money to finance popular public infrastructure such as roads, schools, sanitary facilities and public buildings. It is estimated that more than $100 billion of illegal loans have been made, with very little prospect that local governments will ever repay them.

In recent months, the government, having been both a willing and an inadvertent contributor to these corruptions, has naturally decided to institute an anti-corruption campaign against the banks. What is being learned is the reality that, in such a corrupt environment, corruption existed in most banks from top to bottom. If bank senior officers were creating big scandals, lower level officials were getting their smaller pieces of the action.

The Chinese banking systems was of course never designed to function as successful private organizations and were simply another form of SOE. Their leadership was appointed by the Chinese Communist Party through the banking ministry that also exercised political and managerial oversight over them. Bank decisions about who to lend to were controlled by this oversight ministry and the CCP, largely along political rules for reward of friends, punishing opponents and waiting for bribes from others. Typically, banks were forced to lend to other SOEs even when it was known that they were in serious deficit and lot unlikely to be able to repay. In effect, the banks were forced to finance SOE incompetence because the government did not want to reveal that incompetence publically. SOEs continue to be wards of the government and cannot be allowed to fail.

Provincial and municipal government were caught in a legitimate bind; they had been delegated an increasing range of public responsibilities by the central government without the funds to implement. Local officials are desperate for money, and it is therefore to their advantage to arrange lending for any enterprise that might be taxed to generate future revenues, and to set up the banks to take the fall if things went wrong. Too many of these local officials proved to be too inexperienced to handle their heavier responsibilities, and too many proved to be corrupt.

Bank regulation has, not surprisingly, been slow to develop. China now has a bank regulator – the China Bank Regulation Commission (CBRC) but its efforts have been woefully weak. It has been given few resources, and its political support has been spotty. Even if reform efforts prove to be honest and sincere they will still seem puny compared to the enormous dimensions of the problems. Thus, banks are not yet really regulated. There is only a general legal limit for any given loan of 70% of the costs of construction or the value of the land use permit. There has been little or no control requiring banks to require adequate loan security; or to list asset capacity as a loan prerequisite; or to move forcefully to deal with bad debts; or to provide some adequate resources to deal with their potential bad debts. Everybody seems to know that the banking system is teetering on the brink of disaster, but the negative forces that keep it that way are still too powerful to permit more than modest marginal reforms.

In many developing countries, economic development really only meant three things: first, enhanced opportunities for centrist elites to profit; and second, the expansion and elaboration of urban informal economies; and third, the great increases in housing for the emerging urban middle class. China, which resisted reality for so long, finds that it has built too many high rise apartments for its emerging elites and far too few more modest homes and apartments for the great tide of new urban residents. Similarly, the failure, in India, to deal with urban residences has produced some of the worst urban slums in the world.

Example: European Reforms Mean Less for More

Not all perverse politics is in less developed countries. The burgeoning budget of the European Union is seen as being so out of hand that six of the Union's largest contributors – Austria, Britain, France, Germany, the Netherlands and Sweden signed a letter demanding a budget ceiling equal to no more than 1% of their joint GDP, less than the 1.24% proposed for the budget for the fiscal years 2007-2013. The European Union has repeatedly warned of waste and mismanagement in the budget on projects characterized as wasteful, counter-productive and often plain fraudulent. A recent World Bank report attacked many of the subsidies set aside for the poorer countries as "ineffective, based on incorrect and/or unsubstantiated economic policies, badly designed, poorly carried out, and creating undesirable economic incentives." (48) Another report, commissioned by the EU itself stated that "the budget was a historical relic based on outdated and now irrelevant policies such as agricultural subsidies, while funds are lacking for newer and more valuable priorities such as education and research and development." (49) For perhaps the first time, economic difficulties in Germany, serious political rifts among the member countries, and the extensive need for assistance to the new east European member states are persuading the largest contributor members that they can no longer afford these political perversions.

Example: Egypt and the Muslim Brotherhood

Egypt has constantly been fighting two battles: the first is against a stubbornly inadequate and incompetent economy, and the second is against the Muslim Brotherhood (MB) which is so extensive and widely regarded that it rivals the government itself. In the World Bank report on "business environment", Egypt ranks 126th out of 178 countries rated. This puts it ahead only of Iraq, Syria, Sudan and Iran in the Muslim world. The official government has long been committed to the difficult task of unraveling the complex State Socialist government and economy erected by Gamel Nasser in the 50's and 60's, and moving the economy toward more of a competitive market base. The Muslim Brotherhood, however, still seems to believe in the need for a strong and invasive State, which will force the development of "a pious community and pious individuals", but the MB has also repeatedly admitted the need to arrange that the instruments of the State are properly monitored and constrained. The MB in recent years repeatedly emphasized the need to constrain the powers of the national President. Thus, when Muhammad Morsi of the MB was elected in what was admitted to be a free and open election, it was a great shock to the country, and especially to the military to see that he immediately sponsored and obtained a revision of the Constitution to expand the powers and authorities of the President in major ways. The military leadership thought they saw in this move a MB that has lost its head and pulled a sneak attack on the nature of the government. They saw Morsi as representing a narrow clique violating the very principles that the MB had recently formulated. Thus, Morsi was seen as having run amok, become dangerous, and subject to removal from office.

But then, the military itself overplayed its own hand and did not allow the new interim government that they installed after Morsi much real independence to forge a more truly civilian solution to the problem. In effect everything that everybody did seems to have been badly wrong. Major rapid change does not seem possible for a famously incompetent government: a vast, unpredictable, venal, corrupt, irrational bureaucracy famous for its vast web of regulations controlling everything, constantly being amended, often hostile to public interests, badly administered, and very, very corrupt.

SECTION FIVE

PERVERTING THE JUSTICE SYSTEM

When the regime of Peru's president Alberto Fujimori ended, the new government began to search for the discredited former head of the Peruvian intelligence service, Vladimero Montesinos whose career illustrates the extent that a secret intelligence organization can also become the oppressor of the people and a heavy player in various oppressive activities. To begin with, Montesinos used the intelligence service as a means of gathering blackmail information against political opposition, judges, and other public officials. But even more, he is accused of having run a nation-wide structure of criminal activities including arms dealing, drug trafficking, embezzlement, blackmail and bribery. He was accused of having used an arms dealer to recruit a former prime minister, Mr. Federico Salas, whose compliance was "bought" at the cost of $10,000 per month which equaled his official salary as president. His personal corrupt activities were largely run out of his official office, and it convinced many that the intelligence organization was the national headquarters for vice.

Montisinos has been accused of regularly shaking down both legitimate and illegitimate businesses, and one drug trafficker for example testified that it cost him $50,000 per month for good old fashioned "protection". His access to state bank accounts and ministry budgets let him loot the treasury, and he was estimated to have stolen as much as several hundred million dollars, most of which has simply disappeared. He repeatedly interfered with government contracting decisions. In one case, he was said to have induced the Peruvian government to buy more than 20 obsolete aircraft from Russia and Belarus, and to have paid bills for the aircraft totaling approximately $770 million. In retrospect, an estimate of the value of those planes was closer to $120 million, and the government never found out what happened to the balance of $650 million. In all of these pathological activities, Montesinos and the intelligence agency were officially protected against law enforcement intervention or judicial review in the name of "national security" and the secrecy laws surrounding intelligence information. In addition to his other sins, Montesinos left the intelligence service in a mess –overstaffed with all of the wrong kinds of people, still trying to do the wrong kinds of things, and generating little real intelligence.

Guarding National Borders

Mr. Ronald K. Noble, Secretary-General of Interpol points out that it is very easy to rob a bank electronically; no mask and gun are needed. Organized criminal groups will go online and steal small amounts, maybe $1-2 thousand from medium sized accounts. They might do this in bank A for a month, then shift to bank B. This theft is seen as too small to be cost-effective to pursue. It is cross border, expensive to investigate, difficult to track, and crosses legal jurisdictions.

Interpol now has <u>20 million</u> stolen or lost passports and visas in their data base. In 2009, they did 300 million searches. "In 2009, there were over 500 million international arrivals where passports were **not** checked against the Interpol data base, which contains records on over 11 million stolen passports and 9 milliion other documents. Interpol has the technology to identify false passports being used by war criminals, terrorists, assassins, drug traffikers and fraudsters, but there are only about 40 countries that do routinely screen passports. Where countries do real screening, crooks simply tend to shift their activity elsewhere. Every time somebody is arrested for any form of terrorist or narcotics violation, his/her fingerprints, photos and DNA is taken, but there are dozens of national borders that are so porous that they are all but useless. The emergence of literally dozens of vicious terrorist organzations, including the newest, the Islamic State of Iraq and Syria (ISIS), simply means that the threats will become horribly worse. Mr. Noble offers a "wish list" of what would constitute adequate of national borders:

1. It is in every country's best interest to make sure their borders are monitored 24 hours a day, seven days a week.
2. All countries should screen passports of all international air arrivals against Interpol data bases.
3. All prison escapees, known terrorists or other dangerous people should be reported to Interpol.
4. Track and prevent movement of corrupt officials, especially in law enforcement.
5. Track and prevent the movement of members of terrorist organizations; put more serious attention on intelligence collection that exposes intents to attack.

In Mexico, one study concluded that the Mexican people have such little confidence in their justice system that 4/5ths of victims don't even bother to report crimes. The police are notoriously corrupt and ineffective. Police forces are divided by function: one branch can only prevent crime, but cannot investigate, much less seek prosecution. This force is seen as little more than 300,000 "security guards" who are underpaid and under motivated. The second force is under the Procurators Office and does the investigation and preparation of cases for prosecution. This national force of 54,000 is seen as overwhelmed and subject to extreme political pressure. Only 15% of cases are heard in open court – a serious invitation for corruption in judge's chambers. This situation is highly pathological and it is created and sustained by perverse political motives. The under staffing of police, investigators, prosecutors and judges is deliberate, since the corruptors have no desire to see criminal justice become too successful. The courts themselves badly need reform, and too much power resides with the prosecution which is free to cut deals with the accused, or to "forget" cases where there is political influence brought to bear. There is also a nasty history of torture and forced confessions.

In Iran, the purist religious doctrines of the ruling Islamic regime do not prevent the flagrant politicizing of the police and courts. Often, accused persons are interrogated not just by the police detectives but by the intelligence arm of the police and/or the investigators from the national intelligence ministry.

In Indonesia, the general understanding has been that the whole court system is not about justice but is run along business lines; that is, justice is a commodity that is sold for a profit. Staffs to judges have arranged meetings with potential contestants in a law suit in order to solicit bids. It is made clear that, if and when the judge hears the case the highest bidder will win. Similarly, it has been useless to oppose the actions of companies or state owned enterprises that are blatantly favored by the regime since "the fix" is automatically in. One of the most blatant of such relationships exists between the government and the powerful state oil enterprise TEXMACO. This enterprise has often run amok, and in one case, it ran up $1.9 billion in unpaid loans – from state owned banks. But the President and the ruling party and the Attorney General informed the Minister of State Enterprises to drop all collection efforts; in other words, to convert the loans into give-away grants. Obligingly, the courts have refused the requests of other litigants to schedule any hearings.

In the Dominican Republic, an enormous scandal involved the country's largest bank, the Banco Intercontinental, whose president was a man of legendary generosity to his friends in high office, including gifts of automobiles, lavish foreign vacations, use of bank credit cards and expensive jewelry. The bank had run up huge losses in excess of $2 billion, and the bank president and others had apparently been secretly siphoning off funds for years. Government auditors and an external auditing firm admit that they were "deceived". One must conclude that they were either incredibly bungling, or that they were bought off. What was the response of the government to the scandal? It was to take over the bank and promise to cover all of its debts and pay cheated depositors. In order to finance more than $1 billion of this obligation, the governor of the central bank went shopping for a foreign loan. The World Bank and IMF were understandably reluctant to commit their funds to pay for a combination of private swindling, political corruption, and government incompetence. The IMF held up a $600 million loan; and it was in part motivated by an additional action by the Dominican Republic government to invest an equal amount of its own scarce funds to buy back two privatized electrical distribution companies which formerly had been suspect state owned enterprises. As usual, IMF has absorbed considerable criticism. Politically, if IMF extends such a loan it will be blamed for its insistence on loan repayment and fiscal prudence which might result in cuts in populist social programs. If IMF refuses the loan, it will be accused of abandoning a poor country with a fragile economy.

Nigeria is constantly confronting various forms of massive unrest among the huge population of the country with a police force that even its senior officers and Nigerian justice officials admit is under-strength, ill equipped, and very demoralized. Nigerian citizens would add that the police force is also corrupt, incompetent and brutal. The 135,000 strong force has an appalling record of arresting innocent people in order to extort money from them while accepting further illegal payments from crooks to leave them alone. Many police forces routinely obtain a percentage of the profits of crooked enterprises. It is also widely suspected that investigators are often used to collect political intelligence for use against opponents of the regime. Crime clear-up rates are appallingly low, police and forensic facilities range from the ridiculous to the nonexistent, and few officers or investigators can ever expect any professional training. President Olusegun Obasanjo ordered the recruitment of 40,000 new police but cynics pointed out that the capacity to properly train these new officers did not exist. For the public the cynicism is even deeper – who needs an additional 40,000 ill trained corrupt and brutal thugs who are called police?

Example: Brazilian Justice Overwhelmed

Brazilian law enforcement has an ugly reputation for its perverseness and brutality. The entire Brazilian law enforcement system from top to bottom is infamous for its general incompetence. The government creates confusion by maintaining two police forces in each province: a military-like uniformed service, and a more civilian force of detectives. The uniformed police are in fact, internal security, and are used to intimidate the population. The civilian force often has cases taken away from it if they might actually stop corruption.

Courts are in total disarray. There is widespread perception that judicial decisions are bought and sold. There are far too few public prosecutors, judges and court staffs to meet the overwhelming case load and most court officials including judges have obsolete skills. The government itself files hundreds of trivial cases of little impact even if decided. The judicial process allows for endless appeals on minor technicalities, and in many cases, decisions in one court are not seen as binding on other courts, leading to second filings. The whole process is impossibly complicated and arcane, leading to extreme time delays. In 2003, the Brazilian Supreme Court muddled through more than 160,000 cases. The likelihood of a satisfactory court outcome is so low that many people decide never to try. Bankruptcy judgments are almost impossible, thus harming bank and consumer lending, since a purchaser can file for bankruptcy and avoid payment. Housing mortgages are almost non-existent because the government or lenders are unwilling to attempt foreclosures which are considered "socially undesirable" and politically unpopular. Despite this miserable track record, the Brazilian Congress has long resisted any serious efforts at judicial reform despite the creation in 2003 of a new Secretary of Judicial Reform in the Ministry of Justice.

The incompetence is so great that the violence in Brazilian society has grown at alarming rates. Street violence is universal. Late night clubs and bars are "black holes" of violence, drunkenness, brawls, killings, and frequent of robberies of patrons. People are mugged, robbed, shot and killed at any hour. Drug dealing is common, and always seems to be violent, both for its gang wars, attacks against customers, drug overdosing, and deaths from poisonous drugs. Kidnapping has become a new "cottage industry". Not only are wealthy people kidnapped for ransom, but even average people on the street are seized and forced to draw money from their bank accounts, or be ransomed by relatives for relatively small amounts. The police are both hated and feared. They have a record of violence and brutality, not just against crooks but against the very citizens they are supposed to protect. Many police arrest citizens for little or no reason in order to extort a bribe for their release. Small businesses are shaken down for "protection" money – by the police. Often, the investigation of crimes will be undertaken (poorly) only if a bribe is paid. Police also extort money from drug dealers, fences and other criminals, either as a share of the loot, or for ignoring criminal activity. While urban police are busy lining their own pockets, rural and poor urban areas are totally neglected. Protests or gatherings of almost any kind are subject to police harassment which may precipitate rioting and protests which the police put down with brutal efficiency, attacking both rioters and innocent bystanders alike.

Prisons are a disgrace. They are overcrowded, run brutally by cabals of inmates. Conflicts between ethnic groups are common, and guards cannot or will not do much about it. Prison life is marked by drug and sexual abuse, assaults and murders. There are riots almost every month that are totally beyond the control of the prison guards, who are forced to call in riot police or even the military. What results is heavy violence, with hundreds of prisoners injured or killed. Escapes are common, many of them by prisoners simply bribing their way out. Public prosecutors offices are weak and understaffed, and the courts are widely seen as incompetent or corrupt. They are slow to act even when cases are finally brought before them, and the perception is that many cases are decided not on their merits, but on who offers a judge the most money.

These examples illustrate a situation where a whole body of laws and the existence of a full law enforcement system is essentially meaningless. Despite the work of researchers, scholars, reformers, good government advocates and others, the reality is all too often a law enforcement system that is unrelieved pathology – the "in" crowd has learned how to beat the system for their own private benefit, and the majority of the population are victims. It is almost impossible to say where to start to reform a whole system that has gone bad.

Nor are developed countries without blame. While perverse justice system practices are less prevalent, major systemic difficulties are apparent. In Japan, which is often considered the safest country in the world, the criminal justice system is now the target for serious efforts at reform. One of the main concerns is that the police have too long been able to exercise almost unchecked authority against suspects, and that neither public prosecutors nor judges have resisted this authority. Lost in this system are the rights of the accused. Alleged wrongdoers can be held for weeks without being charged. Suspect interrogation may be conducted without any defense attorney present, and often these interrogations are never documented. The police have become uncomfortably capable of extracting confessions under these conditions, and this may lead to a sense that careful investigation of the evidence is not necessary. Judges and public prosecutors tend to be excessively cautious and all too willing simply to accept what is presented to them by the police, particularly if it includes a "confession". Overall, there is the growing feeling that the system has become far too complacent and bureaucratic. Justice is exceedingly slow and lax. It was not until February of 2004 that a judge finally got around to delivering a verdict against the perpetrators of the Aum Shinrikyo cult poison gas attack in a Tokyo subway more than nine years earlier which killed many people and injured thousands more. If a major case of this nature can languish for years, what does the record reveal about the system's response to lesser accusations?

Even the United States has a long history of criminal justice incompetence, ranging from the all but uncontrolled activities of the Klu Klux Klan in the period following the civil war until the mid-thirties; to the use of police to quell riots such as the Haymarket affair in the 1880's, the Pullman strike of 1894, the corruption of police in the 1930's Chicago of the Capone era. In a more recent example, Mr. Clarence Norman, the leader of the Brooklyn Democratic Party organization, one of the largest political organizations in the country, was arrested for grand larceny resulting from an investigation of an incestuous process of selling judgeships in Brooklyn using the threat of denial of Democratic Party support for uncooperative nominees. In the process, evidence has been unearthed that, in his position of power, Mr. Norman has been accused of multiple billing of expenses to the state of New York (where Mr. Norman is also a state assemblyman), the city of New York, and the Democratic Party. He is also accused of skimming off Party funds and transferring them to his personal bank account. In addition, several of the judges that Mr.

Norman succeeded in getting appointed are also accused of various wrongdoings, including accepting bribes from defense attorneys, and making secret donations to Norman's various enterprises.

Courts and Judges

Courts have extraordinary power because they are supposed to be the ultimate point of decision on issues of great national importance. But courts can be perverted when they are too vulnerable to perverse political leadership. Said another way, it is always the urgent intent of a dictator or tyrant to find a way to get control of the courts. Ways must be found to protect the ultimate power of the courts and use them to actively counter the pathologies of a tyrant or dictatorship. The courts must act as the protectors of the people against their own government, but this is a role that is not even adequately defined, much less universally accepted. What can the courts do to counter government pathology?

What many judges have done is to use a specific case situation to state a broader principle of justice that represents a counterforce to political distortions of the law. Actions of a regime are difficult to constrain where the laws themselves are unclear, distorted, deliberately misinterpreted, improperly extrapolated, or simply ignored. Faith in the rule of law is not enough against legislative bodies that create pathological laws. Courts should seek ways to initiate specific interpretations challenging the validity of perverse laws, or to act as a counterforce to political distortions of the law. In authoritarian regimes, judges may need to take a more assertive position as a counter to pathological legislative bodies and dictators, even recognizing that there may be serious risks in doing so. There would be great public value achieved if judges could go beyond the role of determining legality and help to educate the public about the nature of government pathology. Perhaps some form of "advisory opinion" about perverse laws would serve such a purpose. If judges can't or won't guard the rule of law, who will? And yet, in many Muslim countries, religious leaders still retain a serious role in interpreting the laws as a counter force against a dictatorial government.

In the case of widespread corruption in a regime, one answer may be the creation of special courts with unique authorities to serve as anti-corruption protections. If the courts are not able to create such special mechanisms themselves, legislative action may be needed to do so. In other cases, it may be possible for court leadership at least to initiate a concentration of effort against pathology and corruption by deliberately giving priority to any such cases.

Courts are still able to make law if they have the courage to do so and can be protected. Courts may initiate specific interpretations of the legal validity of laws, as a counterforce to political distortions of the law. A most important and serious task is to serve as a counter to a pathological legislative body. Courts must take steps to defend themselves by setting up a defense mechanism against corrupt appointments of judges by the political leadership, perhaps through a shift to elected judges. If possible, courts should be given an independent source of funding so that they can resist deliberate efforts of a regime to keep them weak and under funded, and increasingly, there is the need to provide better security of judges and pubic prosecutors against physical attack or to investigate allegations of corrupt approaches.

Public Prosecutors

Public prosecutors such as district attorneys in states and localities, or a national justice ministry have become a serious source of pathology. Even when public prosecutors are part of a career service, they are still under the direction of politicians who may create pathological laws and then demand that they be enforced. Decisions about when to prosecute, or when there is insufficient evidence are very complex and ambiguous and subject to too much interpretation. These decisions can be "gamed" because there are very few mechanisms for determining when a prosecutor has indulged in selective decisions to favor pathological or corrupt motives. There may be back room maneuvers to settle out of court either by potential defendants or by other elements of the government, and this also is an endless source of corruption. One possibility may be some system where the courts have some form of oversight function over prosecutors, who in turn have oversight over the police; and then the creation of an independent anti-corruption organization to oversee the honesty and effectiveness of this review system.

The Police

There are three general situations in which the police force can be used pathologically. The first is when the political leadership deliberately uses the police as an instrument to oppress citizens and to destroy or hamper the effectiveness of opposing political parties or individual dissidents. Often, the laws themselves make such oppression legal, and the police have little choice but to enforce these perverse laws. As illustrated by the case of Vladimir Montesinos in Peru, the police, along with intelligence officers may be used to gather information that can be used to blackmail or intimidate persons who oppose or merely criticize the regime. Police brutality is widespread, and is seldom deterred by lack of cause or evidence. Citizens are falsely arrested, often for political reasons. Illegal searches and seizures are common, and citizens are unwilling to complain because complaining can be highly dangerous.

The second perverse situation is when the police are pathologically incompetent. Many police forces are staffed with officers with little or no professional training. Such forces are simply unable to cope with the criminal forces in the community. Far too few criminals are ever caught. If caught, the gathering of evidence is bungled or flawed or wholly inadequate. Any crime beyond the most simple is never really investigated. Forensic capabilities are usually inferior or not even available when needed. Arrests do not hold up, and criminals go free. Departmental leadership is typically unskilled in management, far too bureaucratic and paper-driven, and far too willing to cave to political interventions.

The third situation is when the police themselves are corrupt, and in fact, around the world, there are few elements of government where corruption is more prevalent. It is likely that a police officer can make more money by <u>not</u> making an arrest because criminals offer them bribes to look the other way, and many officers including senior officials are on "retainers" from criminal gangs to provide protection for their activities. Mafia-like gangs in dozens of countries maintain close and profitable links with police organizations. A serious problem in China is smuggling, and often it is the police who help smugglers land their goods, and provide them with police escorts. Individual citizens can be intimidated into making payments to avoid harassment or threatened arrest, and police routinely extort money from businesses for supposed protection. It is little wonder that, in country after country, the police are universally hated and feared.

In Nigeria, the police confront massive unrest and threatened civil disobedience with a police force that even its senior officers admit is demoralized, badly trained, poorly equipped and ridiculously underpaid. Nigerian citizens are bitter in their complaints that the police force is also corrupt, brutal, vicious and indifferent to citizen rights. The police force has almost 135,000 members, but it destroys its effectiveness through its appalling record of extorting money from people by threatening with the alternative of arrest. In addition, it often permits criminal elements to flourish by offering them protection for bribes, and it will solicit bribes from individual crooks to look the other way. The government has been known to fail to prevent, and even to encourage vigilante mobs who are supposedly motivated by a desire to "prevent protests against the government."

Prisons

The state of most prison systems is shameful and a national disgrace and few in power seem to care. Prisoners are treated like animals, and pathological treatment of prisoners by their fellow prisoners is either tolerated by prison administrators, or is totally out of control. Inmates are often able to bribe guards for preferential treatment or allowing inmates to pursue criminal (or economic) activities either inside or outside of the prison itself. Prison administrators themselves can subject prisoners to blackmail, extortion or bribes for even normal services. Often, prisoners are treated as a form of slavery, performing work for the state itself, or "rented out" to external contractors. Prison administration can steal funds, distort purchases, loot government contracts for goods and services, engage in creative bookkeeping or "lose" prisoners who bribe their way out.

SECTION SIX

THE DILEMMA OF MILITARY ESTABLISHMENTS

Most contemporary wars are civil wars involving two or more power groups fighting political wars for power with little or no real justification. Usually there is no real prospect that either group is competent to manage the country and run a government, and thus neither side deserves to win. While in the past many insurrectionist groups were communist and therefore had a supposed concept and philosophy, the basis for wars are now primarily two: that the "ins" are incompetent crooks and the "outs" will be better; and that ethnic, religious, or regional groups are being oppressed and need to be protected.

These civil wars are especially intractable because accusations against the incompetence of the incumbent government are all too often true, and because religious or ethnic conflicts usually have some legitimacy and reactions to oppression or neglect are emotional and irrational. They are more like big feuds, with past outrages justifying the next outrages. Such wars appear totally incomprehensible to outsiders seeking a basis for mediation. Many such conflicts are never really won or lost but fumble on forever.

Given weak and corrupt governments, it takes very little real force to mount an insurrection, and there seems to be lots of people to volunteer. Rebel leaders lack the knowledge or skills to govern, or any real sense of purpose or public policy. Mostly, their only ability is that of a local bandit chief who can hold together a few hundred armed fighters. Even if the rebels triumph, the new government seldom proves better than the old. Peace may be imposed through dictatorial methods, but the basic conflicts are not resolved.

In these conflicts, the real losers are the citizens and the economy. Prior to WW II, casualties in the civilian population were relatively low at around 10-15% of all casualties. WW II changed that, and the civilian and military casualties were about 50/50. Now, the civil war style means that up to 75% of all casualties are civilian; and even most of the young men coerced into fighting on both sides are civilians rather than professional soldiers.

What is now being more fully realized is that such wars usually result in the long term destruction of the economy, the public infrastructure, and the personal assets of citizens. The high cost of armaments and supplies for both sides drains resources from the economy and squanders them on inconclusive destruction. For the government, taxes are raised and funds are diverted from other more needed public services. As public infrastructure is destroyed or deteriorates rapidly there is little or no money or workers to maintain and repair much less to catch up with the real needs of citizens. The whole economy is disrupted. Small businesses are destroyed or vandalized. Sources of industrial supplies and equipment dry up, or can no longer be afforded. This pattern fatally deteriorates the base of confidence in the government, even when there may be public support for resistance to the insurgents. For the insurgents, resources are obtained by blackmail and seizure, or from outside sources; and this sours the public on the insurgents. People are forced to learn a harsh lesson: failure to demand and support an effective government may result in utter catastrophe.

Military Authority and Power

Dictatorships, oppressors of the people, supporters of tyrants, deposers of bad governments, neutral shield of the country, defenders of the revolution, trusted defender of the nation -- military establishments have been all of these things and more.

In the period following World War II, there have been 40-50 significant military coups d'etat and in some countries, there have been successions of military regimes replaced by civilian governments that were again overthrown.

It seems surprising then that the historical pattern shows very few successful long term military regimes. Of 40 military coups since WW II, many have survived for only brief periods of 3-5 years, and at least 23 military regimes have been ultimately replaced (with varying degrees of success) by some form of civilian government. This is even true where military regimes have had long runs: South Korea after 30 years; Nigeria after 36 years (with a brief 4 year civilian government); Peru for 20 years; Ghana for 26 years.

Several military coups have however resulted in permanent long term tenure where the government either remained a military regime, or it evolved into a civilianized structure still mainly controlled by the military. These regimes include Argentina, Egypt, Guinea, Libya, Myanmar (former Burma), Pakistan, Somalia, and Indonesia until 1998. But whether or not the military actually controls the government, in most countries it becomes and remains a powerful and often controlling influence. In several countries, the military establishment that emerged from a great revolution earned (or assumed) the mantle of "Guardian of the Revolution" – a role with substantial support from the public, who accepted the military as a sort of guarantor and last resort protection from oppressive, corrupt or incompetent civilian rule. In some cases, there may have been real or apparent threats to the post-revolution governments, but in most cases (e. g. the USSR, the Peoples Republic of China, Turkey, Vietnam, or Cuba) the reputation of defenders of the revolution has been used as justification for leveraging or even overthrowing the civilian government.

Characteristics of Military Establishments

Perhaps the most valuable asset of any military establishment is the long tradition of insistence on rigid discipline, top down authority, and obedience to command. These make sense under battlefield conditions, but are often ill adapted to the far less rigid realities of civilian rule. Military commanders thrust into civilian roles seem to find it difficult to accept the need for negotiation with elements in society. They prefer simply to issue orders and are often surprised and outraged when orders are challenged or ignored. Military officer training may produce good management skills but not necessarily good political skills.

Military establishments, whether in control of the government or not, seem to share other common characteristics. They tend to be ultra conservative, preferring the status quo however bad, to any urges for reform and change. Most seem to respect technology, but are better at utilizing it for military rather than civilian purposes. Most seem to become "bottomless pits", where no military expenditure seems excessive and social services programs never seem to win out in competitions for funding. The political arts of negotiation and compromise are poorly accepted or understood, and independent organizations such as public interest groups in civil society seem to be confusing, disruptive and often threatening.

One of the most important characteristics of these military establishments is the degree to which they could become financially self sustaining. In the USSR, the unstinting support of the military in the face of the Cold War permitted it to gain control of many vital sectors of the Soviet economy such as the electronics industry in which the military had unquestioned top priority to the exclusion of almost every other need. In Indonesia, the military owned and operated hundreds of profit making companies ranging from production of military hardware down to luxury hotels and restaurants, none of which had anything whatever to do with military readiness. Similar ownership was also true in the Chinese Red Army and elsewhere. This relative financial independence extended as well to any portions of the military budget which came through the civilian government. In most cases, there was little or no review of military budget proposals. Nobody in the oversight processes of the executive or legislative had the temerity to challenge even the smallest of budget items, and almost always the military request was quickly rubber stamped.

In modern day Russia, the government has been able to confront the greatly weakened military establishment and force military controlled assets into privatization. In Indonesia, the surge of revulsion against the undemocratic and corrupt regime of President Suharto, and the overthrow of his regime was in large part attributed to the dominant and brutal military establishment. This led to the final death of the cover story of military "protection of the revolution". A revitalized and newly democratic Indonesian government is finally in a position to wrest away from the military hundreds of its economic assets. Even the Chinese are doing the same with the "glorious Red Army". Based on its successes in moving toward a more productive market based economy and the extraordinary reduction of the numbers of people living in poverty, the Chinese government has steadily withdrawn economic elements from control by the military, and this has meant that the military has been made more dependent on funding coming through civilian control.

Military regimes have produced some of the worlds most vicious and tragic failed governments. And in many cases, the military is able to avoid even its basic military role, through the sponsorship of paramilitary organizations which are funded by the government to fight its battles against various forms of insurgency. The military stays in its barracks and lets the paramilitaries do the fighting. Generals wear their brilliant, medal bedecked uniforms in their military headquarters, but seldom lead troops in the field.

Sudan is a somber example of the failure of a military government to rise above its own narrow elitist motives. Sudan gained independence from Egypt and Great Britain in 1956. Within two years, the military has seized power, and is in power still. The military regime was very narrowly confined to Arab Islamists, with an extraordinary overlay of Marxist/Leninist doctrine, and it set out to impose, by force if necessary, both Arabization and strict Islamic law on a widely diverse country of 25 million people. They succeeded in alienating the devout elements of the Muslim community as well as the Christian/Animist South of the country. The result was two civil wars: one from 1960 to 1972, and the second which began about 1982 and is still not fully resolved. Thus, over the 40 year period of national independence, 34 years have been spent in self destructive civil conflict and the current war is the longest running in modern African history. It is usual to characterize the main conflict as being religious – the Muslim North vs. the Christian/Animist South. But the regime in Khartoum has also excluded non-Arab Muslims in parts of the country, and many of the motivations for conflict are not religious at all but deal with efforts to impose centrist authoritarian control over a population that is in fact a loose array of very localized tribal, village or town interests who want mainly to be left alone to work out their own futures. The main insurgent group in the country is called the Sudan People's Liberation Army (SPLA). Initially, and especially during the first civil war, these insurgents failed to recognize the disaggregated nature of local interests and found it difficult to recruit soldiers willing to fight outside of their own native territory. But in the second civil war, it was the insurgents that learned how to build alliances with many local interests where the only common theme was opposition to the centrist minded regime in Khartoum and its threatening policies of imposing a strict Islamic dictatorship on everybody. After 1989 the military regime used savage repression, purges and executions, banning of communist organizations, removal of public officials, and banning political parties and the media. The SPLA however initiated elements of civil government in areas they occupied, where the main policy was one of relying on and reinforcing local participation and chiefs as voices for the populace.

Throughout this whole period, the government in Khartoum attempted to use the involvement of its neighbor states in crushing its opposition. But these attempts were arrogant and self serving, and often involved intervention in other countries in the form of supporting their own rebels. For example, Khartoum supported rebels against the government of Ethiopia; in turn the Ethiopian government became active supporters of the SPLA, supplying funds, weapons, training camps and a safe haven for SPLA forces. In the last analysis, the Arab minority elite that controlled the government could no more effectively come to grips with other countries than it could find a basis for dealing with its own population, and it ended up isolating itself from Ethiopia, Eritrea and Uganda, and incidentally, Libya as well. Meanwhile, the SPLA has been able to form working arrangements with a wide range of local interests by paying attention to local grievances, not pressing any single doctrine or unitary enforcement, and generally liberating local customs and life styles from the threat of the religious, economic and political threats of the central regime. South Sudanese militia forces fought the Sudanese military to a stalemate. Then, a referendum was agreed to in which 98% of South Sudanese voted for independence, which was achieved in July of 2011. Tragically, S. Sudan has since fallen victim to a harsh and brutal ethnic civil war which still continues.

In Sierra Leone, independence from Great Britain in 1961 led to another much despised military regime that eliminated parliamentary governance and the creation of a one party state in 1978 and precipitated a 25 year civil war. The government armed itself by paying for the weapons used to terrorize its own citizens with sleazy concessions for development of diamond mines and timber reserves. The Revolutionary United Front (RUF) was not a very attractive alternative, yet in the 1980's, RUF had begun to receive substantial help from Liberia which finally invaded Sierra Leone to exploit its massive diamond mine wealth. By 1991, the RUF had gained enough strength to launch more serious attacks against the government, and were joined at times by elements of the army. This unholy alliance pursued one of the most brutal and horrible civil wars on the African continent. Thousands of innocent people were murdered in their homes or on the streets, massacred in shops, thrown from the upper windows of buildings, buried alive, hacked to pieces, and had their eyes gouged out. Hundreds of buildings were burned down, and families were burned to death in their homes, apparently just for thrills. These unspeakable horrors were committed by the governments of Liberia and Sierra Leone, and the military in both countries had willingly become the instruments of terror and oppression of the very people they were supposed to protect. By 1999, national repugnance and UN intervention with 17,000 troops, finally drove the parties to the negotiation table and produced a cease fire in 2002 which held to the point that the 11 year old war could be declared to be over. Here again, the military regime had little to offer the country except harsh centrist control. It had little or no skill in dealing with the civilian population, had no intention of negotiating or compromising, had no interest in civil administration, allowed the deterioration of civil government, social services and public infrastructure, and wallowed in incompetence and corruption.

Indonesia occupied E. Timor in 1975 when the Portuguese withdrew, and the elite government in Jakarta treated it like a colony. The military governor in each province was the real power and his job was to suppress any glimmerings of independence. In August of 1991, a public referendum was held with remarkable results. 98% of the registered voters turned out, and almost 80% voted against continuing to be part of Indonesia. But the military leaders refused to accept such results, and unleashed their military forces to suppress the citizens. In town after town, they looted, killed, raped and burned. Whole villages and even public markets were torched. Almost every person either fled into the hills or tried to make it across the border to West Timor. In the brief space of three weeks, everything of value had been destroyed. E. Timor was left with nothing – no government, no economy, no personal homes or possessions.

SECTION SEVEN

CORRUPT PUBLIC MANAGEMENT

Government Grant and Contract Pathologies

All governments contract for goods and services, in many cases as a preferred alternative to having work performed by staffs of regular civil servants. The ability to contract out work is a vital policy and management tool. Each contract is a binding agreement between the government and commercial suppliers of goods or services and is enforceable in law. In addition, governments may use the instrument of a "grants-in-aid" which are usually made to other levels of government such as states or municipalities. Grants are essentially an award of funds to a recipient for the performance of some defined activity which may range from the conduct of scientific research to information processing or the provision of some public service such as health care centers or municipal transit services. Grants are usually of two forms: one is a categorical grant paid for the performance of a defined "category" of work such as assistance to the handicapped or the provision of low income housing; the other is a formula grant where the amount of the payment is calculated under a defined formula such as population, population density, average income or age ranges.

Contracting is justified where the government lacks some specific skills or institutional capacity, or where the work needs are temporary and would not justify hiring permanent civil servants, or where contractor performance would produce cost savings or superior performance. Contracting may be used for a tremendous range of activities from scientific research to the purchase of paper and pens. It is important to understand that, when a government agency contracts for work it never relinquishes its ultimate responsibility for that work. Some public official must be responsible for defining what will be contracted out and for the supervision of the resulting contract. The public official must draft specifications for a contract that defines what the government needs, and defines standards and controls to be imposed on the contractor to assure that the government needs are met. The public official must oversee the performance of the contractor to assure that the work is performed in accordance with defined specifications or statements of contract objectives. The official must make sure that all contracted work is in fact performed – no performance should mean no payment. There must be evaluation of costs under the contract to make sure that they are justified and realistic. Goods and services must be inspected or evaluated to make sure that they meet the terms of the contract.

There are many forms of contracting. State socialist governments created state owned enterprises as a form of contractor, and gave them responsibility for whole segments of the national economy such as energy production or telecommunications. The most widely used approach however is for a government agency to define separate specific contract requirements and seek a specific company to carry out the work, and millions of contracts of this kind are maintained each year by governments around the world.

If there is a single most important policy to be followed in government contracting, it is to seek competition from interested companies for each contract. Competition is vital in assuring that the government has really sought out the best combination of cost and performance from the private sector. Often, the unwillingness to seek competition is an ominous signal about what the government is doing. "Sole sourcing" is justified only in limited instances where only one company can perform the work.

While the use of contracting is vital in the work of most governments, it is also perhaps the single most important source of corruption and perverse policies and operations. Every element of contracting from the initial decision to contract down to detailed operations is highly vulnerable despite government protective mechanisms. Many governments have corruptly contracted for things that they do not really need as a perverse way to pay off certain companies or as the source of bribe seeking by government officials. A good example is the purchase of expensive military hardware even though there is little military threat. Even where the need for a contract is justified, there may be rules for determining who is eligible to bid which are perverse. For example, eligibility may be limited to domestic companies, even where it is clear that foreign companies might offer better products or capabilities. Bids may be confined to state owned enterprises in recognition of their monopoly position. Eligibility criteria may be skewed to give unfair advantage to a single company – often one that is willing to pay for the privilege. A "sole source" decision may be driven by the prospects of later payoffs.

The whole process of soliciting bids and evaluating them to determine which company will receive the contract is highly sensitive. Legitimate bids may be rejected for many technical reasons so that "friends" of the regime may win the bid. One of the major sources of fraud is called "bid rigging" where bidders and public officials collude to fix the outcome of the competition in advance. Public officials can and do provide insider information (at a price) to their favored companies to make sure that they win. Another form of corruption is called "bidding in" – a deliberate understatement by a bidder of the expected cost of the contract in order to win the bid. The contractor relies on the high potential of raising costs once they have the contract. Many so-called contract cost overruns are the inevitable and plotted outcome of bidding in the first place. The whole bidding process may have been a false front to mask the fact that the winner has already been selected by the public officials involved. A bidder may simply offer a bribe to the selecting official. Even where some formal process of bid evaluation is used, the selecting official may have the authority to ignore the technical evaluation of bidder's competence and make a prejudiced selection.

Once a contractor begins work under the contract, whole new forms of corruption become possible. The work itself can be pathological: shoddy work, substandard materials, failure to perform required work, unwarranted expenses, overstated costs, deliberate cost overruns, and many more failures. Cost may be overstated. The government may be billed "phantom charges" for work or supplies not actually provided. The workforce may be overstated and phantom wages and benefits billed to the government. Work delays may be deliberately created to pump up costs. Management salaries or overhead costs may be excessive. Unfortunately the contractor may feel that the quality of government oversight is so poor that such illegalities will never be caught. In other cases kickbacks are simply made to public officials to turn a blind eye to such cheating. Government managers and inspectors may not be competent, or may be too few to cover all contracts. Performance is not evaluated, costs are not verified, goods are "lost" or stolen, and accounts are not audited. Where a contractor is caught in an illegal or improper act, the overseeing government official may be bribed or coerced to ignore the fact. Even the protections of auditors or inspectors may be frustrated through bribes or political pressure. The point is that corrupt contracting is one of the great failings of governments all over the world, and it is oppressive in the sense that, by theft and misappropriation, it deprives the citizens of these countries of hundreds of billions of dollars, often desperately needed for vital social services.

Fighting Contracting Corruption

Each year, a government may have hundreds or even thousands of contacts in force, with additional contracts or contract renewals being let. Most governments suffer from inadequate resources to oversee these contracts, and in some cases, this shortage of oversight capability is deliberate, where corrupt politicians and officials want to keep oversight as ineffective as possible. The single most effective curb against contract corruption continues to be the mandated use of competitive bidding. A carefully drafted law mandating competition can be used as the basis for defending agency contracting practices, and giving leverage to reformers and those officials in agencies who genuinely want fair and legal contracting to prevail. If citizen groups or commercial companies want to try and keep the government legal, it could do nothing more effective than becoming advocates of public, open competition for all contracts.

But a legislative mandate for competition even if it is achieved, is far from enough. Much depends on the willingness and ability of public officials to implement such laws fairly and free of corruption, and this is not easy. Each agency of government should be required to supplement the law with a carefully defined and published set of procedures for bid competition. All bidders should be made aware of these procedures, and bidders can and should police each other to make sure that the procedures are followed. The reputation of each bidding company can be tested by checking their performance on previous contracts and their financial and management ability to carry out the contract must be evaluated. The initial contractor selection process is critical because it is here that the likelihood of corruption will first manifest itself. If bad public officials and companies capture the contract at this point, it is likely that subsequent operations under the contract will be a constant problem.

Another significant protection is created when the government has the authority to debar bidders from future contract opportunities if there is evidence of collusion, factual misrepresentation or intent to conceal relevant information. Debarment is an administrative action, and it puts the burden on the alleged offender to upset the decision either by law suit or by appealing for help from political allies who may regard it as dangerous to interfere. Even informally, any rumors or partial evidence of improper bidder practices can be made known to other contracting organizations in both government and the private sector.

Since corruption involves both sellers and buyers, every government agency must start with the premise that some improper approaches will take place. This means that the measures to protect against improper actions by the government's own staff are just as important as protections against outsiders. Special oversight of bidding processes can be provided by auditors, inspectors, or even outside investigators, and it should be made clear to the staff that such assessments are to be expected. Each agency should have formal procedures which clearly state that any form of bribery, collusion or improper information disclosure will be sought out and punished. The evaluation of bids should be conducted by multi-person teams, and their evaluation and recommendations should be in writing and signed.

The most difficult problem comes where the decision rests with a political official who is not controlled by the mechanisms applied to the career staff. Many ministers or agency heads have broad and unchecked authority under agency enabling statutes. They may make arbitrary decisions based entirely on their own judgment, and on political factors not considered in the staff technical evaluation. Factors such as the geographical location of bidding companies, or contributions to political campaigns, or the desire to reward the allies of the regime are not uncommon. Few career officials will have either the authority or the courage to challenge such political distortions. In some countries, provision is made for a "Tender Board" or Contract Review Board that has independent authority to review the outcomes of bid processes and challenge any instance of serious impropriety. But again, these boards may be ineffective unless they have the courage to press their objections. At the very least, their challenge of a contract selection can serve to fix public attention on the suspect decision.

During the performance of each contract, there should be multiple responsibilities. First, the official in charge of the contract must be made clearly responsible for its effective management. This is the first and most important line of defense against impropriety, and no amount of post audit can substitute for it. This responsibility includes real time determination that the demands of the contract are being met, that only authorized work is performed and billed, that all costs are realistic and appropriate, and that costly overruns are avoided. In support of these contract managers may be allies in the agency who will audit, inspect or investigate contractor performance if necessary. Every single activity under the contract can be manipulated. Auditing and inspection should be performed "real time" and not left to post audits months after the fact.

The Pathologies of Public Finance

Whatever the problems experienced with the World Bank and the International Monetary Fund, it is necessary to hold a clear understanding of the national problems that make countries turn to these institutions for loans in the first place. Almost always, national governments get into monetary panic situations through their own policies. Sometimes it really can't be helped. Events beyond the control of a given country such as world wide recessions or shifts in the value of goods that a country exports can precipitate a fiscal or monetary crisis and create the need for short term financial assistance from outside of the domestic economy. In fact, this is the kind of dilemma for which the IMF was created in the first place. The IMF can help finance a temporary deficit, bridge over short-term recession problems, back local financial liquidity to stave off investor panic, or help negotiate debt restructuring to avoid peaks in debt repayment. But the basic assumption is that the IMF can and should be involved in short term assistance and that it remains the responsibility of the borrowing country to correct its economic problems itself. But this is exactly the dilemma: what if governments cannot or will not take the necessary steps to correct their political and structural mistakes?

How do governments get themselves into such deep financial difficulties? Perhaps the most pervasive answer is that many governments are so inherently poor that they can never achieve financial soundness. But this answer is simply not acceptable. Poor countries have proven to be capable of rapid improvement. Nor does the plea of poverty solve anything. In poor countries, the intelligent management of government income and expenditure simply becomes surpassingly vital, and most financial crises stem from perverse politics and financial mismanagement – not from relationships good and bad with international lending institutions. George Ayittey in his book "Africa Unchained" lists how Africans themselves lose their own money:

Corruption:	$148 billion
Capital flight:	$ 20 billion
Expenditure on military:	$ 15 billion

Civil war damage	$ 15 billion
Food imports	$ 18 billion
Total other leakages	$ 216 billion

"If Africa could feed itself, if the senseless wars raging on the continent would cease, if the elites would invest their wealth – legitimate or ill-gotten – in Africa, and if expenditures on arms and the military are reduced, Africa could find itself with the resources it needs for investment" (50)

Even rich governments face the need to balance the demands for government services against the realistic ability to generate government revenue from the national economy. One of the common failings in developing countries is that the demands for public programs such as health and education will congenitally exceed the wealth generated by the economy, or the ability of the government to lay its hands on enough of that wealth to finance vital public programs. Taxation is always difficult and never popular, yet achieving adequate taxation is one of the critical responsibilities of governments. The problem however is that governments often lack the strength of purpose to bite the taxation bullet, but they find it too easy to make big promises for the provision of more social service and public infrastructure. Thus, a major pathology occurs when there is deliberate and knowing over-commitment without any reasonable understanding about how the money for meeting such commitments will be obtained. Shifts in financial wellbeing can occur with confusing swiftness. Until three or four years ago, most countries in the OECD were running budget surpluses. Now, their combined deficit is in the range of 3-4% of GDP. The United States has experienced similar downward spirals. Budget decisions are heavily related to political populism – the cutting of taxes at the same time that the government promotes more funds for popular public programs. Every government suffers from this problem yet most are able to struggle along without foundering. But what most governments know but choose to ignore is that once such commitments are made, they are almost impossible to abandon or reduce. Beneficiaries of government programs become resistance blocs to stoutly oppose any reductions in their benefits. Defense of these benefits is very strong and implacable and makes retrenchment almost "mission impossible". In France, even modest reductions in labor related benefits have produced such massive public resistance that it toppled one government and has tarnished another. Political control of the national annual budget of the government becomes absolutely essential, but such control runs counter to low value political instincts.

The way in which most governments see themselves getting out of the budget dilemma is to rely on policies to "grow" the economy at a faster rate, expecting that a richer economy can then be tapped for government revenue to cover budgetary commitments. But this nirvana is often beyond reach, at least in the short term future, and the fiscal problems still have to be faced.

Another solution is often seen in government borrowing, and in less developed countries borrowing has been from both private banks and from international lending institutions. Such borrowing is usually for the purpose of supporting national programs of economic expansion, again with the assumption that expansion will generate the funds to pay off the borrowing. But many developing countries have failed with this strategy, and they become the victims of over borrowing and become heavy and continuous dependents of lenders. Dependence on borrowing seems to lead not to greater financial discipline but yet further dependence. Often borrowed funds become the means of trying to cover annual fiscal deficit problems. As the financing of external debt increases, too much of the revenues of the borrowing country are needed for the debt, further exacerbating the shortage of funds for social services and public infrastructure. Some governments will deliberately and cynically maintain this dependency, hoping to foist the problems created by their own lack of restraint and accountability more or less permanently onto the lenders. In internal political terms the cynical government is then able to blame the lenders for "lack of adequate help", or for the outrage of wanting their loans to be repaid, or for pushing for the kinds of fiscal restraint that the borrowing government does not have the courage to undertake itself.

Similarly, many governments in developing countries play the same game with aid coming from foreign donor countries. In some countries, where donors are willing to provide aid for national problems such as lack of health care or serious shortages in elementary and secondary education, the reliance on such outside donations is cynically used to withdraw the recipient government's own financial investments and leave the problem more or less permanently to the donors. Some budgets in developing countries now draw on donors for as much as 40% of the domestic budget, and donors find themselves so enmeshed that they can't draw back. The most classic of such cases is that of U. S. aid to Israel which has been extensive for more than fifty years, with no end in sight. Israel also receives very substantial donations from American citizens and these funds are a critical component of national income. While American official aid is ostensibly for domestic social programs they do permit the Israeli government to shift its own internally generated funds to military and police expenditures.

Even aside from the international interrelationships for government finance, the same political lack of will and responsibility pervades internal fiscal discipline. Promising "more" or "better" is endlessly attractive politically. Taxation, program reform, fiscal discipline, or governmental retrenchments are always politically repugnant. Yet public debt has declined in developed countries from a high of about 78% in 1996 to about 65% today, while emerging economy debts have risen from about 60% in 1997 to almost 72% today. In the United States, one of the mantras of the Republican Party has been their advocacy of budget constraint, avoidance of big government and the prudent provision of public services. Yet the actual course of events is that the Republicans happily join with the so-called "tax and spend" Democrats in loading up the annual budget with new or expanded public programs. Some of the European socialist countries such as France and Germany are now facing intractable consequences of previous commitments, in large part driven by the aging of the baby boomers and in part by the high costs of social programs generally. The collapse of the Soviet Union destroyed the whole basis for provision of social programs, all of which now require painful redesign and restructuring and refinancing. Part of the pain comes from the growing realization of the extent to which the "cradle to grave" commitment was entirely false. Most social programs and public infrastructure were totally inadequate and even non-existent under the Soviet brand of socialism.

As summarized in the Economist magazine: "There are some striking differences in the structure of budget finances in emerging and developed countries. The first is that government revenue amounts to an average of only 27% of GDP in emerging economies (compared to 44% in rich economies) as a result of inefficient tax systems and larger informal economies where collection of taxes is all but impossible. This means that debts loom much larger in relation to tax revenues. Revenues are also more variable in emerging economies because of their bigger economic ups and downs. Another difference is that interest payments are almost twice as high as the share of GDP in rich countries. They are also more volatile, because poor country's foreign-currency and short-term debt make up a larger share of the total. The IMF looked at 26 cases during the past three decades in which emerging economies' debt declined significantly. Of these, 19 involved defaults, which limit government's subsequent ability to borrow and thus cramped their growth. In the other 7 cases, debt ratios were reduced by fiscal restraint." (51)

There are many cases in which adequate provision has not been made to cover unfunded future expenses. These debts include the rise in pensions, both public and private, and the escalation of health care. In other countries, subsidies have been paid to strictly private companies despite the fact that they are perfectly capable of taking care of themselves. Government subsidies might be justified as short term assistance in special situations such as encouraging development of an important new technology or to enable creation of new export capabilities. The trick is to prevent such subsidies from becoming permanent. Governments should adopt a deliberate policy of not subsidizing profit making organizations. They should avoid programs that permit rent seeking. They should concentrate on loans or loan guarantees and keep corporate subsidies out of the yearly budget. If governments want to do something constructive for corporations – and consumers – they should concentrate on promoting economic competition.

The situation in China is being set up on a very high risk basis. The Chinese Communist Party (CCP) has captured an extraordinarily large portion of national wealth, through its control of the main income sources: earnings by thousands of State Owned Enterprises (SOE), control of most bank lending, control of savings, and high levels of taxation. One of its deliberate strategies has been to shift some very large costs for things like health care, public infrastructure and environmental protection down to Chinese provinces, counties and cities. As a consequence, these governments are desperate for money, and the liabilities of such governments have climbed to about $2.9 trillion, including the obligations of shaky quasi government borrowers. That is, these local governments have created a whole range of government linked special organizations such as development banks, development associations, and construction project enterprises. These special organizations are all empowered to borrow money and have done so in huge amounts. It is legally expected that local governments back these borrowings and are responsible for their payment, but there is a lot of speculation that such governments would do one of two other things: they could repudiate the debt, or they could seek to shift the debt to the national government, which they have often done before. But the magnitude of such indebtedness is now so great that any repudiation or shift would create a monstrous financial crisis. In truth, China is by a wide margin the most indebted country in the world.

A rather recent phenomenon is the emergence of development banks – special purpose financial organizations to attract money for specific economic problems such as rural or urban development, expansion of energy utilities or construction of harbors and ports. These banks are a good idea, but whether any of them succeed is a reflection of the nature of the government that creates them. If the government creates improper subsidies, then chances are that a development bank will too. If a government is corrupt, so too will be its development banks. If a government is honest and stays out of the subsidy and reallocation games development banks can be very useful. But still, many are vulnerable to pressures from their clients and prove unable to say no to bad propositions. Some state owned policy banks are very politically skewed and simply divert funds from more efficient private markets. Many government bank restructuring programs are in reality bailouts of irresponsible banks and other lending institutions. In many cases, banks persuade governments to absorb the cost of bad loans or permit them to be converted into equity, which merely rewards bad management at taxpayer cost. Where short term loans are converted into long term loans, this may simply lock in bad loans for a longer period of time, thus delaying a more fundamental solution. In the end, it appears that direct government intervention into the allocation of financial resources generated only more difficult problems for both big business and the banks. Nor can the government really prevent bank greed and incompetence.

The whole arena of a strategic industry or "national champions" as typified by military industrial complexes or "commanding heights" industries has also skewed the allocation of scarce development money. Policy loans severely constrained the independence and freedom of action of central banks, including their ability to adjust the pace of money flow as a means of controlling inflation. A tendency to be preoccupied with large important companies has led to a neglect of small and medium business financial needs. Many governments believe that helping big business is the path to greater economic development, ignoring statistics that show that real growth takes place in small and intermediate firms. Concentration on public sector state owned enterprises has meant limiting lending available to the private sector. And any enterprise that is subsidized and protected by the government is a candidate for overextension and lack of cost consciousness.

Human Resources Management: Corrupt Appointments

In almost every country, human linkages are often more important than the formal structure of agencies. This is especially true in governments where the official structure is weak and ill conceived, or in governments that are authoritarian rather than democratic or merit based. Thus, the appointment of key leadership to government posts is always carefully controlled to favor the hand of the leadership of whatever kind. The only question may be the basis for selection of key appointments. The most favored basis is political loyalty, but other criteria may be shared interests or common goals, including "causes" such as environmentalism or the alleviation of poverty. Many countries allocate top positions in the government based on the strength or popularity of specific groups. In some governments with many political parties, this allocation may mean the allocation of such positions to each of the parties in the controlling coalition. In developing countries, there is a tendency to allocate based on the divisions in the country such as race, religion, tribalism, clans or even villages or important families. The power to appoint thus becomes the source of many kinds of pathology.

In corrupt governments, appointments designed to perpetuate and extend networks of corrupt officials into the arenas where corruption is most profitable. The acid test for appointments is merely loyalty to the leadership, and not merit or skill. Loyalty is most likely to be to an individual and not the institutions of government. Ability may not be totally ignored; many appointments, even in pathological regimes are from "the brightest and the best", but still the criterion is "the best from among the loyalists".

The narrower the range of selection of top people the more it is visibly seen as unfair since it deliberately ignores large segments of the population and is seen as "in your face" prejudice. The loyalist group, whatever its competence, is seen as the ultimate "special interest" grip on power. The whole government is seen as a special interest bloc, and the consequence of this special interest cronyism extends itself into skewing or manipulating the values of public programs, and in centrist governments. In most cases this control extends itself into penetration of the whole national economy. The most recent high visibility situation of this kind was that of Saddam Hussein who not only gave important posts to his sons but he rather blatantly put much of the government into the hands of people from the village where he grew up.

Such tainted appointments can be expected to be carried down below the crucial top positions. Unless the number and location of authorized positions is tightly controlled, the agency can be filled with numerous, largely meaningless jobs such as "special assistants" or "assistant deputies" or "deputy assistants" which are perfect payoff jobs for loyalist hacks. Elaborate corrupt networks are buried in the more formal structure of the agency. At each level, the boss is expected to develop whatever corrupt practices are possible, with the illicit profits shared upward to the agency head. Such a perverse structure is self-concealing and self-protective, and it presents a formidable resistance to any efforts for reform.

Finally, one of the more popular political games played with agency workforces is the hiring of large numbers of low level employees in redundant jobs. One favorite is drivers, often one (plus auto) assigned to each senior officer of an agency. These drivers may actually drive only one or two hours a day. Another is "tea ladies" who trundle carts from office to office, dispensing tea and snacks, when obviously employees could service themselves. Production lines, warehouses, auto maintenance facilities, mail rooms, janitorial services, file rooms and security guards are all places where staffs can be enlarged. Since the amount of actual work is relatively finite, the result is that each employee does less work, and the concepts of efficiency and productivity are largely abandoned.

There are ways to counter the growth of such entrenched pathological structures, but all of them rest on the ability to find honest and courageous people to replace the crooks. A new agency head, for example, can remove the worst of the corrupt relatively quickly. There may not be the need to have hard evidence of malfeasance, but only a serious suspicion of it. Even lower officials who may have legal tenure in the civil service need not be kept in positions where they can do damage. For example, in 2001, the new head of Mexico's Customs Agency fired more than 90 people, including virtually all of the top managers in the first major purge of government officials by President Vicente Fox who took office in December of 2000, following campaign pledges to eradicate corruption. 45 of 47 supervisors were fired along with 50 commanders of the federal police force whose officers work with customs agents at the border checkpoints. The Customs Service has long been notorious for corruption ranging from small bribes from individuals to major collusion with drug cartels shipping huge amounts of illegal narcotics. One amusing illustrative example of the corrupt services available allowed a three ton circus elephant to be smuggled into the country because the circus owner paid a $4,500 bribe to customs agents not to "see" the elephant as it was shipped across the border from the United States.

Effective bureaucracies, if allowed to do so, can guard the decisions and processes by which money flows, or assets are conveyed. But one of the troublesome aspects of most bureaucracies is that, with many offices and multiple authorities involved, it is often very difficult to determine who actually decided what. Authority to commit money or assets should be severely limited to as few officials as possible, and the decisions to commit should be recorded in writing and available for review. After the commitment decision is made, the next action involves the management of the activities leading to payment. For example, the decision to contract for goods or services is followed by the negotiation of a contract, and procedures for payment. In many cases, an independent "certifying officer" is used to double check that each action is properly authorized and correct. In any event, the credo of the auditor is still highly relevant: "Follow the money!"

Section Eight

Government Regulation
As Oppression

The essence of regulation is to force people and institutions to change the way they act and think. Thus, enforcement is a vital part of any regulatory authority -- in fact, the crucial part. But it is very hard to decide when such enforcement goes beyond reason and becomes an instrument of oppression. Regulation tends to become an end in itself. There is such a thing as "the regulatory mind". The tendency is for a body of regulation to be broadened and deepened; to be extrapolated in application; and to be pushed down into second and third levels of detail. Many oppressive regulations are unwarranted extrapolations of a basically sound statute. Regulations may be a form of legislative abdication -- or at least deferral --- because legislative bodies do not have the front end understanding of the whole consequence of the creation of a regulatory policy, nor the technical expertise to legislate specifics.

Why do Governments regulate? There are, of course many legitimate reasons. Some such as the following are for economic policy reasons:

1. To promote economic "efficiency": i.e. to preserve market competition, to prevent excess profits, or to promote fair prices for value received.
2. To induce competition in any given market.
3. To control entry into a market place: controlling the issuance of licenses to do business; setting minimum standards of business or individual professional performance.

4. To require disclosure of economic information such as ownership, financial assets, level of debt, or legal challenges.
5. To prevent unacceptable public risks: examples include information about stock issues or financial risks (e.g. the savings and loan disaster).
6. To provide national uniformity of certain ground rules (e.g. conflicts of regulatory authority between the federal government and the states).
7. To limit competition in certain sectors (i.e. public utilities, maritime transport)
8. To redistribute income (i.e. minimum wage, labor protection)
9. To allocate scarce resources (e.g. FCC allocation of broadcast rights; access to natural resources on public lands).
10. To control economic outcomes (e.g. banking stability; home mortgage security; performance standards; anti-trust controls, etc.).

Other regulations are for social policy reasons:

1. To provide national or specific standards to assure equity, fairness and equality in issues of race, gender, ethnicity, cultural beliefs.
2. To preserve and enforce public/private rights (i.e. voting, civil rights, health and safety protections).
3. To prevent injustice (e.g. cheating, misrepresentation, failure to perform under contracts, freedom from civic or government abuse of authority, etc.).
4. To prevent or control anti-social behavior (e.g. sexual harassment).
5. To redistribute public power and prevent the abuse of power (requirements for public participation in government decisions; appeals against government actions, etc.).

In examining this listing of the legitimate purposes of regulation, it is unsettling but illuminating to recognize how each power can be perverted and made either pathological or corrupt or both. Regulation has become one of the most powerful tools by which governments enforce their will. The power to regulate can be given to almost every government agency at all levels, and it is used to redirect institutional and individual behavior by defining what is prohibited and what is "allowed". The proliferation of regulations is so great in some countries, nobody including those who write them and enforce them understands them all, much less understanding their consequences, which can be enormous.

To quote Bhagwati: "Few outside of India can appreciate in full measure the extent and nature of India's controls until recently. The Indian planners and bureaucrats sought to regulate both domestic entry and import competition, to eliminate product diversification beyond what was licensed, to penalize unauthorized expansion of capacity, to allocate and prevent the reallocation of imported inputs, and indeed to define and delineate virtually all aspects of investment and production through a maze of Kafkaesque controls. This all-encompassing intrusiveness and omnipotence has no rationale in economic or social logic; it is therefore hard for anyone who is not a victim of it even to begin to understand what it means. The origins of this bureaucratic nightmare lay, for sure, in the combination of two major factors: first, the inability to trust the market when scarcities are acute and the tasks are challenging; and second, the failure to understand that markets will generally work better than central planning as a resource allocation device."

The problems of destructive regulation are ubiquitous, and often at their worst in less developed countries. Some countries believe that regulations can be used to force organizations to pay their workers more money, with no recognition of the economic realties of the organization. For example, a minimum wage regulation may be set so high that many smaller businesses can't comply and are driven out of business or forced into the informal economy. Labor standards may require such exceedingly expensive compensation for released workers that companies avoid hiring them in the first place. In one African country for instance, night and weekend work are forbidden, and the minimum wage is 82% of the average value-added per worker. To discharge an employee an employer must first retrain him, place him in another job and pay him a lump sum equivalent to a year and one half of his regular wages. Similarly, bureaucratic complexity makes the creation of new businesses extraordinarily costly and time consuming. According to the Economist: "In Congo it takes 215 days, costs close to nine times the average annual income per person, and firms must start with a minimum paid-up capital of more than a third of that preposterous fee. These rules are generally regarded as stupid and pointless. [3]

There is virtually no serious intellectual reasoning that helps to define the limits of regulation. Almost nothing in society and life is unregulated, and nobody can say when it should stop and at what level. The basic questions are the hardest to answer: how safe is safe? How safe is safe enough? What, in society should be left essentially unregulated? When and why does regulation become excessive and pathological? For the regulatory mind, the answer seems to be Never!

Another hard question is how far the imperatives of governance and the need to execute public policy should be permitted to overpower the rights of individuals and of institutions? Most people favor control of private sector institutions, at least with respect to public health and safety, but are often not aware of how their own individual rights are also constrained

Governments have proved universally and notoriously unable to regulate themselves. State owned enterprises and other government monopolies are far greater threats to public wellbeing than private monopolies ever were, and many are deliberately exempt from regulatory controls. Laws intended to protect the public are often drawn too broadly, giving too much room for perverse interpretation, and the abuse of power. Political leaders can and do violate even well defined regulations. Many regulations contain the power to allocate valuable resources, and this has proved to be an enormous source of corruption.

Each regulatory authority defined in some enabling statute has precipitated enormous volumes of second and third level regulations generated by the responsible regulatory agency, so voluminous and

---

[3]

complicated that nobody can understand them all, and bureaucrats may play the game of "selective" application of the regulations they choose to enforce. Most regulations are highly technical and complex, and it very difficult to find a basis for challenging those that are seen as unnecessary or perverse. This is the major source of power for the government interpreters of these regulations, and of potential corruption in governments. In many developing countries, salaries are low and police, customs officers, building inspectors, tax officials and contracting officers may cynically regard corrupt income from the interpretation of regulations as an "alternative form" of compensation.

Problems of Regulatory Enforcement

Even in moderate and respected governments, enforcement can be a very corrosive role since it is used to make people or institutions do things that they may not want to do, and the more intrusive the regulations, the more likely it is that they will be resisted by both people and institutions. Ultimately, excessive regulation can breed suspicion of government itself. Political ambition or an excess of regulatory zeal may produce regulations that are managerial "missions impossible" – dreams or hopes of perfection rather than practical rules that are capable of being achieved. In countries with multiple layers of government, there are serious problems of duplication of regulatory power and conflict of authorities. In Europe, the European Union structure has emerged as yet another "super-national" layer of regulation imposed on the already complex structures of the member states.

There are not any agreed upon definitions or even intellectual limits on the theoretical power of governments to regulate, and there is a tendency of regulators to expand and extrapolate the range and depth of their regulations. Abuses of regulatory power have created a growing feeling that governments can and do go too far, and there are no effective means to limit the expansion of such power. Regulation is intensely bureaucratic: complicated, technical hard to understand, and often lacking adequate justification for their creation. Enforcement is usually costly and time consuming, requiring long time delays, and excessive paperwork. And regulations, once imposed can prove to be highly rigid, difficult to change, and almost immortal.

One of the risks associated with government regulation is that the regulated industries learn to play the "game" better than their government supervisors, and in effect, capture the regulatory apparatus, by fair means or foul. Then, regulations can be softened or avoided, enforcement can be fended off, oversight can be made friendlier, and price or cost control regulations mysteriously turned to the advantage of the regulated.

But most of the time, the power of the government is so strong that a pathological regime can easily use regulation as a form of tyranny designed deliberately to enhance the power of an authoritarian regime, and provide the basis for reward of one's friends and punish one's enemies. It is also possible to avoid the consequences of regulations that would quash corruption such as prohibitions against bribery, influence peddling, money laundering, concealment of assets, extortion, malfeasance, misfeasance, and others.

This has led to a new interest in what effective alternatives to regulation could be used, including the following:

1. Societies may want deliberately to decide more carefully that there should be some functions in society that need not be regulated (religion? personal privacy?). The basic question is whether there are elements of society that can be trusted to conduct their activities with only general community oversight and not official government regulatory oversight. The attitude of an authoritarian regime? We trust nobody.
2. The public can be protected by public education instead of, or in partial implementation of situations needing control. Voluntary controls are feasible in many areas and should be tried before government application of controls. Despite experiences like Enron, Parmalat or Credit Lyonnais, most corporations exercise voluntary use of independent auditors

to provide public assurance of legality and probity as a vital element of business conduct.

3. Professional standards are a widely used and highly effective means of assuring publicly acceptable outcomes. Doctors are strongly motivated to observe professional ethics in the treatment of patients. Professional engineers are motivated to build bridges or dams that will not collapse. Teachers and university professors usually want to teach the truth. Professional managers have personal reputations at stake, and in many cases, managerial experience and judgment are superior to hard regulatory mandates.

4. Instruments other than regulation may be employed. The tax system can be used to design rewards or penalties to achieve acceptable outcomes in lieu of regulation. There may also be rewards/penalties available through fiscal allocation.

In Less Developed Countries (LDCs), the experience is that regulations become the instrument of ruling elites to augment or preserve their own position. Whether it is by corrupt practice or simply by the exertion of threats within the bureaucracy, regulations are employed to serve the elites and not the general public.

Regulations are tough to deal with because they are so complicated and technical. This means that there is little public understanding of them. At best, this can be mitigated by careful public education and explanation. At worst, public ignorance is deliberate and highly prized by the holders of power. Governments can select from an almost unlimited variety of tools in the regulatory tool kit: price regulation, import/export limitations; quotas, tariffs; granting or withholding of licenses and permits; health and safety regulations for every segment of the economy; franchising and licensing; controls for anti-trust, anti-monopoly and anti-cartel mechanisms; and control of the right to do business. It can be seen that regulations -- limitless in their scope, obscure in their technical detail, open to extrapolation and interpretation, and selective in their application -- are the ideal tools for government centrists, whether they be democratic representatives, socialists, dictators, or tyrants.

Overregulation is common, and it can be deliberate and political. Politicians find it easier to write broad regulatory authority; it gives them endless opportunities to control a power base that makes everybody else pleaders for something. Overregulation simply gives officials more points of leverage to broker their own power, and their very volume and complexity creates the basis for "selective" regulation where officials can choose what to enforce and how, and in the process, regulators can become petty, tyrannical, mean spirited and, especially, corrupt. If policy is the arena of the big tyrant, regulation is the arena of the petty tyrant.

Regulatory statutes when enacted are usually followed by a "lock-in" of clientele interests, and regulatory statutes are enormously difficult to change -- especially if change involves a shift in power. Thus, a regulation may be "forever." This should suggest that regulatory statutes should be carefully drawn, but many are not. The attitude of most politicians seems to be the urge to draft a vague general law conveying sweeping powers and with no sense of limitation. This then provides a platform for forcing outsiders to come to them to negotiate the consequences. The results of these protracted negotiations are then "sealed" into the basic law, which tends to accrete immutable detail.

In most governments, the tendency in regulation is highly centrist. That is, where there are regional and municipal governments, it is their desire to have some regulatory authority of their own, to accommodate regulation to local circumstances. But the centrist government argues "if it is right to enforce a regulation, it is right that it be enforced all over the country with little latitude for variation." It has long been reasoned that the political capital is best expended in passing a single national law, than in permitting regulatory variations to exist at lower levels of government.

The Indian License Raj Becomes the Regulation Raj

Why is investment so hard in India? One might point to a long history of state socialism suspiciously applied by a bureaucratic cadre so virulent that it became known as the License Raj, where some approval chit from the government was required for simply everything. The government has been trying to reduce this kind of mammoth restriction by substituting general regulation for detailed action by action pre-approvals. But the consequence seems to have been that the License Raj has simply morphed into the Regulation Raj, where everything seems to violate one or more of the government's 400,000 regulations. Of course, each regulation is capable of being broadened and deepened and enthusiastically extrapolated.

The Regulation Raj prospers within a government which is uniformly, confused, inept, erratic, and untrustworthy. The political vulnerability to special interest politics and the political willingness to be bribed plays havoc with even the most important of the License Raj's cherished turf. The Indian government also has a long and shameful history of coziness with criminal elements in the country and a reputation for "selective" enforcement of its criminal justice laws and regulations. The government has essential control over the uses of land, and many applicants for government approval of some land action complain bitterly of up to 4 or 5 years of unbelievable bureaucratic equivocation. Disputes that land in court must function in a highly litigious environment, with excruciating delays in legalistic bureaucracy. People forced from their homes by some official land taking fear that they will be under compensated – or not compensated at all. Every organization or person who benefits from government largess and subsidy becomes a fierce defender of their preferment.

Example: Regulation vs. Market Competition

The promotion of competition in market places is a concept much admired by economists, but often viewed by politicians with fear and loathing. Two major trends in the economic policies of governments following WW II were actively opposed to market competition. In the Soviet Union, in Soviet bloc countries, and in other socialist states, the "market" meant the private sector, which was viewed with suspicion by governments, and was excluded from many of the most important sectors of the economy in favor of state control or heavy regulation. Also, in many developing countries, a natural desire to encourage and support the development of local economic producers, in both the public and privates sectors, led to extensive commitment to a policy of "import substitution" which tried to develop local sources to replace goods or services that came from outside of the country. To implement these policies, a wide range of regulations were developed. In order to control the entry of foreign goods into a country, governments developed a formidable array of regulatory controls. In some cases, foreign imports were simply banned. In a somewhat more sophisticated version, all imports were banned except those that the local economy really could not live without, such as machine tools or certain kinds of metal products for production facilities, medical supplies not locally produced, or supplemental supplies of things that the local economy could not produce in sufficient quantities. In other cases, imports were allowed, but they were subjected to various forms of entry controls such as quotas limiting the quantity of items allowed into the country, or high tariffs as taxes on imports – sometimes set deliberately so high that importation was simply infeasible.

This approach remains an evergreen for politicians who can be on both sides of the import argument. With quotas or tariffs, they have been able to say that imports are allowed; for internal consumption, it is pointed out that the real effect was that importation was effectively denied. A similar outcome has been achieved by the use of technical specifications relating to public health or safety, which can be effectively "gamed" to favor what local enterprises produced, and foreigners did not. For example, Washington state apples, among the most popular in the U. S., were somehow deemed by regulation to be "unsafe" for the Japanese public. Similarly, for many years, foreign companies were not allowed to bid on government construction contracts in Japan because they supposedly lacked "technical and managerial experience", even when they were considered highly qualified in their own countries, and in other international construction experience.

The presence of foreign corporations in many countries has also been constrained, again for largely political and doctrinal reasons, rather than for economic rationality. Many countries have simply been chauvinistic – no foreigners allowed, even as investors in local enterprises. Others have felt that, within a general policy of import substitution, foreign investment in local companies was a form of sneaky penetration. It has been common for countries to prevent foreign presence because they feared competition with state owned enterprises, and some potential deterioration of government investment in them. Where foreign investment is allowed, it has often been limited to a percentage of ownership, certainly less than a controlling interest. Finally, ownership of land or property was prohibited, especially in socialist/communist countries where land and property were government owned. One of the most pathological consequences of such policies is that, in a world where development funding is limited and severely competitive, governments have foolishly prevented foreign direct investment, trading off long term economic advantage for short term political gain.

The same kinds of political or doctrinal issues dictate regulatory controls in the domestic economy. The import substitution policy led to government subsidy of local industry, often at great public cost. Preference has often been given to SOEs over private entities, even where SOEs were demonstrably inefficient economic competitors. For example, the government could regulate in order to make some SOEs monopolies, with no other competitors allowed. Another example could involve regulations that require a state owned electricity enterprise to furnish power to a state owned manufacturing enterprise at highly subsidized costs. Regulations have been used to control the number and size of businesses in each economic sector by refusing to grant permission for companies to enter that sector.

The volume and value of contracts issued by governments has been an extremely important component of the total economy, especially in socialist and developing countries. It is therefore not surprising that regulations controlling the deployment of government contracts are very important and highly sensitive. As in so many other instances, SOEs can be given "capture" of contracts within their sectors and private bidders ruled out. In other cases, legal or technical provisions act to favor SOEs even where private bidders are permitted. Indeed, the special legal differences between State Owned Enterprises and private sector enterprises have been carefully constructed to favor SOEs, and such legal differences in turn justify differences in regulatory controls. It is not coincidental that one of the most serious arenas of government corruption in the world – bribery, kickbacks, and bid rigging, over billing, and downright theft – has been in the murky world of government contracting.

One area in which economists and politicians seemed to have been on the same wavelength was the need for full disclosure of economic risks, and information about the financial strengths and weaknesses of economic enterprises. For economists, disclosure is seen as a prerequisite for rational economic decision making. For politicians, disclosure is seen as critical to the protection of the public from unknown risks. Yet the facts seem to be that disclosure which is so popular in theory has been largely neglected in practice, because, among the corrupt, disclosure is deadly. Governments themselves and their SOEs are notorious for the ominous secrecy of their information. Most SOEs are closed doors, and there are seldom any regulations at all that require them to disclose their costs, expenses, profitability, financial strength, or debt.

One of the facts that emerged from the breakup of the Soviet Union and the conversion of Soviet style governments elsewhere was the remarkable fact that there was no feasible way to compute the value of former state properties. They simply did not even know how to do it, much less have any motivation to do so. The cost of construction was not known; assessment of the deterioration and obsolescence of factories and equipment had seldom been attempted; the value of land was never computed because the land itself was state owned. Potential investors had to start over, discarding misleading official estimates and making their own more realistic evaluations of value. Reliable accounting practices for income and costs simply did not exist. Governments clearly had lied and cheated in the publication of limited economic information about the state of the national economy, about sector strengths and weaknesses, and about individual enterprises. Labor costs were highly unrealistic, since the cost of many things such as employee benefit and pension obligations were shared between an enterprise and the government. There have been huge unfunded obligations such as the cost of future pensions or the cost of replacing obsolete equipment that were carefully concealed. Many enterprises had, for political reasons been required to hire redundant workers. In the last analysis, the true value of an enterprise would be defined by its ability to earn a profit in the market place, and the obsolete SOEs of Socialist economies were simply not competitive.

Regulation of Social Risk

Regulations tend to fall into two broad categories – economic and social. Economic regulation is universal because it relates so significantly to the broader issues of economic development. Social services regulation has had its greatest impact in developed nations, especially Europe, and the European Union is now very strongly asserting its influence in unifying and extending social services protections. In addition to the more traditional health and safety regulation, a powerful new wave of environmental and conservation concerns have triggered the proliferation of regulations in these arenas. Social services regulations tend to have high public acceptance and support, and are relatively free of corrupt practices. But there are many nations, mostly developing countries, where these protections are not nearly adequate. In part, this is due to the fact that many of the developing countries are barely surviving, and have trouble finding funds for more than the bare essentials of life. In part, social services themselves tend to lag behind the demands of economic development that preoccupy poorer countries. There is a significant correlation between national wealth and the ability to afford social services programs. Where a country is marginally able for example, to afford an adequate national health care capability, it is marginally able to enforce laws mandating universal health care, and regulations that seek to enforce levels of service that cannot be afforded. Environmental protections are often neglected not only because of their costs and the complexities of their enforcement but because they are regarded as creating negative inhibitions to some form of industrial or commercial development. But industrial waste may be dumped into lakes and rivers because it is deemed too expensive to dispose of them properly. Power companies pollute the air with effluents from their smoke stacks because they do not want to bear the costs of cleaner but more expensive fuels, and because corrupt government enforcers are paid to ignore problems.

It is not unusual therefore to find implementation of the legal or regulatory base that is handsomely enunciated in broad fine sounding commitments falls far short of achieving such promises. Socialist/communist countries in particular undertook a "cradle to grave" philosophy which placed an almost impossible burden on the State. Thus, when governments were unable or unwilling to live up to these commitments, loss of confidence in the government was inevitable. Each regulation requires often very complex and expensive enforcement which has seldom been fully achieved, since it is far easier to write a regulation than it is to see to it that it is enforced. In some countries, the political and bureaucratic thrill of creating regulatory mandates has produced absolutely ridiculous situation where thousands of detailed regulations are on the books. This allows those in charge to "select" those regulations they choose to enforce, an opportunity seldom missed by the corrupt. Even where government ministries are trying to act responsively, they have often lacked the numbers of trained staff to reach all of the people and institutions required to live under regulatory mandates, and it has proved relatively easy to ignore such mandates, or to get around them.

The lack of adequate staff is often pathological in the sense that the shortage is deliberate in order to limit enforcement, and as a false fiscal saving. Regulations written for political visibility prove impossible to implement. Inspectors, who are generally underpaid and overworked, often find it easier to decide when and how to enforce by the simple process of soliciting bribes to assure inaction. "Speed bribes" are paid to overworked officials in order to get approvals or clearances put at the head of the queue. There are thousands of cases where construction inspectors are bribed to turn a blind eye to serious violations of construction standards, and often buildings, roads, or bridges collapse as a consequence. Doctors in state hospitals may face hopeless patient loads, and decide to provide medical service first to those who are willing and able to pay extra. Corporations that build facilities in places where they can take advantage of cheap labor often collude with governments to keep the cost of labor down. This may lead to neglect in the development of health and safety protections in the work place, or the ever popular "selective" enforcement of such regulations.

The Allocation of National Resources

The most valuable and enduring resources of a nation are its people and the land. In former communist countries, and in many developing countries, the land has been the property of the State and little of it is held by private owners. In Africa ownership is often tribal and less than 10% of the land and housing is formally owned by private parties. The absence of clear title to property presents serious obstacles to its use as collateral for loans or even for conveying property to one's heirs. This failure to allocate land to private holders has enormous consequences not only for the individuals but for the economy as a whole. The great bulk of land in Africa represents a huge undeveloped resource. Hernando de Soto, a Peruvian economist estimated that in 1997, the total value of African's informally owned houses and farmland was roughly $1 trillion. That is nearly three times the Sub-Saharan annual GDP and more than 70 times the amount of aid the continent receives each year. The failure of clear title to property causes entrepreneurs to hesitate to develop their assets because they fear that their efforts may be usurped by some shift in government policy. Foreign investors are similarly inhibited from starting businesses or improving local property unless they can be guaranteed a firm legal title.

All of these dilemmas can be resolved, but it requires a high priority effort by the government to make change happen. In some cases, politicians cling to state ownership because they like the power and authority it conveys. In most cases however, a paucity of knowledge and experience exists about how to redraft legislation, rework regulations, and undertake the administrative burden of dealing with hundreds of thousands of cases for the privatization of land and property disposals.

Example: Israeli Regulation as Tyranny

One of the governments that make the most use of regulations as instruments of control is Israel. As a part of the accords reached at Oslo in 1995, the West Bank territories occupied by Israel in 1967 were divided into three areas: Area A assigned to the Palestinian Authority for full administrative and security control; in Area B, the PA had administrative control, but Israel retained security control; Area C is under the full control of the Israeli government. Israel uses the placement of Jewish settlements in or near Palestinian areas, and the location of a new and massive system of 29 highways and bypass roads as a means of controlling movement and segregating the Jewish and Palestinian populations. In addition, Israel has used the development of Regional Plans as a device to control both economic and social development. And in the last several years, Israel has been constructing a long impenetrable wall to segregate Jewish and Palestinian areas.

Israel has used every conceivable regulatory device to control the lives of its Palestinian citizens. The government justifies such actions in the name of national security even in situations where such justification is obscure and tenuous. The designation of Areas A, B, and C was designed as a means to begin to sort out the ultimate disposition of lands and communities that would become part of a Palestinian state. But Israel has used the designation of these areas as justification for the creation of thousands of regulations to control all movement between them as if they were three foreign countries. It is now harder to move between one area and another than it is to move between countries in the European Union. Movement is controlled in many ways:

1. There are literally hundreds of permanent and semi-permanent check points between these three areas. All Israelis are required to carry personal identity papers, and at the very least, these documents will be checked at each check point. While Jewish citizens are usually given free and immediate passage Palestinian citizens may be denied passage or they may be extensively questioned or delayed while checks are

made of their records in other government data bases. Often, limitations are placed on the Palestinians such as time curfews or limits on visiting places not declared as destinations at the check point. In addition, during times of crisis further temporary check points may be established without notice where Palestinians may be held and interrogated, arrested, or have their goods confiscated.

2. The responsibility for this overwhelming movement control lies with the Israeli military: the Israeli Defense Force (IDF). Thousands of troops, tanks, armored cars, and watch towers are utilized for these controls. The West Bank occupation forces are divided into military command areas and the local commander has wide almost unrestrained authority to issue both permanent and temporary regulations at his discretion and without prior consultation with the civilian populace. In addition, the so called Civil Authority (CA) is in fact a part of the IDF, and under the direct authority of the military commanders. It too has separate authority to issue regulations of all kinds with a similar lack of any necessity for public consultation. As a result, thousands of regulations have been issued just in the arena of movement control alone.

3. Along certain routes that are considered tactically vital, permanent barriers have been created – trenches and mounds of dirt that permanently block passage for anything but foot traffic, which of course is check point controlled. Thus, Palestinians are unable to travel by vehicle, and their movements restricted to what they can reach on foot. The movement of supplies, equipment, food and other civilian goods requires off-loading from trucks at these barriers, hand carrying to the far side, and reloading onto other trucks in order to reach their destinations. In other cases, wide deep trenches have been dug across roads between Palestinian communities, permanently blocking them from vehicle use.

4. In times of crisis, additional temporary check points and physical barriers are set up, and new and more stringent temporary regulations issued. Also, it is common during such times for the IDF or the CA to impose house curfews or whole town curfews banning any but the most local movement.

5. Israel is constructing a large network of highways and bypass roads (i. e. to bypass Palestinian towns). These highways, funded almost entirely by the United States at a cost of more than $3 billion, are accessible only to Jewish citizens and denied the Palestinians. The practical effect of these new highways has been the regulatory seizure of almost 17% of West Bank land and it has been alleged that the location of the routes is such that they deliberately further limit the ability of Palestinians to move about.

These forms of movement control play havoc with even the most innocent of civilian activities. Patients have been denied access to hospitals, doctors or medical clinics; children have difficulty getting to school even for regularly scheduled classes, much less any extra-curricular activity; workers find it difficult to get to their jobs; housewives may not be allowed to go to shopping areas; merchants may not be able to get goods delivered; public transportation has been totally disrupted; maintenance and repair service trucks may not be allowed passage. Farmers may be denied access to their fields, and as a result, crops go untended and rot in the fields, or harvests cannot be transported to the point of sale.

Both the IDF and the CA also use regulations to control almost every form of economic activity in addition to the movement controls. Businesses require licenses to exist, and their activities are subject to hundreds of minor regulations. No building is permitted for either commercial or residential construction with out a license from the CA. Such regulations, if used reasonably and fairly make sense, but the IDF and CA have designed such regulations to favor Jewish interests and to block or control Palestinian interests, and implementation simply furthers this initial prejudice. What is possible and permitted for Jews is denied and impossible for Palestinians. Palestinian citizens find it almost impossible to function in Area C which is reserved only for State activities. Economic and movement controls giver the IDF overwhelming control in Area B in which Palestinian administrative laws and operations are overridden by IDF regulations and on-the-ground control. And even in Area A, supposedly under the full control of the Palestinian Authority the IDF penetrates almost at will, often occupying territory assigned by the UN to the Palestinian Authority and imposing its own regulations.

Other economic controls include forbidding certain kinds of economic activity (for example, Palestinian fishermen have been forbidden to fish, or are cynically allowed to fish only in areas where the absence of fish is well known). In other cases, the construction or repair of public utilities is forbidden. Property is confiscated in the name of national security, including suspect sheep. Crops are destroyed, and valuable olive and fruit trees uprooted in order to provide "fields of fire". Buildings may be bull dozed without notice or warning for similar security reasons.

The new airport in the south of the Gaza Strip (funded almost entirely with U. S. dollars) was at first prohibited from opening. Then, after a brief period of operation it was closed down again by the IDF. The IDF and CA also exercise almost total control over electrical power distribution and over the main water sources and water distribution.

The Civil Administration develops Regional Plans controlling the use of land, the development of communities, the placement of housing, the deployment of public infrastructure, and designation of reserved areas for reasons ranging from military security to provision of parks and other green spaces. These plans are designed without any real community input and protests against Plan provisions are generally ignored. Once approved, they become hard and fast and any deviation from them can be used as the basis for prevention and punishment. There is a constant battle, for example, between limitations in the Plan for housing construction and the needs of individuals or businesses for places to build. Requests for waivers in the Plan are usually hopeless and in most areas, Palestinian housing is seriously overcrowded and deteriorating. Palestinian famillies are constantly building homes on forbidden land, and the CA is constantly tearing down these illegal structures. There are documented cases of bulldozers of the CA knocking down buildings without warning with families still in them. These regional plans universally favor Jewish interests. A dozen industrial parks have been planned and seven are being constructed which will serve Jewish settlements and disrupt the commercial areas used by the Palestinians. One Regional Plan has created a new definition of Metropolitan Jerusalem, extending the western part of the city into a huge area of more than 400 square kilometers of the West Bank and bringing it under the control of EDF/CA regulation. In addition, in May of 2002, the Israeli government announced the unilateral division of all of the West Bank, including all three areas of jurisdiction, into eight subdivisions, ostensibly for more effective "public administration". But this simply means the extension of all of the regulatory powers of the IDF and CA into areas over which they had relinquished control under the Oslo Accords.

In summary, the designation of areas of political authority as approved by the United Nations and both the Israeli government and the Palestinian Authority has been quietly but forcefully undermined by the facts of life of heavy handed regulation by the IDF.

Section Nine

Strategies For Reform

Governance is the ultimate mechanism for directing the affairs of a nation, and it is, of necessity, the exercise of power because it is the primary official and approved instrument for the making national decisions. This remains true even where there is a strong and independent private sector which controls most of the economic life of the country, because even then, the government has enormous influence over the environment in which the private sector functions. If a government is dictatorial and authoritarian, chances are that decision-making is in the hands of a single individual or a small group of elite power holders. If a government is more democratic and representative, the power of the government must be focused by building a reasonable public consensus for major decisions. In either case, second and third level decisions are linked to the functioning of elaborate structures of government agencies with power designated by laws enacted by legislative bodies that own and operate mechanisms for negotiation, compromise, or decision by fiat.

The one absolute essential for curbing perverse political power is to generate and focus public attention on the activities of the political leadership. The public will always be concerned; the real question is whether such concern can develop real leverage on the political leaders. This is not mission impossible; there are in fact many ways in which this leverage can be built. Even in absolute tyrannies, there are tides running which offer opportunities for reformist action. Old tyrants die, and regimes change. Legislatures and judges find windows of opportunity to change pathological laws or call culprits to account. Internal conflicts between elements of the elite may split the regime and open up further opportunities. And even tyrannies can be overthrown, either by internal forces, or by external pressures. It helps to remember that, primarily by internal uprisings, gone are Duvalier and Marcos, apartheid in South Africa, Franco, Ceausescu, the Khmer Rouge, Charles Taylor and Edi Amin, Peron, Mao and many other seemingly invulnerable tyrants. And the world has acted to terminate the regimes of Hitler, Mussolini, Stalin, Tojo, Hussein, and Milosovic.

Public pressure or the reform of bad laws may be almost hopeless in the short run in the face of absolute tyrannies, and the real hope must be placed in the longer term turns of fate. But the most valuable of such public "watchdog" activities can take the following forms:

Despite their frustrations, elections still are the one best hope, because they can be used to legitimize and focus opposition. A regime that is forced to steal an election is also revealing the bankruptcy of its national standing, and the narrowness of its elitist base. In the contemporary world, seriously corrupt elections may now precipitate world-wide attention and cause the monitoring of the next election by international evaluators, giving greater hope to the opposition.

In even the tamest of captive legislatures, there will be some members with the courage to oppose the creation of pathological laws. These people can be visibly supported by others in society, and they can identify bad law proposals so that opposition can be mobilized against them. Citizen groups can help protect honest politicians and public officials by giving them positive visibility and making it more risky to attack them. Hopefully, fewer bad laws can be sneaked through in secret. Existing bad laws stand a better chance of being mitigated or neutralized.

Just as police rely on informers for intelligence, so too can politicians or public officials obtain information from citizens and private organizations about what governments are doing wrong. The worse the regime the greater is the need to make such "whistle blowers" safe, secure and anonymous. But what is really needed are people within the power structure who will listen and perhaps act, and can be trusted not to shoot the messengers. It may be an honest politician, an anti-corruption agency, a newspaper reporter, or a trustworthy public official.

The generation of greater public interest in the machinations of their government is not easy and it may even be dangerous. Public interest relates to the wellbeing of the whole population, and should be clearly distinguished from the more self-serving special interest politics. But even a relatively small group of citizens or a small staffed organization can lock on to an issue such as elementary/secondary education, child care, or the failures of state owned enterprises, or the evidences of corruption. A variety of people have useful skills to contribute: research, writing, evidence gathering, intelligence generation, internet communications and so on. Often, the best sources of such intelligence are from employees of government agencies or state owned enterprises that cannot live with their own corrupt environment.

One of the targets for civic action must be the laws themselves, especially laws that protect the right to oppose the regime. First and foremost, this means the existence of a law that provides for honest elections. In addition, laws are needed that secure the right for people to meet and to protest, and to broaden as much as possible the range of subjects that can be debated without being considered as an attack on the State. Among these subjects should be the right to press for anti-corruption measures, the effective audit or evaluation of agency activities, and the rules under which corruption can be investigated, removed, or prosecuted.

Obviously, any authoritarian regime can probably block any such efforts, and reform may not always be possible. Reform forces must be patient and persistent, and be ready to take any opportunity that comes along and to capitalize on regime weaknesses. The process of reform has to start at the top with the drafting of national laws. There should be constant pressure to define in law if possible that which is not authorized, or is specifically forbidden, or is defined as illegal. Even policy statements that do not convey specific authority can still be used to commit to national goals and preferred actions. The point is that any means of preventing pathology from being locked into law is of enormous value. Any limitation of political excess of power is worth fighting for. Even if these laws are ignored or violated, they still serve as anchors which opponents of a regime can use to justify attacks on tyrants.

Similarly, politicians love to draft broad noble sounding legislative language which seems to promise a government solution to all ills. But reality often is that the broader and more open ended the legislative language, the more power it conveys, and the more vulnerable it is to pathological interpretation. There is usually too great a gap between legislative flights of fancy and the harsher world of implementation. Even in wealthy and stable countries, there is increasing disenchantment over legislative promises not kept. In authoritarian states, wide open legislative mandates are often deliberately sought, since each represents a form of legislative abdication. It transfers all power to the executive and leaves the legislature with no basis for curbing that executive power. Once such wide authority is obtained by the executive, it is extremely difficult to take back, and legislative bodies, having conceded too much, become largely irrelevant.

It is therefore exceedingly important that legislative bodies must be pressed, by whatever forces in the country can be brought to bear, to retain their ability to act as a counter force to the usurpation of power by the executive. Legislatures need to protect their own authority, first by having the courage to resist pressures to corrupt the laws, and then through their own internal control of the law drafting process. In many cases, a two house legislature appears to be superior to a single house because it creates some checks and balances between the two, making it more difficult for executives to seize control. It is also valuable to create a separation between the drafting of laws and the approval of appropriations of the money to implement the law. As an adjunct of this reasoning, legislative bodies should resist any authority of the government to generate revenue that is not officially controlled through the legislative oversight process. For example, in countries such as the old USSR, the Peoples Republic of China, Indonesia, Pakistan and elsewhere, the military budget is often outside of the regular budget and is virtually uncontrolled. In addition, the military often controls production assets that generate revenue, which is used solely for the support of the military establishment. This has helped to generate unwarranted and excessive military power, and has been a direct and powerful enabler of corruption.

Further, legislative bodies must guard the Constitution and important basic authorizing laws by making them harder to change, usually by requiring a 2/3 majority vote for change approval, or even requiring a Constitutional convention to ratify change. The Constitution and supporting legislation should clearly authorize the conduct of political parties, and preferably they should lay down the rules for honest elections in some detail if possible. Even where a dictator is prepared to steal elections, Constitutional definition of proper elections would highlight the nature of such pathology and provide a stronger basis for opposition.

Also if possible, Constitutions or basic laws should provide mechanisms to prevent the abuse of presidential appointment powers. Patronage is one of the most powerful tools of authoritarian regimes, and it conveys five great advantages. First, it is used to make sure that key jobs – particularly those which involve control of money or the allocation of valuable resources – are filled by regime loyalists who will do as they are told. Second, political allies and supporters can be rewarded for past services. In many cases, these payoff jobs are in lesser positions such as "commissions" or "boards" with little or nothing to do. Third, some appointments will be protective. For example, if a law requires the appointment of an Inspector General in an agency, the threat of that office to the corrupt can be mitigated by the appointment of a loyalist or an incompetent to the post. Fourth, appointments can reach down blow the crucial top positions. Unless the number and location of authorized positions is strictly controlled, the agency can be filled with numerous, largely meaningless jobs such as "special assistants", or "assistant deputies" or "deputy assistants", all of which provide comfortable salaries without the discomfort of doing any work.

One of the more political games played with the agency workforce is the hiring of large numbers of lower level employees in redundant jobs. After the disintegration of the USSR, and the conversion of eastern European states, studies indicated that as many as 40% of low level jobs were redundant and existed primarily so that politicians could say that in their socialist economy "nobody is unemployed".

It is also widely true in corrupt regimes that most political appointments will have little or nothing to do with skill or knowledge or competence. The acid test is loyalty to the regime. But what is worse is that, when a regime is corrupt, the power of appointment permits the extension of corruption down into the second and third levels of the organization. This networking is often has an elaborate structure of its own hidden within the more formal structure of the agency. At each level, the boss is expected to develop whatever corrupt practices are possible, with profits shared upward to the agency head. Such a perverse structure is self-concealing and self-protecting, and becomes a formidable obstacle to any effort for reform.

There are ways to counter the growth of such entrenched pathological structures, but all of them rest on the ability to find honest, courageous people to replace the crooks.

Just as the laws must protect against the abuses of the appointment authorities of an agency, laws must provide protection for the conduct of the agency's most important internal processes.

Finally, the machinations of bad regimes can be leveraged from the outside. Globalization is not a phenomenon being experienced only in the corporate world. Government has also built up a globalized structure including the United Nations, the World Bank, the International Monetary Fund, the World Trade Organization, and many regional bodies concerned with economics and human rights. As these international bodies become stronger and more experienced, they have moved to become forces against pathological governments. In addition, many forms of civic community have become globalized, including environmentalism, unions, the health care professions, women's rights, and many others. These institutions have developed their own doctrine; they assert that they represent acceptable standards of what is right and wrong in their chosen fields. The World Health Organization has extensive and comprehensive standards for all forms of health care that are held up for comparison against the practices in individual countries. Environmental organizations define what is right and wrong with respect to threats to air or water pollution, land use, conservation of natural resources, protection of wild life, and avoidance of chemical hazards. All such organizations now are capable of proceeding against what they consider violations of these standards in any country in the world, regardless of political boundaries, and despite traditional concepts of national sovereignty.

Most developing countries are compelled by economic circumstances to resort to borrowing from foreign sources, both public and private, and this gives these external lending institutions exceptional influence over the economic policies and practices of their debtor nations, whether they like it or not. The IMF may demand compliance with stringent conditions of government fiscal and monetary reform as a condition for borrowing or extending loan terms, and increasingly, other non-financial organizations have urged and persuaded to make human rights concerns part of the "structural adjustment" requirements that lending institutions impose. Matters such as women's rights, minority rights, voting reforms, and the adequacy of education or health care have been adopted by international lenders.

The same tides are running in the policies of countries even when they give money away. Most developed nations maintain some foreign assistance programs in the form of donations or grants of funds to troubled countries, and donors are increasingly resistant to the wastage of these funds by crooked or incompetent governments. Even private banks find that there is risk in lending to countries with poor human rights records. After many years of indifference, lending institutions now recognize that they must pay more serious attention to the record of corruption in borrowing countries, since neither voters nor stockholders appreciate the sense that lent money is being squandered or stolen. Over the last few years, all of these external forces have had a tendency to become more interrelated, and to concentrate their reform efforts on the more perverse of their client states. The support of these external organizations also lends credibility and backing to those people within a pathological state who are attempting to oppose its regime.

Robert I. Rotberg, in an article in Foreign Affairs Journal offers a bleak and shocking compendium of the nature of states that suffer massive failure: "Failed states are tense, conflicted, and dangerous. They generally share the following characteristics: a rise in criminal and political violence; a loss of control over their borders; rising ethnic, religious, linguistic, and cultural hostilities; civil war; the use of terror against their own citizens; weak institutions; a deteriorated or insufficient infrastructure; an inability to collect taxes without undue coercion; high levels of corruption; a collapsed health system; rising levels of infant mortality and declining life expectancy; the end of regular schooling opportunities; declining levels of GDP per capita; escalating inflation; a widespread preference for non-national currencies; and basic food shortages, leading to starvation. Failed states ultimately face rising attacks on their fundamental legitimacy." (52)

The aftermath of a catastrophically collapsed state is often a surprisingly fertile time for significant national change for the better. During the height of a powerful authoritarian regime, there is almost no effective leverage that the opponents of the regime can exercise. The grip of the state apparatus is simply too strong. But if somehow a regime can be overthrown, the very emotions that allowed the overthrow to succeed can be used to drive the emotion of reform. The collapse of the Soviet authoritarians, the wave of reform in China, the freedom of black South Africa, the deposing of the Khmer Rouge, the independence of S. Sudan, or the success of the initial Cuban revolution are victories that encourage others to believe that their own dilemmas can be dealt with. When new governments are brought to power, it is seldom clear what they will do or how they will do it. It is vital that the gap between the failure of the old regime, and the period of hardening of the new situation be as productive as possible. One of the first prerequisites is to mount as effective an emergency resuscitation program as possible, and it is here that international organizations are at their best. Emergency aid and funds from foreign donors can largely fill a gap that the weak new government cannot fill themselves. All of the basics of human existence -- food, shelter, clothing, medicines, and physical protection are the top priorities even to the exclusion of all else.

The second priority is certainly the restoration of vital public services, and it makes little difference whether services like a clean water supply, removal of sewage and trash and their related health threats, the restoration of electrical power and the creation of some form of transportation system are provided by the government or by private organizations. Some of these services can be expensive to restore and it is critical to get started as soon as possible, as the painful delays in post-war Iraq well illustrate, as does the lag of governments in the United States to the Hurricane Katrina disaster. In other cases such as the removal of trash or debris, the costs are low and many people are willing to volunteer. Most forms of public regulation must undoubtedly be forgotten in the short run, and if possible much streamlined for the long run. For example, where formerly it might have taken months of bureaucratic clearances (and perhaps a few bribes) to initiate a small business, the government should simply jettison this baggage and turn all small entrepreneurs loose. In fact, the "bottom up" vitality of people starting small enterprises from retailing and customer services to day care centers is the single best hope for rapid economic recovery. The widespread destruction of housing can best be met by temporary shelter not in remote refugee camps but in the old neighborhood communities. The combination of a few shops and some temporary shelter means a return to at least a rudimentary level of communal stability. The government could do a lot worse than to become the supplier of building materials and a central clearing house for the skills needed in both residential and commercial reconstruction. Cheap small loans with long maturity dates are valuable, along with open ended grants of funds to local governments for all forms or revitalization.

These are the places where governments and donor organizations should be committing scarce funds initially. To the extent that additional funds are available, they should be concentrated on short term economic development priorities. The criteria for priority setting should not be political but based on the greatest public need. There should never be a return to the distorted allocations of the power base that got a country into the catastrophic dilemma in the first place, and the collapse of the old regime may represent the best opportunity in decades for reallocation of power and greater equity in its deployment. One of the most challenging of these changes will probably be to recast the military away from the oppressors of the population to its guardians. A great fear in a weakened state is that power will be seized by a small band of armed power seekers who will simply start the horrible cycle all over again. Only the military, under effective partnership with a reform regime has the power to prevent this, and there must be a collateral strengthening of law enforcement capacities for the suppression of street crime and protection of citizens and institutions.

One of the objectives of this sequence of recovery is to prepare the way for the return of the displaced population, who may have fled to safer parts of the country if any, or to refuges in neighboring countries. These refugees may have lost everything but they cannot remain for long as unwanted guests in other countries or as permanent wards of a bankrupt homeland. Often, the last remaining resource left to these people is the most important – their energy and their skills. It is especially important that key skills for recovery be induced to return home. This includes doctors and nurses, teachers, managers, business people, and the providers of vital public services such as police and fire protection and public welfare. These people have options about where they exercise their talents and they may not want to return unless they can be shown a pattern of recovery that assures reasonable stability and opportunity.

One of the most dangerous threats to recovery is the prospect of rapid inflation driven by the scarcity of goods which in turn further drives down the current value of the currency. One of the solutions to this dilemma may simply be to let the informal economy function openly to facilitate the movement of goods and services until the more formal economy can reestablish its capabilities. Such a process should be used to facilitate the restoration of farming as fast as possible and letting farmers sell their produce at the best price possible. This option is likely to be more productive than initiation of (or return to) political price controls that subsidize some elements of the economy and punish others. Similarly a temporary labor market can be created by using external donor funds to undertake rebuilding of vital public infrastructure, which creates at least temporary jobs in construction, distribution and transport. This would be better than some protracted form of public dole.

The longer term ambition for a collapsed state is that it will be able to rebuild a substantial portion of the economy as it was prior to the collapse, and then to use this base as the means to mount a new program of economic development and expansion. Without economic revitalization, it is difficult to see where the revenues will come from to support a revitalization of public social programs and the repair of critical public infrastructure. Many of the less developed countries that have experienced collapse or significant deterioration were socialist states with a high degree of centrist control and dependence on economic policies such as price controls, import substitution and inefficient state owned enterprises that can no longer be subsidized by the weakened and bankrupt state. Such governments will face the sobering necessity of abandoning many strongly held doctrines and policy conceptions about the role of the State. This is precisely the course of action now being followed by the People's Republic of China which has abandoned almost all of the failed doctrines of the communist economic state. The new leadership must become quick studies in moving toward a far more market based and open for two main reasons. First, such an open ended environment may be critical in encouraging a "bottom up" entrepreneurship by individuals that the government could never achieve. Second, if there is any hope of inducing new capital investment from either domestic or foreign sources, investors must be given as much latitude as possible to create viable businesses without government interference. Both import and export controls must be eliminated, and the government must be seen as highly encouraging of all forms of trade. Such openness may downplay in the short run the need for normal government regulation of such concerns as public health and safety or protection of the environment but these forms of oversight can be reinstituted over time. Taxation will always be a problem since it is stoutly resisted even in wealthy countries but businesses can be expected to accept a simple, stable tax system with taxes set at reasonable levels.

Of equal importance is the need for the reconstituted government to come down harshly on all forms of corruption. Many of the old corrupt officials will remain in place since there is probably no one to replace them, but they must be made to understand that a return to the "good old days" will not be tolerated. The best hope for the government lies in honest leadership from the top down, and the creation of small hard-hitting anti-corruption units with real power to investigate and indict. There should also be the recognition that 99% of the population wants fairness and equity and want to be honest if possible but it is essential that the pathology of government corruption is essentially eliminated.

It is possible also to be hopeful that people are better at reconciliation than governments. Too many governments made the fatal mistake of deliberately using the ethnic or regional diversity of the population to foment conflict for perverse political gain. People can be induced by their government to hate each other as the horrible examples in the Sudan, Yugoslavia, Rwanda, Israel and a dozen other countries demonstrate. But if such hatred is unleashed it has proved to be uncontrollable and ultimately has contributed to the destruction of the governments that unleashed it. It is often forgotten that such diverse populations were able to live together in relative peace before the government generated its hate policies. If a renovated government reverses such perversities and begins to promote reconciliation it is likely that the people will respond. South Africa is leading the way in such reconciliation promotion in the form of its Truth and Reconciliation Commission which is a model both in intent and in procedure that any government can emulate.

Government failure and collapse is always catastrophic and destructive, but it may also be a time of great opportunity to get rid of tyrannical leadership, remodel government institutions away from control to facilitation, attack the entrenched apparatus of corruption, and begin the process of restructuring of the economy. Recovering failed governments will find that there is a lot of support for a reform program of this kind from foreign governments and from international organizations and NGOs.

Reform of Macroeconomic Policies

The government must be able to maintain a monetary policy that concentrates on control of inflation and the stability of the economy. Both the government and the private sector must be able to find money to borrow at reasonable rates. The value of the national currency must be maintained and not allowed to fluctuate excessively, and it must trade at a reasonable rate in the international money market. But all too often, the real economic policy in a pathological state is something very different. Pathological leaders use whatever wealth the economy produces to buy power and pay each other off. Such governments become a vast corrupt structure, led by their leaders, universal in its application. The "big men" steal big; the little men steal small and all are fellows in a conspiracy of concealment. The public is lied to, or bought off by populist subsidies. The annual budget of governments are highly vulnerable to the sins of overspending, but the political leadership seldom allows expenses such as salary increases or funds for maintenance and repair unless they have political value. But responsible fiscal policy should be dealing with the legitimate demands for capital expenditures for public infrastructure, funding for a reasonable "social safety net" and the normal day-to-day operations of the rest of the government.

Many countries also suffer from the inadequacies of the tax system. In some cases, taxes are too narrow and inequitable so that some potential payers are allowed to escape. Whole segments of the economy such as the informal economy, or state owned enterprises may dodge taxation entirely. If tax collection and enforcement is weak, chances are that it is the allies of the regime who are let off the hook. Centrist governments may insist on central collection of most taxes, which deprives regional governments and cities of the ability to take advantage of other tax sources that might be more productive. Those governments that are notoriously inequitable and corrupt inevitably create public resistance to taxation and outrage to corrupt tax evasion.

Reform of Trade Policies

Usually there is a great deal of concern about the balance of trade in a given country. Separate but related policies are needed which set the environment for both national exports and national imports. A deficit of trade (i.e. more imports than exports) is usually seen as bad because it drains money out of the domestic economy. In order to improve the balance of trade, many countries try to restructure their economy to promote industries that can export. However, export becomes feasible not because of government policy but because there are many companies that can in fact be competitive in trade markets by offering goods at prices that compete favorably with what is available in other countries.

But the whole pattern of ISI or import substitution strategies, if maintained for too long, leads to what is now perceived to be the sub-optimal investment of scarce public funds. Government ISI policies generally have been interventionist on a broad front. Every ISI country has used an elaborate rationale for public intervention, masking the essential failures, and fooling the public into thinking the government knows what it is doing.

The urge to protect and subsidize ISI public enterprises has led to a cascade of related multiyear planning, heavy regulation of all economic activity, used as weapons of economic control, administered prices, control or modulation of normal market forces, subsidization, cross subsidization, partial or even total control of banking/lending, heavy government oversight of enterprise performance, and the "politics" of state control. It is now increasingly apparent that the track record is one of disappointment in validity of the ISI concept and in the performance of SOEs: chronic losses, inability to avoid import reliance, the high cost of sheltering both industries and labor, and a growing realization of the foolish failure to capitalize on export development potentials. But in many cases, these countries have been frozen by oppressive political protectiveness into their policies despite the wide recognition of clear failures or lost opportunities. Said another way, the risks of government mismanagement are greatest when the forces of the government are perverted and not balanced by real leverage in the hands of the public in their roles as consumers, and also by a private sector that is strong enough to protect its own interests and provide competition to keep the public sector "honest." Yet these are exactly the kinds of outcomes that many regimes say they want to achieve.

The centrist use of state enterprises requires heavy commitments to enforcement of the government's policies. This cost of enforcement is both monetary and fiscal, and societal, and if the policies are wrong, then enforcement is also wrong. There is a lot of evidence that these elites have been too short- sighted, inflexible, self serving, and inclined to let the "politics" of the economy override economic reality. Time and again, great internalized power without effective check or balance has proved to be an overwhelming inducement to corruption and incompetence.

In recent years, some of the most dedicated "ISI" countries such as India, China, and Russia have been forced to abandon these failures. As nations back off from state controlled economies toward more market based economies, the role of the government has also finally tended to shift toward a policy of using the government to promote exportation. Limitations on exports have virtually disappeared and limitations on imports have been eliminated or modified to be more encouraging. Governments have realized that, in order to expand their domestic economies, imports of needed technology and the highest quality of goods at the lowest price is the key to domestic industrial development. Government money that used to be wasted in propping up inefficient local producers is now more available for domestic social services. More countries now help their companies to sell overseas by using their foreign embassies or by setting up special trade offices in countries with high potential for sales. Trade policy is now aimed at upgrading the mix, quality and value of manufactured goods so that they are more attractive or more profitable.

In every country, there is an urgent need for attraction of money to finance capital investment, especially in capital intensive manufacturing. Few developing countries are capable of generating this development money internally through the savings of their citizens, corporations, or state enterprises. Most developing countries must redesign industrial policies that will attract foreign investors, or that will justify loans from international lending organizations. Thus, when a regime is corrupt, oppressive and untrustworthy it scares off the very investment that could save its economy. Some regimes don't get it. Others don't care as long as there is plenty left to loot.

Reform of Financial Policies

Structural adjustment almost always demands the existence of a strong central bank that is committed to the stability of the currency, the availability of adequate lending resources, the liquidity of money, and the safety/security of banks throughout the country. Banking regulation is a growing part of structural adjustment programs. This means that sound, honest banking practices must be insured by bank oversight and auditing; standards defining lending limits and the maintenance of adequate reserves against loans; standards devising lending criteria to prevent loan default; insurance to protect depositors, borrowers and investors against bank failure.

The existence of a viable stock exchange is also crucial since it broadens the means by which small investors can participate and gives businesses a more powerful way to accumulate investment money. Stock markets also represent a way to "evaluate" companies since it represents a collective judgment as to the best places to invest.

Laws are required that provide for limiting the liabilities of investors to actual investments and not to total personal resources, and protection of investors from false or misleading reports about the strength of individual companies. In more sophisticated economies, regulations must be extended to non-bank lending through institutions such as savings and loan institutions, insurance companies, special lending companies.

Governments are also being pushed to clean up their policy act. This must certainly start with repudiation of past anti-private sector biases and adoption of a new willingness to take initiatives to help the private sector rather than hinder it and letting the opportunities be defined by the market rather than stubborn retention of centrist policy control. This is in fact one of the crucial shifts taking place all over the world in both Less Developed Countries (LDC) and socialist states. The final step must then be the elimination of a whole range of government policies designed to control the economy in general and in specific elements of the economy such as energy, banking, communications and transport. At the same time, structures of price controls must be eliminated along with regulatory barriers, especially against things critical to local industry development, especially raw materials, manufacturing equipment.

As governments are able to reallocate and redirect public funds away from economic development, which would be left increasingly to the private sector, they can concentrate their funds and attention toward meeting the huge backlog of needs for social services and public infrastructure. If there are the political guts to do so, this may result in reexamining marginal public programs (outside of the real social safety net) with the intent of elimination or serious cutback of the less useful programs and those which are obsolete, ineffective or excessively expensive. Often, this means the need to trim bloated public employee numbers and to retrench inflated wages or benefits. Fixed costs such as building operations or maintenance and repair that have long been neglected may require a lot of new and urgent attention. And finally, politicians must face up to reform of their national tax systems to eliminate favoritism, raise tax levels, or find new sources of revenue that can be exploited. Interestingly, governments that lack themselves the courage to seek higher taxes can "hide behind" the demands of external lenders. This trap has been especially serious in socialist countries where governments have spent decades and countless amounts of money propping up failed state owned enterprises forcing banks to close out their bad debts with dependent corporations and making them face up to economic reality.

Governments all over the world, when faced with the disasters following greedy lending make the initial (political) decision to bail out economically inefficient enterprises. If they do so in some major way, they have made two mistakes: poor reallocation of lending funds; and poor diversion of fiscal resources. Private borrowers have a vested interest in cheap credit and inflation -- which helps them pay off loans in cheapened money. For governments, cheap credit may be inflationary, which the government is expected to prevent; and it forces tax increases which either raises the cost of public programs or reduces their impact. Rather than subsidize companies, governments should promote enlargement of, and competition among lending institutions. A popular new development is the formation of special development banks, for such concerns as agricultural lending, urban development, regional infrastructure development, or small business assistance. Development banks are a good idea, but whether they succeed is contingent on the nature of government in the first place. That is, if governments create improper subsidies, then development banks will simply be a more targeted way to subsidize. If governments are corrupt, so too will be their development banks. If governments are honest and stay out of reallocation games, development banks can be useful.

But even if the government stays neutral, many such banks are effectively captured by their clientele. State owned "policy" banks can become very politically skewed and simply divert funds from private markets. Many government restructuring efforts are in reality bailouts of irresponsible banks and other lending institutions. In many cases, governments, through ownership of SOEs or pressure on private banks, force them to make very bad loans in the name of bad politics. In many cases, banks then persuade the government to absorb their bad loans or to permit them to be converted into equity or long term loans, which simply enriches the bad banks. Where short term loans are converted into long term loans this simply ties up money in the bad loans for a longer period of time. In addition, in the effort to create competition, governments often allow lending by such institutions as insurance companies, non bank financial intermediaries with lower levels of oversight. In the end, direct and selective intervention by the government in the allocation of financial resources tended to generate more difficult problems for both big business and the banks. The whole arena of "strategic industry" building also skewed the allocation of lending -- to defense industries for example, or to "commanding heights" industries controlled and subsidized by governments. Policy loans severely constrained the independence and freedom of action of central banks. Their inability to adjust the pace of money flow then weakened their ability to impact inflation. In many places, the concentration of financial resources on big companies meant the choking off of funds available for smaller companies or for the private sector in favor of the public sector. This hurt the economy in the long run. Also, the greed of these large companies egged on and protected by the government leads to overextension and contributes to massive failures during recessions. The perversion of banking systems has been one of the major tools of oppressive and corrupt regimes.

Curbing Management Corruption

Given the will, there are many ways in which management corruption can be prevented or mitigated. Some involve broad government-wide management policies which can be mandated in law or implemented through individual agency adoption. Perhaps the most important is the use of maximum feasible competition in all government activities that allocate resources – systems such as awards of contracts, grants, loans, or the use of public lands or facilities. This may also include careful control of licenses for valuable assets such as broadcasting wavelengths or the allocation of access to airport gates.

It is also vitally important to require internal transparency of agency operations. The processes by which agencies carry out their programs should be clearly defined, made as simple and understandable as possible, and widely published for all employees who can then know what is acceptable and what is not. This transparency must also extend to the outside through published summaries of agency authority and operating procedures. This can and should be accompanied by some form of public review and comment before important divisions are made, or key processes changed. Special emphasis, often neglected, should be placed on making visible which officials make key decisions and why.

No public official, including political leadership should be authorized to have what are generally known as "slush funds"; that is, funds that are available without controls or justifications or audits. Somewhat more problematically, it may be vital to develop some forms of protection for career officials from the unwarranted intervention of political leadership into decisions that should rest on merit or competition. Obviously, political leadership is necessary but what should be restricted is the tendency of politicians to meddle in management decisions such as contract awards. It is axiomatic: bad politics makes bad management.

In addition to these broad policies, there are many measures to increase the likelihood of detection and prevention of corrupt practices. Inspectors General or some equivalent should be legislatively mandated in every public agency, with strong independent powers of investigation and discovery. Either independently or as a part of an Office of Inspector General, a skilled corps of auditors should be authorized to insist on the examination of all agency records and actions. Every program manager should be charged with the responsibility of assuring that each program is free of corruption or mismanagement even before the auditors arrive.

There is an old axiom for auditors and inspectors: "follow the money". Special attention should be given to the creation and enforcement of close controls over financial flows from initial collection of revenue by the government to the authorization by legislatures of funds for expenditure by the agencies. Within each agency, authority should be limited as to the numbers of officials who can authorize the commitment of expenditures – the fewer the better. A second internal control should be maintained through the use of separate officials who can approve the actual disbursement of funds. Then, there should be management reviews and post-audits of whether the funds were actually used properly and for the purposes for which they were authorized.

Experience shows that perhaps the best "auditors" of agency actions are not necessarily official auditors, but the general public and sometimes employees of an agency who have inside knowledge of what is happening. Good confidential methods should be available for the public to lodge complaints or report corruption. The best intelligence about government corruption often comes from its victims. Those agencies that operate hotlines are often amazed and gratified by the numbers and sharpness of public responses. Internal agency whistleblowers may also be remarkably valuable but this often is punished by agency officials who have something to conceal, even if it is only their own mismanagement. Whistle blowing is a term coined to highlight the fact that agency employees who witness corrupt practices are motivated to try and stop them. The key problem is for the employee or a member of the public to have a safe place to go with this kind of knowledge, and the sense that there will be some institutional response to justify the risk.

In a corrupt or pathological organization, employees may become victims. They must be protected in some way from the arbitrary and capricious acts on the part of agency leadership, including unwarranted firings, transfers, or demotions. Most employees probably want to be honest, but they can't be if they are subject to threats, coercion and intimidation, or if they are ordered to carry out what are clearly illegal or improper orders. Often, it is actually bureaucracy that protects them. If policies and authorized procedures within an agency are clearly defined in some detail, the employee then has a basis for resisting or fending off an order is improper or illegal.

Finally, in truly scandalous governments, corruption is not just ignored, it is organized and encouraged. Even where the apparatus for controlling corruption exists, it may be ignored or circumvented. What the public deserves and wants to see is that the corruptors are caught and removed, and that corrupt acts receive serious punishment. For situations of entrenched corruption in agencies, it may be impossible for the organization to purge itself from the inside and the only alternative may be the creation of external anti-corruption campaigns mounted and enforced from outside of the agency. Thus, it is vital that there exist a forceful government-wide posture against corruption and a set of instruments by which this posture can be carried out. Most countries have various forms of oversight agencies: Inspectors General, government-wide auditing and evaluation agencies, a government-wide budget review organization, and often, a contract review and oversight board. There is a growing tendency too to create a special anti-corruption agency with strong independent powers.

But of critical importance is the participation of the national legislative body. It was argued earlier that the rule of law can become perverse if the laws themselves are pathological and this is a sin laid at the door of parliaments and congresses. The fact that such legislative bodies can be dominated and perverted by tyrants does not relieve them of the ultimate responsibility of maintaining the integrity of the base of national laws and fiscal appropriations. Part of this responsibility involves the oversight of the executive agencies of the government, and these agencies can be aided and abetted in preventing corruption if the laws themselves make it clear exactly what practices are defined as illegal or improper. Further, anti-corruption controls can be deliberately incorporated into laws and mandated in more detailed government regulations. Legislatures can and should maintain their own forms of transparency and openness to public comment, review, complaint and education. Legislation can even be created that mitigates the worst forms of political patronage, both within the civil service and among top political appointments. It is even possible, if not likely, that the opportunities for corruption may be substantially reduced by the elimination of useless or wasteful public programs and activities. Every public official at senior levels should be required to disclose the state of their personal finances; however, a mistake often made is not to extend this requirement to politicians.

In an extreme environment of embedded and institutionalized corruption, some governments have turned to a promising new approach – popularly called a "watch dog agency". These agencies are not designed for routine auditing or inspection but have the single purpose of mounting government-wide anti- corruption attacks. The record of watch dog agencies is mixed, with some such as that in Singapore cited as highly effective while others are all but useless. In assessing the track record of these agencies, certain characteristics have emerged as critical to their success:

1. Such agencies may be established at the government-wide level or placed in individual agencies of government but in either case, they must be independent and must report to the highest possible level. Most are created by special legislation that establishes the needed independence. Many such laws provide that the reports of the watch dog organization must be submitted either to an agency head or to the legislature. The staffs should be politically neutral and not beholden to any organization or persons other than those who appoint them.

2. The agency should be deliberately weighted to provide the maximum capacity to do operational field investigation – on-the-ground rooting out of corruption.

3. The authority of the agency should be powerful. It must be given the authority to investigate any situation, have open access to all government records, including the legal authority to subpoena such records. It should also have the right to interrogate any individual or to investigate the private records of persons where corruption is suspected.

4. Authority should extend beyond the government itself into the institutions that are engaged in government financed activities such as state owned enterprises, contractors, grantees, local governments to which government authorities have been delegated, or to those holding government licenses or charters.

5. In addition to the power to investigate, many watch dog agencies have also been granted "intelligence gathering" authority which opens up such tools as wire taps, surveillance, and clandestine ways to penetrate suspect groups or organizations.

6. There should also be the means by which secret access is provided to whistleblowers or the general public who want to report suspected corrupt practices without fear of retribution. This access should include reports against politicians, since

one of the greatest inhibitors of ant-corruption criticism is the fear of political retaliation.

7. The independent capability to prepare cases for prosecution is vital, since one of the "choke points" that a regime can most effectively control is that of the actions of public prosecutors who are public employees, subject to direction from their political superiors.

But the creation of one or more anti-corruption agencies is no guarantee of an effective attack on the problem. For example, most countries in Southeast Asia have such agencies, but few function effectively, mostly because of lack of political support, or adequate response by agency management. In the Philippines, seven anti-graft laws enacted over a period of several years has yielded only spastic results because of lack of enforcement. Public prosecutors are notably reluctant to develop cases. Even those cases that are brought before a court may languish for months or years. The usual approach to muzzling these agencies lies in appointment powers of the president who may appoint either incompetents or loyalists to the regime whose primary role is to blunt any embarrassing initiatives.

Missing The Good Tides

Having gotten to this point, it may be therapeutic to recognize that a lot of good positive tides are running in the world:

1. There has been a gradual broad increase in world wealth, much of it taking place in the most poverty-stricken places such as China, India, and parts of Africa. As a consequence, the world has seen the greatest reduction of the numbers of people in abject poverty in modern world history.

2. The world economic is paying off better, and it has been made infinitely stronger and more stable, more inclusive, more equitably distributed between nations, and more profitable.

3. Despite widespread predictions to the contrary, the world supply of energy, far from becoming exhausted, is now greater than ever and, over the long run, the relative cost of energy has been declining, thus stimulating many national economies.

4. Absolutely extraordinary and remarkable inventions and advancements have emerged from a broad range of technologies. Industrial production has been widely automated. Millions of engines and motors are smarter, more powerful and cheaper. Human communications have been utterly revolutionized forever. The medical profession has access to thousands of new medications, treatment techniques, and equipment. New chemicals, seeds, plants and farming techniques have greatly improved agricultural productivity, ending ominous predictions of impending world starvation. Every form of transportation has been vastly upgraded. Even the average household appliance has been made more user friendly.

5. Social systems are building capability. Civil societies are stronger, and people are better able to force attention to their needs and concerns. People are becoming more knowledgeable

about the threats to health, the consequences of bad habits, the problems faced by neglect of the environment, the vital need for adult education and skill building, and the fundamental need to expand and deepen the economy to create jobs and reduce poverty. Life expectancy is climbing, pre and post-natal care is more available, infant mortality is decreasing, the elderly are better cared for, curable diseases are actually being cured, sanitation is being improved, and countless millions upon millings of lives have been made better.

If all of this is true, why then are there still Governments from Hell? And why then are there now hundreds of non-government groups (some created and supported by governments) that are vicious, utterly evil thugs and murderers? WHY?

Perhaps there is no really satisfactory answer to this question, and it is simply the nature of humanity. Running a government is extraordinarily complex and difficult. Almost every situation is likely to be murky, confusing and laden with controversy. There will be options and choices, good and bad. Why do so many governments knowingly and deliberately make the bad choices? Why do they overlook governance designed in Heaven in order to choose governments designed in Hell?

Nobody knows.

Attachment A

Countries Experiencing State Terrorism

1. Afghanistan
2. Algeria
3. Angola
4. Argentina
5. Bahrain
6. Bolivia
7. Bosnia
8. Brazil
9. Cambodia
10. Central African Republic
11. Chechnya
12. China, Peoples Republic of
13. Columbia
14. Democratic Republic of Congo
15. Egypt
16. Eritrea
17. Ethiopia
18. Ghana
19. Haiti
20. India
21. Indonesia
22. Iran
23. Iraq
24. Israel
25. Jordan
26. Kenya

27. Kuwait
28. Lebanon
29. Liberia
30. Libya
31. Malaysia
32. Malawi
33. Mali
34. Mexico
35. Nigeria
36. North Korea
37. Pakistan
38. Palestinian Authority/Gaza
39. Peru
40. Philippines
41. Russian Federation
42. Rwanda
43. Saudi Arabia
44. Serbia
45. Sierra Leone
46. Somalia
47. South Africa
48. Sudan
49. Syria
50. Thailand
51. Tunisia
52. Turkey
53. Uzbekistan
54. Venezuela
55. Vietnam
56. Yemen
57. Yugoslavia
58. Zambia
59. Zimbabwe

END NOTES

1. Page 11: Bhagwati, Jagdish, "India in Transition: Freeing the Economy", Oxford, Clarendon Press, 1993.

2. Page 21: See Rotberg, Robert I., "Failed States in a World of Terror", Foreign Affairs Journal, July/August, 2002, and Rotberg, Ed. "When States Fail", Princeton U. Press, 2004.

3. Page 37: World Bank, "Anticorruption in Transition: A Contribution to the Policy Debate", pp. 3-10.

4. Page 58: See Hutchings, Graham, "Modern China: A Guide to a Century of Change", Harvard U. Press, 2001; and Winchester, Simon, "The River in the Center of the World", Picador, Henry Holt and Co., 2004.

5. Page 59: Economist, Sept. 11, 2013, p. 48.

6. Page 63: Waterbury, John, "Exposed to Innumerable Delusions: Public Enterprises and State Power", Cambridge U. Press, 1995.

7. Page 63: Shliefer, Andrei, and Vishney, Robert W., "The Grabbing Hand", p. 110.

8. Page 69: See Zaeef, Abdul Salam, "My Life with the Taliban"; Mohadessin, Mohammad, "Islamic Fundamentalism: The New Global Threat", Washington, D. C., Seven Locks Press, 1993; Esposito, John L. "Unholy War: Terror in the Name of Islam", Oxford U. Press, 2002; Brown, Vahid, and Rassler, Don, "Fountainhead of Jihad: The Haqqani Nexus, 1973-2-12, Columbia U. Press, 2013; Chandler, Michael, and Gunaratna, Rohan, "Countering Terrorism", London, Reaktion Press, 2007; Rashid, Ahmed, "Taliban", Yale U. Press, 2000.

9. Page 72: See UKEssays.com. and the Economist, April 12, 2014.

10. Page 76: See the Economist, August 31, 2013.

11. Page 98: See Williams, Paul D., "War and Conflict in Africa", Cambridge, Polity Press, 2011; Herbst, Jeffery, "States and Power in Africa", Princeton U. Press, 2000; Cockcroft, Laurence, "Global Corruption", U. of Pennsylvania Press, 2012; Ejiofer, Tony, "Nigeria in Quagmire", XLibris, 2010.

12. Page 101: See Jang, Jin-sung, "Dear Leader: My Escape from North Korea", Simon and Schuster, 2012; and Lankov, Andrei, " The Real North Korea", Oxford U. Press, 2013.

13. Page 106: Magnarella, Paul, "The 1994 Rwanda Genocide", E-Intel Relations, 2014. Also, Goose, Stephen D., and Smyth, Frank, "Arming Genocide in Rwanda: The High Cost of Small Arms Transfers", Foreign Affairs, October, 1994.

14. Page 109: Shah, Anup, "Sierra Leone", Global Issues (Human Rights Watch), 2014. See also "Sierra Leone Civil War: Analysing the Causes", SLCivilWar, February, 2012, and BBC News Africa, "Sierra Leone Profile", September, 2014.

15. Page 117: Index of Economic Freedom, published with the Heritage Foundation and the Wall Street Journal, 2014.

16. Page 123: Rotberg, Robert I., "Africa's Mess, Mugabe's Mayhem", Foreign Affairs Journal, Sep./Oct. 2002.

17. Page 126: Conquest, Robert, "The Great Terror: A Reassessment", Oxford U. Press, 1990.

18. Page 129: Ibid.

19. Page 133: Feinstein, Andrew, "The Shadow World: Inside the Global Arms Trade", New York, Picador Press, p. 442, 2012.

20. Page 133: Ibid, p. 443.

21. Page 133: Ibid, p. 447.

22. Page 140: Sorman, Guy, "The Empire of Lies: The Truth About China in the Twenty-First Century", p. 162. New York, Encounter Books, 2008.

23. Page 144: The Economist, Aug. 3, 2013.

24. Page 145: Bingman, Charles F. "Reforming China's Government, p. 250, XLibris, 2010.

25. Page 154: Chehab, Zaki, "Inside Hamas: The Untold Story of the Militant Islamic Movement", New York, WWW.NationBooks.org., 2007.

26. Page 165: The Economist, Sep. 14, 2013.

27. Page 171: Constable, Pamela, "Fragments of Grace", Washington, D. C., Potomac Books, 2004.

28. Page. 181: De Soto, Hernando, "The Other Path", New York, Perennial Press, 1989.

29. Page 183: Esposito, John L., "Unholy War: Terror in the Name of Islam", Oxford U. Press, 2008.

30. Page 197: The Economist. See editions of April 24, 2003; June 26, 2003; and November 1 2013.

31. Page 209: See Ayittey, George B. N., "Africa Betrayed", St Martins Press, 1992; Ayittey, "Africa in Chaos", St. Martins Press, 1999; Ayittey, "Africa Unchained", Palgrave Macmillan, 2005.

32. Page 212: Ibid.

33. Page 213: National Geographic Magazine, "Bringing Water and Life to the Nuba Mountainss of Sudan", July 24, 2010.

34. Page 214: Dreze, Jean, and Sen, Amartya, "India: Economic Development and Social Opportunity", Oxford, Clarendon Press, 1995. See also Dreze and Sen "An Uncertain Glory: India and its Contradictions", Princeton U. Press, 2013.

35. Page 221: See Adrianova, Anna, "Venezuela After Chavez: An Economy on the Verge", Economist, Nov. 26, 2013. See also the Economist, Mar. 5, 2013, and the Economist, Mar.9, 2013.

36. Page 222: Quoted from Michael Lipton, U. of Sussex, Great Britain, in Easterbrook Greg, "The Progress Paradox", Random House, 2003.

37. Page 223: Ibid, p. 287. See also Bingman, Charles F., "Why Governments Go Wrong", iUniverse Inc., 2006.

38. Page 224: Dollar, David and Kraay, Aart, "Spreading the Wealth", Foreign Affairs Journal, January/February, 2002, pp. 120-133.

39. Page 225: Bingman, Charles F. "Why Governments Go Wrong", iUniverse Inc. 2006, pp. 189-194.

40. Page 233: Rotberg, see End Note 2.

41. Page 237: Economist, Jan. 11, 2014.

42. Page 245: Ejiofer, Tony, "Nigeria in Quagmire", XLibris, 2010.

43. Page 246: Waterbury, John, "Exposed to Innumerable Delusions", Cambridge U. Press, 1993.

44. Page 248: Economist, May 4, 2013.

45. Page 252: De Soto, Hernando, "The Other Path", New York, Perennial Press, 1989.

46. Page 255: Bhagwati, Jagdish, "India in Transition", Oxford, Clarendon Press, 1993.

47. Page 258: See Bingman, Charles F., "Why Governments Go Wrong", p. 221, iUniverse, 2006

48. Page 268: See for example" Denizer, Cevet, Kaufmann, Daniel, Kraay, Aart, "Good Countries or Good Projects? Macro and Micro Correlates of World Bank Performance", 2013; Pantle, Sabina, "Changing Norms is Key to Fighting Everyday Corruption, 2013. Claasen, Bianca, Kraay, Aart, "Corruption and Confidence in Public Institutions: Evidence from a Global Survey", 2009-2012.

49. Page 268: See Inman, Phillip, "Record World Debt Could Trigger New Financial Crisis", Guardian, 2009. Al Jazeera, ""EU Report: Corruption is Widespread in the European Union". February, 2014.

50. Page 291: See Ayittey, George B. N., "Africa Unchained", Palgrave Macmillan, 2005.

51. Page 293: Economist, April 7, 2005.

52. Page 319: Rotberg, Robert I., "Africa's Mess, Mugabe's Mayhem", Foreign Affairs Journal, Sep./Oct. 2002.

SOURCES

Section One: Background

Country Reports on Terrorism, U. S. Department of State November 2009.

Corruption Perceptions Index 2012, Transparency International

Most Dangerously Polluted Cities, AllCountries.org. 2011.

Thematic Map: Population Below the Poverty Line, indexmundi. com/map, 2011.

Inequality-adjusted Human Development Index, Human Development Report, 2010.

"A Mixed Bag", Economist, July 13, 2013 p. 42.

"A Haven for Malcontents", Economist, July 13, 20113, p. 42

Hanson, Stephanie, "Corruption in Sub-Saharan Africa", Council on Foreign Relations, 2009.

Cockroft, Laurence, "Global Corruption", U. of Pennsylvania Press, 2012.

"Africans Let Down by Governments", BBC News, 2004.

"Bureaucratic Corruption in Africa: The Futility of Cleanups", The Cato Journal, Vol. 16, No. 1, 1996

"Study Warns of Stagnation in Arab Societies", The New York Times, July 7, 2002.

"AU in a Nutshell", African Union, 2013.

Williams, Ian, "Arab Human Development Report Takes an Honest Look at Region", Washington Report on Middle East Affairs, October, 2002.

Lynch, Marc, "The 2009 Arab Human Development Report", 2009.

"The World's Ten Most Authoritarian Leaders", World Policy Journal, Fall, 2012.

"How Anti-Rohingya Bengali Islamist Extremist Terrorists Campaigns Started", Burma News, June 13, 2012.

'Human Development Report: Five Arab Countries Among Top Leaders in Long Term Development Gains", United Nations Development Programme, November, 2010.

"Miserable and Weak Again", Economist, Nov. 16, 2013.

Rihani, Samir Dr., "Arab Human Development Report: Part of a Bigger Jigsaw", Globalcomplexity.org/AHDR, 2005.

United States Department of State: National Consortium for the Study of Terrorism and Responses to Terrorism: Annex of Statistical Information, Country Reports on Terrorism, 2012.

"Muslim Statistics (Terrorism), WikiIslam, December, 2013.

Lomborg, Bjorn, "The Skeptical Environmentalist"

"Through A Border Darkly", Economist, August 16, 2014, p. 33.

"Life in Gaza", Washington Post, August 3, 2014, p. A15.

"The State of Africa", Washington Post, August 3, 2014, p. A13.

"Nasty Neighbourhood", Economist, Aug. 2, 2014, p. 41.

World Development Indicators, "Poverty", 2004.

"HDI – Human Development Index 1975-2005, The World Factbook, October, 2008.

"Muslim Countries of the World", Muslim Educational Trust, 2011.

Gleick, Peter H. "Three Gorges Dam Project, Yangtze River, China", The World's Water 2008-2009.

"List of Ottoman Empire Territories", Wikipedia, July, 2011.

Feldman, Noah, "The Fall and Rise of the Islamic State", Council on Foreign Relations, Princeton U. Press, 2008.

Chandler, Michael, and Gunaratria, Rohan, "Countering Terrorism: Reaktion Books, 2007.

Kinzer, Stephen, "Crescent and Star", Farrar, Straus and Giroux, 2001.

Diner, Dan, "Lost in the Sacred", Princeton U. Press, 2009.

Boston, Andrew G., Ed., "The Legacy of Jihad", New York, Prometheus Books, 2005.

Williams, Paul D. "War and Conflict in Africa", Cambridge, UK, Polity Press, 2011.

Ayittey, George B. N., "Africa Unchained: The Blueprint for Africa's Future", Palgrave Macmillan, 2005.

Ayittey, George B. N., "Africa in Chaos", St. Martins Press, 1998.

Ayittey, George B. N., "Africa Betrayed". St. Martins Press, 1992.

Mohaddessin, Mohammad, "Islamic Fundamentalism: The New Global Threat", Washington, D. C., Seven Locks Press, 1993.

Zogby, James J., "What Arabs Think", Zogby International/The Arab Thought Foundation, 2002.

Rotberg, Robert, Ed., "When States Fail: Causes and Consequences", Princeton U. Press, 2004.

Villalon, Leonardo A., and VanDoepp, Peter, Eds., "The Fate of Africa's Democratic Experiments", Indiana U. Press, 2005.

Chellancy, Brahma, "Asian Juggernaut", Harper Business, 2006.

Smith, Lee, "The Strong Horse", Anchor Books, 2010.

Ottaway, Marina, and Choucair-Vezoso, John, Eds., "Beyond the Façade: Political Reform in the Arab World", Carnegie Endowment for International Peace, 2008.

Esposito, John, and Mogahed, Dalin, "Who Speaks for Islam?" Gallup Press, 2007.

Esposito, John, "Unholy War: Terror in the Name of Islam:, Oxford U. Press, 2002.

Wright, Robin, "Rock the Casbah, Simon and Schuster, 2011.

Zia, Rukhsana, Ed., "Globalization, Modernization and Education in Muslim Countries", New York, Nova Science Publishers, 2006.

Kuran, Timur, "The Long Divergence", Princeton U. Press, 2011.

Viorst, Milton, "Sandcastles" The Arabs in Search of the Modern World", Alfredd A. Knopf, 1994.

Otto, Jan Michiel, Ed., "Sharia Incorporated", Leiden U. Press, 2010.

"The New Arab Revolt", Foreign Affairs, issue of May/June, 2011.

Rashid, Ahmed, "Taliban", Yale U. Press, 2000.

Kennedy, Hugh, "The Great Arab Conquests", De Capo Press, 2007.

Wright, Robin, "Dreams and Shadows: The Future of the Middle East", Penguin Books, 2008.

Nasr, Seyyed Hossein, "The Heart of Islam", Harper One, 2002.

Bueno De Mesquita, Bruce, and Smith, Alistair, "The Dictator's Handbook", Public Affairs, 2011.

Bhagwati, Jagdish, "Free Trade Today", Princeton U. Press, 2002.

Hayek, F. A. "The Fatal Conceit" The Errors of Socialism", U. of Chicago Press, 1988.

The Quran: The Dilemma, Volume I, TheQuran.com, 2011.

Levitt, Matthew, "Hamas: Politics, Charity, and Terrorism in the Service of Jihad", Yale U. Press, 2006.

"UN and Government Specialists Discuss Global Anticorruption Efforts in Brazil", United Nations Development Programme, November, 2012.

Yergin, Daniel, and Stanislaw, Joseph, "The Commanding Heights", Simon and Schuster, 1998.

Cockcraft, Laurence, "Global Corruption", U. of Pennsylvania Press, 2012.

Fuller, Graham E. "The Future of Political Islam", Palgrave Macmillan, 2003.

Herbst, Jeffery, "State and Power in Africa", Princeton U. Press, 2000.

Henderson, Harry, "Global Terrorism", Checkmark Books, 2001.

Roy, Olivier, "Secularism Confronts Islam", Columbia U. Press, 2007.

Global Corruption Report, 2004, Transparency International, Pluto Press, 2004.

Cole, Juan, "Engaging the Muslim World", Palgrave Macmillan, 2009.

Bingman, Charles F., "Governments in the Muslim World", iUniverse Press, 2013.

Bingman, Charles F., "Changing Governments in India and China", Schiel and Denver Paperbacks, 2011.

Bingman, Charles F., "Reforming China's Government", Xlibris Press, 2010.

Bingman, Charles, F. "Why Governments Go Wrong", iUniverse Press,2006.

Cruvellier, Thierry, "The Master of Confessions: The Making of a Khmer Rouge Torturer", Paris, Editions Gallimard/Versilio, 2011.

Sallam Zaeef, Abdul, "My Life with the Taliban", Columbia U. Press, 2010.

Brown, Vahid, and Rassler, Don, "Fountainhead of Jihad: The Hiqqani Nexus", Columbia U. Press, 2013.

Ryan, Michael W. S., "Decoding Al-Qaeda's Strategy: The Deep Battle Against America", Columbia U. Press, 2013.

Section Two: Country Analyses

Narizhnaya, Khristina, "Russia Go West", World Policy Journal, Spring, 2013.

Denyer, Simon, "China Earthquake Reignites Debate on Rush to Build Large Dams", Washington Post, Aug. 6, 2014.

Gutierrez, Hernan, "Columbia: Overview of Corruption and Anti-corruption" U4 Anti-Corruption Resource Centre, March, 2013.

'Passing the Baton", Economist, Aug. 2, 2014.

'Sri Lanka Profile", BBC News South Asia, September, 2013.

"Sri Lanka: Torn Between Yesterday and Tomorrow", DW.DE, May, 2014.

"China Dams the World: The Environmental and Social Impacts of Chinese Dams", E-International Relations, June, 2014.

Gleick, Peter H. "Three Gorges Dam Project, Yangtze River, China", Water Briefs, The World's Water, 2007.

Kurtz, Michael, "Corruption in Argentina", Politics and Policy, March, 2012.

"Argentinians Protest Against Their Government, Corrruption and Crime", The Guardian, Nov. 9, 2012.

"Corruption in Argentina", De Argentina, March, 2013.

Schmall, Emily, "Argentina: Back to Peronism", Foreign Affairs Journal, Fall, 2012.

Kurtz, Michael, "Corruption in Argentina", Politics and Policy, February, 2003.

"Argentinians Protest Against Their Government, Corruption and Crime", Associated Press/Argentina, November, 2012.

"Corruption in Argentina", TravelSur.net/notes, March, 2003.

"Sri Lanka Profile", BBC News, 25 Sep. 2013.

"Sri Lanka: Torn Between Yesterday and Tomorrow", DW.DE, May, 2014.

"Ethiopia's 'Oppressed' Muslims", Ze-Habesha Website, Oct. 10, 2013.

"Muslims in Ethiopia Suffer Discrimination and Alienation", Crescent International, May, 2012.

"Muslim Protests Raise Slender Hopes of Change in Ethiopia", DW.DE, September, 2013.

"An Armed Force that Comes Out From Oppression", ECAD Forum, September, 2013. Ze Habasha Website, Oct. 11, 2013.

Mauro, Ryan, "The 'Christian' Dictator or Eritrea, Isayas Afeworki –Al-Qaeda's Funder", Front Page Magazine, 2013.

"Terrorism Statistics: Eritrea vs. Malaysia, NationaMaster.com, November, 2013.

Crimi, Frank, "The Makings of a Terrorist State", Frontpage Magazine, Nov. 20, 2013.

McElroy, Damien, "US Threatens Eritrea Over Support for al-Qaeda-linked Terrorists", The Telegraph, Apr. 17, 2009.

"Cambodia: "Talking About Genocide – Genocides", Peace Pledge Union, January, 2014.

Das, Gurcharan, "India Unbound", July, 2009.

Xin, Li, "India Through Chinese Eyes", World Policy Journal, Winter, 2013-2014.

McKenna, Ed, "Ethiopian Government Choking Muslim Unrest",

Davydova, Donata, "China Against Terrorism", nbenegroup.com, January, 2014.

Chung, Chien-peng, "China's 'War on Terror': September 11 and Uighur Separatism, Foreign Affairs, July-August, 2002.

"Chinese Police Kill Eight in Xinjiang 'Terrorist Attack'", Reuters, Dec. 30, 2013.

Hamid, O., "China's Growing Jihadist Problem", The Diplomat, Aug. 14, 2012.

Smith, Craig S., "Tunisia is Feared to be a New Base for Islamists", New York Times, Feb. 20, 2007.

"Democratic Republic of Congo Economic Outlook", African Development Bank, 2013.

Calavan, Michael M., Briquets, Sergio Diaz, O'Brien, Jerald O., "Cambodian Corruption Assessment", US AID, May-June, 2004.

"Nigeria's Corruption Busters", United Nations Office of Drugs and Crime, November, 2013.

"World Report Vietnam Country Chapter", World Report, 3013.

Stanton, Joshua, "North Korea Sponsors Terrorism", The Weekly Standard, Aug. 13, 2013.

Bechtol, Bruce E. Jr., "North Korea and Support to Terrorism: An Evolving History", Berkeley Electronic Press, 2010.

"Kenya: Trotting Ahead", Economist, Mar. 15, 2014.

"Liberia Profile", BBC News, Oct. 11, 2013.

"Bolivia Assessment", InfoPlease, 2014.

"Banyan: The Year of Killing With Impunity", Economist, Mar. 1, 2014.

"Nigeria's Image in Africa: Big Country, Thin Skin", Economist, Feb. 15, 2004.

"Sudan: Downhill", Economist, Feb. 1, 2014.

"Corruption in India", Wikipedia, 2012.

Smith, Daniel Jordan, "A Culture of Corruption: Everyday Deception and Popular Discontent in Nigeria", Princeton University Press, 2008.

"Anti-Terrorist Unit (Liberia), Wikipedia, November, 2013.

"Algeria's Leaders: The Dead Live Longer", Economist, Sep. 21, 2013.

"China and Africa: Little to Fear But Fear Itself", Economist, Sep. 21, 2013.

"The Palestinians: Lonely Hamas", Economist, Sep. 7, 2013.

Takeyh, Ray, "Hidden Iran: Paradox and Power in the Islamic Republic", Council on Foreign Relations, Time Books, 2006.

Desman, Ann, "Turkey Decoded", London, SAQS, 2008.

Haqqani, Husain, 'Pakistan: Between Mosque and Military", Carnegie Endowment for International Peace, 2005.

Dreze, Jean, and Sen, Amartya, "An Uncertain Glory: India and It's Contradictions", Princeton U. Press, 2013.

Conquest, Robert, "The Great Terror", Oxford U. Press, 1990.

Pan, Philip P. 'Out of Mao's Shadow", Simon and Schuster Paperbacks, 2008.

Dreze, Jean, and Sen, Amartya, "India: Economic Development and Social Opportunity", Oxford, Clarendon Press, 2002.

Shapiro, Judith, "Mao's War Against Nature", Cambridge U. Press, 2001.

Bresnan, John, "Managing Indonesia", Columbia U. Press, 1993.

Cohn Stephen Philip, "India: Emerging Power", Brookings Institution Press, 2001.

Saich, Tony, "Governance and Politics in China", Palgrave Macmillan, 2004.

Starr, S. Frederick, Ed., "Xinjiang: China's Muslim Borderland", M. E. Sharpe, 2004.

Ahmad, Ehtisham; Diang, Gao; Tomsi, Vito, Eds., "Reforming China's Public Finances", International Monetary Fund, 1995.

Roy, Sara, "Hamas and Civil Society in Gaza", Princeton U. Press, 2011.

Section Three: Neglect Of Social Services

Lomborg, Bjorn, "The Skeptical Environmentalist", Cambridge U. Press, 2001.

Urban, Frauke and Nordensvard, Johan, "China Dams the World: The Environmental and Social Impacts of Chinese Dams", E-INTERNATIONAL RELATIONS, January, 2014.

"Muslims in Ethiopia Suffer Discrimination and Alienation", Crescent International, May, 2012.

"Venezuela's Progressive Conscience", Economist, Apr. 20, 2014.

"Ranking of World Health Systems", World Health Organization, 2006.

"Violence Against Women in Latin America" Everyday Aggression", Economist, Sep. 21, 2013.

"Environment: Browner but Greener", Economist, Feb. 1, 2014.

"Education in Kenya: Classroom Divisions", Economist, Feb. 22, 2014.

"Corruption in the African Healthcare System: Where is the Aid Money Really Going?", Global Health Policy at NYU-Wagner, Dec. 15, 2011.

"Pakistan: Causes of Poverty", Asian Development Bank, 2001.

'Official Laws Against Women in Iran", WFAFI, 2005.

Pegg, David, "The 25 Most Dangerous Cities on Earth", Geography and Travel, Oct. 31, 2011.

"Islam in Egypt: Manipulating the Minarets", Economist, Aug. 2, 2014.

"Race and Religion in South-East Asia: The Plural Society and its Enemies", Economist, Aug. 2, 2014.

"Drugs Trafficking in the Caribbean: Full Circle" Economist, May 24, 2014.

"China: Improving Health Care: Congratulations! Inoculations!", Economist, Jul. 26, 2014.

"Education in Northern Nigeria: Mixing the Modern and the Traditional", Economist, Jul. 26, 2014.

"Nigeria's Yobe State Closes Schools to Avoid Attacks by Islamic Militants", Huff Post World, November, 2013.

"Islamic Terrorists Kill at Least 40 Students in Attack on Nigerian College", Fox News.com, Sep. 29, 2013.

"World Report 2012: Vietnam", Human Rights Watch, 2013.

"Moving Out of Poverty in Morocco", World Bank Group, 2013.

"Jordan: Poverty Assessment", World Bank Group, 2012.

"Tunisia: Poverty Alleviation: Preserving Progress While Preparing for the Future", The World Bank Group, 2011.

"West Bank and Gaza: Deep Palestinian Poverty in the Midst of Economic Crisis", The World Bank Group, 2012.

"Yemen: Poverty Update", The World Bank Group, 2011.

"Sustaining Gains in Poverty Reduction and Human Development in the Middle East and North Africa, The World Bank Group, 2012.

"Poverty Status in Afghanistan: A Profile Based on National Risk and Vulnerability Assessment, 2007/2008. Islamic Republic of Afghanistan, 2014.

"UNDP Human Development Report (2006): Morocco, UNDP, 2010.

"Development Program Touches the Lives of Morocco's Poorest Millions", The World Bank Group, 2010.

"Morocco Fights Poverty Through 'Human Development' Approach", TheWorld Bank Group, August, 2010.

Frost, Martin, "The Strategies Behind the Poverty Reduction in Iran and the Middle East", martinfrost.ws/htmlfiles

Nissaramanesh, Bijan, Trace, Mike, and Roberts, Marcus, "The Rise of Harm Reduction in Islamic Republic of Iran, The Beckley Foundation Drug Policy Programme, July, 2005.

"Overview of Education in Ethiopia" School of St. Yared, 2013.

Chaya, Nada, "Poor Access to Health Services: Ways Ethiopia is Overcoming It", Population Action, April, 2007.

"Environmental Accountability Transparency in the Haze", Economist, Feb. 8, 2014.

"Drug Addiction in Iran: The Other Religion", Economist, Aug. 17, 2013.

"Cancer in the Developing World: Worse Than AIDS", Economist, Mar. 1, 2014.

"Government of Afghanistan Releases Latest Data on Poverty and Food Security", Islamic Republic of Afghanistan, Ministry of Economy, Mar. 4, 2012.

"2010 Human Rights Report: Pakistan", U. S. Department of State, Bureau of Democracy, Human Rights and Labor, April, 2011.

"The Global Competitiveness Report 2010-2011, World Economic Forum, 2010.

Campanella, Thomas J., "The Concrete Dragon: China's Urban Revolution", Princeton Architectural Press, 2008.

Section Four: Pathological Economics

"Passing the Baton", Economist, Aug. 2, 2014.

"North Korea: Better Tomorrow?", Economist, Mar. 8, 2014.

"Energy and the Amazon: Drilling in the Wilderness", Economist, Apr. 26, 2014.

"State-controlled Airlines: Flags of Inconvenience", Economist, Aug. 16, 2014.

"Lighting Rural India: Out of the Gloom", Economist, Jul. 20, 2013.

Schumpeter: "Decluttering the Company: Businesses Must Fight a Relentless Battle Against Bureaucracy", Economist, Aug. 2, 2014.

"Corruption in the Economy: Is Anti-graft Anti-growth?", Economist, Aug. 2, 2014.

"Argentina's Debt Saga: No Movement", Economist, Aug. 2, 2014.

"Relations with Russia: Putin Pivots to the East", Economist, May. 24, 2014.

"Free Exchange" Sun, Wind, and Drain", Economist, Jul. 26, 2014.

Buttonwood: "Trillion Dollar Boo-boo", Economist, Jul. 26, 2014.

"Brazil's Economy: All Systems Slow", Economist, Jul. 26, 2014.

"Argentina's Debt Saga: Unsettling Times", Economist, Jul. 26, 2014.

"Mexico's Economy: Jam Manana", Economist, May 24, 2014.

"Democratic Republic of Congo Economic Outlook", African Development Bank, 2013.

"Market Economy Does Good in Vietnam", Saigon; SGGP English Edition, Jul. 15, 2014.

"Viatnam's Economy Continues to Perform Below Potential, World Bank Says", Thanh Nien Daily, July 9, 2014.

"Vietnam Economy Profile 2013", CIA World Factbook, 2013.

"Middle East and North Africa Region (MENA) – Iran: Development Progress, The World Bank Group, September, 2006.

Chellaney, Brahma, "China's Dam Frenzy", World Affairs, December, 2011.

Weisbrot, Mark, Ray, Rebecca, and Johnston, Jake, "Bolivia: The Economy During the Morales Administration", Center for Economic and Policy Research, December, 2009.

"Nationalizing Utilities in Bolivia: From Tap to Socket", Economist, 2014.

Neuman, William, "Turnabout in Bolivia as Economy Rises from Instability", New York Times, Feb. 16, 2014.

"Ethiopia: Economic and Political Governance", African Economic Outlook, 2014.

"Manufacturing in Africa: An Awakening Giant", Economist, Feb. 8, 2014.

Pakistan's Economy: The Urdu Rate of Growth", Economist, Feb. 15, 2014.

"Taiwan's Economic Isolation: Desperately Seeking Space:, Economist, Jul. 13, 2013.

Section Five: Perverting The Justice System

"Justice Delayed", Economist, July 18, 2012.

"Protests in Venezuela: A Tale of Two Prisoners", Economist, Feb. 22, 2014.

"Sri Lanka: Bring Up the Bodies", Economist, Mar. 8, 2014.

"Organized Crime: Earning With the Fishes", Economist, Jan. 18, 2014.

"Prisons: Rough Justice", Economist, Aug. 2, 2014.

"The Death Penalty: Strike Less Hard", Economist, Aug. 3, 2013.

"Ethiopia and the Press: The Noose Tightens", Economist, Aug. 9, 2014.

"Neither Truth nor Justice", Economist, Aug. 9, 2014.

"Corruption Abets Terror in the Philippines, Says US", Asia News Network, Feb. 6, 2013.

"Corruption in South Africa: A Can of Worms", Economist, Oct. 18, 2011.

"Drug War: Get the Facts", DrugWarFacts.org, 2014.

Forero, Juan, "Columbian Government Shaken by Lawmaker's Paramilitary Ties", The Washington Post World, Nov. 18, 2006.

"Security in Kenya: Little Law, Less Order", Economist, May 10, 2014.

Section Six: The Dilemma Of Military Establishments

Shinn, David, "China Confronts Terrorism in Africa", China-US Focus, November, 2013.

"Peru: The Curse of Inca Gold: Players: Vladimiro Montesinos", FRONTLINE/World, October, 2005.

"A Holy Mess: Kidnapping in Nigeria is Out of Hand", Economist, Sep. 14, 2013.

'Indian Military Power: All at Sea", Economist, Aug. 17, 2013.

"Columbia's Armed Forces: General Exit", Economist, Feb. 22, 2014.

Cohen, Stephen P., and Dasgupta, Sunil, "Arming Without Aming: India's Military Modernization", Brookings Institution Press, 2010.

Overland, Martha Ann, "Vietnamese Fight Back Against Cop Corruption", TIME/WORLD, Mar. 25, 2009.

"Africa's Jihadists on Their Way", Economist, Jul. 26, 2014.

"Thailand: Peace, Order, Stagnation", Economist Aaug. 9, 2014.

Forero, Juan, "Columbian Government Shaken by Lawmaker's Paramilitary Ties", The Washington Post World, Nov. 18, 2006.

"Mexico: Cartels Pay Corrupt Cops $ 100 million a Month", Latin American Herald Tribune, July 20, 2014.

Hendawi, Hamza, "Revolutionary Guard Tightens Hold in Iran Crisis", Seattle Times, Jul. 26, 2009.

"Violence in Mexico: Lawless Land", Economist, Jan. 18, 2014.

"Mali: Five Key Facts About the Conflict", The Guardian, Jan. 22, 2013.

Kandell, Jonathan, "Augusto Pinochet, Dictator Who Ruled by Terror in Chile, Dies at 91, The New York Times, Dec. 11, 2006

"A Peace Agreement in Mindanao· A Fragile Peace", Economist, Feb. 1, 2014.

"Pakistan and the Taliban: to Fight or Not to Fight:, Economist, Mar. 1, 2014.

"Pakistan and the Taliban: Jawing with the Enemy", Economist, Feb. 8, 2014.

Farah, Douglas, "Report Says Africans Harbored Al Qaeda; Terror Assets Hidden in Gem-Buying Spree", The Washington Post, Dec. 29, 2002.

Shambaugh, David, and Yang, Richard H., "China's Military in Transition", Clarendon Press, 1997.

Shambaugh, David, "Modernizing China's Military", U. of California Press, 2004.

Flanagan, Stephen J., and Marti, Michael E., "The People's Liberation Army and China in Transition", Honolulu, Hawaii, University Press of the Pacific, 2004.

Section Seven: Corrupt Public Management

"Bureaucracy in China: Cadres, Hassles, The Hukou and Dead Souls", Facts and Details, 2013.

"Climbing Trees to Catch Fish", Economist, Aug. 17, 2013.

"Not Quite the Usual Walkover", Economist, Jul. 13, 2013.

"Masses of Meetings", Economist, Jul. 13, 2013.

"Choose Pemex Over the Pact", Jul. 13, 2013.

"Politics in Venezuela: Whose Hand is at the Tiller?", Economist, Aug. 2, 2014.

Onwuka, Azuka, "It Pays to be Corrupt in Nigeria", The Punch, Feb. 27, 2013.

"Constitution and Political System, Socialist Republic of Vietnam", Embassy of Vietnam in the United States of America, July, 2014.

"South Africans Suffer as Graft Saps Provinces", New York Times, Feb. 18, 2012.

Pol Green, Lydia, "In South Africa, Lethal Battles for Even the Smallest of Political Posts", New York Times, Nov. 30, 2012.

Graham, Eric, "South Africa: Corruption Exposed at Orkney and Grootvlei Mines", World Socialist Web Site, WSWS.org, September, 2012.

Olano, Maria Virginia, "Colombia: A Country Torn Between Peace and Coruption", OCCRP, 2012.

Weiner, Lawrence, "How Mexico Became So Corrupt", The Atlantic, Jun. 25, 2013.

Althaus, Dudley, "Death and Corruption: Organized Crime and Local Government in Mexico", InSight Crime, October, 2013.

Entelis, John P. "Morocco's 'New' Political Face", Project on Middle East Democracy Policy Brief, Dec. 5, 2011.

"Malawi's Mess: Banda and the Bandits", Economist, Dec. 7, 2013.

Hamner, Joshua, "When Jihad Came to Mali", New York Times Review of Books, 2013.

"Corruption in South Africa: Nkandla in the Wind", Economist, Apr. 12, 2014.

"Journalism in Pakistan: The Silencing of the Liberals", Economist, Apr. 26, 2014.

Takeyh, Ray, "Iran's Weak Hand", Washington Post, Nov. 7, 2013.

Yang, Dali L. "Remaking the Chinese Leviaathan", Stanford U. Press, 2004.

Section Eight: Government Regulation As Oppression

Gleick, Peter H. "Three Gorges Dam Project, Yangtze River, China", The World's Water 2008-2009.

"Tangled: The Rich World Needs to Cut Red Tape", Economist, Feb. 22, 2014.

"Government Regulation and Rural Taxation in China", Perspectives, Vol. 5, No. 2, June 30, 2004.

Min Jie, Yu Xiaodong, "Bloated Bureaucracy", News China Magazine, Feb. 12, 2014.

"Indian Bureaucrats Have 'Terrific Powers', Rated Worst in Asia", The Times of India, Jan. 11, 2012.

Watt, Louise, "The Big Story: China's Leaders Take Aim at Railways Ministry", AP, Mar. 10, 2013.

Levitt, Tom, "China's Top-Down Food Safety System is Failing", China Dialogue, Sep. 24, 2013.

INDEX